BEATING
THE
ODDS

BEATING THE ODDS

Jump-Starting
Developing Countries

*Justin Yifu Lin and
Célestin Monga*

PRINCETON UNIVERSITY PRESS
Princeton and Oxford

Published by Princeton University Press,
41 William Street, Princeton, New Jersey 08540

In the United Kingdom: Princeton University Press,
6 Oxford Street, Woodstock, Oxfordshire OX20 1TR
press.princeton.edu

Jacket art courtesy of Shutterstock and Texture Fabrik

Jacket design by Faceout Studio

ISBN 978-0-691-17605-5

British Library Cataloging-in-Publication Data is available

This book has been composed in Garamond Premier Pro and Eutopia

Printed on acid-free paper. ∞

Printed in the United States of America

1 3 5 7 9 10 8 6 4 2

Contents

Acknowledgments

English novelist and poet B. S. Johnson once invited readers to write their own name in the acknowledgments of his book if they thought they deserved to be there. Brendan Pietsch, a professor of religious studies who wrote an academic book from a dissertation project, realized after almost ten years of working on it that he couldn't possibly come up with a full list of all the people who had helped. In his acknowledgments, he facetiously chastised those who made him go through the pains of writing—presumably including his future readers: "I blame all of you," he wrote. "Writing this book has been an exercise in sustained suffering. The casual reader may, perhaps, exempt herself from excessive guilt, but for those of you who have played the larger role in prolonging my agonies with your encouragement and support, well . . . you know who you are, and you owe me."

Fortunately, we never experienced any serious discomfort or pain in writing this book. In fact, we very much enjoyed tackling the most exciting topic in economics, which is to try to understand why some nations achieve prosperity while others find themselves embroiled in misery. We benefited enormously from the wisdom and advice of many friends and colleagues, whom we would like to thank without implicating: Joseph Stiglitz, L. Alan Winters, Finn Tarp, Kaushik Basu, and our students at Peking University and the University of Paris 1 Panthéon-Sorbonne. Our work was made easier by their thirst for knowledge, and the commitment and support of Youssouf Kiendrebeogo and Wei Guo, our research assistants.

Special thanks are due to Justin Yifu Lin's mentor, Mr. Runsheng Du, the father of China's rural reform, who passed away in 2015 at the age of 102, to UNIDO Director General Li Yong, and to UNIDO goodwill ambassador Helen Hai, chief executive officer of the Made in Africa Initiative, who has been enthusiastically piloting the implementation of the ideas in this book in several African countries. We extend our gratitude to Akin Adesina, Mustapha Nabli, François Bourguignon, Edem Kodjo, Geremie Sawadogo, Fabien Eboussi Boulaga, Cilas Kemedjio, Ambroise Kom,

Elizabeth Asiedu, Hippolyte Fofack, and Tertius Zongo for their constant encouragement. We were also blessed with the unflinching support and patience of our families (Yunying, Leon, and Lindsay; Mami Madé, Anne-Mireille, Stephanie, Kephren, Maélys, Bradley, and Hélène).

Last but not least, we would like to thank UNU-WIDER for generous funding support (UNU-WIDER-ICA 605UU-1032) for preparation of this book.

BEATING THE ODDS

Introduction:
The Art of Engineering Prosperity
in Unlikely Places

Anyone who visits the township of Diepsloot, northeast of Johannes-burg, South Africa, is immediately struck by startling images of poverty and dignity, and by conflicting emotions. Amid the well-known, headline-grabbing stories of despair that provoke anger and sadness—street fights, rapes, hijackings, armed robberies, mob justice—there are also puzzling facts that, in contrast, incite joy and hope. The poor people who live in Diepsloot are among the hardest working and most entrepreneurial in the world. There are shops everywhere, generally run by illiterate but savvy women and young people whose energy and faith in their own agency rede-fine entrepreneurship. In a place with no electricity, no running water, and little police presence, they wake up every day at dawn and work hard all day, fighting adversity in all forms, including crime and the high probability of being randomly harassed by a corrupt tax official. Because they have settled on public land without authorization, have invested their meager savings or loans obtained from friends and family in their business ventures, and have no access to administrative protection or legal recourse, they are vulnerable to violence and injustice. And yet they enthusiastically believe in their abil-ity to create value and prosperity and to control their own destiny.

WHY SO MANY BEAUTY SALONS IN A TOWNSHIP?

Perhaps most surprising about Diepsloot's effervescent entrepreneurship is the high concentration of barbershops and beauty salons. This is no Hollywood, Paris, or Milan where one would expect promoters of non-tradable services to focus so much on beauty. Yet in almost every corner of this low-income neighborhood, there is a hair, makeup, and skin care

1

shop with workers and customers focusing on the arts of elegance and the aesthetics of the body. As one watches them devote their energy and imagination to such matters, in the middle of one of the poorest neighborhoods in this most unequal society, many thoughts come to mind—beyond that it provides further evidence of the resilience of the human spirit. One can choose to see in such activities evidence of the dark nihilism described by Nobel Prize–winning novelist V. S. Naipaul. In many of his travel books he laments the deplorable fate of the African continent and often mocks the "strange" set of priorities and the belief systems of the people there. "Africa has no future," he once said; "Africa [is] drowning in the fecundity of its people" (Naipaul 2010). In addition to being factually false, such a cynical view misses the true significance of the ethical quest that underlies the entrepreneurial drive of the people in places like Diepsloot.

A more philosophical explanation of the burgeoning of barbershops and beauty salons there—and for that matter in almost all poor neighborhoods in the developing world—would be the following: poor people, just like everyone else, have high ideals for their actions and behavior, such as requiring that their decisions conform not only to the economic utilitarianism of survival (income and employment) but also to moral standards of self-love and self-respect, such as being "clean," "good-looking," "elegant," "free from contempt," or "desired." On the basis of these ideals, they do not let themselves be defined solely by the hardship of their socioeconomic conditions. They pursue excellence in the reaffirmation of their dignity even in the most difficult situations. True, South Africa's particular political history and the many subtle ways people in Diepsloot are overcoming the hideous legacy of apartheid may also be valid explanations. But beyond the hysteresis of humiliation, the quest for beauty and self-esteem is primarily evidence of the collective belief that even in such a difficult environment, there is always a sense of possibility.[1] As Martin Luther King, Jr., famously observed, "Only in the darkness can you see the stars."

A third and also plausible explanation for the high prevalence of micro enterprises specializing in beauty in as unlikely a place as Diepsloot is simply the hypothesis that the risk-return ratio is lower in that sector. The capital needed to start a business in the beauty industry is lower than in other industries, and the demand for such services is fairly stable, if not growing. Whatever the reason for this phenomenon, the highly unusual concentration of businesses specializing in the aesthetics of the body in South African townships is much more than a metaphor: it reflects the intense dynamism of entrepreneurship on a continent still considered poor and doomed to perpetuate its past mistakes.

Economic development, which started with the Industrial Revolution, is a process of continuous improvement in labor productivity through industrial and technological upgrading. It is fueled by entrepreneurship and facilitated by an enabling government that provides appropriate infrastructure and institutions and encourages learning and knowledge sharing (Lin 2012a, 2012b; Stiglitz and Greenwald 2014). An important part of the process is the willingness and ability of entrepreneurs to take risks and create businesses that generate income, employment, social cohesion, and a collective sense of self-worth and common purpose. But this process can be sustainable only if state resources complement the efforts of individuals and private firms to overcome externalities and solve the coordination problems that often underlie the constraints in finance, infrastructure, employee skills, and the regulatory environment. No single entrepreneur or private firm can credibly overcome an infrastructure gap, the lack of employee skills, or imperfections in the regulatory environment required for reducing transaction costs in new industries. And no country in the world has the administrative and financial resources to blindly build all the airports, roads, railways, and other sector-specific infrastructure that entrepreneurs need, or to randomly train the workforce that industries require to take off and be sustainable. What is needed is selectivity, identification, and targeting of industries in which an economy has a comparative advantage—that is, low factor costs of production compared with producing similar goods or services in other countries.

The history of successful economic development includes only a handful of countries that have supported the natural human drive for entrepreneurship, have gone through the process of creative destruction—which stimulates structural transformation (reallocating resources from low- to high-productivity sectors)—and have constantly moved up their value-chain ladder so that their economy's comparative advantage slowly but continuously changes as their endowment structure changes.[2] Conversely, the history of failed development has primarily included governments whose leaders were unable to work with the private sector and other development stakeholders to channel the government's limited resources and capacity into building the necessary infrastructure and improving the business environment in a way that helps private entrepreneurs reduce their transaction costs in new industries that reflect the economy's latent comparative advantage.[3]

High-income countries such as the United States have long taken pride in the extraordinary drive of their small entrepreneurs and the intensity of their private sectors—and rightfully so. But the economic development literature has not always shed sufficient light on the delicate but essential role of the state, which is always necessary, if not to ignite new industries, at least to help them become viable competitive segments of the economy, especially in an increasingly globalized world where cooperation and connection to networks are integral elements of success.[4]

In contrast, low-income countries—where the entrepreneurial drive is as strong as elsewhere—struggle to connect private efforts and creativity with public and government resources. These countries often fail to identify broad strategic areas in which their economies have latent comparative advantage and to use their limited resources and bureaucratic capacity to coordinate and provide necessary improvements in hard and soft infrastructure. These improvements would reduce transaction costs, help industries become self-sustaining, and create employment. Instead, the countries maintain macro- and microeconomic distortions and compound political economy problems that are the result of their bad policies and weak institutional and regulatory environment. That is precisely why they remain low-income economies in a world where infinite possibilities for shared prosperity have opened up—possibilities spurred by changing patterns of global growth, redistribution of roles in the production of goods and services, a generally rising tide of trade, accumulation of human capital and talent in many places, and changing dynamics of migration and capital flows. That is a pity. In fact, in addition to failing to help the development of latent comparative advantage industries, most developing countries implemented structural adjustment policies advocated by proponents of the Washington Consensus: they attempted to eliminate all distortions without realizing that many of them came from second-best institutional arrangements. Those arrangements provided protections to firms in priority sectors of the previous import-substitution strategy. Without protections, those firms would not have been viable. But if the distortions were eliminated abruptly, many nonviable firms in priority sectors would have collapsed, causing a contraction of gross domestic product (GDP), a surge in unemployment, and acute social disorder. To avoid those dreadful consequences, many governments continued to subsidize the nonviable firms through other disguised, less efficient subsidies and protections (Lin and Tan 1999). Transitional and developing countries thus recorded even poorer growth performance and stability in the 1980s and 1990s than in the 1960s and 1970s (Easterly 2001).

Countries that have undergone successful transitions, such as China, Mauritius, and Vietnam, adopted a pragmatic, gradual, dual-track approach. The government continued to provide transitory subsidies to protect the old comparative-advantage-defying sector, but it liberalized and facilitated entry into the new comparative-advantage-following sectors. Their overall business environment and infrastructure have remained poor, but their governments played an enabling role in creating increasingly large enclaves favorable for the development of industries with latent comparative advantages.

There are many win-win opportunities out there for all countries, regardless of their income and current conditions. There is room for higher rates of inclusive growth, including in countries with very poor business and governance environments. The beauty shop owners and other micro entrepreneurs of Diepsloot could thrive and prosper if the government were more deliberate in designing and implementing a strategy that identifies sectors with strong competitive potential and facilitates their connection with global trade networks and value chains.

The challenge of economic development is not just to ignite high growth rates but also to maintain development without excessive protection and unsustainable subsidies (Hausmann, Pritchett, and Rodrik 2005) and to ensure that the broadest segments of the population benefit from wealth creation. Distortions most likely will continue to exist, as they are necessary to avoid the collapse of old sectors. The new sectors, consistent with the country's latent comparative advantage, require the government's facilitation to reduce transaction costs by improving hard and soft infrastructure so that businesses can become competitive and prosper in domestic and global markets. The government may also provide some incentives to the first movers in the new industries to compensate for the externalities they generate. It can do this by providing tax holidays without distorting prices or giving monopolies.

This book confronts one of the most common misconceptions of economic development theories: the misguided notions that economic prosperity can occur only in places with an excellent business environment and that growth is the result of painful and politically difficult reforms. It also sheds light on the ways economic transformation can be engineered even in countries with a suboptimal institutional environment and weak overall physical and human capital. Building on *New Structural Economics*, its growth identification and facilitation framework operationalization tool, and other works we have written in recent years, it makes the case against the false economics of preconditions (Chandra, Lin, and Wang 2013; Lin 2012a, b, c; Monga 2013a, b; Lin and Monga 2012, 2013, 2014).

This book argues that it is possible for a low-income country (which by definition must have poor infrastructure and a weak institutional environment) to develop industries in which it has latent comparative advantage—provided that the government plays an enabling role by using its limited resources and implementation capacity strategically to create a localized good business environment in industrial parks or zones that facilitates the entry and growth of those industries. The country will then have low factor costs of production in such industries, and the industrial parks or zones will offer circumscribed environments with adequate infrastructure and institutions to reduce transaction costs. As a result, even though the overall business environment remains poor, the production costs (factor costs and transaction costs) for the targeted industries can be competitive internationally. This can allow the economy to attract foreign investment, likely by active investment promotion through government managerial expertise. The economy can also generate the backward and forward linkages necessary for knowledge and learning externalities and sustained success. This is the secret formula for jump-starting dynamic growth in a poor country.

In a nutshell, this book draws lessons from economic history, economic theory, and economic analysis to highlight the often forgotten fact that economic development always occurs in places where almost every one of the preconditions for success is missing or suboptimal. From that observation, the book offers a pragmatic and realistic road map to generating shared prosperity anywhere in the developing world. It underscores the facilitating role of an enabling state, sheds light on the most effective patterns of public-private partnerships, and stresses the need for economists and policy makers to stay away from ideological postures and the legacy of distortions and ill-advised development theories (old structuralism and market fundamentalism).

This introduction sets the stage for the book by presenting stories of economic miracles from the most unlikely places and different country contexts and by linking them to the broader narrative of economic development as it has occurred around the world since the Industrial Revolution.

PERFORMING ECONOMIC MIRACLES IN THE DESERT

In Cecil B. DeMille's classic film *The Ten Commandments* (1956) on the biblical story of the Exodus, widely considered by critics to be a cinematic masterpiece, there is a defining scene in which Moses is expelled from Egypt, where he had tried to free the Hebrew slaves from bondage. The pharaoh Rameses, who considers death to be too easy a punishment for his enemies, condemns Moses to "suffer by living" and banishes him from the kingdom where they were raised as brothers. When sending him off to the Sinai Desert for a slower, more painful, and certain death, Rameses says sarcastically: "Here is your kingdom, with the scorpion, the cobra, and the lizard for subjects. Free them, if you will. Leave the Hebrews to me!" Moses vanishes slowly over the horizon, armed with only a symbolic scepter given to him as an emblem of his insignificant authority in the wilderness. Yet, as the story goes, Moses is able not only to overcome the worst possible forms of adversity in the desert but also to free his people.

Yes, this is a biblical story. Still, it is impossible even for a nonbeliever to travel in Israel some two thousand years later and not feel the intrinsic magic of the place known as the Holy Land. Nowhere is that feeling more overwhelming than in the Negev Desert, where the human spirit and ingenuity have conquered this "vast expanse of moonscape rock and sand that has been a desolate hothouse since pre-history" (Auerbach 1987). This is the lowest point on Earth, 1,200 feet below sea level, with an average of 355 sunny days and barely an inch of rain each year, and where daytime temperatures often exceed 120°F and nights can fall below freezing, yet agricultural production and exports have increased dramatically over the decades. The land long considered uninhabitable is now home to nearly one million people and hundreds of thriving agricultural settlements. Melons, tomatoes, eggplant, peppers, dates, zucchini, and avocados from the desert are shipped to the markets of Europe weeks or months before local harvests. Some farmers harvest crops three or four times a year, growing large quantities of food per acre—four to six times what a farmer in the United States might grow yearly (Auerbach 1987).

Many of these crops are genetically engineered and irrigated with salty water from large aquifers beneath the desert. Despite the difficult climate of this area full of rocks and dust and sparsely vegetated, agricultural production is boosting the country's economy. Cotton yields in the Negev are higher than those in California, Arizona, or Egypt; peanut yields outstrip those in U.S. states such as Georgia and West Virginia, where geography and climate offer considerable advantages. In this unimaginably inhospitable place, Israelis also decided a few decades ago to develop wineries, which are now producing millions of bottles of table wine, including for export. They have engineered spectacular economic success in a place with extreme temperatures and not very fertile soil, and where water, if available, is saline or very expensive.[5] Labor is scarce and therefore also expensive.

Israel's remarkable success in greening the Negev has been hailed as a technological and biological breakthrough and a revolution in managing land and water resources in a poor and difficult desert environment. Israel is unique among developed economies in that its land and water resources are nearly all state owned. Another unique characteristic of Israeli agriculture is the dominance of cooperatives, known as kibbutzim and moshavim. Although the management systems are being gradually privatized, the cooperatives still account for about 80 percent of agricultural output. For several decades, government interventions through central planning of agricultural policies, allocating quotas, controlling prices, protecting against imports, and providing subsidies helped expand agricultural production and exports. Reforms are now in place to remove these policies but only gradually (OECD 2010).

Skeptics may dismiss Israel's agricultural miracle as a costly, capital-intensive fantasy that only a high-income country could afford. Few developing countries could indeed mobilize the capital, technology, and skills to achieve similar agricultural success in the desert—especially in a country where the relative share of agriculture has declined over the past two decades, with its share in total employment and domestic output falling to under 3 percent and 2 percent, respectively. But the main lessons from this story are the economic successes that can be achieved even in the most unlikely places when good policies are implemented to support and facilitate the emergence of competitive industries. Israel has become a world leader in agricultural technology, particularly farming in arid conditions, by exploiting a latent rather than "natural" comparative advantage, one built on knowledge and technological progress and financed at high cost, with strong support from the state. Just like the people in Diepsloot, the Israelis in the Negev Desert have shown entrepreneurial skills, creativity, and resilience. But they have benefited from the strong support of an enabling state that has helped identify latent comparative advantage and removed binding constraints to facilitate the transition of agriculture and resources into dynamic manufacturing and service sectors in the economy.

CHINESE POTATOES: A PARADOXICAL STORY

Despite being the fourth most important world crop, surpassed only by wheat, rice, and maize, the potato has never been the fanciest product in human food systems. In its more than five centuries of history, it has been adopted and adapted as a highland subsistence crop on all continents and has become an important dietary staple. Yet its reputation remains as a popular if not second-class product, perhaps because it was originally an "antifamine food." According to Ellen Messer (2000, 187), it "has been credited with fueling the Industrial Revolution in eighteenth-century Europe but blamed for the mid-nineteenth-century Irish famine. . . . [It] also became a central and distinctive element of European regional, and then national, cuisines." With the globalization of diet and taste that gradually occurred after World War II, multinational companies such as McDonald's developed various forms of standardized, industrially produced potato fries, chips, and other frozen and processed convenience foods based on potatoes, which opened new markets.

When Chinese authorities identified potatoes in the early 1990s as a potential income source to be encouraged, few people even in China thought it was a good idea. Even in places such as Anding County in Gansu Province, where the crop had long been cultivated, it was seen as a secondary crop with a larger market risk than, for example, wheat, for which the government had guaranteed purchasing prices to farmers. Moreover, in the aftermath of rural reform in the 1980s, individual farmers had reclaimed land-use rights and could make their own production decisions. The state could not force them to switch their cropping patterns away from wheat to potatoes.

To persuade farmers that the potato was consistent with the region's comparative advantage and offered excellent income perspective, local officials first mobilized village cadres to experiment with large-scale potato production on their land. Although the farm gate price was rather low, the first potato adopters saw large financial gains because the higher potato yields largely offset the lower price relative to wheat (Zhang and Hu 2011). The yield was good: even at a lower price per kilogram, merely switching production from wheat to potatoes would double the total gross agricultural income. In addition to the higher financial reward of planting potatoes, many farmers could afford to buy high-quality seed potatoes, thanks to funding from the government. Anding County's apparently hostile natural environment still suited potato cultivation, and the dry climate reduced the need for pesticides. Land quality could be improved through irrigation.

The increase in potato production attracted many traders eager to take advantage of poor farmers but who knew nothing about price information in urban wholesale markets—most had never even traveled to big cities where their crops' prices were determined. There were too many middlemen—agents, outside traders, wholesalers, retailers—between farmers and consumers, and asymmetric information allowed them to capture most of the profits, which resulted in some farmers reverting back to wheat production in the early 2000s.

An analysis of the county government's supply chain revealed that lack of market information and weak collective-bargaining power among farmers were the main reasons for their low share of income from potatoes. The county government helped establish a farmers' association to train local farmers who could also become traders. Even farmers with minimal education were given a month of marketing training at the School of Economics and Management at Lanzhou University, which allowed them eventually to increase their bargaining power in the industry. When farmers received higher prices for their output, they produced more potatoes. The rapid increase in market share of potatoes allowed the potato trade association to build wholesale markets financed through a public-private partnership in Anding County, which helped obtain pricing information in a much cheaper, timelier, and more accurate way than collecting the information from wholesale markets all over China. Taking into consideration potato production's seasonal nature, the authorities worked with farmers to help them develop new and better product varieties and offered subsidies to build storage facilities and to stimulate the creation of a potato-processing industry. Working with banks to secure loans for investors, the local government supported the processing industry's development, which created value addition, helped absorb the low-quality potatoes left over from the consumer market, and provided a floor price for those low-quality potatoes. This brought additional income to farmers and generated tax revenues. The support allowed farmers to store the potatoes a little longer, smooth out supply during the year, and sell their products at a good price all year long.

In sum, sensible industrial policy by the local government led to a remarkable transformation of what used to be one of the poorest regions in China. It has now become China's potato capital. Potatoes account for more than 60 percent of cropland in the county, and more than 30 percent of the rural population is involved in activities related to potato production, marketing, and processing. In addition, 60 percent of farmers' income comes from potato production. When potatoes were first identified as an important potential income and employment source in the region, many experts had shown disdain for what they thought would simply be another failed, state-led industrial policy. They stressed China's poor business environment, the skills shortage, and the geographical site, which seemed unsuited for potato production. As Xiaobo Zhang and Dinghuan Hu (2011, 5) note, "The harsh natural environment in Anding County is comparable to, if not worse than, many sub-Saharan African countries. Yet both land and labor productivity in Anding County have improved dramatically over the past three decades. Thus, the successful agricultural transformation of Anding County can provide some useful lessons for other countries at similar stages of development."

Again, such a successful story can be seen as purely anecdotal, and skeptics would dismiss it as another epic tale that only China could pull off because it would be too complicated for the average poor country with (presumably) poor organizational capabilities to handle. That would be the wrong conclusion to draw. In fact, Chinese authorities did nothing extraordinary in building the potato cluster—except perhaps to follow commonsense principles and lessons from economic analysis. Just like Israelis in the Negev Desert, they worked with farmers and investors to pick an industry that was consistent with the economy's latent comparative advantage. And they designed and implemented a simple policy package that could help remove constraints on production and sales and quickly yield widely shared results. To facilitate the cluster's establishment, they studied the competitiveness of the industry through value-chain analysis, identified the main bottlenecks, and provided incentives to investors (land at a discounted price to build factory buildings and localized infrastructure, such as electricity and water supply). The results have been spectacular for all stakeholders.

THE MALIAN MANGO'S PROMISING TALE

Even low-income African countries with very poor business conditions can achieve rapid success in specific industries or sectors comparable to that of high- and middle-income countries such as Israel or China. One of Africa's recent economic success stories, chronicled by Punam Chuhan-Pole and Mwanka Angwafo (2011), is that of Mali's mango exports. A single number sheds light on this most unusual case story: between 1996 and 2006 mango exports from that poor Sahelian, landlocked country into the European Union rose by 600 percent, and in 2014 they reached nearly thirty-eight million tons, allowing millions of farmers to increase their incomes and improve their livelihoods. It all started in the early 1990s at a time when the country's business environment indicators were quite weak—even in 2014 Mali ranked very low on the World Bank's Doing Business indicators, 155th out of 189 economies in the world.

Value added in agriculture was 46 percent of GDP in 1990, and the sector employed about 80 percent of 1990's labor force. But the country lacked most of the basic infrastructure required to open many productive rural areas to trade's benefits. Only 11 percent of the country's road network was paved (25 percent in 2011). There were only thirteen fixed-line and mobile telephone subscribers per 100 people at the peak of mango exports to the European Union in 2006, lower than that year's average for low-income countries (seventeen per 100 people). Less than 10 percent of firms had a line of credit. Governance indicators also were poor, at least as measured by the most commonly used indices: in 1996, for example, Mali scored only a meager 9.3 for government effectiveness on the World Governance indicators (WGI) in percentile ranks, which run from 0 to 100, with higher values reflecting better outcomes. Most of these business and governance indicators remain poor even today.

Still, Malian authorities decided to refocus their development strategy on their country's comparative advantage. Considering the good geographical and weather conditions prevailing in the southern part of the country, they selected labor-intensive agriculture as a sector with strong growth potential. Several horticultural crops were considered as possible targets for economic diversification efforts, including cashews, tomatoes, shallots, and mangoes. Mangoes became a prime candidate both because of the excellent agriclimatic conditions for growing them in the southern regions of Bougouni and Sikasso and because of the fast-growing demand for them in European markets (Sangho, Labaste, and Ravry 2011). Further, the private sector had already identified mangoes as a competitive product, and smallholder farmers throughout the country relied heavily on them as an important income source.

But despite the high quality of Mali's fresh fruit and vegetables, the poor state of infrastructure, the high cost of air freight, and the failure of the state to provide research and extension services and to help build adequate storage facilities were severely limiting marketing and exportation. As a result, many of Mali's mangoes were either lost because they could not be conserved or purchased and processed for export by operators based in Côte d'Ivoire, thus depriving the country of opportunities for value addition.

In 1992 the government prepared a national rural development strategy, the Schéma directeur du développement rural, emphasizing commercial agriculture, export promotion, and value addition, and began directing resources toward those ends. With assistance from the donor community (notably the World Bank and the U.S. Agency for International Development), the government also established an agricultural trading and processing pilot project in 1996, the Projet d'appui à la valorisation et à la commercialisation des produits agricoles (PAVCOPA), which sought to promote agribusiness and exports. It allowed stakeholders to find effective ways to get the product to market, while innovations in transport and logistics systems allowed farmers and exporters to achieve economies of scale.

The state also played its facilitating role by helping with market research, analyzing value-chain costs, benchmarking, and assessing industry constraints. It provided technical assistance and training in the control of plant diseases. These policy actions led to a virtuous circle of positive externalities. There was clear improvement in the average quality of fruit exported from Mali—sea container rejections due to fruit flies, for example, dropped considerably. Backward linkages at the production level also emerged as relationships between exporters and farmers became stronger and based on win-win business deals.[6] Mali was also able to get a foothold in the fair trade niche market.

The initial takeoff in the growth of mango exports has led to a transformation of the subsector and stimulated private-sector interest. It has also provided further evidence that successful economic stories can occur even in the most unlikely places when the government and the private sector work closely to identify the most promising competitive industries—those consistent with the economy's comparative advantage—and to design a manageable and targeted reform program for removing the most binding constraints to their development. Much remains to be done to ensure long-term sustainability of the vibrant mango industry in Mali and to make it a strong pillar for the country's agribusiness strategy (building and retaining capacity through skills and workforce development programs, strengthening the necessary infrastructure and logistics, implementing a realistic industrial and technological upgrading strategy, connecting better to international value chains to improve business and learning practices, and ensuring stable access to finance). But the mango industry's emergence in a country among the less well prepared for international business success confirms the effectiveness of development programs based on latent comparative advantage.

BEYOND ANECDOTAL EVIDENCE: ECONOMIC DEVELOPMENT'S KNOWNS AND UNKNOWNS

In 2002 U.S. secretary of defense Donald Rumsfeld, preparing to wage war on Iraq, was asked at a press conference about the lack of a clear link between Saddam Hussein's regime and terrorist organizations. In his usual feisty style he responded: "As we know, there are known knowns; there are things we know we know. We also know there are known unknowns; that is to say we know there are some things we do not know. But there are also unknown unknowns—the ones we don't know we don't know."[7] His comments, which instantly became part of the global geopolitical lexicon, were reminiscent of Confucius's well-known prescription for wisdom: "To know what you know and what you do not know, that is true knowledge."

The three economic success stories discussed above obviously do not provide a strong enough basis to derive complete knowledge about economic development. They could just offer anecdotal evidence and partial truths, perhaps useful as peculiar historical narratives but not sufficiently comprehensive and legitimate for building rigorous economic theory.[8] When approaching issues of causality and the search for the determinants of complex social phenomena, one should always be aware of omitted variables' existence, "white noise processes" (random processes of random variables that are uncorrelated), the many limitations imposed on theoretical reasoning by the "knowns," the "unknowns," and the mysterious patterns of interaction between them. It was Rumsfeld again who, in response to the question of why the U.S. Army could not find weapons of mass destruction in Iraq after overthrowing the Saddam Hussein regime and taking control of the country, said: "Absence of evidence is not evidence of absence"—another statement with which economists and econometricians would agree.

Such awareness of the difficulties surrounding the understanding and formulation of causal inference in economics and the daunting challenges of elaborating theories of development that are both intellectually rigorous and useful (yielding clear, positive results) to policy makers in individual countries may explain the reluctance of some of the most influential minds in the profession to offer policy prescriptions. After studying in depth the thirteen economies with very different forms of governance that managed to grow at more than 7 percent for periods of more than twenty-five years after World War II, the Growth Commission (led by Nobel laureate Michael Spence) identified a series of stylized facts associated with sustained and inclusive growth: openness to the global economy, macroeconomic stability, high saving and investment rates, market allocation of resources, and good leadership and governance.

But the commission was quick to conclude:

We do not know the sufficient conditions for growth. We can characterize the successful economies of the postwar period, but we cannot name with certainty the factors that sealed their success, or the factors they could have succeeded without. It would be preferable if it were otherwise. Nonetheless, the commissioners have a keen sense of the policies that probably matter—the policies that will make a material difference to a country's chances of sustaining high growth, even if they do not provide a rock-solid guarantee. Just as we cannot say this list is sufficient, we cannot say for sure that all the ingredients are necessary. . . . A list of ingredients is not a recipe, and our list does not constitute a growth strategy. (Commission on Growth and Development 2008, 33)

Robert Solow, another Nobel laureate, widely considered the father of modern growth theory, is as circumspect when discussing the puzzling issues of economic development. When asked why many great minds in economics too often avoid the challenge of elaborating economic development theories, he explains that the subject matter is just too complicated to be taken lightly. He adds that his own work attempts to account for the main features of U.S. economic growth, not to provide an economic development theory. One can only admire Spence's and Solow's humility. But as Robert Lucas—yet another Nobel laureate—famously observed, the search for economic development recipes is of crucial importance. "Is there some action a government of India could take that would lead the Indian economy to grow like Indonesia's or Egypt's?" Lucas wondered. "If so, *what*, exactly? If not, what is it about the 'nature of India' that makes it so? The consequences for human welfare involved in questions like these are simply staggering: once one starts to think about them, it is hard to think about anything else" (Lucas 1988, 5; italics in original).

This book takes up the Lucas challenge but takes a route to the quest of knowledge that differs from conventional approaches. Starting from the observation from historical data that the entire world was poor until about the Industrial Revolution (Maddison 2001), the book seeks to highlight lessons in economic development from other countries' experiences. In fact, looking back to the unexpected economic successes in Great Britain, the United States, Japan, and elsewhere during or after the Industrial Revolution and throughout the twentieth century, one can piece together again a broad picture and knowledge of economic development, which always takes place in suboptimal environments—not after a long list of structural reforms is implemented. Yet the dominant discourse still sets the linear, teleological path to economic progress, which poor countries can implement only with difficulties and with no guarantee that they will yield good results.

Since Plato's *Theaetetus*, philosophers have been concerned about defining precisely what knowledge is useful and how to acquire it. Their general formula that "knowledge is justified true belief," which is taken to mean "believing what is true and having sufficient reasons for it," is of little practical use to economists and policy makers in the development business. Many researchers have devoted themselves to elaborating various theories by which, they argue, all analyses of economic and social problems must justify themselves if they are to claim rigor, coherence, and validity.

True, no consideration of economic development strategies can take place outside an at least implicit theory that underlies it. As Murray Krieger (1976, 7) reminds us, "Our choice is not between having a theory or not having one; for have one (or two or three or more incompatible ones) we must. Our choice is rather between having an awareness of those theoretical issues which our criticism inevitably raises and going along without such an awareness." But there is always a limit beyond which the drive to theorize brings fewer and fewer knowledge benefits and more and more dangers of distraction.[9]

The problems posed by theory's hegemony have been well recognized in economics (Sen 1977). They are even more acute when one realizes that "theory and assumptions are synonyms" and that "other synonyms of assumption are hypothesis, premise, and suppositions" (Manski 2013, 11). But in attempting to move in the opposite direction, researchers may have gone too far. The surge in empiricism—often derived from John Locke's idea that one gains any true knowledge mainly through experience and now reflected in the wide reliance on randomized control trials as the dominant tool of analysis in development studies—has also led to an almost religious belief in the intrinsic value of number games. Yet these so-called evidence-based methods, often postmortem evaluations of projects whose lessons are not transferable from one area to another, also fail to inform policy choices because they do not really enhance the ability to predict whether government programs will be effective (Cartwright and Hardie 2012). They often lead to misleading or useless certainties.

In this book, whose theoretical foundations we explored in previous publications (Lin 2012a, b, c; Lin and Monga 2013; Monga 2013b), we opt for a methodological approach that draws lessons and insights from economic history and theory and uses empirics from economic analysis and policy practice. It starts with the observation that in an increasingly globalized world economy in which technological development allows the use of factors of production in locations that maximize returns and utility, countries gain mutually by trading with each other—if their strategies focus on revealed and latent comparative advantage, determined by their endowment structure. By following carefully selected lead countries, late-comers can emulate the leader-follower, flying-geese pattern that has well served economies catching up since the eighteenth century.

These ideas—which build on insights articulated by David Ricardo (1817), Alexander Gerschenkron (1962), K. Akamatsu (1962), and others—embody the new structural economics approach. They shed light on how structural transformation occurs in environments with suboptimal social, economic, and institutional conditions. The prospects for sustained and inclusive growth are even greater for low-income economies that enjoy the benefits of backwardness. Moreover, the economic success and eventual "graduation" from low-skilled manufacturing jobs of large middle-income economies such as China, Indonesia, Brazil, and Turkey to higher-wage in-dustries opens unprecedented opportunities for lower-income countries. This book advocates implementing viable strategies to capture this new op-portunity for industrialization, which can enable low-income economies to set forth on a dynamic path of structural change and lead to poverty reduction and prosperity.

Chapters 1–4 of this book challenge the conventional thinking on de-velopment and the false economics of preconditions. They argue that the traditional approaches to the development problem—focusing the diag-nostics on the many constraints and obstacles to growth such as governance or lack of human capital or the infrastructure deficit—are misguided. They also argue that the current dominant discourse in economic development, which still sets the linear teleological path for developing countries, makes policy making there difficult, if not impossible, and subjects the outcomes to randomness and chance. Conceiving sustained economic growth as the result of numerous structural reforms to improve "governance" and the business environment in poor countries is historically and conceptually unrealistic. The reason? Such approaches use what high-income countries have or are doing relatively well as references to determine what a devel-oping country lacks or cannot do well. They then advise the developing country to obtain what the high-income countries have or to do as the high-income countries are doing. Such approaches often fail to take into account the different preconditions of development between developing countries and high-income countries.

Chapters 5–7 lay out concrete steps for achieving high growth even in poor institutional and business environments by focusing on what a poor country could do well based on what it has. Almost all low-income economies can achieve high and inclusive growth if economists and policy makers reject the determinism of preconditions and instead facilitate the development of industries in which the country has latent comparative advantage—and if the enabling government uses its limited resources and implementation capacity strategically to create a localized good business environment in industrial parks or zones. The main ingredients of a winning strategy? Selecting industries with competitive potential and targeting reforms that are least disruptive and yield the highest payoffs.

1

The Tyranny of Litanies

In some African cities, traffic police who engage in petty corruption by routinely stopping motorists to obtain cash from them are known for their ability to come up with endless justifications for doing so. The goal of these rogue cops is not to catch bad drivers who commit traffic violations but to find ways to squeeze money from whomever they stop. After randomly pulling motorists over and checking first that they do not have political connections or are not a high-level authority, they search for an infraction with which to cite the driver—if the driver is unwilling to give them cash. They usually start by requesting the registration and insurance for the vehicle. If this paperwork is in order, they will not hide their discontentment. They then request the driver's license. Again, they will not conceal their displeasure if the driver is able to provide a valid license. They then must find something else to justify a citation. After they go through a list of other nonmoving violations or infractions (defective or improper vehicle equipment, seat belt or child-restraint safety violation, etc.), their logical next request is to ask to see the pharmacy box. Yes, in many countries motor vehicles on the road are required to have a pharmacy box. No one knows what it must legally contain, and rogue police use its absence as an excuse to issue a traffic ticket.

Some motorists heroically resist complying with such extortion and are well prepared for encounters with the police by keeping a pharmacy box in their car. When confronted with such drivers the disgruntled police ask a final, unanswerable question: "Can you prove that you were driving at the appropriate speed limit when I pulled you over?" adding with a sarcastic smile, "I stopped you because you were driving too fast!"

In such bad-luck situations it is impossible to escape punishment. The only remaining question is whether the motorist will choose to play the game, plead guilty to a phony charge, and pay the bribe or will pursue the heroic fight to prove compliance with laws and regulations. If the motorist wishes to contest a traffic infraction, the police will take away the vehicle's registration and promise a hearing to be set by the court. The hearings are supposed to take place before a magistrate or judge. Of course, no motorist wants to take the chance of relinquishing important documents to rogue police, so the rational (less risky and frankly less costly) option is to plead guilty to whatever traffic violation the driver is being accused of and then make a deal with the police, often in the form of a couple of dollars paid as a ransom to avoid further harassment.

The discourse on economic development is often reminiscent of this kind of uneven interaction. When asked why only a handful of countries have managed to perform well since the Washington Consensus policies were launched in the 1980s, many experts tend to behave like the rogue police on the streets of Africa. They offer ever-changing explanations that they present as irrefutable truths. Defending their intellectual agenda even in the midst of obvious failure and disappointments, they come up with a litany of reasons for the failure of their prescriptions—typically a wide range of reasons about poor implementation—that policy makers in developing countries cannot dispute. This justification strategy of constantly putting the blame on the recipient allows the proponents of the Washington Consensus to require further compliance by poor countries. Like the helpless motorists on some African streets, policy makers must accept whatever recommendations are imposed on them.

Of course, it would be unfair to characterize the honest but difficult search for answers that motivates most development economists and experts as equivalent to the immoral and illegal behavior of renegade police. But the fundamental tactics often used to justify a predetermined and liturgical discourse and to enforce a priori decisions are similar. They are often based on false diagnostics and rely on rhetorical sophisms. This is why policy makers in low-income countries often confess that they constantly feel pressure from powerful development experts whose opinions carry weight and can determine whether a small economy has access to external funding. In many such countries, Washington Consensus policies still represent the dominant intellectual framework for policy analysis and justify all prescriptions for reforms (Monga and Lin 2015; Mkandawire 2014; Mkandawire and Soludo 1999; Mkandawire and Olukoshi 1995). Questions about the sources of low growth, low employment creation, and persistent poverty are given successive answers that are meant only to reflect and validate a predetermined truth. After trying in vain to offer alternative views of the problems of development, government officials find themselves in the same situation as the African motorists. The opportunity cost of asserting different opinions and of taking the chance to pursue different strategies is simply too high. It becomes rational to just go along with the prevailing truth and conventional thinking—and to accommodate policies that have little chance of yielding the expected positive results.

This chapter examines some of the policy issues often presented as the causes of poor economic performance and underdevelopment. It identifies the most commonly posited causes—insufficient physical capital, bad business environment and poor governance, weak human capital and absorptive capacity, low productivity, and bad cultural habits (laziness)—and explains why they are inconsistent with both the historical and the empirical evidence.

INFRASTRUCTURE: A REAL CONSTRAINT BUT A CONVENIENT CULPRIT

The most common policy precondition given by many economists for improved economic performance in developing economies is the quantity and quality of infrastructure. Since at least Adam Smith, economists have known that transport infrastructure plays an important role in economic growth and poverty reduction. Starting with the work of D. Aschauer (1989), B. Sanchez-Robles (1998), and D. Canning (1999), researchers have offered compelling theoretical and empirical analyses to support infrastructure's role. While the empirical arguments about the specific conditions under which infrastructure is beneficial are far from being fully settled, there is broad consensus that under the appropriate conditions, infrastructure development can induce growth and equity, both of which contribute to poverty reduction. Infrastructure services increase total factor productivity (TFP) directly because they are an additional production input and have an immediate impact on enterprises' productivity. Indirectly they can raise TFP by reducing transaction and other costs, thus allowing a more efficient use of conventional productive inputs. In addition, infrastructure services "can affect investment adjustment costs, the durability of private capital and both demand for and supply of health and education services. If transport, electricity, or telecom services are absent or unreliable, firms face additional costs (e.g., having to purchase power generators), and they are prevented from adopting new technologies. Better transportation increases the effective size of labor markets" (Dethier 2015).

It is conventional wisdom that all economies rely heavily on various types of infrastructure and investments to improve conditions and performance and to move people and goods more efficiently and safely to local, domestic, and international markets. All countries need effective transport, sanitation, energy, and communications systems if they are to prosper and provide an adequate standard of living for their populations. Decent roads, railways, seaports, and airports are essential for the sustainable growth of key industries such as agriculture, industry, mining, or tourism—particularly important in developing economies. Good transport infrastructure improves the delivery of and access to vital social services such as health and education. Without a well-functioning transport system, much activity in most countries would grind to a halt.

Transportation infrastructure has substantial economic benefits in both the long and the short run. Investments that create, maintain, or expand road and railway networks can improve economic efficiency, productivity, and economic growth. These investments can also support employment in construction and in the production of materials, with the increased spending by the workers hired in these sectors generating positive ripple effects throughout the economy. The short-run effects can vary depending on the state of the economy. At the peak of a business cycle, when the economy is operating at or close to full potential, the benefits of hiring workers for infrastructure projects could be partially offset by the diversion of these workers from other productive activities, and the investment of public funds may "crowd out" some private investment (EOP 2011). But economies around the world are generally operating significantly below their full potential, with underemployment and unemployment still high. In such excess-capacity situations there is little risk that increased spending on construction materials and increased private spending by newly hired workers will divert goods or materials from other uses. In fact, with large amounts of resources sitting idle, the opportunity costs of using them for infrastructure investment are greatly reduced. Therefore the value of making such investments is high at a time when the global economy continues to have substantial underutilized resources, including more than 200 million workers seeking employment.

Yet many developing countries suffer from a large infrastructure deficit, which hampers their growth and ability to trade in the global economy. Asia still demonstrates a massive gap in infrastructure funding.[1] The situation in Latin America and the Caribbean is no better. César Calderón and Luis Servén (2011) compare the evolution of infrastructure availability, quality, and accessibility across the region with that of other benchmark regions. They focus on telecommunications, electricity, land transportation, and water and sanitation. Overall they find evidence that an "infrastructure gap" vis-à-vis other industrial and developing regions opened up in the 1980s and 1990s. They also estimate the quantitative growth cost of the region's infrastructure gap.

Africa's infrastructure challenges are even more daunting. Compared with other regions, Africa has a low infrastructure stock, particularly in energy and transportation, and the continent has not fully harnessed its information and communication technology potential. Inadequate infrastructure raises the transaction costs of business in most African economies. Studies by the African Development Bank estimate that inadequate infrastructure shaves off at least 2 percent of Africa's annual growth, and that with adequate infrastructure, African firms could achieve productivity gains of up to 40 percent. The situation is particularly worrisome in the agriculture sector. Calestous Juma (2012) notes:

> A large part of the continent's inability to feed itself and stimulate rural entrepreneurship can be explained by poor infrastructure (transportation, energy, irrigation, and telecommunication). The majority of Africa's rural populations do not live within reach of all-season roads. As a result they are not capable of participating in any meaningful entrepreneurial activities. On average, in middle-income countries about 60 percent of rural people live within two kilometers of an all-season road. In Kenya . . . only about 32 percent of the rural people live within two kilometers of an all-weather road. The figure is 31 percent for Angola, 26 percent for Malawi, 24 percent for Tanzania, 18 percent for Mali and a mere 10.5 percent for Ethiopia.

Unfortunately, too many experts draw the wrong conclusions from these diagnostics. Identifying a problem correctly does not necessarily translate into a good understanding of its meaning and implications. One should be careful not to misinterpret Albert Einstein's admonition, "If I had an hour to solve a problem I'd spend fifty-five minutes thinking about the problem and five minutes thinking about solutions." While the infrastructure gap must be resolved, it is a mistake to postulate—as many development experts do—that it necessarily prevents developing countries from initiating a process of sustained economic growth.

Poor infrastructure is indeed a major binding constraint on economic performance, but it is not an insurmountable barrier for launching economic transformation, especially with today's globalized economies, decentralized global value chains, increasingly freer trade, mobile capital flows, and migration of skilled workers. Economic development and infrastructure building can evolve in parallel and feed each other. No country in human history started its process of economic development with good infrastructure—certainly not Great Britain in the late eighteenth century, the United States in the early nineteenth century, or China in the late twentieth century, where there was only a very small network of highways. Yes, Africa's infrastructure gap is a major bottleneck to economic growth and welfare. But it is a mistake to expect that economic development can be launched successfully only *after* that gap is filled—in fact, it may never be filled, even when the continent's annual GDP per capita reaches $100,000. Infrastructure development and maintenance are matters of constant concern for policy makers—even high-income countries need continuous industrial and technological upgrading.[2]

Moreover, by assuming that the infrastructure gap is *the* culprit for poor economic performance and that it should be resolved *before* sustained growth can take place, many experts and policy makers tend to adopt generic, costly, and unrealistic solutions to the problem. Asia's overall national infrastructure investment needs are estimated to amount to $8 trillion over the 2010–2020 period, or $730 billion per year—68 percent of which is for new capacity and 32 percent for maintaining and replacing existing infrastructure (ADB/ADBI 2009; The Global Competitiveness Report 2011–2012). These are staggering numbers. India's infrastructure needs for the next decade are estimated to vary between $1 trillion and $2 trillion. Africa's infrastructure gap is estimated to amount to $93 billion per year (Andres et al. 2013). In South Africa alone, a country considered the most industrialized on the continent, infrastructure needs are still so large that the government unveiled in 2012 a three-year, $97 billion plan to upgrade roads, ports, and transportation networks aimed at accessing coal and other minerals. That is more than the combined annual GDP of Ethiopia, Tanzania, and Mozambique.

By approaching economic growth as a linear and teleological process in which all infrastructure constraints must be addressed before positive dynamics can take place, proponents of the Washington Consensus have generally recommended policy reforms that amount to privatizing the infrastructure sector and devoting more public and private money to it (Foster and Briceño-Garmendia 2010). Such recommendations, which involve untargeted policies and broad reform programs that are often politically difficult to implement, may or may not yield positive results.

The inadequacy of the broad infrastructure policies recommended to developing countries mirrors the unrealistic and daunting reform programs prescribed in the Washington Consensus framework. No country with limited financial and administrative resources should be expected to seriously adhere to the long list of reforms identified as conditions for generating economic growth. Each reform may or may not make sense individually. Without prioritization, these dozens (if not hundreds) of difficult policy prescriptions are politically unfeasible and certainly do not reflect the real, binding constraints in potentially competitive industries. This is why successful developing countries typically do not blindly follow them. The puzzling inconsistencies in the Doing Business rankings are evidence that the recommended reforms are problematic. Several of the top-performing countries in the world for the past twenty years are consistently ranked quite low when it comes to the ease of doing business: Brazil is 132nd, Vietnam 98th, and China 91st, behind such star economies as Kazakhstan, Azerbaijan, Tunisia, Belarus, and Vanuatu (Doing Business 2013).

Table 1.1, which lists the thirty fastest-growing economies of the past two decades, provides evidence that the quality of the business environment, at least as measured by popular indicators, does not seem to matter: except for Singapore and Malaysia, the remaining economies score rather poorly on the Doing Business indicators.

A more pragmatic approach is to focus the government's limited resources and implementation capacity on the creation of "islands of excellence," or carefully selected areas with good infrastructure and business environment (even in countries with a poor overall infrastructure and

Country Name	Average Real GDP Growth Rate 1992–2012	Ranking on GDP Growth Performance	Ease of Doing Business Rank for 2012	Ease of Doing Business Rank for 2013
Equatorial Guinea	19.2	1	164	166
China	10.1	2	99	96
Bosnia and Herzegovina	10.8	3	130	131
Liberia	10.4	4	149	144
Cape Verde	9.3	5	128	121
Macao SAR, China	8.9	6		
Bhutan	7.8	7	146	141
Qatar	7.6	8	45	48
Vietnam	7.4	9	98	99
Cambodia	7.4	10	135	137
Lao PDR	7.3	11	163	159
Uganda	7.2	12	126	132
Mozambique	7.2	13	142	139
India	7	14	131	134
Angola	7	15	178	179
Ethiopia	6.9	16	124	125
Chad	6.8	17	189	189
Rwanda	6.6	18	54	32
Singapore	6.5	19	1	1
Panama	6.3	20	61	55
Myanmar	6.2	21	182	182
Dominican Republic	6	22	112	117
Malaysia	6	23	8	6
Ghana	6	24	62	67
Jordan	5.9	25	119	119
Burkina Faso	5.9	26	154	154
Kuwait	5.9	27	101	104
Bangladesh	5.8	28	132	130
Sri Lanka	5.7	29	83	85
Azerbaijan	5.7	30	71	70

Source: Authors' calculations.

business climate), to facilitate the emergence of competitive industries—those that exploit the economy's latent comparative advantage.[3]

REALITIES AND MYTHS OF A WEAK HUMAN CAPITAL BASE

If, despite its importance and relevance, the infrastructure gap is not a constraint that *completely* prevents economic growth from taking place in low-income countries, then what is the problem? Following the logic of the rogue police on the streets of Africa, the most obvious suspect should be human capital (generally defined as "the knowledge, skills, competencies, and attributes embodied in individuals that facilitate the creation of personal, social and economic well-being"[4]), and for very good reasons: human capital is indeed generally weak in developing nations.

Human capital theory, which emerged in the early 1960s, argues that schooling and training are investments in skills and competences and that individuals make decisions on the education and training they receive as a way of augmenting their productivity—a rational expectation of returns on investment (Schultz 1960, 1961; Becker 1964). Subsequent studies have explored the interaction between the education and skill levels of the workforce and technological activity, explaining how a more educated/skilled workforce allows firms to adopt and implement new technologies, thus reinforcing returns on education and training (Nelson and Phelps 1966). James Heckman (2003, 796–97) explains how human capital improves productivity:

> First of all, human capital is productive because of its immediate effect on raising the skill levels of workers. So, for example, if an individual is trained to be a better accountant, the accounting performance of that individual will rise. If a worker is trained to fix an engine, the worker will be more productive in fixing engines. These are the obvious direct effects of making people more skilled. But human capital also improves the adaptability and allocative efficiency of resources in society. It allows agents to allocate resources more effectively across tasks. It enhances the ability of agents to adapt to change and respond to new opportunities.

Empirical analyses have provided varying degrees of support to these theories, but without solving methodological and measurement issues on the relationship between human capital and economic growth. Zvi Griliches (1970) was one of the first to estimate that one-third of the so-called Solow residual (the portion of output growth that could not be attributed to the growth in labor hours or capital stock) could be accounted for by the increase in the labor force's educational attainments. Robert Barro (1991) and N. Gregorey Mankiw and colleagues (1992) have confirmed these positive relationships through a cross-section of countries at all levels of development.

If one thinks about human capital as a set of talents, skills, abilities, and knowledge that workers can accumulate through various forms of investments to make themselves more productive, then human capital indicators are indeed important clues about growth prospects. From a country perspective, an educated workforce in good health is an important requirement for productivity and growth. It therefore seems logical to assume that the generally low levels of human capital in developing countries explain why such countries remain poor. Would Bolivia, Burundi, or Myanmar have the same income per capita as Norway if they all had similar natural resources and the same amount of human capital? Few people would argue that.

Moreover, in an increasingly globalized world with often free movement of goods, services, knowledge, and skills, can the reasoning between a country's level of human capital and its economic growth rate be that linear? Things are clearly much more complicated in practice than they appear to be in theory. An important debate over the nature and strength of the relationship between human capital accumulation and economic growth in developing countries erupted after Lant Pritchett (2001) released an article with the provocative title "Where Has All the Education Gone?" He analyzed cross-national data and found no association between increases in human capital attributable to the rising educational attainment of the labor force and the rate of growth of output per worker. While he noted that the development impact of education varied widely across countries, it had generally fallen short of expectations for three possible reasons: first, the governance and institutional environment in place could be so perverse that the accumulation of educational capital actually lowers economic growth; second, marginal returns to education could fall rapidly as the supply of educated labor expands rapidly while demand remains stagnant; and third, educational quality could be so low that years of schooling creates no human capital.

True, Pritchett's article was controversial, and its methodology and measurement issues were criticized.[5] It highlighted, however, the unavoidable fact that the relationship between schooling and health indicators and economic prosperity is difficult to disentangle with undisputable analytical rigor. It is not a *homogeneous* function with a clearly defined multiplicative scale. Enterprise surveys show that between 20 and 40 percent of firms in most developing countries identify the lack of appropriate skills as a major constraint to the firms' development. But besides the fact that policy prescriptions should not necessarily be drawn from survey results (see Lin and Monga 2011), country studies reveal a wide variety of reasons that investments in education and health may not necessarily translate into improvements in general economic welfare.

An important and often overlooked issue is the fact that countries at different levels of economic development generally require different types of skills to make their labor force more employable and productive to the fullest potential. An economy like the Democratic Republic of Congo, with $500 income per capita and a labor force of thirty-five million people (most of them with only primary level education), does not need the same type of human capital that a country such as Luxemburg, with $100,000 income per capita and only 300,000 people in the labor force (most of them with tertiary-level education), requires. Because sustained economic growth is a process of industrial and technological upgrading that goes hand in hand with institutional changes, success depends on the ability to launch industries that rely on comparative advantage, which is determined by a country's relative distribution of factors (capital, labor, land, or natural resources). At different levels of development and depending on the dynamics of revealed and latent comparative advantage, which determine the real needs of the economy, countries require different skills.

There is no shame in putting large fractions of the population to work in basic assembly activities or light manufacturing. That is actually what all good-performing economies in the history of economic development have done. The Industrial Revolution had already been going on for more than a century when human capital became a topic of interest in the Western world. The postliteracy schooling of the masses—at the secondary and higher levels—was perceived only at the turn of the twentieth century to greatly enhance economic production. As noted by Claudia Goldin (2001), "In 1900 no nation apart from the United States had more than a trivial fraction of its youth enrolled in full-time upper secondary schooling. The industrial world had already recognized the importance of universal literacy, but post-elementary schooling for the masses was a new frontier." Even in Britain and the United States, which had the two leading economies at the time, had grown closer in per capita income since 1850, and were fierce competitors in product markets, it took a while for policy makers and strategists to consider human capital as a critical component of and contributor to economic welfare.

Likewise, human capital stocks were still weak in many parts of the world when economic growth took off in these regions. Subsequent prosperity allowed the endowment structure of the successful economies to constantly change and adapt, improving human capital. In their review of the evolution of educational institutions and outcomes in Italy over 150 years, Giuseppe Bertola and Paolo Sestito (2011, 26) note:

> Formal education does not appear to have played a major role in the postwar economic boom. . . . In spite of relatively low levels of formal education, for quite a long time Italy proved able to sustain a high and increasing, if geographically unequal, standard of living. This apparent gravity-defying process may be explained by the role of less formal mechanisms of information transmission and training, including the Scuole Professionali vocational track that, in some local contexts, provided suitable skills to the population of highly specialized industrial districts.

Italy's schooling and literacy indicators across regions and over time have improved substantially over the past century, but they were very poor for a long time while the economy was booming. Figure 1.1 shows the relationship between human capital accumulation and economic growth. The average number of years of schooling (defined as the minimum number needed to attain the highest educational title held) among individuals age fifteen to sixty-four in Italy increased very slowly, from 4.1 in 1951 to 10.8 in 2010. Yet Italy was already among the most developed economies in 1951, with GDP per capita of nearly $4,000.

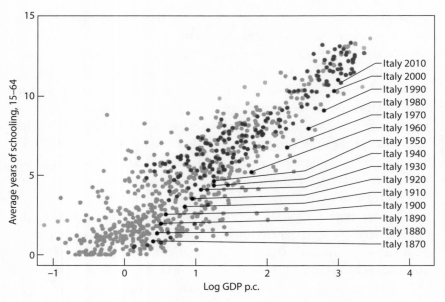

Figure 1.1. Average years of schooling and GDP per capita, 1870–2010.
Unlabeled dots represent various countries for which data is available.
Source: Bertola and Sestito (2011), Monga (2014).

If history is any guide, figure 1.1 implies that there is a strong positive correlation between GDP per capita growth and the average number of years of schooling. Even for industrialized countries such as Italy, progress on years of schooling has been achieved over time, and not as a precondition for economic growth.

In 1980 the mean number of years of schooling in China was 3.7, comparable to Ghana's 3.6 the same year. Still, the Chinese used their weak human capital to engineer what President Barack Obama called "an accomplishment unparalleled in human history": three decades of economic growth at the breathtaking pace of 9.8 percent a year.[6] Even today, despite massive public and private spending in education and remarkable progress, the mean number of years of schooling in China is only 7.5, about the same as in Gabon or Libya and even lower than in Algeria.

China's case is of particular interest to today's poor economies since its spectacular growth performance started only a generation ago. It is a good place to check the validity of some of the popular preconditions for growth—not to search for a "model" to be replicated but to observe what can actually be done even in the most difficult environments. Empirical studies using various methodologies and measurement techniques tend to highlight the important contribution of human capital to China's economic growth. But population growth was the main contributor to total human capital accumulation before 1994, and per capita human capital growth became the primary driving force mainly after 1995 (Li et al. 2009). Human capital formation accelerated only following the major educational expansion increases after 1999—college enrollment in China increased nearly fivefold between 1997 and 2007 (Whalley and Zhao 2010).

In 1978 the capacity for economic policy making in China was still weak and the country was poorer than most other poor countries in the world. Deng Xiaoping was a seventy-four-year old communist leader when he took the helm of a large country inhabited by mainly hungry and angry people. According to Ezra Vogel (2011), one of his biographers, Deng

> was acutely aware that China was in a disastrous state. At the beginning of the previous decade, during the Great Leap Forward, more than thirty million people had died. The country was still reeling from the Cultural Revolution in which young people had been mobilized to attack high-level officials and, with Mao [Zedong]'s support, push them aside as the country of almost one billion people was plunged into chaos. The average per capita income of Chinese peasants, who made up 80 percent of the population, was then only $40 per year. The amount of grain produced per person had fallen below what it had been in 1957.

GDP per capita was $154, about one-fifth that of Ghana or Cameroon.

The senior Communist Party officials who ran the Chinese administration in the 1970s had been forced out and replaced with military people and revolutionary rebels, but they were

> unprepared and unqualified for the positions they had assumed. The military had become bloated and was neglecting the military tasks, while military officers in civilian jobs were enjoying the perquisites of offices without performing the work. The transportation and communication infrastructure was in disarray. The bigger factories were still operating with technology imported from the Soviet Union in

the 1950s, and the equipment was in a state of disrepair. Universities had been basically closed down for almost a decade. Educated youth had been forcibly sent to the countryside and it was becoming harder to make them stay. Yet in the cities there were no jobs for them, nor for the tens of millions of peasants wanting to migrate there. Further, the people who were already living in the cities, fearing for their jobs, were not ready to welcome newcomers. (Vogel 2011)

An avid bridge player, Deng (whose only official title during the final years of his life was "honorary chairman of the Bridge Club of China") believed that dwelling on what might have been or who was at fault for past errors was beside the point and a waste of time. "As in bridge, he was ready to play the hand he was dealt. He could recognize and accept power realities and operate within the boundaries of what seemed possible." (Vogel 2011) Deng did not have a blueprint for generating prosperity and confessed that he "groped for the stepping stones as he crossed the river." He decided that lack of natural resources, weak human capital, absence of infrastructure, or even China's terrible business environment and poor reputation as a communist stronghold would not prevent him from performing economic miracles. He simply felt that he owed it to his people. He adopted a few commonsense principles, which ultimately proved to be the secret recipe for manufacturing the most stunning success in the history of global development and an indictment of the prevailing paradigms, the dominant thinking of the time, and the traditional policy prescriptions from old textbooks.

Deng started with a healthy mix of humility ("we are all to blame," he said) and self-confidence and focused on learning and knowledge. He met with Lee Kwan Yew in Singapore to ask basic questions about how to circumvent the litany of binding constraints that the Chinese economy faced. He encouraged learning from Singapore and South Korea but also from Japan, Taiwan-China, and Hong Kong-China. He challenged other officials to expand their horizons and to travel the world and bring back new ideas, new management practices, and promising new technologies, and to carry out experiments. His approach to problem solving was similar to that of the wise Bateke woodcutters in Congo, who believe that "you learn to cut down trees by cutting them down!" He presided over the development of labor-intensive industries that would absorb large fractions of China's then low-skilled population. That not only opened up the possibility of high participation rates and low unemployment rates but also allowed low-skilled workers to increase their human capital through work and learning and to gain on-the-job training and "soft skills," which prepared them well for the necessary industrial and technological upgrading of China's manufacturing sector. From a macroeconomic standpoint, Deng's labor-intensive strategy also facilitated the emergence of competitive private industries, which in turn helped increase government tax revenue levels and opened up room for the country's savings and investment policies.

For low-income countries such as Bolivia, Burundi, or Myanmar, where the size of the labor force makes it more easily manageable, the lesson from China's recent economic history is encouraging: the weak human capital base is not a radically binding constraint to igniting economic growth. By choosing to make the best of their endowment structure and using the factor that is most abundant (typically labor, land, or natural resources), even countries with very weak human capital can achieve high growth rates. In the process, they accumulate enough savings and capital to progressively upgrade their endowment structure. At lower levels of economic development, poor economies can still perform very well if they exploit their weak human capital to engage in industries that are consistent with their comparative advantage—typically labor-intensive industries at the lower end of the value chain. As they become middle-income economies and advance toward the technological frontier, these countries climb up the value chain and need different types of skills, such as high-level technical and cognitive skills for sophisticated innovation, design, analysis, and problem solving.

The generally poor quality of the education system in many low-income countries is also a recurrent issue often presented in the economic literature as a binding constraint to growth and development. It is indeed a pervasive and serious problem. In many African countries even basic education, an area where there has been substantial progress, is still weak on quality and learning outcomes. Survey results show that 20 percent of seventh graders in Tanzania, one of the continent's top-performing countries, cannot read a paragraph in Kiswahili (Bold et al. 2012). But such survey results lead researchers to conclude too quickly that "higher-quality" educational outcomes (measured as proxies for high levels of human capital) are absolute preconditions for the launching of a credible growth process.

That assertion seems to make sense conceptually but is difficult to validate empirically—and historically. Arguing that the labor force in poor countries is both unsatisfactory and small is reminiscent of the Woody Allen story in which a woman complains angrily that the food in a restaurant is bad, and her companion agrees wholeheartedly before adding that the portions are too small. . . . Moreover, the quality of education and training and the quality of the labor force remain issues of concern to policy makers regardless of the country's level of economic development.[7] And for a good reason: growth and development will always imply changes in the endowment structure and in the economy's comparative advantage—with the rate of change declining as the economy completes the catch-up process (during which it can achieve high growth through imitation) and moves closer to the technology frontier, where finding new niches for progress becomes more and more complicated.

While a poor-quality labor force may appear to be an impediment to economic development, it is a problem that can easily be circumvented. In a world where factors—including high-skill labor—are increasingly mobile and where technological innovations make knowledge transfers and training much less costly than in previous times, poor countries can attract almost all the competencies and expertise they need. They can do this by using revenue from their natural resources (as several Arabian Gulf countries have done for several generations) or by designing and implementing a growth strategy centered on their comparative advantage and developing competitive industries (Mauritius).

Likewise, the existence of a high-quality labor force may not necessarily translate into higher rates of economic growth and poverty reduction. Many developing countries, such as Cuba, devoted their meager fiscal resources to building excellent human capital without ever getting the expected economic development benefits. Countries like India, Ghana, Cameroon, and Kenya prioritized education in the 1960s and 1970s and trained large numbers of well-qualified experts in various domains, often using public spending levied on poor peasants through high taxes. But without accompanying strategies for the emergence of competitive industries and employment creation, these countries saw many of their skilled workers have to leave their home countries, depriving their people of rare talents that were expensively accumulated.

There are some even more puzzling recent examples of such stories. Former president Bingu wa Mutharika of Malawi often recounted how he made the training of world-class nurses one of his priorities. He devoted to it large amounts of public spending, which yielded great results. Malawian nurses quickly became hot commodities around the world, and the British government even launched a recruiting program to attract them. Naturally, the lack of jobs in Malawi forced many of them to leave their country, often the very day of their graduation. This led Mutharika to wonder whether his country, with a gross national income (GNI) per capita of $300 in 2010, should be subsidizing the healthcare system in the United Kingdom, where GNI per capita at the same time was $36,000. When confronted with such incongruities, some researchers stress what they call the brain-drain benefits—namely, the potentially high volume of remittances that migrants can send back to their home countries. These amounts are often not negligible, and various empirical studies indeed show that they can positively affect growth and poverty reduction through many channels (Imai et al. 2012). Yet such analyses omit the unquantifiable positive externalities that poor societies lose when their best-trained young people emigrate. The mere physical presence in Malawi of all the well-educated nurses who left would have brought substantial social benefits to their country. They would have served as precious role models for young people and brought social and economic bonuses to the country. "Education is what remains after one has forgotten everything he learned at school," Albert Einstein once said.

TALES OF THE LAZY POOR:
THE ANALYTICS OF PRODUCTIVITY

The combination of a pervasive infrastructure deficit and weak human capital has led many researchers and policy makers to identify a third factor as a reason countries remain poor: low productivity. The logical conclusion from this popular diagnostic is the need to improve productivity levels before growth can take place. Before discussing the diagnostic's validity, it is worth noting that this conclusion has often been made throughout the history of economic development thinking, sometimes with racial undertones. Before Germany's economy took off in the mid-nineteenth century, British thinkers and political leaders regularly described Germans as "a dull and heavy people" (Hodgskin 1820, 50). As Ha-Joon Chang (2007, 169) observes, "'indolence' was the word that was frequently associated with the Germanic nature. . . . A French manufacturer who employed German workers complained that they 'work as and when they please.'" John Russell, a travel writer, described Germans as a "plodding, easily contented people . . . endowed neither with great acuteness of perception nor quickness of feeling." In words reminiscent of those often heard expressed today about people in low-income countries, Russell asserted that they were not open to new ideas: "It is long before [a German] can be brought to comprehend the bearings of what is new to him, and it is difficult to rouse him to ardour in its pursuit" (Russell 1828, 394).

Before they became perceived as a society of people addicted to hard work, Japanese suffered from similar prejudice. Sidney Gullick, a respected American scholar and missionary who taught and resided in Japan for twenty-five years, wrote in his book *Evolution of the Japanese* (1903, 82) that many of them "give an impression . . . of being lazy and utterly indifferent to the passage of time." Chang (2007, chap. 9) points to the irony of such comments from a man who, despite his strong beliefs in cultural stereotypes of Japanese as being an "easygoing" and "emotional" people "living chiefly for the present," spent most of his life campaigning for racial equality on behalf of Asian Americans.

After touring Asia in 1911–12, British socialist leader Beatrice Webb (1978, 375) dismissed Japan as a country where "there is evidently no desire to teach people to think" and described Koreans as "12 million of dirty, degraded, sullen, lazy and religionless savages who slouch about in dirty white garments of the most inept kind and who live in filthy mudhuts." Similar stories of prejudice have been told about Chinese workers and Indians—including the so-called Hindu rate of economic growth. Interestingly, when the economies of East Asia defied the somber predictions by some of the most influential economists of the 1960s[8] and started picking up, the cultural argument was turned on its head and used again to justify their superior performance. In their search for why South Korea, whose per capita income in 1965 ($150) was about half Colombia's ($280), outperformed Colombia in the span of just two decades ($2,150 in 1985 compared to Colombia's $1,320), or why U.S. garment buyers chose South Korea even though Colombia is nearer, Geert Hofstede and Michael Harris Bond (1988, 8) conjectured that it was because of better selection, better quality, lower prices, and more reliable delivery times. They also noted: "Better management was obviously also involved, but this is too easy an explanation for two reasons. First, the quality of management depends on the qualities of the people to be managed; second, the quality-of-management explanation begs the question of how an entire nation can collectively produce better management than another nation. For the real explanation, we must turn to the domain of culture."

Latin American and African workers also were subject to even worse accusations and suspicions about their mindsets and cultural habits. Mexicans have long been depicted in blockbuster Hollywood movies as lazy. Argentines and Brazilians are often chastised in popular discourse for the so-called propensity to procrastinate, seen as one of the main explanations for why their countries have remained "developing nations" for more than a hundred years.

African workers have been portrayed by mainstream, influential researchers as incapable of economic progress because of cultural choices. Samuel Huntington, author of the popular but misleading concept of a "clash of civilizations," argued that cultural differences explain most of the diverging economic performance of South Korea and Ghana: "Undoubtedly, many factors played a role, but . . . culture had to be a large part of the explanation. South Koreans valued thrift, investment, hard work, education, organization, and discipline. Ghanaians had different values. In short, cultures count" (Huntington 2000, xi). Ghanaians had "different" values? Such as wastefulness, extravagance, laziness, obscurantism, chaos, and indiscipline?

Axelle Kabou (1991) went as far as asserting that the continent of Africa opposes the very notion of economic development. In a similar vein, Daniel Etounga-Manguelle (2000, 69) argued that "the African, anchored in his ancestral culture, is so convinced that the past can only repeat itself that he worries only superficially about the future. However, without a dynamic perception of the future, there is no planning, no foresight, no scenario building; in other words, no policy to affect the course of events."

Such comments would not deserve mention if they did not often come from some leading thinkers and political figures—people whose beliefs and actions shape the dynamics of international economic relations. In 2007, for example, then French president Nicolas Sarkozy made controversial comments in a major speech in Dakar, Senegal, during his first trip to the continent as head of state: "The tragedy of Africa is that the African has not fully entered into history. . . . The African peasant, who for thousands of years has lived in accordance with the seasons . . . , doesn't know anything but the eternal renewal of time.... In this imaginary world where everything starts over and over again there is no place for human adventure or for the idea of progress.... This man (the traditional African) never launched himself towards the future."

One way to examine the economic validity of such statements is to review labor productivity in low-income countries, where it is perhaps the most important driver of growth. The analytical explanation is that poor economies often have limited domestic demand and rely on exports to expand market size for their products and to earn foreign exchange to pay for the imports they consume. Therefore these necessarily "open" economies can increase their per capita consumption in two ways: first, by importing more without selling more abroad—which implies that they have to find the money to pay for the extra imports (borrowing); or second, by obtaining better prices for their exports so that they do not need to borrow to pay the extra cost of their additional imports. The first option is possible only for countries with sufficient reserves and excellent creditworthiness to pay the extra cost, but in any case, it cannot be sustained for a long period of time because the amount borrowed needs to be repaid at some point. The second option is the most realistic, but it implies that African countries are able to convince foreigners to pay more for their exports. This can be done only through higher productivity, that is, by producing better goods and services. This helps explain the importance of terms of trade.[9]

It is therefore worrisome to read news articles about the low productivity in poor countries and the widening gap between most developing countries and industrialized economies. It has been estimated, for instance, that the value of total factor productivity in Latin America relative to the average total productivity in the United States is 0.76 (Pagés 2010). In other words, if Latin America used the amount of capital and labor that is used in the United States, production in Latin America would be roughly three-fourths of U.S. production. Moreover, the TFP in Latin America relative to the United States has been declining in recent decades, and only four countries (Brazil, Chile, Panama, and Dominican Republic) in the region managed to reduce their income gap with the United States between 1960 and 2007 (Powell 2013). In 1955 GDP per capita in Latin America relative to the United States was 28 percent; in 2005 it was 19 percent. Growth accounting exercises indicate that the main reason behind this divergence has been the low productivity growth experienced by Latin American economies since the mid-1970s (Busso, Madrigal, and Pagés 2012). Etounga-Manguelle (1991) quoted figures of labor productivity in various regions in the world and commented sarcastically that the absence of data for Africa was perhaps best for the continent's dignity.

But such stories of low productivity in developing regions of the world can be highly misleading and erroneously interpreted. Helen Hai, the Chinese businesswoman who successfully championed the relocation in 2012 of a major leather manufacturing company from her country to Ethiopia, a landlocked country and one of the poorest in the world, often tells of the lazy African workers that she heard about before she established her factory there. She notes that, in reality, her Ethiopian employees were as committed as others—provided that the rules and the incentive system in place were clear about their duties and guaranteed their rights. She was able to establish a 3,500-worker factory in two years, exporting women's designer shoes competitively to U.S. and European markets. With three months of training, the workers' productivity reached 80 percent of that of their counterparts in China.[10]

While African countries seem to exhibit the lowest levels of productivity of all low-income countries before one controls for any variable and are among the least competitive economies in the world, a more careful examination of the data tells a completely different story. Empirical studies show, however, that firms in sub-Saharan Africa are more productive, on average, than firms in East Asia, eastern Europe, Central Asia, and Latin America after one controls for the quality of the investment climate (Dinh and Clarke 2012). Based on detailed analyses that explicitly control for differences in infrastructure, regulation, access to credit, and other political and geographical differences, firms in Africa actually perform better on average than firms in other regions (Harrison, Lin, and Xu 2014).

What explains the disconnect between the reports of aggregate productivity in the headlines and the more nuanced reality that careful empirical analyses reveal about firm-level output per worker in poor countries? One reason is the often forgotten basic fact that labor productivity is not a proxy for workers' cultural habits or their commitment to hard work. Their productivity increases if technology improves or if capital per worker rises. This is true not only in high-income countries such as the United States and Norway but also in Bolivia, Burundi, and Bhutan. In addition, one must highlight the complementary role of human capital in the growth process. Because physical and human capital have been relative complements throughout the twentieth century, the accumulation of physical capital contributes more readily to growth when augmented by an educated workforce. As better and more advanced technologies diffuse through the economy, the allocation of workers with different skills and education levels to production tasks can be altered through carefully designed and implemented education policies, which in turn improves labor productivity.

Looking at historical data, researchers have established that shifts in the demand and supply of educated, highly skilled workers have transformed the level and composition of human capital embodied in the average worker in the United States, with corresponding effects on labor productivity and growth. Claudia Goldin and Lawrence Katz (2008) provide strong evidence, for example, that the demand for highly educated workers relative to less educated workers increased steadily throughout the twentieth century, except for a brief slowdown during the 1940s. On the supply side, they observe that changes in the distribution of educational attainment in the labor force derive from two sources—workers who obtain an education in the United States and workers of varying levels of schooling who immigrate to the United States. When growth in the demand for educated workers outstrips the growth in supply, the earnings gap between workers with different educations levels, such as those with a college degree versus those with a high school degree, or between workers in occupations that demand high skills versus workers in occupations requiring less formal schooling will increase.[11]

Aggregate productivity gains are therefore often driven by upgrades in the processes, products, or machinery used by firms, affected in turn by investments in human capital and innovation and R&D. In that context, low TFP growth can be the result of barriers that prevent diffusion and implementation of new ways of doing business and the adoption of new technologies (Parente and Prescott 2002). In addition, low aggregate TFP growth can be also explained by a number of policy and market failures that may have determined the selection of firms in the market and distorted the allocation of resources across firms. In such situations, even competitive firms are in fact smaller than they would be in an undistorted economy, and that loss is enough to lower aggregate TFP (Restuccia and Rogerson 2008). It is therefore not surprising that some measures of labor productivity in low-income countries, which does not account for education and demographic dynamics, show lower performance than that observed in high-income countries.

In sum, many of the reasons often put forward in the development literature to justify the poor economic performance of low-income countries (such as insufficient physical capital, weak human capital and absorptive capacity, and low productivity) are generally symptoms of the problem rather than its root causes. No country begins its process of sustained economic growth with the "appropriate" amount of physical or human capital. Likewise, the culturalist argument put forward to explain economic performance does not hold under empirical and historical scrutiny. Economic takeoff and poverty reduction processes have now occurred in countries with widely different cultural backgrounds and political and administrative itineraries. This has led to another line of "prerequisites to economic development" articulated around the notions of institutional and financial development. These factors are discussed in the next chapter.

2

Unpleasant Truths about Institutional and Financial Development

Thomas Edison, the intrepid American inventor who brought to the world the lightbulb and many other enlightening ideas and held more than a thousand patents, had a simple rule for recruiting his engineers. He always invited the short-listed candidates (whom he assumed to all be technically capable of doing the job at hand) for lunch and carefully observed their behavior. His objective was not to check whether they had sophisticated table manners but rather to try to deduce their decision-making process from their most anodyne acts. A key indicator he monitored was some of his guests' propensity to add salt and pepper to their dish as soon as the food was brought to them, without even tasting it. That simple, very common, and often unconscious gesture would disqualify any prospective candidate: it revealed an inept tendency to blindly act on one's instincts and to decide without thinking and checking the evidence.

Many researchers and policy makers working today on institutional development in developing countries may be guilty of the kind of Pavlovian behavior despised by Edison. By simply looking at the current state of institutional development in industrialized countries, they assume they know precisely what it means and how it can be measured. They mechanically compare political, administrative, and financial institutions of countries regardless of their economic development levels. They naturally find gaps between poor and rich countries, and they derive from those a generic reform agenda and policy recommendations that are not based on irrefutable evidence. They also neglect the lessons from the history of very industrialized economies, all of which started their economic development success stories with suboptimal political, administrative, and financial institutions. The broad (and somewhat abstract) intuition on the need to improve governance in all countries has strong moral and theoretical foundations: it is the *right* thing to do to sustain growth, ensure shared prosperity, and build social trust and stable societies. But the conventional wisdom that low-income countries should start their development with the governance institutions of high-income countries is both a non sequitur and a historical fallacy.

This chapter refutes the linear and almost teleological approach in vogue in development economics on political and financial institutions. It briefly discusses the theoretical issues at hand and suggests that policies take into account the requirements of both time and place—the importance of the development level. The chapter acknowledges that institutional development problems are indeed major impediments to economic growth. But contrary to conventional wisdom, it argues that they are often correlated with the level of economic development. Seen from that perspective, the well-known weaknesses in the governance and financial sectors of many poor countries today often reflect their low level of development and the results of failed state interventions and distortions originating from erroneous economic development strategies.

The first part of the chapter deals with the notion of political and administrative institutions through an analysis of the concept of governance. The second part focuses on financial institutions and argues that, contrary to popular belief, third-world countries may not need first-world financial institutions before they reach certain income levels. Instead of posing first-world-type governance and financial institutions as the main prescription and a prerequisite for sustained growth in third-world countries, development economists should design policy frameworks that offer the maximum likelihood of success because they are consistent with comparative advantage and existing firm structure while providing minimum opportunities for rent seeking and state capture. The dynamic development of competitive firms and industries eventually leads to institutional development.

"UNDERDEVELOPED" POLITICAL INSTITUTIONS: THE MYSTERY OF GOVERNANCE

Institutional development is generally acknowledged to be the reflection or result of "good governance." Yet an indication that good governance is still a mystery and a difficult concept to assess, measure, and grasp confidently is the observation by A. Premchand (1993), an economist from the International Monetary Fund (IMF)—a serious organization not known for the propensity of its experts to rely on humor—that governance is like obscenity "because it is difficult to define as a legal phrase."

Perhaps the most comprehensive and authoritative intellectual source on the subject are the Worldwide Governance Indicators (WGI). The indicators are released on a yearly basis by a team of excellent Washington-based researchers and are used widely in academic and policy circles. They define governance as "the traditions and institutions by which authority in a country is exercised. This includes the process by which governments are selected, monitored and replaced; the capacity of the government to effectively formulate and implement sound policies; and the respect of citizens and the state for the institutions that govern economic and social interactions among them." They identify six dimensions that can measure governance: government effectiveness; regulatory quality; rule of law; control of corruption; voice and accountability; and political stability and absence of violence. That conceptual framework is then given empirical life through the use of data sources produced by a variety of think tanks, survey institutes, international organizations, nongovernmental organizations, and private-sector firms. The WGI are therefore aggregate indices that combine the views of a large number of survey respondents, including those representing enterprises, citizens, and experts in industrial and developing countries.

Such a valiant effort to give meaning to the complex notion of governance is certainly respectable. But the theoretical and philosophical underpinnings of the WGI are highly questionable. First, assessing the quality of the traditions and institutions by which authority in a country is exercised is bound to be a subjective exercise based on value judgments. It is therefore susceptible to being a reflection of ethnocentric—if not paternalistic—perspectives. There is no reason to believe that such an assessment should be performed uniformly in China, Alaska, or Zanzibar. In a world where globalization does not prevent people from seeking to assert their subjectively defined cultural peculiarities, even within old nations that were once thought to be stable and homogenous entities but now are sometimes breaking up,[1] one risks falling into the double trap of universalism and relativism. There will always be those who claim that all human societies share the same goals and have adopted global standards and broad principles of good governance embodied in internationally agreed covenants. Yet there will also always be the perception that these global standards of good governance are actually evidence of the Westernization of human values under the pretense of "universality." Both camps have some intellectual legitimacy. That some who reject the good-governance agenda as a hidden attempt to Westernize the world may be defenders of authoritarian practices hidden behind the claim of cultural relativism does not necessarily invalidate all their arguments. After all, even those who are paranoid sometimes have true enemies.

The WGI and other indicators of good governance or democratization do not really help escape the theoretical (universalist-versus-relativist) impasse. Moreover, even if one could come up with an ingredient list that satisfies both the universalists and the relativists, the belief that good governance can be captured quantitatively and measured through subjective perception surveys will remain subject to debate and controversy. Behavioral economics shows that people are often wrong when asked to identify the true constraints that affect even their most important activities and welfare. Econometric analyses show, for instance, that popular survey results such as the World Bank's Doing Business indicators do not correlate well with the actual constraints on private-sector performance (Bourguignon 2006). In other words, even the most successful businesspeople in the world generally fail to intuitively identify the real obstacles to productivity growth and enterprise development. If that is the case, how confident can one be about perceptions, opinions, self-assessment exercises, or assessments of others' well-being? Philosophers have struggled to answer these questions satisfactorily at least since Arthur Schopenhauer's famous essay on the freedom of will.

The relationship between perceptions of good governance and effective political and administrative institutions, on the one hand, and economic performance, on the other, is certainly not as simple as much of the existing economic literature would suggest. In fact, there are fundamental discrepancies between indicators of what is perceived as good governance and indicators of actual economic performance. These discrepancies also reveal fundamental issues of subjectivism and ethnocentrism that are reminiscent of the "orientalism" analyzed by Edward Said (1978) and tackled by several African researchers (Ela 1990; Monga 2015).

A good illustration of the problem can be found in countries' corruption scale rankings, always one of the key pillars of the good governance agenda.

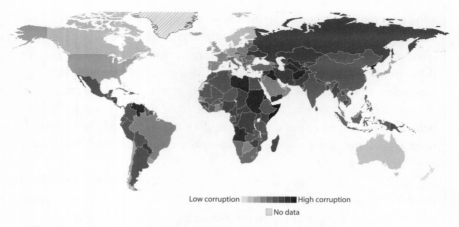

Low corruption ▨▨▨▨▨▨▨ High corruption
▨ No data

Figure 2.1. Corruption in the world: A dichotomy of good and evil? *Source*: Transparency International (2014).

It is puzzling to look at the world map of corruption, the typical and most representative indicator of governance quality. Figure 2.1, from Transparency International surveys, basically shows that the world is divided into two country categories: the highly corrupt countries (in dark grey and black) and the least corrupt ones—presumably with good governance (in light grey). It is difficult to look at this map and not give some credit to the argument of some relativists, as it depicts a "good-governance" Western world surrounded by a "bad-governance" non-Western world. Transparency International is a reputable organization that does good work. But its surveys' visual results, which display a Manichean view of the world, are deeply disturbing.

Given that the fight against corruption is an important part of the good-governance agenda, it is perplexing that corruption has been prevalent throughout human history and still exists, often on a wide scale, even in high-income countries. One simply has to read Robert Caro's four-volume *The Years of Lyndon Johnson* (1982–2012), a monumental biography of the U.S. president and a detailed account of a highly corrupt U.S. Senate, or Jack Abramoff's *Capitol Punishment* (2011) to realize that corruption is pervasive even in old democracies and that a good-versus-evil dichotomy among countries is highly misleading.

Newspaper headlines, empirical studies, and political biographies regularly document the persistence of corruption in the most unlikely places.

In recent years, France gave its former president Jacques Chirac a two-year suspended prison sentence for diverting public funds and abusing public trust. In the United States, four of the past seven Illinois governors were convicted and imprisoned—including Rod Blagojevitch, the first in history to be impeached, who was convicted of numerous corruption charges in 2011, including for trying to "sell" President Barack Obama's former Senate seat to the highest bidder. Even the holy state of the Vatican was shaken by corruption when the press revealed several confidential letters sent to Pope Benedict by the state's deputy governor, Archbishop Carlo Maria Vigano, documenting corruption at its administration's highest level. In Japan—a non-Western, high-income country with old democratic traditions—many high-ranking government officials have been forced out of office throughout the postwar period amid corruption scandals (Mitchell 1996). The problem has extended well beyond the political sphere and into a bureaucracy often considered one of the better managed in the world (Johnson 2001).

Of course, the economic cost of corruption and bad governance may be relatively higher in low-income countries where large fractions of the population remain poor compared with high-income countries. But if corruption—a sign of bad governance—is observed everywhere, a few questions come to mind: What exactly is corruption? Why do some countries seem to thrive despite its prevalence? And what is the real relationship between perceived levels of bad governance and economic performance?

The typical response to the unflattering truths that corruption exists everywhere and no human society can legislate morality is to argue that high-income countries are "less" corrupt than others and their institutions are "stronger"—strength shown by the number of prosecutions. But those elegant arguments are hard to empirically validate. First, it is difficult to rigorously define what corruption means anytime and everywhere, and to measure it comparatively across place and time. Second, many of both the open and hidden transactions between lobbyists and policy makers in the United States, for example, would be considered corruption in other places in the world. Third, aggressive prosecution of corruption is taking place in many low-income countries, yet in those countries such legal actions are paradoxically considered further evidence of terrible governance. A case in point is that of Cameroon, where dozens of politicians and civil servants at the highest levels of power (including a former prime minister, many government ministers, the president's chief of staff, heads of the largest state-owned enterprises, and ambassadors) have been tried and convicted for embezzling public funds. Yet few analysts would consider Cameroon a good-governance country. To the contrary, the more that senior government officials are arrested and sent to jail, the more that experts are convinced that Cameroon is profoundly corrupt.

Defining Corruption: Some Basic Conceptual Issues

The first sign of the inextricable difficulties of corruption analytics—with heavy implications for what the appropriate political institutions in any given country should be—is the vagueness of the definitions that one can find in the literature. The most commonly used definition is the one by A. Shleifer and R. Vishny (1993, 599), who define government corruption as

> the sale by government officials of government property for personal gain. For example, government officials often collect bribes for providing permits and licenses, for giving passage through customs, or for prohibiting the entry of competitors. In these cases they charge personally for goods that the state officially owns. In most cases the goods that the government officials sell are not demanded for their own sake, but rather enable private agents to pursue economic activity they could not pursue otherwise. Licenses, permits, passports, and visas are needed to comply with laws and regulations that restrict private economic activity. Insofar as government officials have discretion over the provision of these goods, they can collect bribes from private agents.

The obvious question that this well-established definition raises is that of legality. What if there are no laws in place preventing government officials from making excessive or arbitrary use of their discretionary power? What if some of their actions, while morally and politically wrong and economically costly, are not strictly illegal? Does corruption intrinsically imply illegality? If it does, then the logical inference from the definition is that some practices may be considered "corruption" in some countries or regions and not so in others. This further complicates the assessment of the extent of the phenomenon and the comparative analysis across place and time.

Corruption can be disaggregated along several dimensions. First, one must distinguish its prevalence, especially in large countries with decentralized or federal political systems. "Corruption can be widespread at the local government level, even if it is controlled effectively at the central government level. The United States and India provide examples where corruption is much more severe in some states than in others" (Knack 2007, 256). Second, the purpose of improper actions characterized as corruption must also be taken into account. Bribes intended to influence the design and content of laws and regulations (state capture) must be differentiated from those intended to change or circumvent their implementation (administrative corruption). Third, there is a need to distinguish among the actor categories involved in various forms of corruption: when poor people are involved, it is often referred to as petty corruption as opposed to grand corruption, which involves high-level officials and political figures. Fourth, corruption may be of a different scale and nature depending on the administrative agency in which it takes place (schools, customs, health centers, and so on).

Transparency International, arguably the most active nongovernmental organization fighting corruption around the world, has chosen a more focused operational definition of the term: "the abuse of entrusted power for private gain." The organization further differentiates between "according to rule" corruption and "against the rule" corruption. Facilitation payments, where a bribe is paid to receive preferential treatment for something that the bribe receiver is required to do by law, constitute the first. The second is a bribe paid to obtain services the bribe receiver is prohibited from providing.

While Transparency International's definition of corruption is much clearer, it raises another series of problems: First, since bribe payments are not publicly recorded, it is virtually impossible to calculate the financial transactions that they entail. Second, bribes do not always take monetary form: favors, presents, services, and even threats and blackmail are just as common. These factors highlight new issues, such as the strength of the judicial system and its ability to effectively handle complaints at the lowest possible cost; the prevailing cultural and behavioral norms; and so on. Even less quantifiable are corruption's social costs. "No one knows how much the loss of an energetic entrepreneur or an acclaimed scientist costs a country. Moreover, any estimated social costs in dollars would be inadequate to the task of measuring the human tragedy behind resignation, illiteracy, or in-adequate medical care."[2] All this explains why it is impossible to measure the true net social and economic cost of corruption, regardless of how it is defined.

In fact, much of the research on governance—regardless of how it is defined—and institutions in general suggests implicitly, if not explicitly, that they are mostly exotic phenomena that can be observed only on a wide scale in countries under a certain income level. Although there is obviously recognition that corruption also occurs in high-income countries, it is treated as an insignificant example of poor behavior by public officials or businesspeople who represent the exception and not the rule. These high-profile, headline-grabbing cases are considered outlier or minority cases (the so-called bad apples) and therefore are either ignored or discounted by mainstream economic research. Nothing could be farther from the truth.

Defining and measuring corruption is a difficult task, not least because it is not always considered a crime but a general classification for a variety of criminal acts, such as bribery, breach of trust, abuse of authority, and misappropriation of public funds. The definitions of these criminal acts differ not only between countries but also within national boundaries. For instance, while all of Japan is subject to one penal code, and therefore a single defini-tion, the United States has fifty different penal codes (one per state) as well as a national (federal) code, resulting in numerous definitions. Moreover, Japan keeps detailed statistics on corrupt acts, whereas the United States has no centralized record keeping for such acts (Castberg 1999).

Still, consider these statistics: between 1987 and 2006, federal prosecu-tors convicted more than 20,000 government officials and private citizens involved in public corruption offenses in the United States.[3] That is an av-erage of 1,000 a year for several decades. The actual number is higher, since these numbers do not include public corruption convictions that result from prosecution pursued by state district attorneys or attorneys general. Also, public officials in any given U.S. state can be corrupt but not charged simply because federal prosecutors do not have the resources or the polit-ical will to bring cases and win convictions; such public corruption cases would not be reflected in the Department of Justice's dataset.

These conceptual difficulties of defining corruption in a rigorous and comparable way across countries explain why social scientists from various disciplines have come up with contradictory theories of corruption and mostly inconclusive empirical evidence on its impact on economic growth and political liberalization.

The Changing Perceptions of Corruption and Governance

The dominant view of good governance as a precondition for economic success is therefore misguided. By focusing on the search for the determinants of global governance standards that often reflect particular political, philosophical, and ideological concepts of power, the traditional literature on governance has so far yielded few results. It has failed to offer a set of actionable policies that poor countries could implement to foster inclusive growth in a pragmatic and incentives-compatible way.

In fact, good governance has been an elusive quest. Since the United Nations Commission on Human Rights identified transparency, responsibility, accountability, participation, and responsiveness to the needs of the people as key attributes of good governance (Resolution 2000/64), the fight against corruption has become the most revealing and the most widely discussed aspect of governance. The academic pendulum on the subject has shifted from praising the economic efficiency effects of corruption to stressing its many economic, sociopolitical, and even moral costs to societies.

Initial theoretical work on corruption underlined its positive role in development. Renowned scholars such as Nathaniel Leff (1964) and Samuel Huntington (1968) argued that corruption may allow businesspeople to be more efficient by allowing them to circumvent bureaucratic procedures and therefore avoid the burden of red tape. Similar arguments were made in subsequent studies: F. T. Lui (1985) developed an equilibrium-queuing model to show that corruption allows the queue to be reorganized in a way that leads to an efficient allocation of time, giving those for whom time is most valuable the opportunity to move to the front of the line. The same efficiency argument can be found in D.-H. D. Lien (1986), who even suggested that corruption actually helps ensure that contracts are awarded to the most efficient firms (those that stand to gain the most from the payment of bribes).

A second strand of the literature has attempted to invalidate these previous analyses, arguing, for instance, that beyond possible changes in the order in the queue, bribes may actually allow civil servants to reduce the speed with which they process business transactions in the queue (Myrdal 1968), or that bureaucratic procedures should be seen not only as causes of rent-seeking activities but as their consequences (Tanzi 1998). Maxim Boycko and colleagues (1995) also stressed the higher degree of uncertainty and costs due to enforceability problems created by corruption.

Others have argued that even taking at face value the suggestion that the most able economic agents in corrupt societies are also engaged in and benefit from rent-seeking activities, such talent reallocation cannot be economically efficient. Susan Rose-Ackerman (1975), for instance, observed that once corruption is entrenched it becomes so pervasive that it cannot be limited to areas in which it might be economically "desirable."

A third and most recent strand of research has focused on the negative effects of corruption (and bad governance more generally) on economic growth. K. M. Murphy and colleagues (1993) suggested that increasing returns on rent seeking may eventually crowd out productive investment. P. M. Romer (1994) made a similar point, emphasizing the idea that corruption imposes a tax on ex-post profits, which may reduce the flow of new goods and technology. Paolo Mauro (1995) offered empirical evidence that the prevalence of perceived corruption may negatively affect economic performance and pioneered econometric work on the subject. His conclusions were confirmed by Philip Keefer and Stephen Knack (1997) and Hélène Poirson (1998), who also observed that corruption substantially reduces economic growth rates. Such problems are said to be even worse in countries rich in natural resources—especially those in the developing world—where opportunities for rent-seeking activities are typically very high.

Despite the insights from all these various waves of research, the problems of corruption and governance and their implications for economic development remain unresolved. Empirical demonstrations of the impact of governance on economic growth are often based on subjective perception indices, the limitations of which are well known. Policy makers in developing countries still have few actionable prescriptions for how to design policies to achieve their economic and governance goals. Moreover, a traditional recommendation for improving governance often involves curbing the power of political leaders—some of whom are not democratically selected. Yet the social sciences literature does not provide an incentives-compatible mechanism for political leaders to improve governance and eliminate corruption. For low-income countries, a potentially more fruitful approach to tackling the problem would be to examine the possible determinants of good governance and infer from these determinants which policies could limit opportunities for rent seeking that contribute to political leaders' personal goals.

The Opportunity Cost of the Good Governance Rhetoric

The opportunity cost of the good governance rhetoric and the obsession that low-income countries must have the same political institutions as high-income countries is perhaps well explained through the story of a fake corruption scandal surrounding the visit of the president of Congo to New York in September 2005. He was there to attend the sixtieth summit of the United Nations. His official purpose was to give a fifteen-minute speech to the UN General Assembly; he also had meetings with other political leaders and members of the world business community.

Questions arose when hotel bill for the president and the fifty-six people in his entourage was leaked to the press. Copies of the bill were headline news all over the world. True, the numbers were grotesque—at least at first sight. They revealed that Denis Sassou Nguesso, the former military man who had ruled Congo from 1979 to 1992 and had been in power again since 1997 after a civil war that left thousands of people dead, had spent $295,000 for an eight-night stay at the Palace Hotel on New York's Madison Avenue, including some $81,000 for his own suite. He was charged $8,500 a night for his three-story suite, which the hotel advertised as one of a quartet of art deco–inspired triplex suites that are unlike any others in New York City, featuring marble floors, expansive views of midtown Manhattan from 18-foot windows, and spacious, private roof-top terraces. The suite featured a master bedroom with a king bed, two additional bedrooms with two double beds, and six bathrooms. It also had its own private elevator. Media reports noted that President Sassou Nguesso had a whirlpool bathtub and a 50-inch plasma television screen, and that his room service charges on September 18 alone came to $3,500. The total charges for room service during his stay amounted to $12,000.

In their voyeuristic quest for juicy details, journalists tried to determine what cost so much money. But the hotel did not itemize the charges. Reporters were left to speculate about the items available on the room service menu, which included Dungeness crab, truffle crumbles, Scottish langoustines, pan-seared foie gras, braised snails in chicken mousse, and other exotic selections. They also made a big deal of the Congolese mission at the UN paying only a $51,000 deposit by check to secure the rooms, and the settlement of the final bill's balance by a $177,942.96 cash payment, "an extraordinary sum for any hotel guest to be carrying" according to one journalist.[4] Presidential aides pulled out wads of $100 notes to settle the bill for twenty-six rooms.

All the more stunning to reporters was that President Sassou Nguesso was at the time the chairman of the African Union, representing the continent's fifty-three countries, and also negotiating with the World Bank and the International Monetary Fund for the cancellation of a large fraction of Congo's debt held by the two multilateral institutions on the grounds that the country could not afford to repay them in full. His government was also talking to the Paris and London Clubs, two informal groups of official and private creditors, respectively, whose role is to find coordinated and sustainable solutions to debtor countries' payment difficulties. It was therefore shocking to political analysts that such a country's leader would choose to stay at one of Manhattan's most expensive hotels.

As could be expected, the news was received with shock and anger, especially by people in Congo, who probably would have liked their tax money spent on other priorities. Outraged by President Sassou Nguesso's apparent extravagance, leaders of nongovernmental organizations and anticorruption movements wrote letters to the World Bank's president urging him to oppose any debt relief operation for Congo until the country's leaders could demonstrate better public finance management skill. Global Witness, a well-known anticorruption group, issued a report claiming that Congo's oil wealth has "for too long been managed for the private profit of the elite rather than for the benefit of its entire population" (Allen-Mills 2008). Not surprisingly, Paul Wolfowitz, then president of the World Bank, was more than inclined to bow to the pressure. It took a forceful response from the office of the executive director for francophone Africa on the board of directors of the World Bank to refocus the debate on Congo's debt relief back on the real issues at hand.

Let's step back and look at the situation in the context of normal diplomatic practices. Why the outrage about a hotel bill of a few hundred thousand dollars for a large presidential delegation on an official visit to the United Nations? After all, hotel suites are expensive in New York in September, especially in the small number of luxury hotels where foreign heads of states are forced to reside—for security reasons—when they attend the annual UN meetings. Would those who cried foul about the hotel bill's amount have preferred that the president of Congo and his entourage sleep on the streets of New York or settle in a two-star hotel somewhere in neighboring New Jersey or Connecticut while attending the summit? Hopefully not: even the president of "poor" Congo certainly deserves the same treatment that his peers from "rich" countries receive during their official trips abroad.

Is Incompetence Worse than Corruption?

There are certainly many important economic and even governance issues to be discussed about Congo and other low-income countries. But the focus on the superficial problem of the hotel bill of a sovereign country's president on an official visit to the United States obscured the real questions of whether the public policies implemented by his government were sound enough to bring strong economic growth and prosperity to his people. While the bill might have been expensive, the only reason it was disclosed to the press was that some of Congo's creditors had filed lawsuits against the country through U.S. and British courts over business debt repayment. These were all "vulture" investment funds that make profits by speculating and buying up poor countries' debt at a discount price. Using a judgment from two British High Court judges that found Congolese officials to be "dishonest" about their country's debt, the vulture fund managers had subpoenaed President Sassou Nguesso's hotel bill and leaked it to the media as corruption evidence. Yet few newspapers that reported the sensationalist tale of President Sassou Nguesso's hotel bill devoted time and resources to investigate the even more important story of these vulture investment funds—what they are, how they function, and how poor countries around the world should deal with them.

One fund manager was quoted saying that the president's hotel suite cost "more per day than the average Congolese makes in a decade."[5] This was probably an exaggeration, but it was beside the point. Would the media have shown the same interest in the story if the hotel bills were run up by a leader from a country with a better reputation? Would these questions have arisen if the president of an industrialized country had spent the same amount of money for a stay in the city? Did anyone calculate the cost for the trip to New York by the U.S. president (including the cost of flying Air Force One from Washington to New York) and compare it to the $30,000 annual income per capita in the United States? Was the problem merely Congo's intolerable poverty level? Or were the attacks against

Sassou Nguesso motivated by other factors—ignorance, class prejudice, racial prejudice, and so on?

Perhaps because he had read news reports and briefing memos on issues such as the Sassou Nguesso hotel bill story, U.S. president Barack Obama used his first official trip to Africa (Accra, Ghana, July 2009) to speak out against corrupt leaders:

> Repression can take many forms, and too many nations, even those that have elections, are plagued by problems that condemn their people to poverty. No country is going to create wealth if its leaders exploit the economy to enrich themselves or if police can be bought off by drug traffickers. No business wants to invest in a place where the government skims 20 percent off the top or the head of the Port Authority is corrupt. No person wants to live in a society where the rule of law gives way to the rule of brutality and bribery. That is not democracy. That is tyranny, even if occasionally you sprinkle an election in there. And now is the time for that style of governance to end.

Those words were met with polite applause. But many African leaders and intellectuals objected to the speech's paternalistic tone and the perceived double standards that underlined Obama's public ethics lecture. Festus G. Mogae, the Republic of Botswana's former president, sarcastically observed in 2009 that Obama's critique of African corruption on his first official visit there seemed quite selective:

> [Obama] has been to the Middle East, to Turkey, to Russia, to Europe, to Britain—Britain where Parliamentarians have been doing their own thing, Germany where Siemens has been indicted for corruption, Russia, and the Middle East, [places] which are not known for their anti-corruption probity. . . . So, while it is right and proper that the President should have raised the issue of corruption, the fact that he only raised it when he got to Africa has the effect of perpetuating the misconception that corruption exists only in Africa.

The story of President Sassou Nguesso's hotel bill illustrates the confusion and fantasies that have too often plagued public policy when the good governance obsession leads to distracting public discourse and focus on the

Figure 2.2. Governance: The forgotten aspects. *Source*: Authors.

wrong development objectives. By devoting attention to valid but less important questions, such stories sidelined the much bigger economic issues of public investment priorities, flawed debt management strategies, and economic policy mistakes throughout the decades that are much costlier to Congo.

Similar stories can be told about many other countries. In the neighboring Democratic Republic of Congo (DRC), the public debate about corruption and good governance was dominated in 2013 by the story of fifteen government officials who pocketed $52 million in mining rents in 2012. Again, that was a valid issue. But the public debate over corruption and good governance never tackled the much bigger problem: that the mining sector represents one-third of the DRC's GDP but only 10 percent of fiscal revenue. This is a clear indication that something is profoundly wrong with the framework for sharing rents between the state and foreign firms. The DRC receives less than 5 percent of revenues generated by mining firms operating in the country, while the ratio is as high as 60–80 percent in the Gulf countries or other African countries such as Algeria. Honest incompetence and bad economic strategies are neglected, despite their potentially serious consequences on productivity and growth (figure 2.2).

Likewise, the African Union has devoted many resources to promoting the findings of its Report on Corruption released by its commissioner on human rights and administrative justice in 2012, which indicates that an estimated $148 billion is lost to corruption every year. Clearly, such waste deserves publicity and reflection, because these funds, often meant for projects such as schools and hospitals, are diverted into the pockets of corrupt public officials. But the sum should be compared to the GDP of more than $2 trillion for the continent and to the much larger sums of money wasted on unproductive public expenditures. Honest policy mistakes that are even costlier than corruption should be part of the governance agenda and appropriately debated.

An Incentives-Compatible Policy Framework for Governance

Most studies on the determinants of good governance go back to arguments similar to those made by either Gary S. Becker (1968) or Anne Osborn Krueger (1974). Becker analyzed corruption as a purely illegal activity and suggested that criminal offenses must be viewed as "economic activities" with external effects and punishment conceived as a form of taxation. From that general framework he conjectured that the probability of committing a crime depends essentially on the penalty imposed and on the probability of being caught. Furthermore, the penalty's deterrent value depends on the authorities' willingness and capacity to enforce laws and regulations and also on people's acceptance of the country's institutions. This implies that effective corruption enforcement rules and good governance in general can take place only in countries with political stability and transparent rules.

In Becker's insightful analysis, corrupt agents expend resources to steal, and society, the victim, experiences negative external effects. Using the Pigouvian solution to negative externalities—to introduce fees or taxes on the externality-generating activity—he suggests that prohibition rules combined with fines or other punishment make up such a fee system. Unfortunately, this kind of after-the-fact remedy to corruption may arrive too late. It may be ineffective in countries where the externality-generating activities (that is, corruption) are not easy to identify owing to prevailing social norms and practices or may be costly to curb. In almost all poor countries, the costs of running a well-staffed, well-equipped, and well-functioning national judicial system are often far beyond what the public sector can afford. The problem is compounded in many African countries where corruption is embedded in societal, economic, and power relations (Monga 1996), and virtually all state institutions, including the judicial system, are caught in the low-equilibrium dynamics of what Richard Joseph (1998) called "prebendal politics."

But "corruption isn't just something that happens to poor countries" (Glaeser and Saks 2004, 1). If one looks at corruption in historical perspective, it is clear that today's high-income countries also went through the same—or even worse—bad governance episodes that can now be observed in sub-Saharan Africa. In the fascinating book *Corruption and Reform* (2006, 3), Harvard University's Edward Glaeser and Claudia Goldin analyze various schemes and patterns of bad governance in the history of the world's greatest democracy. The results are disconcerting. "Conventional histories of nineteenth- and early twentieth-century America portray its corrupt elements as similar, and at times equal, to those found in many of today's modern transition economies and developing regions. Nineteenth-century American urban governments vastly overpaid for basic services, such as street cleaning and construction, in exchange for kickbacks garnered by elected officials. Governments gave away public services for nominal official fees and healthy bribes."

These elements provide a crucial clue to the problems of corruption and governance: that they are endogenous to the economic development level. In other words, low-income countries are by definition places where (perceived) corruption is a problem, and their governance indicators improve with their economic performance. It is unrealistic to expect the Democratic Republic of Congo, a country of less than $200 income per capita, to build governance institutions that are perceived as effective as those of Norway, where per capita income is $80,000.

Figure 2.3 confirms and illustrates that simple historical truth. It shows a clear correlation between the perception of good governance and income growth. If that is the case, then what is crucially needed to fight corruption and improve governance in low-income countries is a development strategy that offers few opportunities for state capture and rent-seeking activities. In other words, the main solution to corruption is to create a policy environment where there are few opportunities and gains for such externality-generating activities. If a government adopts a comparative-advantage-following strategy, firms in the priority sectors will be viable in an open, competitive market, and the government will not need to protect or subsidize them through various forms of distortions. The result will be dynamic growth, fewer rents, and fewer opportunities for rent seeking. By contrast, if the government adopts a comparative-advantage-defying strategy, the result will be just the opposite (Lin 2009).

What does this leave us? If poor governance (at least as measured by perception indicators) is indeed a low-income disease, the obvious way

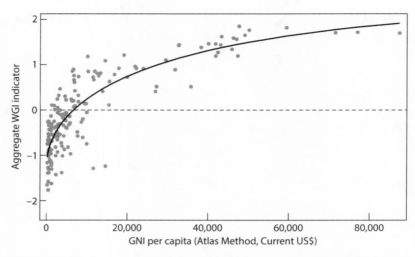

Figure 2.3. Governance performance and GDP per capita: the algebra of mystery.
Source: Lin and Monga (2012).

of achieving good governance is to focus on development strategies and policies that quickly lead to economic growth while minimizing the opportunities for state capture and rent seeking. In sum, "good political governance" is a difficult concept to operationalize, and there is no generic or universal prescription for it. Despite the beautifully formulated language of UN treaties and the official commitment to the good governance agenda by countries from around the world, no international entity or research body has the qualifications to legitimately measure someone else's governance quality. Good political governance should be an important public policy goal and be set freely by the all countries' people and leaders. It should not, however, be a precondition for good economic performance. Sustained economic growth, employment creation, and poverty reduction can be achieved even in very poor governance environments. Moreover, good political governance is always an unfinished process.

Good economic governance is also a noble goal, and its general principles can be widely shared across nations and cultures. But operationalizing it is likely to vary widely across place and time. To succeed at this goal, a policy agenda is needed that focuses on using limited state resources strategically and wisely. Focus areas should include setting economic policy to ensure that only activities that are consistent with comparative advantage are encouraged; ensuring that government at all levels has the tools, incentives, and discipline to facilitate public-private partnerships in the development of competitive industries; and setting rules of the game that are enduring and effective (transparency, time limits, collective action, and so on).

Following the type of policy-oriented approach suggested by Krueger (1974), the empirical literature has identified seven factors as the main causes of corruption:

→ Trade restrictions, which make the necessary import licenses very valuable and encourage importers to consider bribing the officials who control their issue

→ Poorly targeted government subsidies that are appropriated by firms for which they are not intended

→ Price controls whose purpose is to lower the prices of some goods below market value (usually for social or political reasons) but create incentives for individuals or groups to bribe officials to maintain the flow of such goods or to acquire an unfair share at the below-market price

→ Multiple exchange rate practices and foreign exchange allocation schemes. Differentials among these rates often lead to attempts to obtain the most advantageous rate, although that rate might not apply to the intended use of the exchange, and multiple exchange rate systems are often associated with anticompetitive banking systems in which a particular bank with strong political ties makes large profits by arbitraging between markets.

→ Low wages in the civil service relative to wages in the private sector, which often lead civil servants to use their positions to collect bribes as a way of making ends meet, particularly when the expected cost of being caught is low

→ Natural resource endowments

→ Sociological factors such as ethnolinguistic fractionalization (Mauro 1995)

Given that virtually all governments in the world—including those in successful democratic countries—regularly intervene in their economies and set various types of regulations, the important question is: which particular policy circumstances provide the best incentives for good governance? *New Structural Economics* (Lin 2012a) attempts to articulate a response to this question. Leaving aside the last two factors identified by Krueger, it specifically recommends policies and safeguards to ensure that the essential responsibilities of any state be carried out in a way that mitigates the risks of state capture and rent seeking. It suggests the gradual lifting of trade restrictions, price controls, and multiple exchange rates, recognizing that such interventions and distortions are temporarily needed to protect nonviable firms in sectors that defy comparative advantage. It advocates carefully targeted incentives (of limited amount and time), allocated in a transparent manner to compensate for the externality generated by pioneer firms—even in industries that are consistent with comparative advantage.

Such a framework ensures that corruption opportunities are minimal. It favors government interventions only in industries where firms are viable in open, competitive markets, and whose investment and survival do not depend on protection, large budgetary subsidies, or direct resource allocations through measures such as monopoly rent, high tariffs, quota restrictions, or subsidized credits. In the absence of large rents embedded in public policies, there will not be distortions that become the easy targets of political capture. The likelihood of the pervasive governance problems that are observed in many low-income countries can be much reduced when governments facilitate the development of new industries that are consistent with the country's changing comparative advantage, determined by the change in its endowment structure.

The goals of most political leaders everywhere are typically to stay in power as long as possible and to have a positive legacy (if their staying in power is not under threat). Most leaders understand that promoting economic prosperity is the best way to achieve these goals. Development policy based on new structural economics, which advises governments to facilitate the entry of private firms into sectors with comparative advantages, can reduce corruption and bring dynamic growth to a country. Good governance will be the result of such a strategy, because there is no need to create rents that subsidize and protect firms in the priority sectors. Therefore it is an incentives-compatible way for political leaders in developing countries, including those in poor countries, to address challenging governance issues.

"UNDERDEVELOPED" FINANCIAL INSTITUTIONS:
THE ILLUSIONS OF INTELLECTUAL MIMICRY

On the list of the most recurrent obstacles and preconditions to growth and poverty reduction, the next culprit often singled out in the literature as a key constraint to economic development is limited access to finance. As with the challenges discussed earlier, weak institutional development in the financial sector is a major impediment to economic growth, employment creation, and poverty reduction. Because finance plays a substantial role in modern economies, researchers have long debated the relative importance of banks and financial markets in a financial system. The 2008–09 global financial and economic crisis has also led to calls for improving domestic and international financial regulations and supervision.

Money is obviously an indispensable commodity for households and firms. In survey results it also appears to be a major bottleneck for business creation and development. Moreover, bankers and financiers are universally considered villains whose propensity for greed and shortsightedness are such that entrepreneurs everywhere cannot expect their support in their drive for value creation. In her compilation of jokes about them, Anna White (2011) recounts the widely shared belief that "bankers are people that help you with problems you would not have had without them." She also recounts the story of a man who visits his bank manager and asks, "How do I start a small business?" The manager replies, "Start a large one and wait six months."

It is not surprising that the generally weak and underdeveloped financial systems that are so prevalent in low-income countries are perceived as prime suspects in the search for impediments to growth and poverty reduction. At least since Adam Smith and Alfred Marshall, there has been much discussion about financial systems' role in the economy. Joseph Schumpeter, Alexander Gerschenkron, and others pointed to banks as an economic growth engine in industrialized economies. Following the pioneering work of Raymond Goldsmith (1969), Ronald McKinnon (1973), and Edward Shaw (1973), a rich theoretical and empirical literature has advanced the view that the amount of credit the financial sector can intermediate is an important economic performance determinant. It is almost conventional wisdom that finance is not simply a development by-product but an engine propelling growth. Economic research on the subject generally concludes that a large, well-functioning financial sector with deep and liquid markets can generate the necessary credit to support economic growth and reduce growth volatility.

Here again, while the theoretical case for making such a judgment seems quite strong, empirical analyses offer a much more complex story. The theoretical case is as follows: Economic prosperity, the pursuit and result of improvements in physical and human capital and productivity, depends in theory on the efficient and optimal use of productive assets and on including the largest segments of the population in that process. Effective financial intermediation is therefore essential to the smooth unfolding of that process, as agents with excess savings (whether domestic, like households and firms, or foreign) should be encouraged to provide funding at optimal cost to support investment by firms. The state should also establish the appropriate regulatory framework to ensure that these funds are allocated by the financial system to the most productive use, with risk and liquidity levels that allow firms to create value and operate efficiently. Both savers and investors face risk and uncertainty, and the financial system can help them mitigate it or capitalize on it. Savers are generally unable to select the investment project that best matches their personal risk tolerance—except at high costs—and without pooling their money they cannot take advantage of increasing returns to scale in investments (Stiglitz 1998).

Asli Demirgüç-Kunt and Leora Klapper (2012, 2) sum up the intellectual consensus on financial systems' capacity to reduce poverty:

> Well-functioning financial systems serve a vital purpose, offering savings, credit, payment, and risk management products to people with a wide range of needs. Inclusive financial systems—allowing broad access to financial services, without price or nonprice barriers to their use—are especially likely to benefit poor people and other disadvantaged groups. Without inclusive financial systems, poor people must rely on their own limited savings to invest in their education or become entrepreneurs—and small enterprises must rely on their limited earnings to pursue promising growth opportunities. This can contribute to persistent income inequality and slower economic growth.

But empirical research tends to show that the relationship between financial development, economic growth, and poverty reduction is much more complex and varies depending on many other factors, such as the country's development level, the financial structure, and existing regulations. Stephen Cecchetti and Enisse Kharroubi (2012, 1) investigate two simple questions: "Is it true [that financial development is good for economic growth] regardless of the size and growth rate of the financial system? Or, like a person who eats too much, does a bloated financial system become a drag on the rest of the economy?" From a sample of developed and emerging economies, they show that the financial development level is good only up to a point, after which it becomes a drag on growth. Focusing on advanced economies, they also show that a fast-growing financial sector is detrimental to aggregate productivity growth.

These findings raise important questions for policy makers. The types of financial institutions, the criteria under which they are established and can expand, the rules governing the specific market in which they operate, and even the major instruments they use to mobilize savings from households and firms into enterprise investment and household consumption, to monitor investments and allocate funds, and to price and spread risk are indeed key elements for policy consideration. They are important because in market economies, financial intermediation carries strong externalities, which can be either positive (such as information and liquidity provision) or negative and even threatening to the entire economy (such as excessive risk-taking behavior, contagions, and systemic financial crises).

The Quest for Appropriate Financial Institutions

There is a vast body of literature analyzing the relative advantages of various banking structures. But taken as a whole, the existing research has not reached consensus on the strengths and weaknesses of various types of financial structures—defined as the composition and relative importance of various financial institutional arrangements in a financial system—in promoting economic growth.[6] There also is little consensus among researchers on the important policy questions at hand: the strengths and weaknesses of various types of financial structures and why they may promote economic growth in different country settings. The reasons for these gaps in the literature are the neglect of the specific characteristics of the real economy at each level of development and the corresponding needs in terms of financial structure. Understanding the difference in financial structure and how it is related to economic development is indeed essential and can provide policy implications for many countries, especially those developing countries that are making efforts to strengthen their financial system.

Economic research shows that financial markets tend to be more active than banks in countries with higher income per capita (Goldsmith 1969; Demirgüç-Kunt and Levine 2001). The literature has focused on the causal relationship between financial structure and economic growth, that is, whether a market-based or bank-based financial structure is better for economic growth.[7] Bank-based structure proponents argue that banks and other financial intermediaries have advantages in collecting and processing information, while financial markets provide much weaker incentives for agents to collect information ex ante and monitor borrowers (or stock issuers) ex post. Thus financial markets are at a disadvantage in alleviating informational asymmetry, and therefore a financial system with a bank-based structure should perform better in allocating resources and promoting economic development (Grossman and Hart 1982).

Not surprisingly, those who favor a market-based structure focus on the problems created by powerful banks. Bank-based systems may involve intermediaries that have huge influence over firms that may damage economic growth (Rajan 1992). In addition, banks tend to be more cautious by nature, and so bank-based systems may stymie economic innovation and impede economic growth. Furthermore, financial markets are often seen as providing richer and flexible risk-management tools for agents while banks can provide only basic risk-management services.

The economic literature that focuses on banking structure tends to examine whether competitive or monopolistic banking structure is better for economic growth. Some authors suggest that monopolistic banks may extract too much rent from firms, pay lower deposit interest rates, and thus lead to more severe credit rationing, which has very negative effects on economic growth. But others argue that monopolistic banks have more incentive to collect information, screen and monitor borrowers, and form long-term relationships with borrowers; therefore investment projects have more chances to get financed. In a competitive banking sector, borrowers can more easily shift between lenders, so banks may have less incentive and less capability to forge such long-term borrower-lender relationships. Such borrower-lender relationships are especially valuable to start-ups and new firms. Empirical results on this topic are far from conclusive. Some studies show a positive relationship between banking concentration and stability (Beck, Demirgüç-Kunt, and Levine 2007). Others find that new firms grow faster in economies with a more concentrated banking sector, but old firms benefit from a more competitive banking structure (Petersen and Rajan 1995).

Despite their diverging conclusions, these two main schools of thought actually adopt a similar research perspective. They typically start from an examination of the characteristics of various financial institutional arrangements and then offer a discussion of the possible effects of financial structure on economic development. Researchers adopt this perspective probably because they are interested in studying the effect of financial structure on economic growth. Yet its effect on growth may not be appropriately determined if its examination is separated from the examination of how the financial structure is determined. While the research on banking structure has focused on banking concentration, the important topic of the distribution of banks of different size and its economic significance has been neglected. The well-established fact that small businesses, the dominant form of business operations in developing countries, usually have difficulty obtaining loans from big banks suggests that bank size does matter for the allocation efficiency of the banking sector.

A few studies have examined the mechanisms affecting the determination of financial structure. R. G. Rajan and Luigi Zingales (2003), for instance, apply interest group theory to explain the difference in financial structure in countries at a similar development stage. Others have emphasized the legal system's importance in determining financial structure, arguing that legally protecting investors and effectively implementing the law are more critical for operating financial markets than for banks. Thus a bank-based financial system will have advantages in countries with a weak legal system. This logic, however, does not explain the following observed facts: the financial development level and financial structure are usually different in countries with a similar legal origin but at different development stages, and the financial structure in the same country changes as the country's economy develops. In fact, any effective financial development theory should take into consideration the financial structure's endogeneity when analyzing the relationship between financial structure and economic development.

To sum up, much of the literature adopts a supply-side approach. It starts from an examination of the characteristics of various financial arrangements and then discusses the likely effects of different financial systems on economic growth. Financial structure is actually seen as not relevant, and the real economy's characteristics are ignored. It is important to pursue a radically different demand-side approach, one that starts from the analysis of the real economy's characteristics and the real economy's demand for financial services. The reason for such a methodological shift is simple, and a financial structure's effectiveness should be determined by one important criterion: whether the financial structure can best mobilize and allocate financial resources to serve the real economy's financial needs.

Redefining Financial Structure and Its Optimality

Empirical research shows that there is virtually no country—even among industrialized ones—where security markets actually contribute a large part of corporate sector financing. A comparative study by Colin Mayer (1990) devoted to the industry financing of eight developed countries and to evaluating these patterns in the context of alternative theories of corporate finance concludes that the average net contribution of their security markets was close to zero and highlights the deficiencies of equity markets. This does not imply that equity markets do not perform an important function. "They may promote allocative efficiency by providing prices that guide the allocation of resources or productive efficiency through reallocating existing resources via, for example, the takeover process. But in terms of aggregate corporate sector funding, their function appears limited. Instead, a majority of external finance comes from banks." (Mayer 1990, 325).

Two financial structure dimensions critically affect financial systems' efficiency in performing their fundamental functions in economic development: first, the relative importance of banks and financial markets, and second, the distribution of banks of different sizes. Banks are the predominant type of financial intermediaries in low-income countries. Their mechanisms for mobilizing savings, allocating capital, and diversifying risks are very different from those of financial markets. Therefore the relative importance of banks and markets constitutes the most important financial structure dimension. Among banks there is an obvious distinction between the way in which big banks do business and how small banks operate; this has implications for access to services, especially lending services, by different size firms.

Banks were long regarded as central to promoting economic growth and poverty reduction. But in the face of widespread corruption and bank failures in the 1970s and 1980s, which were often compounded by financial repression policies, there was disillusionment with their role, most notably in developing countries. As a result, many influential development institutions, such as the World Bank (1989), shifted their policy advice and advocated the use of both security markets and banks in promoting growth. In fact, a central feature of the economic reform and structural adjustment programs designed and implemented in the Washington Consensus framework was the dismantling of the traditional development finance model (based on bank-based systems, directed credit, public development banks, closed capital accounts, capped interest rates, and active monetary intervention) that had been established in developing countries in the postwar era.

Small banks with very limited assets cannot afford to make large loans; they would have to bear much higher risk resulting from concentrated investments. Thus small banks can only make small loans. Large banks are more able to make large loans and achieve better risk diversification. Since the transaction cost for making a loan is, at least to some degree, independent of loan size, large banks understandably prefer making loans to large firms rather than small ones. Large banks tend to stay away from small businesses but rather focus on large businesses, while small banks specialize in lending to small businesses (Jayaratne and Wolken 1999). This specialization suggests that, in addition to the mix of banks and financial markets, the distribution of different size banks can be an important dimension for the understanding of financial structure and economic development. Thus the distribution of big banks and their smaller counterparts can have a substantial effect on the banking sector's performance.

The new standard financial structure model, which has become conventional wisdom, aims to reflect the imperatives of financial development. It has been influenced by financial market liberalization that is unfolding in the advanced economies, which have moved away from national bank-based systems toward open capital markets—at least until the 2008 Great Recession when the pendulum switched to the other extreme. Conservative governments in the United States and Europe abruptly changed gears and adopted new laws and regulations to rein in financial markets and nationalize banks.

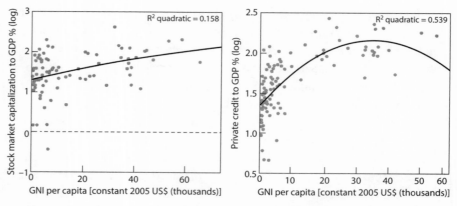

Figure 2.4. Stock market capitalization and GDP (left); private credit and GDP (right).
Source: Authors.

The financial sector reforms implemented in developing countries around the world over the past decades were expected to raise savings and investment levels, reduce macroeconomic instability, increase the rate of growth, and create employment. These objectives have generally not been achieved. Instead, there have been several financial crises since the mid-1990s and a general funding decline for large firms in productive sectors, and small and medium-sized enterprises (SMEs) in general, a major problem for sustainable growth and poverty reduction in the long run (Fitz-Gerald 2006).

Recent analytical work by Justin Yifu Lin, Xifang Sun, and Ye Jiang (2013) shows that each institutional arrangement in a financial system has both advantages and disadvantages in mobilizing savings, allocating capital, diversifying risks, and processing information when facilitating financial transactions. Empirical observations reveal that equity markets become more active relative to banks as a country becomes richer, and that small businesses have no access to equity markets and generally have less access to large banks' loan facilities (figure 2.4).

The explanation for these stylized facts lies in the crucial notion of factor endowment, which itself determines firms' competitiveness—and thus the profitability of financial institutions supporting them. A financial system's efficiency in promoting economic growth depends on its ability to allocate financial resources to efficient firms in the most competitive industries

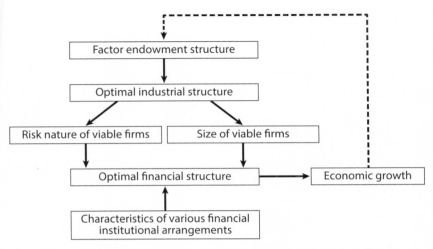

Figure 2.5. The dynamics of optimal financial structure. *Source*: Authors.

in the economy. In other words, the factor endowment in an economy at each stage of its development determines the optimal industrial structure in the real sector, which in turn constitutes the main determinant of the size distribution and risk features of viable enterprises with implications for the appropriate institutional arrangement of financial services at that stage. Therefore there is an endogenously determined optimal financial structure for the economy at each development stage.

The reason is the following: at each stage of its development, an economy has a specific factor endowment structure (that is, the relative abundance of various factors of production, mainly labor, capital, and natural resources), which endogenously determines its optimal industrial structure at that stage (figure 2.5). Enterprises operating in different industries are distinct in firm size, risk, and financing needs. Thus the real economy's demand for financial services at some development stages can be systemically different from that of the same economy at other stages. Only when the characteristics of financial structure match those of the economy's industrial structure can the financial system efficiently perform its fundamental functions and contribute to sustainable and inclusive economic development. Therefore there exists an optimal financial structure for the economy at each development stage. A financial structure deviation from its optimal path will lead to low financial system efficiency and hinder economic development.

While poor regulation and supervision may cause financial crises, a serious mismatch between the financial structure and industrial structure will reduce efficiency in mobilizing and allocating financial resources.

In developed countries where large capital-intensive firms and high-tech firms dominate the economy, financial systems dominated by capital markets and big banks will be more efficient in allocating financial resources and promoting economic growth. In developing countries where small and less risky labor-intensive firms are the main engines for economic growth, the optimal financial structure will be characterized by the dominance of banks, especially small local banks. The optimal financial structure for any country changes as the economy develops, endowment structure upgrades, and industrial structure changes.

The remaining major challenge is selecting the appropriate policy framework for developing sustainable and effective financial institutions. In this regard, governments have an important role to play. Both the equity market and banks require government regulation and supervision to mitigate inherent moral hazard and reduce the occurrence and severity of financial crises. Although a country's endowment structure and the resulting optimal industrial structure are the most fundamental force shaping its financial structure, the government's policy will also affect the actual financial system evolution. In fact, development strategies promoted by governments and related policies are among the most important factors that cause the industrial structure and financial structure to deviate from their optimal structures. If a capital-scarce developing country adopts a comparative-advantage-defying strategy in which the development of capital-intensive industries is the priority, the financial structure will be diverted from its optimal path and channel scarce capital to the government's priority sectors. The "financial repression" in many developing countries is the result of such a development strategy.

Policy makers in developing countries should be mindful of a particularly costly type of hidden distortion: the one that consists of replicating the financial systems in place in developed countries without fully considering the real economy's demand characteristics for financial services. Just like perception indicators of good governance, financial development is a function of a country's economic development level, not a prerequisite to performance.

3

The Economics of Chance:
Policy Prescriptions
as Laundry Lists

In one of his most popular sketches, Ivorian comic Adama Dahico imagines the continent of Africa as a sick patient visiting a medical doctor whose task is to cure her ills. The physician's diagnosis is grim but imprecise despite the doctor's very confident tone, and the causes of the patient's bad health are numerous. The doctor never listens much to the patient yet prescribes a wide range of medications, from drugs to cure the debt to measures to improve economic governance and democracy.

Dahico's satirical sketch is not far-fetched: African policy makers at the highest government levels often confess to regularly finding themselves in similar situations. When they identify an expert who seems to have the credentials to provide them with the right strategy and policy advice, they often end up frustrated. The recommendations are generally either vague and generic or too specific and microscopic, leading to lengthy and complex policy frameworks. Worse, the recommendations typically do not seem to integrate the most precious currency in politics: time. For political leaders, time constraints are indeed hard constraints, as they always compound the already daunting political-economy constraints they face. Regardless of the political regime, time is one of the most precious currencies and must be handled with extreme care. Yet most political leaders are likely to ignore economic development strategies that leave no space for clear, quick wins and little possibility of advertising success.

The situation is made even more complex in low-income countries that were once under foreign domination and where development strategies and policies are designed by external experts and institutions and are therefore perceived as illegitimate—if not as blueprints for perpetual domination. A few years ago, a tense and interesting exchange took place at a Geneva donors' conference devoted to Burkina Faso. High-level representatives of many bilateral and international institutions had gathered with Burkinabe government members to discuss the country's development strategy and its funding needs. Taking the floor to wrap up donor sentiment, a director from one of the Bretton Woods institutions chastised the insufficient progress over decades by the country on structural reforms, despite great hopes. Burkina Faso was compared to "an airplane that had been sitting on the tarmac for years while everybody was waiting for a takeoff that never occurred."

The country's minister for economic development, Bissiri Sirima, did not like being challenged by an official of an international organization whose rigid internal procedures and heavy bureaucracy he knew all too well. He reacted forcefully but with humor by telling the donor representatives in the room that they were treating his country with condescension. He told the audience that before the meeting he had collected the most important policy framework papers prepared for Burkina Faso by the Bretton Woods institutions and counted the total number of recommended reforms imposed on his government as conditions for ongoing programs and projects, which amounted to more than 500 for a single year in all government sectors. His list of policy prescriptions ranged from measures to ensure macroeconomic stabilization to reforms to boost competition in telecommunications or to protect the environment. He concluded: "To satisfy you guys, the government of Burkina Faso must implement 1.5 conditionalities per day for an entire year!"

Minister Sirima reminded the audience that almost every day, cohorts of donor representatives from Washington, Paris, Brussels, and elsewhere arrived in Ouagadougou, often without prior notice, and flocked to government offices asking for meetings not with their technical-level counterparts in the administration but with the president, the prime minister, and other high-level government officials. This constant yet impromptu diplomatic ballet forced his small team and almost all the cadres in various ministries to work day and night just to accommodate requests for documents by the donor community. His unexpected statement brought some humility and common sense to the discussion that followed. It also put to rest the notion that his government had not been making enough progress on reforms.

Yes, development economics has not always been a trustworthy source for those policy makers who need a concrete blueprint for action. Decades of paradigm shifts, from grandiose project financing (interventionist policies) in the 1960s and 1970s to structural adjustment (laissez-faire) in the 1980s and 1990s, have led to randomness and intellectual confusion in economic policy. The disappointing results of various waves of development thinking of the past sixty years have led some researchers and policy analysts to reject many previously held ideas instead of looking carefully at the evidence. Knowledge always builds on ancient wisdom, which is then strengthened through new learning.

This chapter discusses the foundations of the most popular policy prescriptions that are offered to developing countries as blueprints for prosperity. It starts by sketching the historical intellectual background that determined economic policies in colonial times. It then reviews the various waves of development thinking that have dominated research and policy making since World War II. It also highlights some issues with the analytics of growth and the random search for binding constraints in developing countries. It concludes with a review of the disappointing results of the lengthy policy prescriptions that developing countries typically receive and adopt.

COLONIAL ECONOMICS: A SHORT HISTORY OF UNSOUND IDEAS

Among the many lingering consequences of centuries of colonialism in developing countries, perhaps the most distressing is the persistence of bad ideas, often originating elsewhere and adopted (if not imposed) without due consideration of time, place, and circumstances. A quick look at the economic policies implemented by colonial powers in the countries and territories under their control in the nineteenth and early twentieth centuries shows various forms of what Edward Said (1978) called "orientalism," or the propensity for Western thinkers and political leaders to view and conceptualize other societies and civilizations mainly through the lens of their own frameworks and models. Despite their occasional ideological differences, colonial economic policies often reflected a discourse about other nations that essentially accommodated the prevailing modes of Western thinking and neglected the specificities of each society at any time. Moreover, these policies were generally aimed at facilitating and optimizing the exploitation of colonies or at setting up the techno-structure to support broader colonial goals (Austin 2010, 2015).

It is therefore not surprising that in colonial times, the economic debate in the developing world often simply reflected the main ideas that were prevalent in advanced countries. Looking specifically at the economic history of Africa (the region with the most difficult economic development challenges), Ralph Austen (1987) identified two major schools of thought during colonial times.[1] One was committed to the market (or neoclassical) perspective, using the principles subsequently known as "rational choice theory" as the main analysis tool, and another was subdivided into Marxist, dependency, and substantivist theory. As reflected in ensuing macroeconomic debates, these two camps held sharply different assumptions about the motives and behavior of economic agents. Market theorists considered the economic agent's objective to be the use of production factors in a way that maximizes benefits or returns under specific constraints imposed by circumstances while minimizing risks. Structuralists tended to focus on collective goals such as harmonizing the social order that determines the rules of economic behavior (for substantivists) or a hierarchical system in which dominant and subordinate social groups or world regions struggle over economic control (Marxists and dependency theorists).

Analyzing West Africa's involvement in colonial world trade, A. G. Hopkins (1973), a main proponent of the market-oriented school, explained that a market system initially failed in that part of the world not because economic agents rejected it but because domestic resources were not available in sufficient quantity to spur the growth of effective demand. According to Hopkins, economic development there was constrained by low population density and high transportation costs. Thus, prior to the nineteenth century, international trade failed to act as an engine of growth in West Africa because the slave trade, besides being criminal and immoral, created only a very small export sector, one that had "few beneficial links with the rest of the economy."

But at the beginning of the nineteenth century there was a major turning point in African economies' development: trade became more legitimate and more intense as warrior entrepreneurs who had previously dominated the scene faced numerous small producers and traders. This structural shift in export-producing firms was sustained for several decades by internal dynamics in African societies (the emergence of a very industrious class of local entrepreneurs) and France's increasingly important role as a West African colonial power. After the Industrial Revolution the elaboration of military technology and the self-confidence of the bourgeois culture gave European elites a sense that their ways of organizing life stood for both might and progress.

By the end of the nineteenth century this new economy suffered a major setback. A general economic crisis can be explained by economic and political factors: a prolonged fall in the price of palm oil and groundnuts after 1860 and desperate attempts by the slave-trade network oligarchs to maintain their grasp on the economy. Furthermore, trading firms' poor business practices eventually encouraged colonialism: in response to declining profit margins, monopolies became popular and business relations more politicized. Colonial powers felt compelled to become more involved in ruling these territories in a way that suited their political goals.

In the early twentieth century colonial powers tried to present their role in "structuring" the occupied territories' economies with pride. In the 1930s several large expositions were organized in Europe to display what was then considered colonization's accomplishments. These include the launch of major public works; the familiar argument that, thanks to European rule, foreign trade (especially commodity trade) had acted as the main engine of growth, drawing the dark continent into the international economy; and the ability of colonial states to bring together diverse populations and cultures into "harmonious, peaceful nations." According to Hopkins, colonialism marked "a new and broadly speaking, expansionist phase in the evolution of the modern market economy."

In a forceful defense of the economics of colonialism, P. T. Bauer (1976, 149) also writes:

> The colonial governments established law and order, safeguarded private property and contractual relations, organized basic transport and health services, and introduced some modern financial and legal institutions. This environment also promoted the establishment or extension of external contracts, which encouraged the inflow of external resources, notably administrative, commercial and technical skills as well as capital. These contracts also acquainted the population

with new wants, crops, commodities and methods of cultivation and opened new sources of supply of a wide range of commodities. These changes engendered a new outlook on material advance and on the means of securing it: for good or evil these contracts promoted the erosion of the traditional values, objectives, attitudes and customs obstructing material advance.

In other words, "colonialism was a necessary instrument of 'modernization' which would help other peoples to do what they could not have done, or have done as well, by themselves" (Fieldhouse 1981, 43).

The substantivists and Marxist researchers obviously did not share that assessment. They argue that prior to the nineteenth century Africa and Asia had strong trading networks based on the market of locally produced agricultural and industrial goods, despite low economic growth in these regions. G. A. Akinola (1997, 324), for instance, notes that "Africa was Europe's trading partner, not its economic appendage," and that colonialism changed the dynamics. A turning point was the wresting of control of trade from middlemen, like the Swahili states of the eastern African coast and powerful magnates like the king of the Niger Delta state of Opobo. Indeed, several wars aimed at resisting European penetration in the Lower Niger, in eastern Africa, and in the Congo Basin were precipitated by European measures to take control of trade.

The subsequent colonial boundaries and the smothering of precolonial industries through the flooding of African markets with European consumer goods contributed to the colonial economy's export-import orientation—still a dominant feature of African economies today. According to Akinola, "Encouragement was, however, given to the growth of cash crops like cocoa, peanuts, coffee, tea, and cotton, organized so as to ensure that a colony specialized in one major crop, such as cocoa in the Gold Coast and Côte d'Ivoire, peanuts in Senegal and the Gambia, and cotton in Uganda. Even in those areas, there were European firms or prosperous merchants and produce buyers who stood between the African producer and the world market, and skimmed off most of the profit" (325).

Substantivist, Marxist, and dependency theorists have denounced colonialism as exploitation and described pre-independence economic policies as strategies imposed by colonial powers to generate rents for themselves without spurring the oppressed territories' development. John A. Hobson

(1902) linked colonialism to capitalism, arguing that underconsumption in Europe was the main driver of imperialism. By keeping workers' wages very low and consistently investing profits into more production, Western capitalists quickly faced insufficient domestic markets to absorb their surplus. Each national group then pressured their government to find new, protected colonial markets overseas.

Many economists and historians now assess colonial economics mainly as a purely extractive process, designed to produce profits for colonial capitalists, prevent capital accumulation in African economies, and perpetuate such economies' dependency on imports and commodities.[2] In his review of how colonial rule and African actions during the colonial period affected the resources and institutional settings for subsequent economic development, Gareth Austin (2010) sums up the current consensus on the flawed intellectual framework that underlined colonial economics—regardless of the ideological bents of their proponents—and its deleterious effects. He concludes that colonial governments and European firms invested in both infrastructure and (especially in southern Africa) institutions designed to develop African economies as primary-product exporters. In both cases the old economic logic for coercing labor continued to operate, that is, the continued existence of slavery in early colonial tropical Africa and the use of large-scale land grabs to promote migrant labor flows in "settler" economies.

But there were changes and variations. Austin also notes that the main determinant of the differential evolution of poverty, welfare, and structural change was the contrast between "settler" and "peasant" economies:

> It was in those "peasant" colonies that were best endowed with lands suitable for producing the more lucrative crops that African populations experienced substantial improvements in purchasing power and had the most improvement in physical welfare. In the same countries, however, colonial rulers, partly because of fiscal constraints as well as a probably realistic assessment of the short-term economic prospects, did little directly to prepare the economies to move "up the value chain." Thus, the first generation of postcolonial rulers presided over economies which were as yet too short of educated (and cheap) labor and sufficient (and sufficiently cheap) electricity to embark successfully on industrialization. It has taken post-colonial investment in

education and other public goods to move West African economies, and tropical Africa generally, closer to the prospect of a substantial growth of labor-intensive manufacturing, if international competition permits it.

By contrast, "settler" colonies had a worse record for poverty reduction, especially considering the mineral resources in countries such as South Africa and Southern Rhodesia, but they had a better record for structural change. "The large-scale use of coercion was the basis for the construction of white-ruled economies that, especially in South Africa, eventually became profitable enough for a partly politically impelled policy of import-substituting industrialization to achieve some success. Thus the rents extracted from African laborers were channeled into structural change, although the process became self-defeating as it progressed, contributing to the fall of apartheid" (Austin 2010).

WAVES OF DEVELOPMENT THINKING
AND THE LEGACY OF BAD IDEAS

Economists and policy experts specializing in developing countries subsequently amplified and carried out the debates over colonial economics. The first wave of development economics, which emerged as a new subdiscipline of modern economics after World War II, was heavily influenced by structuralism. It suggested that the virtuous circle of development depended essentially on the interaction between economies of scale at the individual firm level and the size of the market (Rosenstein-Rodan 1943). Specifically, it assumed that modern methods of production can be made more productive than traditional ones only if the market is large enough for their productivity edge to compensate for the need to pay higher wages.

But the size of the market depends on the extent to which these modern techniques are adopted. Therefore if modernization can be started on a very large scale, economic development will be self-reinforcing and self-sustaining. If not, countries will be indefinitely trapped in poverty. Although the early structuralists inspired by Rosenstein-Rodan's work were right in emphasizing the importance of structural change, they attributed the lack thereof to market failures, and they proposed government interventions to correct it, most notably by import substitution strategies, many of which failed.

Early structuralists were right to try to close the structural gaps between low-income and high-income countries. But they identified the wrong causes for the gaps. They attributed to market rigidities the low-income countries' inability to establish the high-income countries' advanced industries. On the basis of this assumption, they advocated inward-looking policies to build industries that were not viable in open, competitive environments. Although subsidies and protection allowed some countries to achieve high investment-led growth for a time, that strategy came with costly distortions and was not sustainable in the medium to long term. Certainly the approach could not help countries converge to high-income country levels.

By the 1970s a second wave of thinking led to a gradual shift to free-market policies, culminating in the 1980s and 1990s, and highlighted government failures. With its main policy framework, known as the Washington Consensus (Williamson 1990), it tackled structural analysis indirectly through broad examination of the general functioning of economies and their markets, institutions, mechanisms for allocating resources, regulatory and incentives systems, and so on. The proponents of the structural adjustment programs implemented in many developing countries viewed the restoration of external and domestic balances as essential preconditions for launching economic transformation and change. Their policy prescriptions—stabilization, liberalization, deregulation, and privatization—also often led to economic dislocation and social tensions. The results were at best controversial, and some researchers have even characterized the 1980s and 1990s as the developing countries' "lost decades."

The Washington Consensus shifted the policy pendulum toward market fundamentalism. By focusing obsessively on government failures and ignoring the structural issues, its proponents assumed that free markets will automatically create spontaneous forces to correct structural differences among countries. Yet market failures from externality and coordination are inherent in structural change. Without the government's facilitation, the spontaneous process that ignites the change either is too slow or never even happens in a country. But the Washington Consensus neglected this, even in its "expanded version."[3] The Washington Consensus also neglected to consider that many distortions in a developing country are second-best arrangements to protect nonviable firms in structuralism's priority sectors in the country. Without addressing the firms' viability, the attempt to eliminate those distortions could cause their collapse, large-scale unemployment, and social and political instability. For fear of such dire consequences, many governments reintroduced disguised protections and subsidies that were even less efficient than the old ones.

Because of persistent poverty, and because developing countries were not able to close the gap with high-income countries, the international donor community shifted its efforts to humanitarian projects, such as investing directly in education and health for poor people. But service delivery remained disappointing in most countries. This led to a new focus on improving project performance, which researchers at MIT's Poverty Action Lab have pioneered with randomized controlled experiments. Commenting on the evolution of development thinking from early structuralism/Washington Consensus to project- or sector-based approaches, Michael Woolcock (2012) has written about a shift from "Big Development" to "Small Development." Although it is clearly important to understand the determinants of project performance, it is questionable whether that is really the route to economic prosperity. After all, the few economies that were able to close the gap with the United States did not start their development journey with micro projects but with big ideas.

Reducing poverty and climbing the ladder to prosperity are not easy: from 1950 to 2008 (before the Great Recession), only twenty-eight economies in the world had reduced their gaps with the United States by 10 percent or more. Among those economies, only twelve were non-European and non-oil exporters. Such a small number is sobering: it means that most countries have been trapped in middle-income or low-income status. Yet the policy frameworks that have so far come out of the various waves of development thinking still fail to deliver results. They are ineffective in their diagnosis of the nature or causes of modern economic growth. Moreover, beyond their dividing ideological backgrounds and the swing of the pendulum from market failures to government failures and even donors' failures, they also reflect the legacy of bad ideas in the analysis of the problem: they all identify infinite lists of obstacles and constraints to growth, leading them to offer lengthy lists of policy prescriptions (table 3.1).

TABLE 3.1. MAJOR WAVES OF DEVELOPMENT THINKING: A CRITICAL SUMMARY

Main Features and Policy Prescriptions	Strengths	Weaknesses
EARLY STRUCTURALISM: FOCUS ON MARKET FAILURES		
Suggested that the virtuous circle of development depended essentially on the interaction between economies of scale at the individual firm level and the market's size.	Stressed the importance of innovation and technological change in the growth process.	Ignored comparative advantage and led to the development of industries that were not competitive.
If modernization can be started on a very large scale, then economic development will be self-reinforcing and self-sustaining.	Attempted to close the structural gaps between low- and high-income countries.	Identified the wrong causes of the problem. Attributed the low-income countries' inability to establish high-income countries' advanced industries to market rigidities. On the basis of this assumption, advocated inward-looking policies to build industries that in fact were not viable in open, competitive environments. Although subsidies and protection allowed some countries to achieve high investment-led growth for a time, that strategy came with costly distortions and was unsustainable in the medium to long term. The approach could not help countries converge to high-income-country levels.
The market encompasses insurmountable defects and the state is a powerful supplementary means to accelerate the pace of economic development.		
The way for a developing country to avoid exploitation by developed countries is to develop domestic manufacturing industries through a process known as "import substitution."		
Need to target modern, advanced, capital-intensive industries.		
STRUCTURAL ADJUSTMENT: FOCUS ON GOVERNMENT FAILURES		
Suggested that state-sponsored development strategies necessarily give rise to incorrect relative prices in poor economies and distort incentives.	Used the price system to ensure efficient allocations of resources, encouraging efficiency.	Ignored issues of coordination and externalities that cannot be addressed by market mechanisms.
Viewed the restoration of external and domestic balances as an essential precondition for launching economic transformation and change.		Did not explain how technological diffusion takes place across countries and generates or sustains growth, and why it does not take root in others.
Recommended macroeconomic stabilization, liberalization, deregulation, and privatization.		Policy prescriptions did not include crucial elements for growth and structural change such as human capital or institutions,

Main Features and Policy Prescriptions	Strengths	Weaknesses
AUGMENTED WASHINGTON CONSENSUS: FOCUS ON GOVERNMENT FAILURES		
Recommended that initial Washington Consensus framework be complemented with policy measures to improve social and institutional development.	Drew attention to issues of governance, institutions, and human capital development, generally seen as critical to sustain dynamic growth.	Had same weaknesses as the Washington Consensus. Did not acknowledge issues such as intrasectoral tradeoffs in budget allocations and did not provide a blueprint for benefit incidence analysis. Offered only generic recommendations for good governance and institutional development, which are actually endogenous to growth.
RANDOMIZED CONTROL TRIALS AND MICRO RECIPES: FOCUS ON GOVERNMENT AND DONORS' FAILURES		
Suggested that policies to reduce poverty be based on "scientific evidence" through the use of randomized control trials (RCTs) or social experiments. Extensive use of project and program evaluation.	RCTs are good tools for understanding the effectiveness of specific micro projects and programs, and why they work or fail. Highlight what works and what does not—even though lessons are not necessarily transferable from one context to another. Helped ensure value for money in specific projects and programs. Provide some useful micro feedback to development stakeholders.	RCTs often do not start from a clear strategic assessment of how a particular method would fit the highest-priority knowledge gaps. Assessing the impact of specific projects one at a time without taking into consideration the many sources of heterogeneity relevant to behavior and the interaction effects—the fact that each such project is only one part of a development portfolio that often cuts across sectors—can lead to biases. Provide few insights to policy makers facing strategic macro decisions. Do not allow for a random selection of projects and programs and may exclude other learning opportunities that are at least equally important for improving understanding of economic transformation. RCTs do not provide answers to the main question of economic development, which is why and how some countries succeeded and others failed to fundamentally transform their economies, so the countries remain trapped in poverty.

Main Features and Policy Prescriptions	Strengths	Weaknesses
GROWTH DIAGNOSTICS AND PRODUCT SPACE: FOCUS ON GOVERNMENT AND DONORS' FAILURES		
Acknowledges central role of structural change in economic development and argues that in each country there will be binding constraints on growth, implying that failure in one dimension prevents growth even if all others are satisfactory. Posits that identifying the most binding constraints to growth is key to economic policy. Economic progress occurs because countries upgrade what they produce. This suggests that countries should move from their current products to other, usually more sophisticated, related products. The more closely related the product lines, the easier it is for countries to redeploy their capabilities and make incremental progress.	Stresses the need to prioritize reforms using the information revealed by shadow prices. Provides a simple method (the network of relatedness between products) for industrial and technological upgrading.	Applies to new industries that a given country is attempting to develop and argues that choices of such industries should depend on a self-discovery process by individual firms. But because this approach is not explicitly based on the theory of comparative advantage, the newly selected industries can be developed almost randomly and, in such cases, would likely have the same characteristics as those targeted by the structuralist approach and may not be viable in a competitive market.

THE ELUSIVE ANALYTICS OF GROWTH

When the Institute of Medicine, based in Washington, DC, published its study "To Err Is Human" (1999), which reported that up to 98,000 people a year die in the United States alone because of hospital mistakes, there was consternation and skepticism within the world medical community. The number was initially disputed. In recent years there has been wide consensus among health experts—including doctors and hospital officials—that things are actually much worse: In 2010 the U.S. government itself acknowledged that bad hospital care contributed to the deaths of 180,000 patients in the Medicare program alone in any given year. A recent study by a leading NASA toxicologist published in the very reputable *Journal of Patient Safety* (James 2013) goes much further, showing that deaths due to wrong diagnostics and wrong prescriptions are actually much higher. It estimated that between 210,000 and 440,000 patients each year who go to the hospital for care suffer some type of preventable harm that contributes to their deaths. If such a high number of medical mistakes can occur in a country with arguably the world's best healthcare system, one can only imagine what may be happening in low-income countries that do not collect or publish statistics.

A useful and even more frightening parallel can be drawn from this example to highlight the highly risky nature of the challenging economic development process and the unobserved consequences for societies and nations of the mistakes often made by experts and policy makers in their diagnostics and recommended strategies. No one knows the hidden political, social, and economic costs of the misguided policy advice given to low-income countries over long periods of time. Whatever they are, these costs are certainly extremely high and compounded to affect these countries for generations. This section discusses some of the pervasive problems in identifying constraints to economic growth and the logically misguided and often lengthy policy prescriptions that are derived from erroneous diagnostics.

In trying to answer the most fundamental question in development economics—what should poor countries do to ignite and sustain an inclusive growth process given their specific context and circumstances?—economists have too often relied on cross-country growth regressions, which posit that growth depends on initial conditions, institutions, and policy variables.

But that paradigm has produced disappointing results. There is still divergence in growth performance between developed and developing countries, despite the prediction of convergence from the traditional growth theory—and despite the observation that there has been policy convergence among countries instead of GDP convergence. A related issue is that much of the evidence in the growth literature relies on stationarity (the assumption that all that has been observed in the past will be observed in the future). There is also some evidence that cross-country distribution of world economies may be multimodal, with the existence of "convergence clubs" among countries that are too often stuck at similar levels of economic growth with no clear prospects for further growth (Ben-David 1998).

With such disappointments, some authors have concluded that the policy prescriptions and/or expectations about the effectiveness of Barro-type regressions are necessarily wrong when their generic conclusions are used as a basis for designing policies and selecting levers for action (Rodrik 2012). Another view is that growth researchers may have paid limited attention to heterogeneity (the specific characteristics and circumstances of each country and the many different types of firms and households). A third type of criticism is that growth research exhibits a strong tendency to "linearize" complex models: the traditional approach has been to focus on independent effects of a multitude of growth determinants. This has led to the linearization of complex theoretical models. Yet growth determinants interact with one another. To be successful, some policy reforms must be implemented with other reforms. Thus there is a need to adopt a policy complementary approach.[4] Even if complementarity is introduced into the analysis, the heterogeneity problem remains. If different firms (classified by size, location, ownership, and so on) in different countries at different times perform differently, it follows that generic policy prescriptions of the types often recommended by dominant modes of thinking are likely to be ineffective, if not counterproductive (inappropriate policies not only cost money but also often create social disruptions with long-term consequences).

These disappointments have led to rethinking and to searching for new approaches to economic growth. But this has proved to be a challenging exercise. In fact, despite all the criticism for being nonstructural, linear approximations to a complex reality and yielding results that are not robust, one can still justify the use of cross-country regressions by pointing out that the analytical path forward without them is not clear. First, there is probably as much heterogeneity across states of a country, or individuals in a state, as there is across countries. In other words, the neglect of heterogeneity is not an intrinsic failure of cross-country growth regressions; it applies equally to any other type of regressions. Second, for many macroeconomic questions (such as the effects of policies or institutions on growth), the relevant unit of observation is the country, and there is almost no alternative to using cross-country variation in the data. Finally, it is not easy to carry out a structural or nonlinear estimation using cross-country data, because one quickly runs out of degrees of freedom, and identifying full structural models is hard given the dearth of good instruments.

Such considerations are often put forward to justify the new consensus on growth analytics, which is the following: the various methodological approaches should be viewed as mutually complementary, and thus rather than selecting a "preferred" methodology, the most promising strategy is to judiciously combine cross-country analysis with micro- and country-specific work. On that basis, a three-step approach is often recommended for undertaking good country studies on growth: First, cross-country comparisons can be used to set up the international context and estimate the average effects of broad growth determinants and the potential gains from certain reforms. Second, micro data can be employed to allow for heterogeneity in the economy (across and within countries) and to investigate how constraints to growth operate at the industry/sectoral or firm levels. To gain a fuller understanding of the growth process and policies that will enhance it, one must indeed develop more empirical surveys and carry out better analyses of the dynamics of the investment climate, the distribution of assets, political reforms, and so on. More work using microeconomic data at the firm level could also prove to be a fruitful direction for future research, especially for issues related to employment. And third, country-specific analyses can be carried out to better understand the causality of relationships and the various transmission channels through which policies or institutional changes or foreign aid influence growth.

That broad consensus clearly takes us forward in defining the growth policy problem. But it still falls short of providing policy makers in developing countries with actionable policy levers for generating sustained and inclusive growth and prosperity. Despite not having solved the problem of where exactly policy makers should focus their action to target sectors and industries with the highest potential payoff, development economists and experts have turned their attention to the need for improving the business environment.

THE RANDOM SEARCH FOR THE TRUE BINDING CONSTRAINTS

One lingering effect from the Washington Consensus is the wide consensus among economists that reforms to improve the business environment in all countries—especially developing countries—can help attract and retain investment, thus fostering competitive markets, growth, and job creation. Adopting reforms to improve the investment climate is largely seen as a cost-effective way to promote private-sector development and improve competitiveness. This has led to the burgeoning of a new field of research and the development of new diagnostic tools, products, and services that many important institutions support.[5] It is indeed useful for any given country to analyze the World Bank's well-known Doing Business indicators (which benchmarks laws and regulations across ten policy areas) and its Enterprise Surveys (which examine firm experiences across a similar range of topics). Enterprise Surveys provide the raw material for the bank's Investment Climate Assessments (ICAs).[6]

Firm growth is essential to economic development, and all these databases and tools have generated strong worldwide interest in how best to facilitate economic and industrial growth and in country performance rankings. Yet, despite their usefulness, Doing Business indicators and ICAs, which are at the core of the formulation of economic policies and priorities in many developing countries because they try to capture the policy and institutional environment in which firms operate, have often yielded inconsistent and unsatisfactory results. As with the Doing Business indicators (see chapter 2), the ICA results can be misused or misinterpreted.

ICAs analyze firm performance and the perception of entrepreneurs in a country, and the results link to quantitative data found in investment climate surveys. Firms report various features of their business environment as obstacles to their growth. In a typical survey the managers of a sample of firms are asked to rate each investment climate dimension (such as corruption, infrastructure, and access to financing) on a scale of 1 to 4, corresponding to the degree to which it is an obstacle to firm performance. High mean reported values for particular investment climate dimensions are then interpreted as evidence of the severity of obstacles to growth.

But this may not be the case. Perceptions of the degree to which some investment climate variables are obstacles differ from the actual effect of these variables on firm growth, business performance, or firm productivity. Despite their intimate knowledge of their business processes and operating environment, firms may not fully recognize the true origin of their main problems and may mistakenly identify as a constraint something that is a symptom of another, less obvious problem.

The landmark empirical investigation by Meghana Ayyagari and colleagues (2008) highlights inconsistencies between perceptions of obstacles to growth by businesspeople and the reality of firm performance. It examines which business environment features directly affect firm growth. Using firm-level survey results and the mean reported values for a handful of investment climate variables in a sample of more than 6,000 firms in eighty countries, the authors assess whether each feature of the business environment that firms report as an obstacle affects their growth; the relative economic importance of the obstacles that do constrain firm growth; whether an obstacle has a direct effect on firm growth or acts indirectly by reinforcing other obstacles that have a direct effect; and whether these relationships vary by different levels of economic development and firm characteristics.

In the overall sample drawn from all eighty countries, firms reported taxes and regulation, political instability, inflation, and financing as the greatest obstacles to growth. These investment climate survey results are used to inform policy deliberations at the country level by looking at the ranking of such mean reported values. Thus if the mean reported value for a particular investment climate dimension in a country is high compared with other investment climate dimensions (and also compared with the mean value in other countries), then that investment climate variable is deemed to constitute an obstacle to growth in the country concerned (as shown in table 3.2).

But if one digs deeper, it quickly appears that such a popular methodology for identifying obstacles to firm growth is actually unsound. Careful econometric analysis by Ayyagari and others (2008) reveals that the perception by managers of the degree to which an investment climate variable constitutes an obstacle is often quite different from the effect of that variable on firm productivity, investment behavior, and firm growth. Regression analyses show that financing, street crime, and political instability are the constraints with the greatest and statistically significant estimated economic impacts (highlighted in table 3.3). In other words, managers are often wrong when they respond to surveys and list specific variables that they believe are the binding constraints to their firm's performance. This should not be too surprising: when responding to survey questionnaires, managers may intuitively be thinking about profits or other subjective factors that are not necessarily the true determinants of productivity growth.

The inconsistencies between the results in tables 3.2 and 3.3 can be explained with a model of growth with heterogeneity at a disaggregated level

Obstacle	Mean Reported Value			
	Overall	Bangladesh	Nigeria	Singapore
Taxes and regulation	2.97	3.03	3.10	1.55
Political instability	2.83	3.08	3.43	1.50
Inflation	2.83	2.86	3.21	1.61
Financing	2.81	2.60	3.11	1.97
Exchange rate	2.59	3.09	2.92	1.88
Street crime	2.54	3.07	3.30	1.22
Corruption	2.54	3.61	3.37	1.28
Anticompetitive behavior	2.39	2.40		1.58
Infrastructure	2.27		3.68	1.42
Judicial efficiency	2.16			1.32

Source: Calculations from Ayyagari, Demirgüç-Kunt, and Maksimovic (2008).

Note: Obstacles to firm growth reported by more than 6,000 firms in 80 countries. Reported value between 1 and 4, where 1 indicates no obstacle and 4 indicates major obstacle.

of the type offered by François Bourguignon (2006). One can indeed estimate the effect of a particular dimension of the investment climate, Z^m, on some measure of firm i's performance, y_i (such as firm productivity, investment, or firm growth) as follows:

$$y_i = \sum_m \delta_m Z_i^m + \varepsilon_i \qquad (1)$$

where δ_m is the elasticity of the impact of the investment climate variable m. One should then focus on the product δZ—that is, the impact on firm performance of relaxing a particular constraint—rather than the value or "height," Z, of the constraint itself. In fact, the estimated impact of relaxing investment climate constraints can be quite different from their mean perceived values.[7] The results in table 3.3 show the estimated impact on firm growth of a change in the investment climate constraint by its relevant (overall or country-specific) sample mean. Thus the figures for estimated impact

TABLE 3.3. REALITY OF INVESTMENT CLIMATE VARIABLES: ESTIMATED IMPACT ON FIRM GROWTH

Obstacle	Estimated Economic Impact			
	Overall	Bangladesh	Nigeria	Singapore
Financing	−0.101**	−0.094**	−0.112**	−0.070**
Street crime	−0.096**	−0.117**	−0.125**	−0.046**
Political instability	−0.074**	−0.080**	−0.089**	−0.039**
Inflation	−0.031	−0.031	−0.035	−0.018
Judicial efficiency	−0.011	−0.012		−0.007
Taxes and regulation	−0.006	−0.006	−0.006	−0.003
Corruption	0.013	0.018	0.017	0.006
Infrastructure	0.018		0.029	0.011
Exchange rate	0.041	0.049	0.047	0.030
Anticompetitive behavior	0.043	0.043		0.028

Source: Calculations from Ayyagari, Demirgüç-Kunt, and Maksimovic (2008).

Note: Estimated economic impact is the effect on firm growth of a change in the obstacle by its relevant (overall or country-specific) sample mean.

are the products $\delta_m Z_m$, where the δ_m is obtained from estimating a regression equation such as equation 1.

The inconsistencies between the results in tables 3.2 and 3.3 show the difference between the subjectively reported perception of obstacles to firm growth and the actual impact of constraints to firm performance. These inconsistencies highlight some of the many ways in which the relative importance of different dimensions of the policy and institutional environment and their effects on firm performance can be misinterpreted.

Furthermore, one should not limit the analysis of binding constraints to a unique scenario in which the elasticities of the estimated effects are the same across countries—that is, the case with the estimates underlying the results presented in table 3.3, where the effect of investment climate variables on firm performance is not differentiated across countries or by firm characteristics. It is a big assumption indeed to consider that the elasticity of the impact of political instability on firm growth, for example, must be the same in Singapore, Bangladesh, and Nigeria.

This is where researchers are confronted with data limitations and the analytical tools often used are unsatisfactory. Bourguignon (2006) explains the still unsolved problem that confronts researchers: "The difficulty has been that we face limitations with regard to the number of degrees of freedom. Within the same country, at a given point in time, there is not sufficient variation in the policy environment—there is much more variation in firm performance than there is in the policy environment. Thus, we do not have enough degrees of freedom to estimate the elasticities separately within countries, possibly within sectors, within age and size categories, and so forth."

The issue is one of heterogeneity of countries (where policies evolve over time) and firms (where performance varies depending on size, location, and other factors), which can be addressed with satisfactory analytical tools only if one constantly expands the set of available data. Such a costly solution is neither practical nor realistic. Therefore economists have struggled to identify actionable policy levers behind vaguely formulated investment climate variables such as financing, judicial efficiency, political instability, and taxes and regulation.

The need for taking heterogeneity into account is obvious when one adopts the policy maker's perspective and looks for practical ways to increase the competitiveness of specific manufacturing sectors that could have positive impacts on employment and spur job creation. In contrast with most studies of growth potential in developing countries, which repeatedly yield long lists of general constraints (including corruption, education, infrastructure, and red tape), Hinh Dinh and Célestin Monga (2013) identify a smaller number of more specific key constraints that vary by sector and firm size. Using several methodological tools,[8] they identify six main constraints across sectors and firms that impede the competitiveness of light manufacturing in Tanzania: worker skills; trade logistics; access to finance; access to industrial land; the availability, cost, and quality of inputs; and entrepreneurial capabilities, both technical and managerial. Among small firms, the most important constraints are in land, inputs, finance, and entrepreneurial skills. Among large firms, the most important constraints are associated with land, inputs, and trade logistics (table 3.4). On that basis, they present an in-depth diagnosis of the constraints in four

TABLE 3.4. TANZANIA'S EXAMPLE: NOT EVERYTHING EVERYWHERE IS CRITICAL

Sector	Firm Size	Input Industries	Land	Finance	Entrepreneurial Skills & Networks	Worker Skills	Trade Logistics
Textiles and apparel	Small	*Critical*	Important	Important	Important	Important	
	Large	Important			Important	*Critical*	Important
Leather products	Small	*Critical*	Important	Important	Important		
	Large	*Critical*	Important	Important	Important		Important
Wood products	Small	Important	Important			*Critical*	
	Large	Important	Important			*Critical*	Important
Agribusiness	Small	*Critical*	*Critical*	Important			
	Large	*Critical*	*Critical*	Important			

Source: Dinh and Monga (2013).

light manufacturing sectors in Tanzania that are identified for their good growth potential: agro-processing, textiles and apparel, wood and wood products, and leather and leather products.

Investment climate surveys have two more limitations: First, they do not provide information about industries that do not yet exist but in which a country has latent comparative advantage (Lin and Monga 2011). Second, the industries that are surveyed may not be consistent with the country's comparative advantage, either because they are too advanced (as a legacy of a development strategy that defied comparative advantage) or because they have become fundamentally uncompetitive (as a result of a general wage increase that accompanied the country's development). These two additional limitations make it highly desirable for investment climate surveys to cover only a sample of firms that meet the criteria of viability and can represent the economy's true potential.

PROMISES AND LIMITATIONS OF GROWTH DIAGNOSTICS

The discussion above leaves growth researchers and policy makers with several important questions: Are those searching for the determinants of growth looking in the wrong place? Should the focus be on institutions and institutional *outcomes*, rather than or in addition to policies? How can good institutional outcomes be obtained (assuming that they are not reflecting other factors)? One of the most interesting attempts to deal with nonlinearities in growth research is the growth diagnostics tool suggested by Ricardo Hausmann and colleagues (2008), also known as the "decision tree" approach. It suggests that there are "big principles" that growth requires— markets, openness, sound money, property rights—but that they can take many forms, and that achieving them requires country-specific context and information. In particular, these principles need not take any one precise institutional or policy form.

It starts with the premise that it is much more beneficial for any country to carry out a small number of high productivity reforms—a view driven by the empirical work of Hausmann and others' (2005) on growth accelerations. It then tries to identify in a logical, sequential way what the binding constraints are (using the so-called decision tree); this allows researchers to observe if the problem is due to low returns of some kind (externalities, high taxes, low social returns on labor or capital, low appropriability on issues like property rights, and so on). For any given country, one can then develop an empirical growth diagnostic framework based on both direct evidence that is a systematic focus on a list of "shadow prices" (real interest rates, cost of transportation, returns to education, and so on) and indirect evidence (informality, self-enforcement of contracts, and so on). In short, the approach is supposed to yield an economic agenda consistent with the country's recent growth history that avoids a comprehensive checklist of policies (as they imply no prioritization), the benchmarking of countries (as this is done on outcome variables, not on policies that have been pursued elsewhere), and cross-country regressions (as they capture only averages).

The key idea is therefore to identify the main binding constraints for growth through the information revealed by shadow prices. In an intellectual domain where growth decomposition and cross-country regressions have been the main tools for growth diagnostics, the proposed approach represents a novel and potentially fruitful advance. One can hardly object to the proposition that in each country there will be binding constraints on growth, implying that failure in one dimension prevents growth even if all the others are satisfactory, and that through time and across countries the binding constraint can vary. The growth diagnostics approach therefore makes a strong and convincing case for prioritization.

But operationalizing it in various country contexts still ends up focusing policy recommendations on some of the traditional macroeconomic problems, leaving the impression that the diagnostic's scope was limited. This was inevitable given the structure of the proposed decision tree, limited to a few broad problems. Issues that arise at the micro and institutional levels (and often explain the macro issues observed) are not fleshed out in the approach. The decision tree does not make any distinction between what could be called first-order constraints and second-order constraints. As a result, the diagnostic runs the risk of mixing symptoms and causes of slow growth.

In fact, the notion of "binding" lies uneasily with the model provided by Hausmann and others (2008).[9] This model comprises a two-equation summary of growth whereby, in an economy that is finance constrained,

$$g = \frac{r(1-\theta)(1-\psi)p - \rho}{1-\beta}$$

and

$$r = [\alpha^{\alpha}(1-\alpha)^{1-\alpha}a(1-\gamma)\nu^{-(1-\alpha)}]^{1/\alpha}\frac{1}{1-\sigma}$$

An equation for welfare along the balanced growth path can be written as follows:

$$W_c = \frac{\log[r\theta + \rho(1-\beta)] - \log(1+\delta) - \log(1-\beta) + \log k_0}{\rho} + \frac{r(1-\theta)-\rho}{\rho^2(1-\beta)},$$

where g is growth (balanced)

r is the rate of return on capital

θ is the degree of externality (coordination failure)

ψ is the inefficiency of taxation broadly interpreted

p is the probability of "expropriation" for micro or macro reasons

ρ is the "relevant" international interest rate

β is a financing constraint = borrowing/capital stock

α is the share of private inputs (x) in output; $(1-\alpha)$ the share of public inputs

a is total factor productivity

γ is taxes on output/income

ν is the cost of public services

σ is the subsidy to purchases of (x)

k is endowments

These equations are simply tools for organizing ideas rather than a predictor, and the variables are deliberately left imprecise. This explains why the proposed framework is very macroeconomic. But this raises many questions about sectoral interactions and tradeoffs. First, serious policy discussions about growth always get down to specific industries and sectors—existing ones that are competitive and nonexisting ones with potential (those with latent comparative advantage). Moreover, many of the parameters and variables are microeconomic in essence (from input subsidies to tax elasticities and inefficiencies). Hence the micro components of good diagnostics and policy response should not be neglected.

Second, beyond financing constraints, the model actually has no binding constraints. The equations are continuous so that a little improvement in any right-hand-side variable yields a little growth: improving, say, the efficiency of public services (lowering ν) can be precisely substituted by lowering taxes (τ). The remaining issue of "bindingness" lies in the shadow prices of various constraints that tie together the concepts in the welfare equation or in the interactions among terms in that equation. For example, $\partial W_c / \partial \beta$ depends on the excess of local returns $r(1-\theta)$ over the costs of capital ρ. The advantages of subsidizing firms depend on the shadow value of fiscal resources. This is, as acknowledged by Hausmann and others, an application of second best. So although the growth diagnostics framework is a good systematic approach to developing country case studies, in practice it is more an art than a science. It says little about the costs of removing the constraints and seems to be at odds with the view that reforms must be undertaken jointly to be successful.

OVERDOSE OF POLICY PRESCRIPTIONS AND REFORMS WITHOUT GROWTH

Despite the analytical fragility of many popular methods for identifying binding constraints to growth, policy makers in many developing countries are typically advised to adopt and aggressively implement a set of generic policies aimed at achieving macroeconomic stabilization and structural and institutional reforms. These prescriptions are derived from three simple ideas, the foundations of what John Williamson (1990) called the Washington Consensus: the belief in the virtues of market economy, the importance of macroeconomic discipline, and the need for all economies to open up to trade and foreign direct investment. Williamson (2002, 90) provides the rationale for the still dominant policy package not just as a matter of economic logic but also by pointing to the need for similarity between economic policies in rich OECD countries and poor developing countries. He argues:

> For the most part, [the Washington Consensus policies] are motherhood and apple pie, which is why they commanded a consensus. . . . These are ideas that had long been regarded as orthodox so far as OECD countries are concerned, but there used to be a sort of global apartheid which claimed that developing countries came from a different universe which enabled them to benefit from inflation (so as to reap the inflation tax and boost investment); a leading role for the state in initiating industrialization; and import substitution. The Washington Consensus said that this era of apartheid was over.

On that basis, the typical policy prescriptions recommended to developing countries facing serious large balance-of-payment problems, debt sustainability challenges, a shortage of external financing, and low growth in the 1980s (Monga 2006) were aimed at restoring domestic and external balance and putting them back on the path to long-term sustainable growth. They were designed by the Bretton Woods institutions and encapsulated in structural adjustment programs (SAPs), which combined lending in exchange for reforms. SAPs had two overlapping objectives: macroeconomic stabilization, defined as reducing national expenditure to bring it in line with national output or income, and adjustment, consisting of policies to increase national income or output through more efficient use of resources.

The consensus view within mainstream development economics was that stabilizing the economy typically implies adopting policies that lower the rate of inflation, reduce the current account deficit, restore external competitiveness, and limit the loss of international reserves. The recommended strategy was a contraction of domestic spending, most easily done by a tightening of monetary and fiscal policies. When the imbalances were too large, a real depreciation of the currency was also required. SAPs also provided that stabilization be complemented with policies to increase the national economy's productive capacity and to improve the efficiency with which the country's resources are utilized. Macroeconomic success is achieved when the economy has reached domestic balance (loosely defined as full employment without large distortion in economic policies) and external balance (a sustainable position of the current account balance). The justification was that in an interdependent world, small open economies with low levels of domestic savings like those in the developing world desperately needed to develop trade and attract foreign savings to be able to pay for their imports and investments, use their resources more efficiently, create jobs, raise their income, and reduce poverty.

The policy framework to achieve the dual objectives of stabilization and structural reforms has been summarized by Williamson (2002) as follows:

1. *Fiscal discipline.* This was in the context of a region where almost all the countries had run large deficits that led to balance-of-payments crises and high inflation that hit mainly the poor because the rich could park their money abroad.
2. *Reordering public expenditure priorities.* This suggested switching expenditure in a way that favored poor people, from things like indiscriminate subsidies to basic health and education.
3. *Tax reform.* Constructing a tax system that would combine a broad tax base with moderate marginal tax rates.
4. *Liberalizing interest rates.* In retrospect I wish I had formulated this in a broader way as financial liberalization, and stressed that views differed on how fast it should be achieved.
5. *A competitive exchange rate.* I fear I indulged in wishful thinking in asserting that there was a consensus in favor of ensuring that the exchange rate would be competitive, which implies an intermediate regime; in fact Washington was already beginning to subscribe to the two-corner doctrine.
6. *Trade liberalization.* I stated that there was a difference of view about how fast trade should be liberalized.
7. *Liberalization of inward foreign direct investment.* I specifically did not include comprehensive capital account liberalization, because that did not command a consensus in Washington.

8. *Privatization*. This was the one area in which what originated as a neoliberal idea had won broad acceptance. We have since been made very conscious that it matters a lot how privatization is done: it can be a highly corrupt process that transfers assets to a privileged elite for a fraction of their true value, but the evidence is that it brings benefits when done properly.
9. *Deregulation*. This focused specifically on easing barriers to entry and exit, not on abolishing regulations designed for safety or environmental reasons.
10. *Property rights*. This was primarily about providing the informal sector with the ability to gain property rights at acceptable cost.

Taken in isolation, any one of the policy recommendations seemed reasonable. But as a policy package for low-income countries that are by definition at different levels of development and therefore exhibit different endowment structures, comparative advantages, and capabilities, generic, one-size-fits-all economic strategies with a predetermined sequencing may not yield the expected results. Moreover, in specific country cases, various policy instruments could be used in different ways to achieve intended goals, taking into account social and political constraints, circumstances, and opportunities. Depending on the country and its size, performance, and economic structure, there may also be different ways to move from stabilization to growth and to combine demand-restraining and supply measures.

Not surprisingly, SAPs were controversial from the start, often viewed as economically costly (at least in the short term), politically and socially painful, and not very effective. Several studies, including by the World Bank and the International Monetary Fund, have indeed highlighted the persistent negative consequences of some of the early structural adjustment programs.[10] In fact, the proponents of SAPs seemed more concerned about inefficiencies in the economic systems of developing countries (the so-called deadweight loss triangles) than the need for understanding how firm performance, economic growth, and employment creation take place. The quest for efficiency gains through eliminating distortions in these poorly performing economies took priority over the need for effective growth strategies.

Taking into account lessons from the experience of implementing SAPs and their conventional policy package, the initial list of ten policy recommendations summarized by Williamson (2002) was complemented in the 1990s and 2000s with some of the most obvious missing ingredients: institutional reforms and human capital formation. As a result, a new conventional wisdom in the development industry could be summarized in one sentence: any developing country that can steadily achieve macroeconomic stabilization as generally defined in the prevailing IMF doctrine and implement structural and institutional reforms of the sort that are advocated by multilateral development banks would achieve high growth and reduce poverty. Table 3.5 offers a summary of this conventional package.

Unfortunately there are few developing countries where even these extended policy prescriptions—still mainly based on the Washington Consensus framework and often codified in IMF programs—have yielded the expected economic results. The simple, straightforward evidence of their disappointing results is the weak growth performance of all sub-Saharan African countries that have adopted and implemented such policy frameworks. Even after thirty years of IMF programs, most of them still recorded very low or negative average growth rates (table 3.6).

Disappointing news is actually widespread across the developing world. Indeed, economic reforms based on conventional policy prescriptions have also yielded few positive results in Latin America and in the eastern European countries that underwent big-bang-type transitions from socialism to the market economy. A case in point is that of Bolivia, a resource-rich country with strong growth potential, which remains one of the least developed countries in Latin America. Despite nearly two centuries of independence—it broke away from Spanish rule in 1825—the country has long faced social unrest, pervasive poverty, and illegal drug production. Political instability was seen as one of the main explanations for Bolivia's suboptimal economic performance (much of its history has consisted of a series of nearly 200 coups and countercoups).

Civilian rule was restored in 1982, but the country suffered a major economic crisis in the early 1980s. For about two decades, successive governments implemented Washington Consensus–type reforms, which included pension reforms; fiscal adjustments; central bank independence; decentralizing public administration; opening the economy to foreign trade; capitalizing and privatizing public enterprises; liberalizing prices, exchange rates, and interest rates; establishing a financial regulation and supervision system; and strengthening key public institutions such as the

TABLE 3.5. THE EXTENDED BLUEPRINT FOR ECONOMIC PROSPERITY

Policy Recommendation	Justification
MACROECONOMIC STABILIZATION	
Fiscal discipline	To curb large deficits that led to balance of payments crises and high inflation
Tax reform	To construct a tax system that combines a broad tax base with moderate marginal tax rates
Reordering public expenditure priorities	To switch expenditure in a pro-poor way from things like indiscriminate subsidies to basic health and education
Restrictive monetary policy	To keep inflation in check and gain credibility
A competitive exchange rate	To mitigate external shocks and limit balance of payments deficits
STRUCTURAL AND INSTITUTIONAL REFORMS	
Liberalizing interest rates	To end financial repression and capital flight
Liberalizing the financial sector	To end financial repression and improve intermediation
Liberalization of inward foreign direct investment	To attract foreign savings and stimulate knowledge transfers
Trade liberalization	To eliminate distortions and stimulate competitive exports
Privatization	To eliminate distortions, encourage competition, and alleviate the cost of poorly managed public enterprises on public finance
Public sector reform	To alleviate the burden of the public administration on public finance and make it more consistent with the needs of a "modern" economy
Deregulation	To ease barriers to entry and exit and establish a level playing field among firms
Protecting property rights	To provide the informal sector with the ability to gain property rights at acceptable cost
Liberalizing labor markets	To provide the flexibility that firms need to be able to hire and fire workers
Human capital	To provide the public sector and private sector firms the skills base needed for development
Improve the business environment	To build infrastructure, stimulate private sector development, and remove all binding constraints to growth
Improve governance	To strengthen administrative institutions, fight corruption and rent-seeking, and create a transparent public sector
Sectoral reforms and strategies of various kinds (water, agriculture, electricity, telecommunications, and so on)	To set objectives that are consistent with the medium-term budget framework and the long-term development goals

Source: Authors.

TABLE 3.6. IMF PROGRAM SENIORITY IN SUB-SAHARAN AFRICA AND GROWTH PERFORMANCE

Country	Time Span from First SAP to 2012	First 5 Years	Average Growth After 10 Years	Rate Post-IMF After 15 Years	3.2 SAP After 20 Years
Benin	23	3.8	4.1	4.4	4.3
Burkina Faso	21	4.0	5.4	5.8	5.7
Burundi	26	3.7	0.7	0.0	0.5
Cameroon	24	−4.5	−1.5	0.5	1.2
Central African Republic	32	0.6	0.9	0.4	1.1
Chad	25	4.5	2.8	3.4	6.3
Congo, Dem. Rep.	31	1.9	0.9	−1.7	−2.3
Congo, Rep.	26	−0.3	0.1	0.9	1.7
Cote d'lvoire	31	0.3	0.8	1.0	1.6
Equatorial Guinea	32		0.9	3.1	14.7
Ethiopia	31	−1.2	2.4	2.0	2.7
Gabon	32	3.5	1.9	2.3	2.2
Gambia, The	30	3.4	3.6	3.1	3.6
Ghana	29	3.8	4.2	4.2	4.2
Guinea	30		4.1	4.2	4.0
Guinea-Bissau	31	6.4	5.1	4.5	3.1
Kenya	32	2.8	4.2	3.3	3.2
Lesotho	24	6.2	5.1	4.2	4.1
Liberia	32	−2.5	−4.5	−13.3	−1.7
Madagascar	32	−1.6	0.4	0.2	1.0
Malawi	32	1.3	1.7	1.6	2.9
Mali	30	0.3	1.4	2.0	3.3
Mauritania	32	1.0	2.2	1.8	2.5
Mauritius	32	1.3	4.3	4.7	4.7
Mozambique	25	7.1	5.6	6.5	6.8
Niger	29	−1.5	−0.5	0.6	1.4
Nigeria	29	−3.7	0.8	1.3	1.8
Sao Tome and Principe	27				4.4
Senegal	32	1.6	2.4	1.9	2.6
Sierra Leone	31	0.9	1.0	−1.0	−0.7
Somalia	32	0.1	1.7	1.4	1.4
Sudan	30	0.4	2.7	3.4	4.1
Tanzania	32		3.8	2.7	3.3
Togo	31	−0.2	1.1	1.0	1.9
Uganda	32	2.7	3.0	4.3	5.3
Zambia	31	0.5	1.1	0.3	0.9
Zimbabwe	31	4.4	4.5	3.4	3.2

Source: Authors.

internal revenue and customs offices and the national road administration. In their critical assessment of the results, Luis Carlos Jemio and colleagues (2009, 4) conclude that "while reforms have increased productivity, they have failed to secure the political support necessary to assure long-term sustainability. In contrast, counter-reforms have so far enjoyed extensive political support, but productivity has stagnated since this process started, with declining economic growth and job creation—developments likely to undermine support for the counter-reform process."

The reforms were credited with successfully ending hyperinflation (from 12,000 percent in 1985 to 10 percent in 2006), spurring private investment, stimulating economic growth, and cutting poverty rates in the 1990s. But Bolivia still faced substantial challenges as income inequality remained high and growth was unlikely to reach levels sufficient to relieve the high poverty rate of more than 50 percent of the population. In addition, several social indicators still fell short of Latin American averages. In his inaugural speech in 2006, President Evo Morales commented: "We were told 10, 15, 20 years ago that the private sector was going to solve the country's corruption problems and unemployment, then years go by and there is more unemployment, more corruption, that economic model is not the solution for our country, maybe it is a solution for an European country or African, but in Bolivia the neoliberal model does not work."

Another more recent case of "shock therapy" with unsatisfactory results is that of the nation of Georgia. It was widely perceived as a near-failed state in 2003, but it managed to become a fairly well-functioning market economy in just a decade and ranked eighth in the World Bank's Ease of Doing Business Index (2013). Improvements in infrastructure quality, the business environment, and public finance management along with reduced trade barriers stimulated investments. Annual growth rates even averaged 6 percent between 2004 and 2013. Still, in 2013 Georgia remained one of the few countries in Europe and Central Asia that had not yet caught up to its 1990 real GDP level. Economic reforms generated little net employment creation. In fact,

> labor shedding in the public sector and as an outcome of economic transformation in some of the older sectors meant that there was significant labor churning and little net job creation. New growth sectors, especially in tourism and other service sectors, have not

been able to generate formal employment as effectively as a robust agri-business or manufacturing sector would have. The majority of the work force—more than 55 percent—is employed in agriculture (mostly self-employed), which contributes only 8.2 percent of GDP and is characterized by largely family-based subsistence farming with a relatively small agri-business sector. Low productivity levels in agriculture have contributed significantly to high rural poverty. (World Bank 2014, 2)

Furthermore, poverty and extreme poverty, measured using absolute poverty lines from national statistics, are still high in Georgia compared with other countries in the region.

The implementation of conventional policy packages derived from the Washington Consensus framework led to disappointments well beyond Bolivia and Georgia. From an economic perspective, the 1980s are known to have been a lost decade for many countries in Latin America (Ocampo 2005). Several eastern European economies that underwent transitions in the 1990s and chose to adopt a big-bang reform strategy instead of a more realistic and cautious gradualist approach also ended up bearing much heavier social and economic costs (Popov 2007). Africa's experience with SAPs has generally been even more painful (Soludo and Mkandawire 2003).

In a much cited paper critically reassessing Washington Consensus policies, Dani Rodrik (2006, 973, 975) observed that

life used to be relatively simple for the peddlers of policy advice in the tropics. Observing the endless list of policy follies to which poor nations had succumbed, any well-trained and well-intentioned economist could feel justified in uttering the obvious truths of the profession: get your macro balances in order, take the state out of business, give markets free rein. "Stabilize, privatize, and liberalize" became the mantra of a generation of technocrats who cut their teeth in the developing world and of the political leaders they counseled. . . . The evidence that macroeconomic policies, price distortions, financial policies, and trade openness have predictable, robust, and systematic effects on national growth rates is quite weak—except possibly in the extremes. Humongous fiscal deficits or autarkic trade policies can stifle economic growth, but moderate amounts of each are associated with widely varying economic outcomes.

Looking back, it was apparent that the Washington Consensus policies were overly prescriptive and did not take into account the many ways a particular policy objective can be achieved in different country contexts. A major World Bank study released in the mid-2000s noted that "the principles of . . . 'macroeconomic stability, domestic liberalization, and openness' have been interpreted narrowly to mean 'minimize fiscal deficits, minimize inflation, minimize tariffs, maximize privatization, maximize liberalization of finance,' with the assumption that the more of these changes the better, at all times and in all places—overlooking the fact that these expedients are just *some* of the ways in which these principles can be implemented" (World Bank 2005, 11). It was a stunning acknowledgment that the specific policy instruments and the way to use them, as well as the sequencing of actions, should not have been uniformly prescribed to developing countries in different circumstances.

These policy recommendations also failed to recognize the endogeneity of many government interventions. In developing countries, many market distortions were endogenous to the government's need to protect and subsidize nonviable firms that had been promoted by the government's previous import-substitution strategies. Eliminating protections and subsidies would doom nonviable firms, resulting in large-scale unemployment, slow economic growth, and social and political unrest. To avoid those consequences and to continue to prop up nonviable capital-intensive industries that were still considered the cornerstone of modernization, governments often continued to protect them through new and less visible means after removing previous protections and subsidies in line with the Washington Consensus precepts. The new protections and subsidies were usually less efficient than the old ones, especially in the transition economies of the former Soviet Union and Eastern Europe (World Bank 2002).

In sum, the classical market-oriented prescription of a balanced budget, competitive real exchange rate, and supply-side policies that promote a better resource allocation offered perhaps necessary conditions for a return of growth, but they were not sufficient (Dornbusch 1991). In many developing countries, the lackluster growth performance is often due to coordination failures and issues of externalities that the conventional policy framework did not take into account (Lin 2012a; Serra and Stiglitz 2008). The notion that low-income countries must follow economic policy strategies similar to those implemented in OECD countries is one of the major flaws of the traditional approach to growth.

Many growth researchers have found themselves in an intellectual impasse primarily because they tend to ignore the strongest clue from the past three hundred years: that modern growth is a continuous process of technological and institutional upgrading that must be based on the structure of an economy at a specific time. Growth researchers have neglected Adam Smith's fundamental teaching about the insight to be gained from inquiring into the nature and causes of the wealth of nations. Instead, they have often adopted an unsustainable posture of trying to identify and collect all the factors that may be preventing the ignition and maintenance of growth.

In addition to being a tall order, the list of such factors is likely to be open ended, infinite, and unrealistic. It is therefore not surprising that when confronted with too many variables, growth researchers have been concerned about their models' correct functional form. The cross-country approach imposes too much structure on heterogeneous countries, but the case-study approach does not allow for generalizations. Choosing the high-income model economy as a reference for all low-income countries in the world and searching for growth by relying on generic market-based prescriptions have been unproductive. This approach also led policy makers to focus only on the infinite lists of binding constraints—and therefore overlook ingredients—and to come up with ineffective policy prescriptions.

The disappointments of growth research—most notably from the perspective of policymakers seeking specific and actionable measures to generate prosperity—have led to a reassessment of the validity and usefulness of existing knowledge, and to the development of radically new approaches. Several studies devoted to economic reforms in developing countries in the 1980s and 1990s have concluded somewhat pessimistically that economic growth is too daunting a task and too complex a process to be fully understood through a single general framework. But even the researchers who recommend smaller and more manageable sets of reforms, generally also offer some rather generic prescriptions to policymakers. Taking up the challenge of the search for new growth frameworks, a number of insightful analysts who also believe that there may not be a unique and universal set of rules to guide policy have recommended less reliance on simple formulas and "best practices" (Pritchett 2006), and that policymakers and researchers identify a small number of the most binding constraints on growth in each country, and focus their reform strategies on lifting these (Hausmann, Rodrik and Velasco 2008).

Such approaches constitute real intellectual progress from past waves of research, as they propose policies that make better use of the limited human, administrative, organizational capacity and financial resources in developing economies. However, these new approaches should be complemented by more precise policy frameworks to guide government and private sector actions, and to encourage the process of industrial upgrading and structural change, which is at the core of all successful development strategies. The way forward is therefore to take stock of the insufficient but substantial knowledge that growth research has generated over the decades, and enrich it with a rethinking of economic development that brings the focus back to the deeper issues of structural transformation. The next chapter analyzes the mechanics of failure and the secrets of economic success.

4

The Mechanics of Failure
and the Secrets of Success

One of the most puzzling but edifying stories in sports history occurred in Argentina in early 1978. The country, which had been under authoritarian military rule for many years, was preparing to host the football (soccer) World Cup for the first time and trying to reposition itself on the global scene as a credible economic powerhouse. The stage was being set for the most momentous global event in sports, and the military junta was hoping to seize that unique opportunity to glorify Argentina's past history, showcase its achievements, and restore its blemished reputation. Argentina's economic path had indeed damaged the country's brand: it was already a high-income country in the nineteenth century, well before many of today's leading economies, but lost its luster in the twentieth century and had been caught up since then in the middle-income trap.

The World Cup was therefore more than a sports event and represented even more than an economic opportunity to boost growth through investment and tourism. It was a rare opportunity to reclaim the country's past grandeur and reset its image on the global scene. Everyone in a leadership position understood the moment's uniqueness and knew that there was no margin for error. Football could help erase several decades of suboptimal performance, reposition the country as Latin America's main leader, and even set a new and more prosperous course.

There was a sense of urgency everywhere, perhaps nowhere more so than in the Argentinian national football team, the Albiceleste. Cesar Luis Menotti had a unique philosophy and an unusual strategy for achieving success: he believed in building a team that was cohesive, was well-disciplined, and reflected the strengths of the country's endowments. He never felt that a team could win a tournament simply with an exceptional (and singular) player in its ranks. "He told us that he was coaching us because he believed in our potential," said former player Gabriel Calderon. "He put special emphasis on each individual's strengths. Every player ran out on the pitch crystal clear on what they had to do, and determined to do it" (FIFA 2007).

Menotti implemented his vision by making one of his most controversial decisions: despite saying publicly that the young prodigy Diego Maradona was at the time "the best football player in the world and by far," he indicated that Maradona's exceptional talents and playing skills did not fit the team strategy and would not allow the other Albiceleste players to maximize their assets. In a country where everyone seems to have a strong opinion about football strategy, the decision not to include Diego Maradona in the 1978 national squad was greeted with outrage. The coach did not give in to criticism. He chose to select a veteran but much less known striker named Mario Kempes as the team leader.

The rest is history. Under Menotti's expertise, Argentina played a remarkable tournament and won the World Cup. In the finals on July 25, 1978, the Albiceleste gave the world a stylish, forward-looking game and beat the Netherlands 3–1, with two superb goals by none other than Mario Kempes. It was a crowning achievement for Menotti, still discussed and studied to this day, not only by football fans and experts but also by social scientists who consider that historical event as a salient moment of collective renewal for the country (Miller 2009). In Simon Kuper's words, it has become "a respected academic field [in Argentina], almost like particle physics or neurology" (Kuper 2006, 220).

According to FIFA (2007), the highest international organ of football, "Argentine football, recognized among the finest in the world, owes its lofty standing in no small measure to Cesar Luis Menotti. [His] arrival was a turning point in the organization and planning of international football in Argentina."

The world soccer championship in 1978 did not pull Argentina from the middle-income trap. But several historians and sociologists credit it as a major factor in the country's reemergence as a major powerhouse in Latin America and its heightened sense of national pride that propelled democratic reforms in the 1980s—including, paradoxically, the fall of the military regime that organized it.

Viewing Menotti as the architect of Argentina's political and economic renaissance may be far-fetched. But his daring strategy is one from which development experts and policy makers seeking to generate economic prosperity could learn. It was based mainly on the notion that success is determined by the best use of resources—not on the wholesale import of ideas and factors that may not be sustainable. His strategy's main ingredients could serve as a metaphor for the basic argument in this chapter: any low-income country can achieve sustained and inclusive growth if it properly identifies its endowment structure and uses its most competitive factor(s) to exploit its comparative advantage.

This chapter discusses the mechanics of failure in economic development and the secrets of economic success. It starts with a presentation of the standard model of stabilization and structural adjustment, which has come to dominate development thinking and policy across the world and has survived several decades of critical research. It then explores reasons why the model has endured despite criticism from across the ideological spectrum, especially in the 1980s and 1990s. It also offers an analysis of why traditional policy frameworks derived from the standard model often do not yield results, and it stresses the need to focus growth strategies on coordination and externalities. It is the story of applying realism, humility, and boldness in understanding the economy's prevailing endowment structure, having faith in domestic factors, and designing a dynamic strategy for industrial, technological, and institutional upgrading that sustains progress but at the proper pace—just like Menotti did with his Argentinian World Cup soccer squad in 1978. The chapter ends with a discussion of one of the main "side effects" of the standard model and its growth prescriptions: the extreme dependence on foreign aid ("aid addiction") by many low-income economies, especially those in Africa.

THE UNREALISTIC STANDARD MODEL OF RANDOM GROWTH

Physicists around the world rely on something called the standard model, which explains how everything in the universe is made from a few basic building blocks called fundamental particles, governed by well-identified fundamental forces. That model was developed in the early 1970s, has explained almost all experimental results in physics, and has precisely predicted a wide variety of phenomena. Over time the standard model has become established as a well-tested physics theory.

Aiming to set their discipline as the hardest social science, economists have always tried to build standard models in their various subfields. Despite the ideological and methodological debates that have shaped development economics since its inception after World War II (from early structuralists to proponents of the Washington Consensus and the believers in the virtues of randomization), a dominant framework has emerged that underlies the prevailing conventional wisdom and determines policies throughout much of the developing world. Multilateral development institutions and bilateral aid institutions use it formally or surreptitiously as a framework of analysis of low-income economies and as a tool for deciding whether to give financial aid to recipient countries. Even when the standard development economics model does not directly dictate public financing flows to poor countries, it underpins macro- and microeconomic analysis for major institutions such as the International Monetary Fund to signal their assessment of country performance to private lenders and investors. So it is quite influential.

Its most basic formulation can be found in the IMF growth model (Khan and Knight 1985), which posits that countries that implement stabilization programs can expect major growth dividends, *within a two-year period*! This is supposed to occur first through demand-side policies and later through supply-side measures and policies to improve external competitiveness. The analytical framework underpinning such an optimistic story starts with the real sector where aggregate demand drives the growth of actual output:[1]

$$\Delta y = \alpha \Delta g + \beta \Delta d + \delta \Delta x + \lambda (y^* - y)$$

All lowercase letters denote logs of the following real variables:

y is the country's output
g is real government spending
d is real domestic private credit
x is real exports
y^* is capacity output
$y^* - y$ represents the GDP gap. It is central to the model because it implies that capacity expansion from implementing stabilization and structural adjustment programs automatically translates into higher GDP.

The model relies on a few equations and assumptions. The growth of potential output $y^* - y$ is driven by labor force growth, n, and by the investment ratio, ω.

$$\Delta y^* = \sigma\omega + (1 - \sigma)n$$

But in the model simulations, the labor force and the investment ratio are taken as exogenous. Because there is no credit market, the interest rate is exogenous too, and the growth in real credit to the private sector is also exogenous. All crowding in takes place only by fiat.

Increases in real exports are determined by capacity output and changes in competitiveness:

$$\Delta x = \gamma\Delta y^* + \theta\Delta\Psi$$

Competitiveness is the log of the ratio of exogenous world prices (p^*) to domestic prices in dollars ($e + p$):

$$\Psi = p^* + e - p$$

Inflation, μ, is the result of two factors: the gap between actual real balances, m, and real money demand, m^d, and the exogenous rate of increase of the price of traded goods so that we have:

$$\Delta p = \mu(m - m^d) + \Delta(p^* + e)$$

Although there have been a few more sophisticated versions of this "standard" growth model, the basic building blocks are broadly as presented above.[2] In running this model for their simulations of stabilization policies, Mohsin S. Khan and Malcolm Knight (1985) focus on the expected effects of combining demand- and supply-side measures. To show how growth can be generated, they lay out a stabilization and adjustment scenario that includes a sustained 10 percent reduction in the growth of nominal domestic credit and nominal government spending and an initial one-time 10 percent nominal devaluation. It also includes supply-side measures (an increase in the investment ratio) that raise output by a cumulative rate of 2.5 percent a year.

The model predicts positive growth results, which occur through a stabilization and adjustment process whose mechanics are described as follows: First, the one-time devaluation improves competitiveness immediately and over time, thus stimulating aggregate demand. Second, in the short run, the devaluation raises inflation and thus reduces the growth in real demand—at least for given nominal credit growth. Third, the growth rate reduction of nominal domestic credit and nominal domestic spending reduce the growth in real demand in the short run because the initial inflation does not slow down quickly enough. Fourth, the money supply is determined by the balance of payments, and the inflation rate by the exogenous rate of depreciation and domestic credit creation.

The devaluation and the restraining trends reduce growth in the short run. But after a fairly short period—usually a year—the expansionary effects of devaluation and the benefits of declining inflation for real credit growth yield the expected magic: economic growth rates go up. Prices come down gradually, and inflation declines to settle at a rate projected to be about 10 percent lower than its initial level. Several factors explain the outcome of a much higher growth rate. After the initial negative shock and the reduction in real demand, the decline in inflation eventually stimulates a recovery, which benefits government spending and the private sector. The gain in competitiveness translates into a decline in real imports and the progressive crowding in of real exports, which compensates for any reduction in real domestic demand. Also, because of the exogenous increase in investment, potential output also increases.

Whatever one might say about the Khan and Knight model, which over the decades has become not only a stabilization and adjustment model but indeed the standard model of growth that mainstream macroeconomists and policy makers have used in various incarnations, it must be acknowledged that it is elegant and consistent from an accounting viewpoint. Beyond macroeconomics, it has become the unnamed workhorse model for much of the economic development strategies implemented by many low-income countries around the world—especially those in Latin America in the 1980s and in Africa in the 1990s and 2000s. But from both an analytical and a policy perspective, it was a seriously flawed model that could lead only to disappointment.

VALIDATING A MYTH: HOW THE STANDARD
MODEL SURVIVED ITS FLAWS

James Cameron's landmark science-fiction movie *Terminator 2: Judgment Day* (1991) is the story of a battle between good and evil to protect or kill a boy destined to grow up to become humanity's savior from a computer-controlled Armageddon. The battle pits a new and improved Terminator android called the T-1000, who arrives from the future to eliminate the young hero, against an older model T-800, sent to protect the boy. The T-1000, however, has the ability to morph into any shape, giving it chameleon-like powers and near indestructibility. The movie is reminiscent of the debates over growth models for developing countries, which include good ideas and bad but often end up with the less suitable ones dominating.

Despite its inappropriateness, the standard model of stabilization-adjustment-growth has taken over the economic development discourse to the point of becoming indestructible. Just like the T-1000 in Cameron's action thriller, it has become the nearly indestructible policy framework in most developing economies. Its proponents have consistently managed to present it as the unavoidable path to prosperity, if not to survival. Yet it has many analytical flaws that several generations of researchers have pointed out from the beginning, to no avail.

First, there was the macroeconomic critique from the ideological left, most notably by early and neo-structuralists, who challenged the model from its inception in the 1980s (see, for instance, Taylor 1981, 1988, 1993). Starting with a review of financial, production, and commodity market arrangements in semi-industrialized economies whose characteristics are very different from those of high-income countries, Lance Taylor formulated the key relationships and offers a derivation of investment-savings, liquidity-money (IS, LM) curves, which describe the economy in the short term. His central hypothesis was that standard policies derived from traditional models run a severe risk of making a bad economic situation worse because of their high short-term costs. Stabilization policies that aim to restrict demand but end up reducing supply by even more than they reduce demand will be inflationary.

Populist policies that do not recognize the link between money growth and price growth, or between the real exchange rate and trade performance, often result in total economic and political collapse. But the reverse is also true: governments that embark on orthodox stabilization programs aiming to reestablish equilibrium after, say, two years of extreme hardship may not even survive the first year. So the whole effort may break down because the short-term costs are simply too high (see Dervis 1981). The conclusion is that gradualism is preferable to the shock treatment approach proposed in Khan and Knight–type models and policy prescriptions. These valid observations did little to alter the intellectual dominance of the standard model of stabilization-adjustment-growth.

Then there was the critique from the right—including some mainstream economists. Perhaps the most pertinent from that line of criticism was Rudi Dornbusch (1990, 1991), an economist with bona fide neoclassical credentials who could not be suspected of ideological motives. His paper highlights the absence of income distribution variables in the analysis, which raises serious questions about the validity and likelihood of the linkages in the proposed growth model, especially in Latin American and African countries.

The model posits that successful real depreciation does not affect real aggregate demand even though it almost always implies a decline in real wages. Such benign neglect of income issues is unrealistic. Stabilization and adjustment programs usually take place in countries that have seen their economies driven by expansionary government policies. By putting a stop to that process, these programs create a new policy regime, one that requires shifting the growth engine to the traded sector and private investment. The shift entails fiscal consolidation, which reduces real wages and thus internal demand. Those trends make private firms reluctant to invest. With devaluation, a crucial part of the policy package, a highly competitive exchange rate implies that real wages are very low. Although this may boost exports in the end, in the short run it translates into higher import prices and inflation.

Almost everywhere, devaluations have brought inflation and recession on more than a short-term basis. If the resources freed up from fiscal consolidation are not immediately used to support import substitution—not an automatic process—the expected growth may not take place. Low real wages and fiscal consolidation may create more poverty and social disruptions, as seen in Bolivia and Mexico in the 1980s, and in Africa (Lizondo and Montiel 1989; Dornbusch and Edwards 1989; Christiaensen, Demery, and Paternostro 2002).

The Khan-Knight model also presumes that real depreciation is an automatic way of generating more net exports. This holds true because of an optimistic choice of long-run elasticity of exports and imports. The export side of the economy is modeled as if the competitiveness of industries depends only on the "appropriate" real exchange rate. In other words, the (expected) supply response is not affected by such other factors as the economic viability of industries, access to finance and to global value chains, and evolving international prices (particularly important in many developing countries whose trade is dominated by a few commodities). The model offers a static and rigid analysis of the sources of growth in the economy and ignores the fact that dynamic and sustainable growth reflects a development strategy that focuses on shifting comparative advantages.

Because investment is considered exogenous in the model, one can easily pick any value that allows the proposed linear mechanics of stabilization to yield higher potential output growth and thus actual growth. That is a great leap of faith: the model does not offer any link between growth prospects and even some of its most widely known determinants (investor confidence, credit market conditions, potential return on investment, and so on). There is no discussion in the model of the availability of savings (domestic and foreign) to finance investment. One can presume that the expected gains from fiscal coordination, an essential feature of the model, open room for more credit to the private sector. But the proposed policy of high interest rates could also reduce investment. Yet simulations in the Khan-Knight paper confidently predict that supply-side measures in a typical stabilization and adjustment program could add 2.5 percent to the trend growth rate.

Summing up his macroeconomic critique of the standard model, Dornbusch (1990b, abstract) writes:

> Tradition in discussions of stabilization is to assume that fiscal austerity, competitive real exchange rates, sound financial markets and deregulation provide the preconditions for a resumption of growth. There is, however, a need to distinguish the necessary and the sufficient conditions. Adjustment is strictly necessary, but it may not be sufficient. Asset holders can postpone repatriation of capital flight and investors can delay initiating projects, so that there is an important coordination problem that classical economics does not recognize.

Despite criticism from several waves of development thinking, the standard model has managed to survive its flaws and quietly become the workhorse of growth in many developing countries. Just like James Cameron's T-1000 could morph into any shape, giving it chameleon-like powers and near infallibility, the standard model has adopted cosmetic adjustments to allay criticism, eventually imposing its intellectual dominance.

SORTING FACTS FROM FICTION:
MISLEADING TALES AND REVISIONIST STORIES

When confronted with the disappointing results of growth and economic development based on the standard model, its proponents often argue that the main reason is the reluctance or inability of policy makers in developing countries to implement their framework. They often stress both the lack of ownership of reforms that are often unpopular and politically difficult to implement and policy reversals (Mussa and Savastano 2000). They also point to poor governance and corruption issues and to vested interests that often block reforms.

But the argument does not hold up to scrutiny. The reforms proposed under the label "Washington Consensus" in the 1980s and 1990s and derived from the standard model did not fail in much of the developing world simply because they were perceived as foreign ideas. Throughout their history, all developing countries have implemented many policies designed abroad. Latin American, Asian, and African countries embraced and adopted socialist policies and import substitution advocated by structuralism, even though they too were foreign ideas conceived in the former Soviet Union or in China.

The main reason for rejecting standard policy prescriptions was pure cost-benefit analysis by political leaders in these countries whose poorly performing economies, crippled by several decades of distortions, were already second- or third-best situations. In such delicate environments, traditional reform packages based on the standard model were too economically and politically risky: they carried heavy short-term economic and political costs and offered uncertain future benefits.

Thus the failure to embrace wholeheartedly the first-best reform proposals in many developing countries was not always due solely to state capture by the political elites and vested interests or the lack of domestic consensus. Washington Consensus policies that aimed at liberalizing the economy and privatizing public enterprises in a "big-bang" style also faltered because government interventions were needed to protect nonviable firms in the "priority" sectors created under previous development. The abrupt removal of government protection would have led to the collapse of those firms, creating large-scale unemployment and social instability or the loss of precious foreign exchange and fiscal revenues.

Even in countries where there was consensus on the need to remove those distortions, such as Russia and other Commonwealth of Independent States (CIS)[3] and eastern European countries, governments often felt compelled to reintroduce disguised forms of protection and distortions, which later became even less efficient than the original second-best policy measures. That is why the CIS and the countries of central and eastern Europe that tried the "shock therapy" performed more poorly than those like Belarus, Slovenia, and Uzbekistan, which adopted a more gradual reform approach. An even better way to carry out reform is the dual-track approach invented by Mauritius in the 1970s and followed by China and Vietnam in the 1980s that allows policy makers to reduce political resistance to reform and reach stability and dynamic growth simultaneously.

Some development experts have argued that in Africa there were differentiated strategies and outcomes between countries such as Côte d'Ivoire (which supposedly followed standard policy prescriptions since the 1970s) and countries like Ghana or Tanzania (where governments adopted the prescriptions only in the 1980s and 1990s). But the facts do not support a sharp distinction in performance between Ghana and Côte d'Ivoire. More than fifty years after their independence, both countries are still economically undistinguishable; they are still considered poor. Ghana's per capita income is $1,230 and Côte d'Ivoire's is $1,160. Ghana's first president after independence in 1957, Kwame Nkrumah, was wrong not because of his belief that the government had to play a helping role to overcome market failures in structural transformation but in his attempt to implement a comparative advantage–defying strategy. The economic strategy underpinning Ghana's Second Development Plan, launched in 1959, aimed to modernize the country in record time by developing advanced, high capital-intensive industries. Rather than trying to build a "modern" industrial sector centered on heavy, capital-intensive industries in the late 1950s, he should have facilitated private sector–led, labor-intensive industries in which Ghana had comparative advantage.

Also, celebrating President Félix Houphouet-Boigny's economic strategy in Côte d'Ivoire after the country achieved independence in 1960 is misleading. The country did enjoy rapid growth for more than two decades. But without government facilitation, its economy did not undergo structural transformation. After years of dynamic growth, its economy's exports remained predominately agricultural, like coffee, cocoa, sugar, pineapple, and palm oil. The lack of diversification had three drawbacks: First, growth was never inclusive, and inequality between a small elite and a majority of the people increased dramatically, as shown by several empirical studies, including by the World Bank (Addison and Demery 1985; Christiaensen, Demery, and Paternostro 2002). Second, because of the lack of diversification, the country's economy was not resilient to external and natural shocks. The world recession and a local drought trapped the Ivoirian economy in economic crises, leading to a period of sociopolitical tumult in the 1980s and 1990s, followed by civil war in the 2000s. Third, Côte d'Ivoire's economic performance in the past five decades has been mediocre compared with that of other economies that had a similar starting point but whose governments diversified and upgraded their economies according to their comparative advantages (figure 4.1).

The bankruptcy of the Morogoro shoe factory in Tanzania has also been presented as evidence of a development strategy failure in which the government selects certain industries for support to trigger a structural transformation. In the 1970s the World Bank provided financing and helped furnish the factory with the latest equipment. The plan was to supply the entire Tanzanian shoe market and export the remaining three-quarters of the four million shoes it produced to Europe. The plant was not designed for Tanzania's climate and stopped production in 1990 without having exported even one shoe (Easterly 2002, 68).

The Morogoro factory story could indeed be an interesting business school country case study. But it illustrates the failure of the country's leadership to design and implement an economic strategy that uses comparative advantage. Tanzania has one of the highest cattle populations in Africa and the potential for a thriving leather sector. Based on factor costs of production, the country has comparative advantage in the labor-intensive shoe industry. Its development would not have required rents. The company did

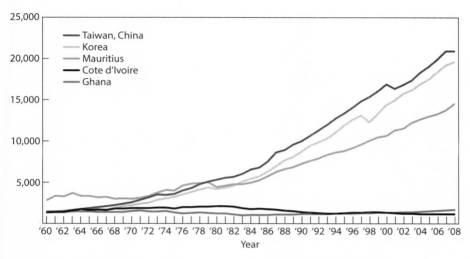

Figure 4.1. Per capita income in a sample of countries, 1960–2008 (in 1990 international dollars). *Source*: Angus Maddison, *Historical Statistics of the World Economy*, 1–2008AD.

not manage to export its products, though, because it not only was state owned and poorly managed but also had little access to international marketing channels. There was also no cluster in the shoe industry, which increased logistical and other transaction-related costs. Tanzania could have developed shoes—and still can—by attracting foreign direct investment through a cluster-based industrial park approach. A case in point is that of Ethiopia. Despite its many policy distortions, it is developing its footwear subsector with some success in a private sector–led, government-helped leather industry, which has generated some 50,000 new jobs in just three years. Few development economists would have predicted such success in a poor landlocked country that lacked most of the usual requirements for growth (see Oqubay 2015).

Another attempt to legitimate policy prescriptions derived from the standard model is the suggestion that recently accelerating economic growth in Africa from about 3 percent a year in the 1990s to almost 6 percent a year in the 2000s is due to the implementation of Washington Consensus policies (Devarajan 2012). Although macroeconomic stability is certainly an important factor, improvement in growth performance by many African countries can be attributed to the global commodity

Dependent Variable	Resource-intensive (1 = Resource Rich)	GNI per Capita (Current PPP, 1999)	Doing Business 2006	Δ Doing Business (2008–2006)	Constant	R2 N
Average annual growth of SSA GDP, 2000–2008	0.0244 (0.0133)**	−0.0001 (0.0001)	0.0484 (0.0384)	0.0946 (0.0904)	0.0609 (0.0095)*	0.1203 35

Note: Ease of Doing Business rankings were transformed to a 0 to 1 scale, with a value of 1 indicating a number one ranking on the Ease of Doing Business variable and a value of 0 indicating the lowest ranking of the year being measured.

* Significant at the 5% level, ** Significant at the 10% level

boom, and the improvement of macroeconomic stability is a result of the growth performance. A simple cross-country regression shows that the most important condition explaining the growth performance in sub-Saharan African countries is the resource intensity of the country. The business environment and its improvement do not have a consistently significant effect on growth performance. Their signs even show their effects likely to be just the opposite. These results invalidate revisionist attempts to credit the Washington Consensus with recent African economic growth (table 4.1).[4]

It has also often been argued that infrastructure and skills deficits explain the lack of structural transformation in African countries. That popular claim is not supported by empirical evidence. Several African countries—such as Ghana, Kenya, Senegal, Cameroon, and Côte d'Ivoire—did not exhibit these severe human and physical capital constraints. Yet structural transformation did not happen in them spontaneously either. Even more to the point is the fact that structural transformation did not occur spontaneously in Tunisia and Botswana, although both countries have very good business environments. By contrast, China, Brazil, Vietnam, India, and Indonesia have achieved remarkable structural transformation and growth despite poor business environment ratings. They were able to undergo significant structural change because their governments helped facilitate their economic development.

A country with a poor business environment does not have to wait until all the distortions and unwise government interventions are removed before it takes off. But the caveat is that it should pursue targeted industries that are consistent with comparative advantage, and the government should proactively help overcome the inherent coordination and externality issues in their growth. Many distortions certainly result from political capture[5] or the need to protect/subsidize nonviable firms (financial repression) or to generate revenues (high tariffs for importing cars). Pragmatism is crucial in such environments. Political leaders always have some discretionary powers and are not necessarily hostages of elite capture. The key to success is to use those discretionary powers in areas where they can achieve quick wins, as discussed below. This requires a good understanding of coordination and externalities.

THE MISSING PARTS: COORDINATION AND EXTERNALITIES

More than the macroeconomic weaknesses and inconsistencies discussed earlier, the neglect of coordination issues and externalities is the main flaw in what has become the standard economic growth model in development economics. In countries that are confronted with unsustainable domestic and external imbalances, stabilization and structural adjustment may be initial conditions for resuming growth—but they are not sufficient. Growth models and economic strategies must adequately account for the microeconomic linkages and institutional requirements that allow economies to overcome coordination issues that no single economic agent can address. They must also stipulate how national economies generate positive externalities across firms and industries. These issues cannot be addressed solely by the market and the price mechanism recommended by the standard model.

To understand why, one must dissect modern economic growth and flesh out more explicitly the dynamics that allow low-income economies—especially those without natural resources—to generate increasing returns on capital and labor and to raise their productivity. An inquiry into the "nature and causes of the wealth of nations" (Adam Smith) should therefore start with a good understanding of the forces and processes preventing small firms and micro household enterprises from blossoming into large and vibrant economic entities that generate jobs and profits, enlarge the tax base, and fuel prosperity. Yet for centuries economists have concentrated their attention on endowments (land, entrepreneurship, financial resources, and quantity of labor that could be exploited for manufacturing within a country), neglecting the need to understand the mechanics and determinants of their evolution over time.

Investigating the real constraints to the Schumpeterian process of creative destruction, which gradually converts the traditional and artisanal production modes from simply accumulating minimum amounts of capital and low-skilled labor into higher levels of output and productivity and eventually to higher standards of living, should start with the systematic analysis of the mechanics of modern economic growth.

What Sustains Growth?

Sustained growth takes places because of continuous technological upgrading, institutional innovation, and structural change. At the core of that process there is an important but often overlooked force: the dynamics of factor endowments, the most revealing feature of the growth process. Identifying what these factor endowments are in each country at any given period, understanding why they are often underutilized or even repressed, and how they change and can be developed and accumulated, should be the aim of models, growth theories, and policy prescriptions. The various dominant waves of development thinking and policy whose findings are encapsulated in the standard model have not done so. Failing to understand those dynamics and to design the optimal policy framework to sustain and stimulate them results in stagnation and underdevelopment. Relying on the standard model is *the* mistake that all poor countries have made.

Qatar, Luxemburg, and Singapore, the three countries with the highest GDP per capita in the world in 2013 (IMF rankings, current Geary-Khamis international dollars), do not have the same economic structure as Malawi, the Democratic Republic of Congo, and the Central African Republic, the bottom three on the list.[6] Because they are at different development levels, the countries in these two groups have different economic structures due to differences in their endowments. For countries in the first group (top performers), the relatively abundant factor in their endowment is typically capital (and natural resources for Qatar), not labor. They tend to have comparative advantage in capital-intensive industries with economies of scale in production. Their economies are driven by large firms and dominated by sophisticated, high-value-added manufacturing and services, which operate in international markets.

By contrast, for the second group (those countries in early development and ranking low on GDP per capita), the factor endowments are typically characterized by a relative scarcity of capital and relative abundance of labor or resources. Their production tends to be labor intensive or resource intensive (mostly in fishery, animal husbandry, subsistence agriculture, and mining) and usually relies on conventional, mature technologies and "mature," well-established products. Except for mining and plantations, their production has limited economies of scale. Firm sizes are usually relatively small, with market transactions often informal and limited to local markets with familiar people.

The amazing stylized fact often forgotten in growth models and strategies is that Qatar, Luxemburg, and Singapore, like all other high-income countries, once had endowment structures broadly comparable to those of Malawi, the DRC, and the Central African Republic today. Qatar started its quest for prosperity as a poor British protectorate noted mainly for pearling and fishing. It lacked infrastructure and human capital (at least as measured by today's quantitative tools) and had very poor governance (again as measured by today's popular and democracy-based indicators). Yet Qatar has stunned the world, not only by escaping the resource curse and resolving its long-standing border disputes with both Bahrain and Saudi Arabia but also by using its immense wealth from oil and natural gas to improve the welfare of its citizens (including establishing advanced healthcare and education systems and expanding the country's infrastructure) and to launch an ambitious economic diversification strategy. Although Qatar's GDP is still driven largely by changes in oil prices and by investment in the energy sector (oil and gas accounted for more than 50 percent of GDP in 2013, roughly 85 percent of export earnings, and 50 percent of government revenues), economic policy is geared toward achieving a balance between an oil-based and a knowledge-based economy, diversifying the country's economy, and guaranteeing a stable and sustainable business environment

Luxemburg, a country with precarious living conditions as late as the early twentieth century, started its own economic growth process as a backward, landlocked republic with often difficult relations with some of its neighbors. Although the discovery of iron ore in the south of the country marked the beginning of Luxemburg's industrialization, "it was neverthe-less the construction of large-scale integrated steelworks—during the two decades preceding the First World War—enabling on-site processing of cast iron into steel and rolled-steel products, that was crucial to the subse-quent development of this economic sector and of the country as a whole" (Letz 2007, 110). The country eventually made the best use of its proximity to France, Belgium, and Germany and diversified its industrial sector to in-clude rubber, chemicals, automobile parts, and other products. Moreover, structural transformation has taken place over time, and the financial sec-tor alone now represents more than a third of the country's GDP.

Singapore was a British naval base in Southeast Asia during colonial times and was made part of Malaya "until its largely Chinese population proved too daunting for a state attempting to define its national identity by a Malay majority. Malaya extruded Singapore because it was not yet ready to cope with so large a Chinese population or, less charitably, to teach Sin-gapore the habits of dependence if it was forced back into what later became the Malaysian Federation" (Kissinger 2000, 9). It had no oil or minerals, lit-tle infrastructure, and a small, low-skilled labor force. Yet under the leader-ship of Lee Kuan Yew, a bold development strategy based on the country's comparative advantage, starting with labor-intensive, export-oriented pro-cessing industries and gradually moving up the industrial ladder to more capital-intensive industries after labor became fairly scarce, made it one of the leading economies in the world in less than two generations.

All of today's high-income economies underwent comparable struc-tural transformation processes. How did they do it? How do economies undergo the kind of structural transformation process that later converts even the resource-poor, landlocked ones into dynamic performers and suc-cessful stories?

The path to economic prosperity that led today's rich countries to their current status can be traced to the way they constantly changed and devel-oped their endowment structure (defined as the relative distribution of fac-tor endowments). Successful economies typically start their journey toward wealth with their initial endowment structure and use it as the central part of the growth strategy and the main focus of economic policies. The opti-mal industrial structure in an economy, that is, the industrial structure that will make the economy most competitive domestically and internation-ally at any time, is endogenous to its comparative advantage, determined by the given endowment structure of the economy at that time. In other words, good-performing economies devote their resources (most notably capital and labor) strategically and pragmatically to industries with latent comparative advantages—those that have factor cost advantages in the international comparison at a particular time. By contrast, poor-performing economies are those that ignore their endowment structure and fail to identify potentially competitive industries.

Because the optimal industrial structure at any time is endogenous to the existing factor endowments, a country trying to move up the technological development ladder must first change its endowment structure. With capital accumulation, the economy's factor endowment structure develops, pushing its industrial structure to deviate from the optimal determined by its previous level. This opens the possibilities for a virtuous circle, or a vicious one: countries that achieve sustained growth are those where firms upgrade their industries and technologies realistically to reflect the changing endowment structure. This allows them to maintain market competitiveness.

If the economy follows its comparative advantage in the selection and development of its main economic sectors, its industries will be highly competitive in domestic and world markets. As a result, they will gain the largest possible market share and potentially generate the largest surplus. Capital investment will also have the largest possible return. Consequently, households will have the highest savings propensity, resulting in an even faster upgrade of the country's endowment structure. Once low-income countries, Qatar, Luxemburg, and Singapore followed their comparative advantage and selected and developed industries that reflected their evolving factor endowments. They started their development by exploiting their geographic location (Luxemburg, Singapore) or their natural resources (Qatar). Other countries, such as the United States, Great Britain, and Japan, exploited their labor-intensive industries. Those strategic choices make their firms competitive, and economic success allowed them to gradually move into more sophisticated and technologically advanced industries in a dynamic that reflects their evolving endowment structure.

Malawi, the DRC, and the Central African Republic have so far failed to do so and have found themselves stuck in a vicious circle: they did not develop the labor-intensive industries that could have allowed their economies to strive. But in an increasingly globalized world where large middle-income economies such as China, Brazil, India, or Indonesia open up new economic opportunities for low-income countries (Lin 2011), there are reasons for optimism. Developing countries that follow their comparative advantage to develop their industries can also benefit from the advantage of backwardness in the upgrading process and grow faster than advanced countries. Enterprises in developing countries can benefit from the industrial and technological gap with developed countries by acquiring industrial and technological innovations that are consistent with their new comparative advantage through learning and borrowing from developed countries. With rising wages and labor costs in good-performing middle-income countries, low-income countries around the world can even attract basic-assembly manufacturing and create much needed jobs (Monga 2014).

Why Are the Opportunities Not Being Seized?

The conventional policy frameworks implemented in much of the developing world and derived from the standard growth model use the industries and institutions in high-income countries as the targets for their development policies. In designing a growth model and a policy framework, the key question should be how to ensure that the economy grows in a manner consistent with its comparative advantage so that the economy can be competitive internationally. The import-substitution catch-up strategy, promoted by structuralists, required governments to give priority to capital- and technology-intensive industries, which prevailed in high-income countries and thus defied developing countries' comparative advantages. Firms in those industries were not viable in open and competitive markets. Entrepreneurs would not voluntarily invest in those industries, which were doomed to fail in competitive markets, without government protection and subsidies. Structuralism mistakenly regarded market failures as the cause of developing countries' inability to develop advanced, capital-intensive industries and called on the government to protect and subsidize nonviable firms in comparative-advantage-defying industries.

The Washington Consensus reform, advocated by neoliberalists, encouraged developing countries to adopt market institutions similar to those of high-income countries but failed to recognize the endogeneity of government interventions and the need for the government to facilitate structural change. In developing countries market distortions were endogenous to the government's need to protect and subsidize nonviable firms that had been promoted by the government's previous import-substitution strategies. Eliminating protections and subsidies would doom nonviable firms, resulting in large-scale unemployment, slow economic growth, and social and political unrest. To avoid those consequences and to continue to prop up nonviable capital-intensive industries that were still considered the cornerstone of modernization, governments often continued to protect them through new and less visible means after removing previous protections and subsidies in line with the Washington Consensus precepts.

The new protections and subsidies were usually less efficient than the old ones, especially in the transition economies of the former Soviet Union and eastern Europe. In addition, neoliberalism threw the baby out with the bathwater, vehemently opposing any government role in facilitating structural change. The goal of most firms everywhere is profit maximization, which is, other things being equal, a function of relative prices of factor inputs. The criterion they use to select their industries and technology is typically the relative price of capital, labor, and natural resources. Therefore the precondition for firms to follow the comparative advantage of the economy in their choice of technologies and industries is to have a relative price system that can reflect the relative scarcity of these production factors in the endowment structure. Admittedly, such a relative price system exists only in a competitive market system. In developing countries, where this is usually not the case, it is necessary that government action be taken to improve various market institutions to create and protect effective competition in the product and factor markets. The standard growth model, which reflects blind faith in the virtues of the market and skepticism about government interventions, does not discuss this government role.

Successful industrial upgrading also requires constant adjustment and upgrades of the factor endowments. An economy with GDP per capita of less than $1,000, like Malawi, does not need the same types of physical and human capital or the same type of institutions that a high-income economy with GDP per capita of nearly $150,000, such as Luxemburg, needs. Moreover, legitimate and enduring institutions, whose role is essential in facilitating sustained growth and stability, are hard to design and build, especially in low-income countries that are often mired in sociopolitical conflicts. Table 4.2, which displays the pace of change of institutional quality indicators using progress in the twenty-four-year period 1985–2009 as the basis of comparison, shows that it is indeed a slow process. Even for the

TABLE 4.2. THE SLOW PROCESS OF BUILDING INSTITUTIONS

Institutional Quality Indicators 1985–2009	YEARS TO GO FROM "FRAGILE" TO "LOW-INCOME" STATUS	
	Fastest 20 Reformers	Fastest Ever Reformer
Bureaucratic quality	20	12
Corruption	27	14
Rule of law	41	18
Government effectiveness	36	13

Source: Devarajan and Pritchett.

fastest twenty reformers, it took an average of thirty-six years to improve their indicator of "government effectiveness" from that of a fragile country (say, Afghanistan) to that of a low-income country (say, Bangladesh). Even the fastest ever reformer still needed thirteen years to make that relatively small improvement. Progress on the indicators of the rule of law is even slower, typically requiring decades even for the most incremental steps. This underscores the need to design growth strategies that are realistic and not based on rapid changes in the quality of institutions.

Historical precedents show that most people in low-income countries depend on agriculture for their livelihood. The kind of technology, institutions, infrastructure, and human capital required for facilitating that type of production is limited and relatively simple. Even with low-skilled labor, such countries can manage to sustain high growth rates for long periods by exploiting the advantages of backwardness and by relying on judiciously located infrastructure, targeting potential competitive industries, and building well-functioning but basic financial and governance institutions. Improvements in agricultural technology are key to increasing farmers' income and reducing poverty. But economic development also requires continuous diversifying and upgrading to new, more capital-intensive industries. Without such a structural change, the scope for sustained increase in per capita income will be limited.

By contrast, high-income countries display a completely different endowment structure. They are at the technological frontier and need first-rate infrastructure, a well-educated labor force, cutting-edge production processes, advanced financial systems (such as developed stock or equity markets), and excellent governance institutions (for instance, sophisticated legal systems).

The various types of "hard" infrastructure (power, telecommunication, roads, port facilities, and so on) and "soft" infrastructure (regulatory and legal frameworks, cultural value systems, and so on) that are needed must comply with the necessities of national and global markets where business transactions are long distance and large in quantity and value.

Developing countries can choose from a whole spectrum of industries with different capital intensity. They must select industries with latent comparative advantages determined by their current factor endowments and turn them into their competitive advantages with the government's facilitation in overcoming externality and coordination problems. If the government plays such a facilitation role, the economy can generate the largest possible economic surplus and have the largest incentive to save and accumulate capital in the quickest possible way. By upgrading endowments, they can move up the industrial ladder (Ju, Lin, and Wang 2015). When they move up the industrial ladder, they also increase their scale of production, because of the indivisibility of capital equipment. Their firms become larger and need a bigger market, which necessitates corresponding changes in power, transportation, financial arrangements, and other soft infrastructure.

Industrial upgrading and diversification also increases risk faced by firms. As firms move closer to the global technology frontier, it becomes more difficult for them to borrow mature technology from advanced countries. They increasingly need to invent new technologies and products and thus face more risk. With changes in the size of firms, scope of the market, and nature of risk, along with the upgrading of the industrial structure, the requirements for infrastructure services, both hard and soft, also change. If the infrastructure is not improved simultaneously, the upgrading process in various industries may face x-inefficiency, a problem discussed by Harvey Leibenstein (1957).

Following Comparative Advantage

Why have Qatar, Luxemburg, and Singapore succeeded in designing and managing that process but the DRC, Malawi, and the Central African Republic have so far failed? Firms in today's high-income countries chose to enter industries and adopt technologies that were consistent with the comparative advantage determined by changes in such countries' factor endowments. That strategic choice allowed their economies to be most competitive. As competitive industries and firms grew, they claimed larger domestic and international market shares and created the greatest possible economic surplus in the form of profits and salaries. Reinvested surpluses earned the highest return possible as well, because the industrial structure was optimal for that endowment structure. Over time this approach allowed their economies to accumulate physical and human capital, upgrading the factor endowment structures and the industrial structures and making domestic firms more competitive in more capital- and skill-intensive products.

That kind of comparative-advantage-following approach in economic development may appear to be slow and frustrating in countries with major poverty challenges such as Malawi, the DRC, and the Central African Republic. In reality, it is the fastest way to accumulate capital and upgrade the endowment structure, and the upgrading of industrial structure can be accelerated by better access to technology and industries already developed by more advanced countries. At each development level, firms in developing countries can acquire the technologies (and enter the industries) that are appropriate for their endowment structure, rather than having to reinvent the wheel (Gerschenkron 1962). This possibility to use off-the-shelf technology and to enter into existing industries is what has recently allowed some East Asian newly industrialized economies to sustain annual GDP growth rates of 8 and even 10 percent.

As a country climbs up the industrial and technological ladder, many other changes take place. The technology used by its firms becomes more sophisticated, and capital requirements, the size of markets, and the scale of production increase. Market transactions increasingly take place at arm's length. A flexible and smooth industrial and technological upgrading process therefore requires simultaneous improvements in legal, financial, and educational institutions and in hard infrastructure so that firms in the newly upgraded industries can reduce transaction costs and reach the production possibility frontier (Harrison and Rodríguez-Clare 2010).

As suggested by the numbers in table 4.2, it is difficult to build the new types of legal, financial, and other "soft" (or intangible) and "hard" (or tangible) infrastructures that are constantly needed to facilitate production and market transactions and gradually allow developing economies to reach their production possibility frontier. Moreover, the improvement of these hard and soft infrastructures requires coordination beyond individual firms' decisions. No private firm would or should be solely entrusted to make decisions on building ports, airports, or highways, or to make (possibly self-serving) changes in commercial or banking laws. Clearly, individual firms cannot internalize all these changes cost effectively, and spontaneous coordination among many firms to meet these new challenges is often impossible. Change in infrastructure requires collective action or at least coordination between the provider of infrastructure services and industrial firms. For this reason, it falls to the government either to introduce such changes or to coordinate them proactively. This essential piece of the growth and development puzzle has been missing in the standard model and in the traditional development policy framework.

Another major challenge in industrial upgrading is indeed that firms need to have information about production technologies and product markets. Competing with other firms in industries that are mature and well known, with few barriers to entry and little regulation, can be relatively easy. New entrants simply have to ensure that their cost structure is competitive and that the prospective customers are willing to give their goods and services a chance. Effective marketing strategies and well-negotiated deals with suppliers and banks typically help new firms succeed in those industries.

Things are more difficult when firms consider entering new industries—even those that are consistent with the economy's latent comparative advantage. If information about production technologies and product markets is not freely available, each firm will need to invest resources to search for it, collect it, and analyze it. For individual firms in developing countries, industrial upgrading is therefore a high-reward, high-risk process. First movers that try to enter new industries can either fail—because they target the wrong industries—or succeed—because the industry is consistent with the country's new comparative advantage. With success, their experience offers valuable and free information to other prospective entrants. They will not have monopoly rent because of competition from new entry. Moreover, these first movers often need to devote resources to train workers on the new business processes and techniques, who may be then hired by competitors. First movers generate demand for new activities and human capital that may not have existed otherwise. Even when they fail because the new industries are not viable, that negative experience also provides useful knowledge to other firms. Yet the first movers must bear the costs of failure alone. In other words, the social value to the economy as a whole of the first movers' investments is usually much larger than their private value to specific firms, and there is an asymmetry between the first movers' gain from success and the cost of failure.

Economic development is therefore a dynamic process marked with externalities and requiring coordination. Although the market is a necessary mechanism for resource allocation at each development stage, governments must play a proactive, facilitating role for an economy to move from one stage to another. They must intervene to allow markets to function properly. They take the following steps:

→ Provide information about new industries that are consistent with the new comparative advantage determined by change in the economy's endowment structure.
→ Coordinate investments in related industries and the required improvements in infrastructure.
→ Subsidize activities with externalities in industrial upgrading and structural change.
→ Facilitate new industries by incubation or by attracting foreign direct investment to overcome the deficits in social capital and other intangible constraints.

Today's high-income countries went through successful structural transformation processes because they followed their comparative advantage in their growth and development strategy. They opened up their economies at a realistic pace, produced goods and services consistent with their endowment structures, and exported to the international market while importing whatever products were not in their comparative advantage. Their trade dependency ratio became endogenous to their comparative advantage and larger than would have otherwise been the case. Their economies also became competitive, and their endowment structure and industrial structure were upgraded at the fastest pace possible. They could achieve sustainable if not strong fiscal positions because they could reap the benefits of dynamic growth and had no need for subsidizing nonviable firms. Their economies were also able to generate more job opportunities and less unemployment.

That strategy also shielded them from homegrown crises due to fiscal crises, currency mismatch, or uncompetitive industries. Because of their external competitiveness and limited reliance on capital inflows for growth, they built strong external accounts, and their governments are in a strong position to adopt countercyclical measures if there are shocks to the economy from global crises. Their competitive stance also yielded large economic surpluses (profits) for firms, which led to high savings for the economy. Competitive industries also imply high return on investment, which provides incentives to save and invest. Moreover, good public investments can enhance the economy's growth potential, reduce transaction costs on the private sector, increase the rate of return on private investment, and eventually generate enough tax revenues to liquidate the initial costs.

Adopting a market system to allocate resources as recommended by the standard model is indeed a necessary condition for an economy to follow comparative advantage in its development, because it minimizes distortions as private firms are set up to pursue profits. But it must be complemented by recognizing a facilitating state role in industrial upgrading.

Beyond the standard growth model's incompleteness, perhaps the most serious consequences of adopting it and its unrealistic policy prescriptions have been the extreme dependence of many low-income countries—especially in Africa—on foreign aid. Such dependence has contributed to their poor economic performance over long periods and distorted the public debate over development strategies.

AN UNPLEASANT SIDE EFFECT:
THE SOFT ADDICTION TO FOREIGN AID

Many developing countries that have followed the conventional policy prescriptions derived from the standard growth model have become trapped into low-growth and persistently high-poverty situations, which limit their ability to borrow domestically and externally, even for potentially productive activities. In such situations, they often have no other recourse for financing than to rely on foreign aid. Debate has raged since the 1950s over the effectiveness of foreign aid to developing countries. This section does not discuss the arguments on various sides of the debate, as they are well known. Moreover, from the new structural economics perspective, aid is not an absolute precondition for sustained growth because any country can design and implement a successful economic development strategy if it focuses on its comparative advantage and turns it into its competitive advantage in a pragmatic way. It would then be able to build industries that are economically viable and quickly reap the benefits of trade and globalization. But aid could help poor countries move faster toward their industrial and technological goals if it is targeted to finance countries' infrastructure in the industries representing their latent comparative advantage. The next section summarizes the diverging views and emerging consensus on aid effectiveness and then examines the often neglected "addiction to foreign aid."

Careful What You Wish For

Since the release of the Meltzer Report in 2000, which cast doubts on the effectiveness of the large international financial institutions in charge of the development business, there has been much debate and confusion over issues surrounding foreign aid.[7] Many skeptics have pointed out that stated objectives of foreign aid and the often repeated commitments by bilateral and multilateral aid institutions to foster economic growth and reduce poverty in the poorest nations have not succeeded. They have also argued that foreign aid should be stopped or at least completely revamped (Easterly 2003, 2006).

But the publication of the millennium development goals and the United Nations post-2015 agenda has given impetus to some aid optimists. Although acknowledging that a large gap remains between the promise and achievement of aid, other authors have argued that poor countries cannot have access to enough private financing to support their development needs—and certainly not for the delivery of public services in rural areas where there are market failures. They advocate for major increases in international financial assistance to the poorest nations, especially those in Africa. This viewpoint is more forcefully made by Jeffrey D. Sachs (2014):

> We are living in a world of great wealth. We need not accept the fallacy perpetuated by the rich that global resources available are quite so "modest," when total aid to sub-Saharan Africa in 2012 amounted to roughly 0.1 percent of the GDP of the donor countries (around $45 billion per year). We can and should mobilize more support. Just fractions of 1 percent of GDP of the rich countries can make a profound difference to ending extreme poverty throughout the world. Of course, we should also certainly agree to focus on what works,

and take effective programs to large scale. The positive evidence since 2000 shows that well-designed aid has made a tremendous impact.

Sachs has made similar arguments throughout the years (see, for instance, Sachs 2005), and his position has recently received strong endorsement by influential global philanthropists such as Bill and Melinda Gates.

The controversies are too often plagued with misunderstanding and confusion about the definition of aid and the empirical strategies used to investigate its impact. That is why others have adopted a more nuanced position, highlighting the complexity and the nonlinearity of the aid-growth-poverty-reducing relationships, the possibility of decreasing returns to aid (Hansen and Tarp 2001), the need to take into account the specificities of country conditions and policy environments (Burnside and Dollar 2000), or the importance of distinguishing aid categories (humanitarian aid versus aid to support human capital or infrastructure) and temporalities (differentiated effects between the short and the long term).[8] Channing Arndt, Sam Jones, and Finn Tarp (2015) go further and widen the evaluation to outcomes including proximate sources of growth (such as physical and human capital), indicators of social welfare (such as poverty and infant mortality), and measures of economic transformation (such as share of agriculture and industry in value added). They conclude that aid has over the past forty years stimulated growth, promoted structural change, improved social indicators, and reduced poverty.

Foreign aid is, by definition, an inexpensive new financial resource that savings-constrained developing countries could use to support productive investment. But empirical analysis of long-term aid patterns shows evidence of addiction[9]—defined as reliance on aid to a point where the social, economic, and political costs outweigh the potential benefits—in many African countries, with deleterious effects on economic development (Monga 2014a). The phenomenon described here as *aid addiction* goes well beyond the *aid dependency* thesis criticized by Paul Collier (1999), which focuses only on the financial and economic aspects of aid. Besides the well-known macroeconomic issues associated with high volumes of aid, aid addiction extends the scope of analysis to the sociopolitical implications of excessive dependency on foreign assistance.

Such a comprehensive approach has several implications. First, aid addiction is a broad concept, encompassing the different economic and financial aspects of what happens to a country that relies excessively on external generosity—mostly charity from Western countries with various political motives for their support. Second, aid addiction implies not only that external financial help is a key determinant of the government's capacity but also that the state is incapable of operating without financial help from outside. Third, beyond economics and finance, beyond public-sector issues, aid addiction has potential consequences for society at large and for the negative expectations, attitude, and behavior of private agents.

Aid can be a formidable catalyst to economic growth and poverty reduction—but only if used with moderation. As the logical outcome of conventional growth strategies that rely on the standard model, aid addiction therefore raises a variety of policy issues, among which are the following:

→ Macroeconomic and financial risks created by large financial inflows—reflected in real exchange rate appreciation and unpredictable fiscal revenue performance

→ Uncertainty in public and private investment and major instability in medium- to long-term economic projections

→ High correlation between changes in private consumption and aid inflows—as foreign assistance is the main source of financing not only for public investment but sometimes also for recurrent costs, including civil service salaries

→ The propensity of the private sector to request some form of "signal," "guarantee," and "insurance" from the donor community before engaging in economic activities—even those with clear positive rates of return

→ Extreme dominance of foreign institutions in the design, implementation, monitoring, and evaluation of public policies

→ Extraversion and ineffectiveness of government agencies and political institutions whose policy agenda has to conform to the objectives set by the donors and to externally determined incentives and rules

→ Limited role for the state in the economy—either as a direct player or as regulator—and only in sectors that may or may not be consistent with the economy's comparative advantage

→ Distorted expectations and fragile accountability systems because public policies are not legitimized by domestic constituencies but geared toward satisfying unelected foreign actors

META-ECONOMICS OF AID ADDICTION
AND STANDARD GROWTH RECIPES

Although the economic impact of the policy prescriptions derived from the standard growth model and its corollary, the extreme dependency on foreign aid by many low-income countries, have often been debated in the economic literature, the noneconomic aspects of the conventional development strategy have not been considered systematically. Those meta-economic side effects of aid addiction include the lack of economic policy ownership and distorted expectations in developing countries. They can carry heavy political and psychological costs.

Distorted Expectations and Compulsive Behavior

Just as drug abuse creates dysfunctional behavior, aid addiction affects almost all stakeholders involved (donors, policy makers, government, and social institutions), often leading to various forms of a compulsive and psychological need for financial flows. In aid-addicted countries, disbursing official development assistance (ODA) flows grants foreign donors the legitimacy to set the country's development objectives and priorities, determine the strategic framework and policy measures to achieve them, and establish the measuring and monitoring criteria—even though in the end no donor institution is ever willing to take responsibility in case of failure. In the 1980s and 1990s, low-income countries that had programs with the IMF and World Bank were required to sign off on policy framework papers (PFPs) that were prepared in Washington and taken to the country for "discussions" that lasted a few days. These long PFPs spelled out in great detail all the sectoral priorities of the country (determined by the donor community and reflecting their values) and the hundreds of conditionalities that would determine disbursement. Low-income countries that could not agree with the experts of the Bretton-Woods institutions could not access external financing, because other multilateral, bilateral, and even private financiers would require the IMF stamp of approval ("signaling") before considering funding of programs or projects.

In the late 1990s and early 2000s, the IMF and the World Bank acknowledged that such a modus operandi was suboptimal. With the launch of the various debt relief initiatives and under the pressure of many nongovernmental organizations, the PFPs were abandoned and replaced with poverty reduction strategy papers (PRSPs) that were supposed to reflect greater ownership of policy priorities and development strategies by the countries getting ODA. Yet despite some cosmetic changes in processes, the Bretton Woods institutions retained a de facto veto right on policies. Under the excuse that all proposed development strategies and policy priorities should be "consistent with the macroeconomic framework" prepared by the IMF, many country programs and projects often were not validated and cleared by the Washington experts. They were deemed "too expensive" or "too ambitious" and simply rejected.

Many donor community representatives consider themselves— sometimes without even realizing it—rulers of the states in which they operate. Knowing well how important their financial support is to state functioning and country stability, these unelected foreigners act as colonial proconsuls, although they understand little about the history, culture, or social dynamics of the countries where they happen to be assigned, generally for short periods. A Dutch minister for development cooperation confessed that "donors have to be much more helpful than in the past. We do not have an unblemished record. We have regularly bothered developing countries with our latest lobbies. We have imposed counterpart and recurrent costs on their budgets, without talking to them first to find out if it was a good idea to start such and such a project in the first place. We have been micromanaging" (Herfkens 1999, 484).

Such arrogant attitudes from the donor community tend to distort expectations from domestic policy makers, political leaders, and even society at large. From the head of state to the lowest-ranking civil servants, and from business leaders to ordinary citizens, many people tend to expect the donor community to set their country's "development" agenda, to determine the macroeconomic framework consistent with such an agenda, to design the "proper" economic strategy and even choose (or at least give their clearance on) the major investment projects to be implemented, and to decide on the "adequate" number of civil servants and the wage bill that the state can afford. These distorted expectations lead to a silent, collective resignation from the responsibilities associated with leadership and even citizenship. This creates a policy vacuum filled by external players, who have no difficulties imposing their own "vision" of what the country should become and their policies to materialize it.

In high-aid countries, collective resignation often translates into (and is worsened by) the strong opposition or the skepticism of civil servants and private agents toward economic policies advocated by the donor community. Opinion polls in high-aid countries show that few people express satisfaction with the condition of their national economy: 34 percent in Ghana, 26 percent in Malawi, 22 percent in Tanzania, and 19 percent in Zambia.[10] The only exception seems to be Uganda, where a majority is satisfied with economic conditions (62 percent). Moreover, most people believe that their living standards have worsened over time. When asked specifically about structural adjustment programs promoted by international financial institutions like the World Bank and the IMF, fewer people claim to comprehend something about them than are aware of "democracy": in Uganda, the numbers are 55 percent and 74 percent, respectively (Bratton, Lambright, and Sentamu 2000).

Limited Policy Space and Trust

Distorted expectations created by addiction to foreign aid is most noticeable in the realm of public policies. It often leads to difficulties in building trust and establishing full partnerships between the donor community and policy makers in recipient countries. William Easterly (2009) gives anecdotal evidence of the problem by describing the steps that beleaguered government officials in low-income countries must take to receive foreign aid:

> Among other things, they must prepare a participatory Poverty Reduction Paper (PRSP)—a detailed plan for uplifting the destitute that the World Bank and IMF require before granting debt forgiveness and new loans. This document in turn must adhere to the World Bank's Comprehensive Development Framework, a 14-point checklist covering everything from lumber policy to labor practices. And the list goes on: Policymakers seeking aid dollars must also prepare a Financial Information Management System report, a Report on Observance of Standards and Codes, a Medium Term Expenditure Framework, and a Debt Sustainability Analysis for the Enhanced Heavily Indebted Poor Countries Initiative.

He notes that each document can run to hundreds of pages and consume months of preparation time. He also observes that Niger's 2002 PRSP was 187 pages long, took fifteen months to prepare, and set out spending programs with such detailed line items as $17,600 a year on "sensitizing population to traffic circulation."

Easterly's comments highlight another feature of the meta-economics of extreme reliance on foreign aid. Through the prism of conditionality and ownership of reforms, they raise the issue of trust between policy makers in recipient countries and the donor community. Conditionality is usually defined as the link between approving or continuing financing by an external creditor or donor and implementing specified elements of economic policy by the country receiving this financing.[11] The reason often put forward by donors is that it gives safeguards to creditors to ensure that successive tranches of financing are delivered only if key policies are on track. It also gives assurances to recipient countries that they will continue to get financing provided that they continue to implement the policies envisaged.

But conditionality has several other rationales. It represents a form of inducement—with aid offered as an incentive for reform. It is also a form of paternalism when external players claim to know best what development path should be followed by recipient countries. It is a means of restraint, a commitment device to make policy choices credible for private agents, and a signaling mechanism to indicate to external investors that the government is adhering to market rules and is improving its business climate (Collier et al. 1997; Killick 1997). Some policy makers in developing countries resent conditionality as infringing on national sovereignty and weakening ownership of their development strategies. Others seem more inclined to accept it, even unwillingly. When the National Assembly of Chad changed the oil revenue law passed in 1999 as a condition for the World Bank's support for the Chad-Cameroon pipeline, the Bretton Woods institution reacted in January 2006 by cutting $124 million in financial assistance and freezing a government escrow account in London with $125 million in royalties. President Idriss Deby publicly complained about the "imperialistic" conditionality of the World Bank. But Côte d'Ivoire's Laurent Gbagbo declared: "If you seek money from outside, those who give it to you also impose their analysis of the crisis and its solutions."[12]

How did things get to that point? Conditionality, which was not mentioned in the Articles of Agreement of the IMF or the World Bank, has changed over the past fifty years. Its scope was enlarged in the late 1980s with the recognition that in some cases, balance-of-payments problems were rooted in structural rigidities and distortions. The launch of structural adjustment programs led to adopting new financing instruments, which required policy and institutional actions well beyond the IMF's traditional

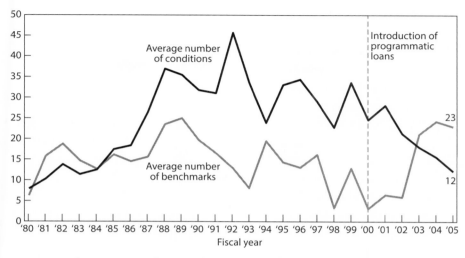

Figure 4.2. Average conditions and benchmarks in World Bank lending operations, 1980–2005. *Source*: World Bank (2005b, 10).

areas of focus (promoting macroeconomic stabilization and an open exchange system). The World Bank also went beyond its initial agenda of investment project financing to advocate correcting structural imbalances in production, trade, and prices. Both institutions have now acknowledged that they may have gone too far in attaching conditions to their low-income country financing. Figure 4.2 shows the declining trend in the average number of conditions in World Bank lending operations between 1980 and 2005, though benchmarks have increased since fiscal year 2000.[13]

Another important aspect of the meta-economics of aid addiction is its political economy. A review of the criteria and justification for transferring significant funding to African countries led Carol Lancaster (1999, 498) to observe that "donors still provide aid for non-development-related goals, including maintaining spheres of influence (as in the case of France), garnering votes for favored issues in the United Nations (as in the case of Japan, which wants a seat on the Security Council) or promoting commercial interests (as is often the case with France, Italy, Japan, and others)."

Too often, their reason for choosing which "development" project they are willing to fund has little to do with recipient country priorities but is determined by political motives and the desire to see their flag hanging over a building and television cameras celebrating their nation's greatness. Dutch minister Herfkens (1999, 485) confirms: "One of the reasons aid has failed is because donors wanted their contribution to be visible. So, we built hospitals or schools: you will find them all over the developing world, with a plaque on them expressing the gratitude to the Dutch or Swedish people, opened by this minister or that, but totally run down because no one ever thought about who finances the medicines, or the salaries of the teachers or nurses."

Against this background, it can be argued that addiction to foreign aid is a chronic economic "disease" characterized by a strong craving for ODA flows that are not necessarily funding the most competitive industries or supporting the most potentially productive sectors. It also carries clear adverse administrative and sociopolitical consequences. Lessons from successful economies and economic history and policy shed light on the principles of economic pragmatism that should be at the core of sustainable and inclusive growth strategies. They are discussed in the next chapter.

APPENDIX 4.1

How does one identify aid addiction symptoms? A straightforward way to proceed is to gather empirical evidence to support the proposition that foreign assistance has consistently represented a very large source of income for an increasingly large group of African countries, yet "aid-addicted" countries have not performed better on average than other countries.

Basic Statistics and Facts

Analyses focusing on the continent of Africa—which has attracted the most external financial assistance since the early 1960s—show that the biggest recipients of aid have grown accustomed to external financial support to the point that substantial parts of their public spending (investment and recurrent) could not be financed without the constant flow of foreign money. As with addiction, these countries tend to need higher levels of foreign assistance simply to maintain the same economic level.

During the past five decades, more African countries have indeed relied on foreign assistance for bigger parts of their national incomes. In 1965 six countries received 10 percent or more of their gross national income in foreign aid, as measured by ODA. In 2012 twenty-one did (table A4.1).

Confirming these trends, the number of countries relying heavily on aid for long periods to the point of addiction has also been substantial. A

Aid (% of GNI)	1965	1975	1985	1995	2005	2012
	NUMBER OF COUNTRIES					
Less than 2	3	3	8	8	15	12
2–5	13	13	5	5	4	10
5–10	9	9	11	7	11	8
10–15	3	6	8	10	7	14
15–20	1	5	4	6	5	4
More than 20	2	3	9	13	10	3

Source: Authors.

country is considered to be *aid addicted* if it consistently ranks above the global median in ODA flows to GNI for thirty years or more.[14]

The data also show a strong correlation between the amount of aid received over time by various countries and aid addiction, which confirms that extreme reliance on foreign aid has indeed become a form of addiction for a large group of African countries (figure A4.1). This phenomenon, which can be termed *aid hysteresis*, also indicates that contrary to other parts of the world where aid was used to ignite private financial flows and boost trade

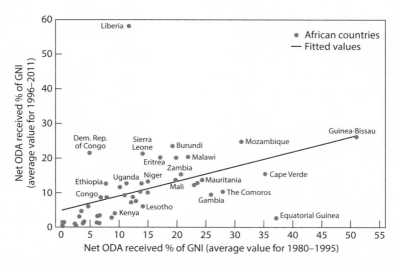

Figure A4.1. Hysteresis in aid flows (aid as percent of GNI). *Source*: Authors.

and economic development, few African countries have designed and implemented an effective exit strategy from high aid flows. As noted above, there has been a long debate over aid effectiveness (especially the effect of aid on growth), with strong arguments made on all sides. Without getting into the controversies, one can simply examine whether, in light of aid addiction and aid hysteresis, there are substantial differences in macroeconomic performance and social indicators between countries that rely consistently on ODA flows and others. A straightforward comparison between "high-aid" countries and "others" is implemented in the next section.

Have Aid-Addicted Countries Performed Better than the Others?

We use a panel dataset of forty-nine African countries for which data are available from 1960–2010. To calculate the aid-addiction threshold, we take the average of the ODA-to-GNI ratio over this period for each country.[15] The threshold is defined as the sample median of the ODA-to-GNI ratio: countries with a ratio above (below) this median are considered as aid-addicted (other countries). One advantage of the sample median (over the sample mean) is that it is insensitive to outliers. The two country groups are presented below.

We use a probit model to estimate the propensity scores.[16] The dependent variable is our treatment variable, that is, the aid-addiction dummy assigned 1 for aid-addicted countries and 0 otherwise. The idea is to estimate the probability of being addicted as a function of the real GDP per capita (PC), a dummy indicating if a country is a heavily indebted poor country (HIPC), trade openness, and Country Policy and Institutional Assessment (CPIA)-related institutional quality. The underlying hypothesis here is that these regressors are the country characteristics donors look at to allocate ODA. The results reported are intuitive (table A4.2). GDP PC is negatively related to the probability of being addicted, reflecting that ODA is allocated to low-income countries. Being an HIPC is positively associated with the probability of being aid addicted.

This result suggests that HIPC are likely to be aid addicted and accords with the negative coefficient of GDP PC. On average, countries with a lower ODA resource allocation index are likely to be aid addicted. This result is surprising given that the aim of donors is to allocate ODA to countries with better institutions, but this also confirms that low-income countries (LIC) are likely to have poor institutions. But the results on

**TABLE A4.2. PROBIT ESTIMATES TO GENERATE
THE PROPENSITY SCORES**

Dpdt var.:	=1 if aid-addicted
Ln Real GDP PC	-0.601***
	(0 .150)
1 if HIPC	0.469**
	(0.203)
CPIA fiscal policy rating	0.940***
	(0.281)
IDA resource allocation index	-6.093***
	(1.004)
CPIA public sector management and institutions	4.154***
	(0.617)
CPIA policies for social inclusion/equity	1.816***
	(0.472)
Trade openness	1.25e-03
	(2.82e-03)
Constant	1.656***
	(1.009)
Number of Observations	301
Pseudo R2	0.262

Note: Standard errors in parentheses. Asterisks denote significance as follows:
*** $p < 0.01$, ** $p < 0.05$, * $p < 0.1$. CPIA are Country Policy and Institutional
Assessment indicators from the World Bank. IDA is the International Development Association.

the CPIA subindexes are consistent with what we expect. Having better institutions—for fiscal policy, public-sector management, and social inclusion—increases the probability that a given country experiences good access to ODA. Trade openness is positively related to the likelihood of being addicted, but its coefficient is not statistically significant.

The results on the macroeconomic stability aspects are reported in table A4.3. From 1960 to 2010, aid-addicted countries experienced fast growth in real per capita income. This result reflects a "catch-up" situation where countries with initial low income tend to converge toward rich countries, notably because of the diminishing returns to capital. But labor productivity (captured by GDP for each person employed) is lower in aid-addicted

MAIN RESULTS AND DISCUSSION

The first step here is to construct a control group as similar as possible to aid-addicted countries, based on the propensity scores. These scores are predicted by the probit model for each country as the probability of being addicted, given the regressors in the estimation. The matching idea is therefore to compare a given aid-addicted country with the comparison country (or country group) with which it is the closest, by propensity scores. To this end, we use three alternative matching approaches: the nearest neighbor matching with replacement, the radius matching, and the kernel matching. The nearest neighbor matching consists of matching each aid-addicted country with control countries that have the closest propensity score. The radius matching matches each aid-addicted country to control countries with estimated propensity scores falling within a given radius. As for the kernel matching, it matches a given aid-addicted country to all control countries weighted in proportion to the closeness between treated unit and the control unit.

The main focus of this study is to estimate the impact of addiction on country outcomes, classified in three broad categories: macroeconomic stability, economic and social development, and access to basic infrastructure and business environment. So in the second step the country characteristic comparisons are implemented using each of these categories.

countries, possibly owing to a relatively lower labor cost in these countries. Aid-addicted countries also tend to experience lower internal imbalances (measured by inflation) but higher external imbalances (captured by the current account balance). There is no statistically significant difference in fiscal balances between aid-addicted and other countries. Although macroeconomic stability is a central target for policy makers, the most important goal for developing countries is economic and social development.

Table A4.4 presents the results using economic and social development indicators. The big picture here is that while aid-addicted countries are

TABLE A4.3: AID ADDICTION AND COUNTRY PERFORMANCE (AVERAGE TREATMENT EFFECT ON THE TREATED)

MACROECONOMIC STABILITY

	Nearest Neighbor Matching			Radius Matching			Kernel Matching		
	ATT	Average		ATT	Average		ATT	Average	
		AA	Others		AA	Others		AA	Others
Real GDP per capita growth	0.543 (0.462)	2.637	2.093	0.572* (0.295)	2.666	2.093	0.598 (0.709)	2.666	2.068
Ln GDP per person employed	-0.087 (0.094)	7.730	7.817	-0.129** (0.051)	7.687	7.817	-0.292 (0.212)	7.687	7.980
Fiscal balance (% of GDP)	-0.263 (1.970)	-0.332	-0.068	-0.311 (1.817)	-0.380	-0.068	1.888 (2.416)	-0.380	-2.269
Tax revenue (% of GDP)	2.027 (1.311)	15.929	13.901	1.935* (1.109)	15.837	13.901	1.806 (1.898)	15.837	14.030
Ln [1+Inflation, consumer prices (annual %)]	-0.381*** (0.119)	1.881	2.262	-0.327*** (0.062)	1.935	2.262	-0.574*** (0.178)	1.935	2.510
Current account balance (% of GDP)	-8.526*** (1.736)	-11.852	-3.326	-8.169*** (1.190)	-11.495	-3.326	-2.403 (2.427)	-11.495	-9.091

Standard errors in parentheses. Asterisks denote significance as follows: *** p<0.01, ** p<0.05, * p<0.1. AA stands for aid-addicted countries. ATT is the average treatment effect on the treated. The treatment effect on the treated (TOT) is defined as follows: $TOT = E[Y_i(1) - Y_i(0) | T_i = 1]$, where i refers to individuals, $E[Y_i(1) | T_i = 1]$ is the average outcome of the treated conditional on being in a treated area, and $E[Y_i(1) | T_i = 1]$ is the average outcome of the non-treated (control group) conditional on being in a treated area. In this case, "conditional on being in a treated area" means "conditional on having access to ODA". So, the TOT is the difference in outcomes from receiving the program as compared with being in a control area for a person or subject i randomly drawn from the treated sample.

TABLE A4.4. AID ADDICTION AND COUNTRY PERFORMANCE (AVERAGE TREATMENT EFFECT ON THE TREATED)

	Nearest Neighbor Matching			Radius Matching			Kernel Matching		
	ATT	Average		ATT	Average		ATT	Average	
		AA	Others		AA	Others		AA	Others
ECONOMIC AND SOCIAL DEVELOPMENT									
Social spending (% of GDP)	1.298*** (0.480)	7.432	6.134	1.623*** (0.329)	7.758	6.134	1.055* (0.561)	7.758	6.702
Education spending (% of GDP)	0.465 (0.385)	4.420	3.954	0.541** (0.260)	4.496	3.954	0.228 (0.415)	4.496	4.268
Health spending (% of GDP)	1.176*** (0.146)	3.230	2.054	1.223*** (0.119)	3.278	2.054	0.708*** (0.171)	3.278	2.569
Poverty headcount ratio at $1.25 a day	14.237** (7.220)	58.217	43.980	12.251*** (3.671)	56.232	43.980	9.596 (10.047)	56.232	46.636
GINI index	1.805 (2.607)	43.642	41.837	0.508 (2.088)	42.346	41.837	-0.806 (2.564)	42.346	43.152
Income share held by lowest 20%	0.049 (0.521)	6.028	5.979	0.304 (0.430)	6.283	5.979	0.422 (0.514)	6.283	5.860
Pupil-teacher ratio, primary	3.043* (1.836)	47.217	44.173	5.152*** (1.452)	49.325	44.173	9.758*** (2.181)	49.325	39.567
School enrollment, primary (% net)	-1.675 (2.386)	75.345	77.021	-2.908* (1.723)	74.113	77.021	1.391 (2.753)	74.113	72.721
Primary completion rate	2.409 (2.807)	65.398	62.989	-0.754 (1.882)	62.234	62.989	-5.895* (3.457)	62.234	68.130
Life expectancy at birth	0.418 (0.783)	55.462	55.044	0.755 (0.548)	55.800	55.044	-1.647* (0.965)	55.800	57.447
Literacy rate, youth	-12.347** (5.718)	57.480	69.828	-11.710*** (4.368)	58.118	69.828	-5.210 (8.609)	58.118	63.328
Children in jobs	0.912 (4.811)	38.319	37.406	-1.230 (2.680)	36.175	37.406	-6.659 (7.239)	36.175	42.834

	(1)	(2)	(3)	(4)	(5)	(6)	(7)	(8)	(9)
Mortality rate, infant	0.172 (2.691)	108.7	109.854	-2.807 (1.812)	67.075	69.882	6.171* (3.549)	67.075	60.903
Immunization, DPT	6.092*** (1.941)	80.784	74.692	6.670*** (1.187)	81.362	74.692	0.256 (2.967)	81.362	81.106
Immunization, measles	8.392*** (1.738)	79.315	70.923	9.014*** (1.116)	79.937	70.923	3.551 (2.620)	79.937	76.385
Maternal mortality ratio	-7.153 (57.944)	572.846	580.000	-19.978 (41.687)	560.021	580.000	41.691 (71.564)	560.021	518.330
Malnutrition prevalence, height for age	6.406*** (2.319)	41.068	34.662	6.873*** (1.761)	41.535	34.662	8.425*** (3.018)	41.535	33.110
Malnutrition prevalence, weight for age	3.871** (1.834)	22.264	18.392	3.052* (1.489)	21.445	18.392	4.963** (2.230)	21.445	16.481
Prevalence of undernourishment	4.204** (1.889)	26.846	22.641	7.928*** (1.496)	30.570	22.641	12.666*** (2.254)	30.570	17.904
Births attended by skilled health staff	-1.987 (3.426)	52.990	54.978	-3.984 (2.890)	50.994	54.978	-4.110 (5.034)	50.994	55.104
Hospital beds (per 1,000 people)	0.358** (0.161)	1.209	0.850	0.398** (0.166)	1.248	0.850	0.387 (0.251)	1.248	0.860
Unemployment, total	3.122*** (0.781)	9.353	6.230	2.734*** (0.627)	8.965	6.230	4.422*** (0.821)	8.965	4.542
Unemployment, youth	3.953*** (1.114)	14.329	10.375	3.414*** (0.874)	13.789	10.375	6.293*** (1.232)	13.789	7.495
Vulnerable job	2.716 (1.726)	91.650	88.283	2.988*** (0.831)	91.271	88.283	2.988* (1.675)	91.271	88.283
Labor force, total	-1.545*** (0.146)	14.287	15.832	-1.218*** (0.124)	14.613	15.832	-1.234*** (0.174)	14.613	15.847
Labor force, female	-0.064*** (0.022)	3.745	3.809	-0.036** (0.015)	3.772	3.809	-0.092*** (0.026)	3.772	3.865

Note: Standard errors in parentheses. Asterisks denote significance as follows: *** $p < 0.01$, ** $p < 0.05$, * $p < 0.1$. AA stands for aid-addicted countries. ATT is the average treatment effect on the treated.

spending relatively more on social sectors, they experience poor economic and social development, on average. Social spending, especially spending on health, is relatively high in aid-addicted countries compared with other countries. But aid-addicted countries experience higher numbers of people living on less than $1.25 a day.

The pupil-teacher ratio, child mortality, malnutrition prevalence (height and weight for age), undernourishment, and unemployment (total, youth, and vulnerable) are significantly higher in aid-addicted countries compared with other countries. Child immunization (DPT and measles) rates and hospital beds are also relatively higher in aid-addicted countries, consistent with their relatively higher health spending. But life expectancy at birth, youth literacy rate, primary school enrollment, primary school completion, and labor force (total and female) are importantly lower in aid-addicted countries than in others.

The differences between aid-addicted and other countries in income inequality (measured by the GINI index and the income share held by lowest 20 percent), children, jobs, maternal mortality, and the ratio of births attended by skilled health staff are not statistically indistinguishable from zero. Economic and social development indicators considered here are "final" development outcomes, but we also need to look at "intermediate" development outcomes that give opportunities to improve development outcomes.

In this regard, we looked at the country differences by access to basic infrastructure and investment climate quality (table A4.5). The results suggest that aid-addicted countries are very different from other countries from the perspective of intermediate development outcomes. In terms of basic infrastructure, while access to electricity is relatively lower in aid-addicted countries, access to water and sanitation facilities is relatively higher in these countries than in others. But on quality of the business environment, aid-addicted countries perform better than other African countries. The procedures to enforce a contract and the time required to register property are significantly lower in aid-addicted countries, reflecting the influence of donors on the investment climate quality.

The treatment effect on the treated (TOT) is defined as follows: $TOT = E[Y_i(1) - Y_i(0) \mid T_i = 1]$, where i refers to individuals, $E[Y_i(1) \mid T_i = 1]$ is the average outcomes of the treated conditional on being in a treated area, and $E[Y_i(0) \mid T_i = 1]$ is the average outcomes of the nontreated (control group) conditional on being in a treated area.

TABLE A4.5. AID ADDICTION AND COUNTRY PERFORMANCE (AVERAGE TREATMENT EFFECT ON THE TREATED)

	Nearest Neighbor Matching			Radius Matching			Kernel Matching		
		Average			Average			Average	
	ATT	AA	Others	ATT	AA	Others	ATT	AA	Others
MACROECONOMIC STABILITY									
Access to electricity (% of population)	−8.381*** (2.638)	18.443	36.825	−19.266*** (1.750)	18.443	37.710	−36.527*** (12.648)	18.443	54.971
Access to improved water source (% of population with access)	3.890** (1.706)	68.826	64.936	2.763** (1.237)	67.7	64.936	−1.816 (2.229)	67.7	69.516
Access to sanitation facilities (% of population with access)	3.305* (1.906)	29.662	26.356	1.619 (1.351)	27.976	26.356	5.828** (2.565)	27.976	22.147
Procedures to enforce a contract (number)	−3.147*** (0.604)	38.544	41.691	−3.260*** (0.403)	38.430	41.691	−1.791** (0.822)	38.430	40.221
Time required to register property (days)	−14.551* (8.801)	81.110	95.661	−13.867*** (5.137)	81.793	95.661	−6.888 (13.114)	81.793	88.68

Note: Standard errors in parentheses. Asterisks denote significance levels as follows: *** $p < 0.01$, ** $p < 0.05$, * $p < 0.1$. AA stands for aid-addicted countries. ATT is the average treatment effect on the treated.

In this analysis, "conditional on being in a treated area" means "conditional on having access to ODA." So the TOT is the difference in outcomes from receiving the program as compared with being in a control area for a person or subject i randomly drawn from the treated sample.

Country Lists

Aid-addicted countries: Burkina Faso, Burundi, Cabo Verde, Central African Republic, Comoros, Equatorial Guinea, Eritrea, Ethiopia, Guinea-Bissau, Lesotho, Liberia, Malawi, Mali, Mauritania, Mozambique, Niger, Rwanda, São Tomé and Principe, Sierra Leone, South Sudan, Tanzania, Gambia, Zambia

Non-aid-addicted countries: Angola, Benin, Botswana, Cameroon, Chad, Congo, Côte d'Ivoire, Democratic Republic of Congo, Gabon, Ghana, Guinea, Kenya, Madagascar, Mauritius, Namibia, Nigeria, Senegal, Seychelles, Somalia, South Africa, Sudan, Swaziland, Togo, Uganda, Zimbabwe

To sum up, although the results are mixed, aid-addicted countries, on average, are mostly different from others in terms of economic and social development and basic infrastructure and investment climate. On the macroeconomic stability side, the two main factors are inflation and the current account balance.

5

Ambitious Pragmatism:
First-Order Economic Principles

"It is better to be pleasantly surprised than to be disappointed," the old saying goes. The late president of Ghana, Kwame Nkrumah, must have meditated on these words after he was deposed in a military coup d'état in 1966. Back in 1957, when Ghana became the first African country to gain independence, it was expected to quickly become the beacon of hope for the continent and for many other third-world countries. There was excitement about its economic prospects throughout the developing world. Kwame Nkrumah, who led the country's quest for independence, seemed well prepared for the challenge. A well-educated, well-meaning, and charismatic leader, he also seemed to have all that was needed to succeed. A gifted speaker and committed Pan-Africanist, Osagyefo Kwame Nkrumah, as he was called affectionately by his people, could mobilize and mesmerize crowds with speeches that integrated historical analyses with ethical concerns and geopolitical explorations. He had the vision of a bright future for his country, the passion to make it happen within the framework of the United Nations of Africa, the inner strength to dominate Ghanaian popular and political support, and the necessary wit to make big things happen. He even recruited several internationally respected scholars to serve as his senior advisors, including Sir Arthur Lewis, one of the greatest economic minds of the time and to this day the only black person ever to win the Nobel Prize in economics.

Yet Nkrumah's grand vision for Ghana and Africa did not materialize. His economic development strategy failed to deliver results and brought anger and political turmoil to the country. Once seen as liberator, he was quickly branded a dictator, and a group of military officers had no difficulty deposing him while he was on an official visit to North Vietnam and

China. He lived an unhappy exiled life in Conakry, Guinea, until his lonely death in 1972. Ghana's grand experiment in African transformation not only fell short of expectations but also demolished the myth of a vibrant, united, and prosperous Africa. Ghana was a well-endowed economy with a great location, strong traditional institutions that had not been weakened by the colonial British, and a population of only 6.6 million at the time of independence. It was supposed to take off and lift Africa out of centuries of poverty. It failed to achieve its objectives.

Since Nkrumah's failure, Ghana has gone through its ups and downs but has mostly underachieved—despite being the second largest world cocoa producer, being well-endowed with natural resources, and having millions of well-trained workers within and outside its borders. Ghana remains heavily dependent on international financial and technical assistance. Nearly six decades after independence, Nkrumah's country is still underperforming. Growth has been insufficient to reduce poverty, and most of the labor force—whether highly skilled or not—is still underemployed if not unemployed. Gold and cocoa production and remittances are major sources of foreign exchange. Its economy continues to revolve around agriculture, which accounts for more than one-third of gross domestic product and employs about 55 percent of the workforce, mainly small landholders.

What happened?

Ghana's story has largely been Africa's story and that of many other developing countries. Former Tanzanian president Jakaya Kikwete complained about the vexing mystery of his country's remarkable growth performance (7 percent on average for fifteen years) that nonetheless has sometimes been accompanied by increased poverty. At the African Union Summit in January 2012, he shared some of the criticisms that he often heard from his fellow citizens whenever he brought up his country's stellar macroeconomic performance. He told the old Tanzanian joke about how people who feel good about themselves often convince themselves that life is good for everyone around them. "When you have had enough food and are full you tend to think that everyone is in the same situation," the president said with a sarcastic smile.

Equatorial Guinea is an even more perplexing case. It is currently the continent's only high-income economy. Yes, with gross national income per capita of $32,000 (PPP) in 2014, Equatorial Guinea should have propelled itself into the very select club of elite countries where major decisions about the world's future are supposed to be discussed. So Equatorial Guinea, of all places, has beaten the odds.

Or has it? Its spectacular economic growth is due to oil. The country's population is only about 700,000. Yet there is still something terribly frustrating about its tale of economic turnaround: poverty levels are still high (77 percent according to the latest figures), and the authorities have not yet managed even to vaccinate all of the country's 150,000 children. Its "triumph" is reminiscent of the story of the H. G. Wells novel *The War of the Worlds* in which the Martian characters are extremely smart and able to do almost anything except invent the wheel.

Unsatisfactory success and frustration are not unique to Equatorial Guinea. Rwanda president Paul Kagame has often wondered publicly why his country, consistently rated among the top performers in the World Bank's Doing Business indicators and other popular international rankings, still has not been able to create employment.

People in Africa are increasingly impatient about the abstract macroeconomic performance benefits that are being celebrated in political speeches and public discourse. They also are not convinced by the technical explanations of why high rates of economic growth may not translate into good jobs and improved economic and social well-being. (These include high growth but from a very low base, high population growth, GDP increases often due to a boom in industries such as security or healthcare, growth benefits being used to finance investment rather than consumption, and so on.) And not surprisingly, the skepticism in fast-growing countries where the wealth is not shared is matched by the anger and deep social tensions in slow-growing countries. As a result, Africa's economic transition is fraught with economic insecurity and danger, and there is always the risk that the unprecedented opportunities for change may be wasted or even squandered.

Compare Ghana in 1957 or Tanzania in 2012 or even Equatorial Guinea in 2014 with China in 1978 when Deng Xiaoping became its leader. As discussed in chapter 1, China was in a disastrous state in 1978. Yet it managed to ignite and sustain spectacular growth over several decades. Annual GDP growth averaged 9.8 percent over the thirty-five-year period from 1978 to 2013, and annual growth in international trade was 16.6 percent. China is now an upper-middle-income country, with a per capita GDP of $6,800 in 2012; more than 680 million people have escaped poverty (Lin 2014). This extraordinary performance has far exceeded the expectations of anyone at the outset of the transition, including Deng Xiaoping himself, the architect of China's reform and opening-up strategy.

What did Deng Xiaoping know or learn that Kwame Nkrumah and other frustrated African leaders did not? Was there anything unique to the Chinese culture, history, or country conditions that allowed Deng to succeed where others were doomed to fail? This chapter draws on lessons from history to argue that policy disappointments such as Ghana's mainly reflect failure not of politics but of economic thinking and policy making. There are now enough both failed and successful experiments in economic development for researchers and policy makers to draw on.

The chapter highlights the possibilities for poor countries to transform into middle- and even high-income economies and stresses the benefits of such transformations for the world economy as a whole. It starts with a discussion of the role of agricultural development in developing countries today, stressing both its potential contribution in the short term and its limitations in the medium and long term. It then details some first-order economic principles for success, pointing to the need for structural change, which occurs only through industrialization. For the process to be successful, economic policy should aim at "ambitious pragmatism," which requires calibrating the pace of economic takeoff with the existing economic structure and country development level reviewed in the chapter's final section. Ambitious pragmatism is possible only if policy makers reject the determinism of preconditions and are willing instead to learn and draw inspiration from the experiences of dynamically growing countries with similar endowment structures but with higher income per capita.

PARADOXES OF AGRICULTURE
AND INDUSTRIAL DEVELOPMENT

Economics has become such a fragmented subject nowadays that few people, even among experts, remember that, for a long while, the entire discipline was devoted exclusively to the study of agriculture. "Until 200 years ago all economics was agricultural economics," said John Kenneth Galbraith (1977). Agricultural economists are often frustrated with the intellectual and policy neglect of their subdiscipline in development thinking and policy. From their perspective, the importance of agriculture in economics in the global quest for prosperity and in the search for solutions to poverty seems both obvious and inescapable. Yet recent intellectual trends in mainstream economics have often given priority to the issues that dominate headlines: the global financial crisis and its aftermath for the world economy; monetary and fiscal policies to resume global growth; the implications of technological innovation and globalization for traditional forms of employment; and so on.

For decades, influential institutions such as the World Bank and the IMF that defined the core of development economics and its most popular policy frameworks did not really focus on agriculture.[1] In fact, since the creation of the two Bretton Woods institutions after World War II, their proposed development strategies have changed quite often. Advocacy of policy frameworks centered on the provision of public investments to launch and support capital-intensive industries to "modernize" poor economies was the thrust of their strategy in the 1960s and 1970s. Macroeconomic stabilization and structural reforms (restrictive fiscal and monetary policies, privatization, deregulation, and liberalization) dominated their policies in the 1980s and 1990s, and the development of social sectors through better evaluation by randomization techniques of (micro) projects and programs that deliver their expected results has been their major focus since the early 2000s (Lin and Monga 2014). These evolving policy frameworks have reflected the changing intellectual paradigms that have characterized development thinking since its inception in the 1940s. It is true that at both the theoretical and policy levels, agriculture was not consistently and prominently featured in development strategies.

The charge that agricultural development has been left out of development theories and policies—especially since the late 1970s and the advent of free-market-inspired poverty-reduction strategies—is often amplified by important nongovernmental organizations working with peasants and farmers in developing countries, especially when they find themselves at the front line of humanitarian dramas and famines caused by natural disasters or by conflicts and wars. Why on earth would political leaders across the world not devote most of the available resources to supporting agriculture, they ask? To these advocates, the social benefits of setting that crucial sector as the top priority appear to be beyond dispute.

For developing economies, the theoretical case for agricultural transformation is indeed quite strong. In addition to the most obvious macroeconomic economic benefits (export and foreign exchange revenues and fiscal revenue), agricultural transformation pushes agricultural productivity to converge to economy-wide levels and generate positive growth externalities for other activities.

> Expanding agricultural production through technological change and trade creates important demands for the outputs of other sectors, notably fertilizer, transportation, commercial services, and construction. At the same time, agricultural households are often the basic market for a wide range of consumer goods that loom large in the early stages of industrial development—textiles and clothing, processed foods, kerosene and vegetable oils, aluminum hollowware, radios, bicycles, and construction materials for home improvements. (World Bank 1982, 44–45)

The virtuous circle goes further: a dynamic agricultural sector generates and sustains modern services in rural and urban areas, stimulating new activities of various kinds, from intermediaries such as brokers and underwriters to accountants and lawyers. Nonfarm enterprises (repair services, shops, basic public services) emerge and provide new sources of better livelihood for the poor.

At face value, agricultural development is therefore an obvious economic policy priority, not only for low-income countries but for the world community. "Everyone knows that the spectacular industrial revolution would not have been possible without the agricultural revolution that preceded it," wrote Ragnar Nurkse (1953, 52). Agricultural development also plays an important role as the first step toward industrialization. W. Arthur Lewis (1954, 433) offered a good explanation of one crucial aspect of that role: food production.

> If the capitalist sector produces no food, its expansion increases the demand for food, raises the price of food in terms of capitalist products, and so reduces profits. This is one sense in which industrialization is dependent upon agricultural improvement; it is not profitable to produce a growing volume of manufactures unless agricultural production is growing simultaneously. This is also why industrial and agrarian revolutions always go together, and why economies in which agriculture is stagnant do not show industrial development.

Despite these intellectual insights, the understanding of the role of agriculture in economic development has remained a challenge, and many researchers have highlighted the paradoxical dynamics of structural transformation processes (Clark 1940; Kuznets 1966; Chenery and Syrquin 1975). They have noted that, on the one hand, sustained economic growth in all regions of the world was characterized by the persistent declining importance of agriculture (irrespective of country conditions, the prevailing ideological postures, or the existing political, economic, and social institutions), mirroring the growing importance of the manufacturing and urban-industrial and modern service sectors. On the other hand, rapid agricultural development also appeared to be a precondition for sustained growth and economic development.

The paradox was only apparent. As noted by C. P. Timmer (1988, 277), "the need for rapid agricultural growth and for the decline in the agricultural sector's share of output and the labor force are not contradictory, of course, but the apparent paradox gave rise to a widespread misperception that agriculture is unimportant—that it does not require resources or a favorable policy environment—because its relative share of the economy declines." During the structural transformation process the share of agriculture in the economy (measured by its contribution to national income) declines steadily. At the same time, the share of labor working in the agricultural sector declines too but at a much slower pace. This differential creates a "structural lag" (Timmer 2014), which makes workers in the agricultural sector poorer than those in other sectors.

That transition typically also involves changes in demographics: the surplus labor moving out of agriculture into cities in search of higher-income job opportunities is often accompanied by a surge in birthrates (eventually followed by a decline). In successful cases of structural transformation where markets and governments play their respective roles effectively, these parallel transitions (sectoral and demographic) balance themselves out, and the economic conditions for workers in all sectors end up being generally comparable: real wages are the same, just as poverty levels are; labor, goods, and financial markets become interconnected, and there are good physical linkages allowing for commodity outputs to move from farms into the modern urban food systems. In sum, when structural transformation occurs smoothly, surplus labor moves out of low-productivity subsistence farming into higher-productivity modern sectors and allows sustained economic growth. Countries that experience it also achieve food security and record rapid reduction in hunger and poverty.

The analytical explanation of the apparent paradox of agriculture has been studied extensively (Johnston 1970, 1973; Anderson and Hayami 1986). First, with rising incomes in successful cases of structural transformation, the share of expenditures for food declines (the so-called Engel's Law). In a closed economy with constant prices, this phenomenon explains a big part of the declining share of agriculture in the economy—it does not matter how fast the agricultural sector grows. As a result, the gross value of sales of farm products will grow less than gross domestic product.[2] Second, in cases of successful structural transformations, the rapid increase in agricultural productivity due to technical change and the adoption of new technology typically leads to a decline in the long-run terms of trade of farm products. Such lower prices generally worsen the already lower demand created by Engel's Law and push workers out of the agricultural sectors. Despite their increased productivity levels, the remaining smaller number of farmers often feel the pain of lower demand for their products and lower prices, which explains why policy makers in all countries at any level of development feel compelled to provide agricultural subsidies (World Bank 1986).

In sum, the complex nature of the patterns of agricultural transformation, the delicate political economy issues of losers and winners among social groups, and the often ineffective policy choices made by policy makers largely explain the failed transformations that have plagued many poor countries. Such failures of agricultural transformation are often exacerbated by rapid population growth, the pervasiveness of small farms with little possibilities for scale economies, and the forced exodus of workers off the farm and into low-productivity jobs in the rural nonfarm sector or in the urban informal and services sector. The two puzzling stylized facts that created the illusion of an agricultural paradox (agricultural growth and decline of the relative importance of the sector in GDP) are therefore not mutually exclusive as assumed by early development economists. Yet the mainstream intellectual paradigm for development in the 1950s hastily suggested that agriculture should be squeezed on behalf of the more dynamic sectors of the economy.

Fortunately, the process of agricultural transformation and its potential benefits to the entire economy are now well understood, beyond the initial insights provided by Nurkse and Lewis. They can be summarized in four phases, which can be presented in a linear manner to facilitate the exposition but do not necessarily occur in a sequential manner. Historical and cross-section analyses show that the process generally starts with an increase in agricultural productivity per worker, which creates a surplus. In the second phase, the surplus can be tapped through taxation, government intervention, or factor flows and utilized to develop the nonagricultural sector.[3] Resources flow better out of agriculture when rural and factor markets are better integrated with those in the rest of the economy. Well-functioning markets and well-targeted government interventions to improve potentially profitable infrastructure can allow for a third phase in which the agricultural sector is progressively integrated into the macro economy. In the fourth phase, agricultural productivity rises to reach that in other sectors, and the role of agriculture becomes indistinguishable from that of others.

But the unfolding of this four-phase process is always delicate, especially since it involves challenging political economy issues and policy frameworks that vary in each phase and requires strong, transparent, and well-informed collaboration between government institutions, stakeholders in the agricultural sectors (farmer's associations, international development institutions, etc.), and the private sector at large (including investors, traders, and financial institutions). Policy makers must be well aware of the tradeoffs and have a good sense of which particular social groups gain or lose, as workers move out of rural agriculture to gain higher wages in the urban industrial sectors. Green revolutions have been launched in many parts of the developing world, but few have delivered the expected results. They often failed for various reasons: adequate rainfall, irrigation, or flood control was not available to farmers; the technology adopted and promoted by governments did not fit the country climate and soils; national research systems were not available or effective to support farmers in their attempts to adapt international varieties to local conditions; the lack of insurance products led farmers to try too many crops on very small plots, with little prospects for reaching the critical mass that would be necessary to make them credible players in competitive markets often dominated by large international groups; in countries with rigid land laws and regulations and no land reform, prices and other incentives were inadequate and farmers could not access financial systems; government policy failed to encourage the use of collective action mechanisms by farmers (especially cooperatives); transport and marketing network were nonexistent or deficient (in some African countries farmers are still more than a day's walk from the nearest road); and so on.

Because of the failure of agricultural transformation in many developing countries, the largest segment of the labor force generally found itself trapped in low-productivity subsistence agriculture, or in informal sector activities. There have also been instances where the agricultural transformation process remains stalled at the first or second phase, leaving farmers highly vulnerable to shocks of various natures. For instance, cotton producers in West Africa or sugar producers in Thailand have long suffered the negative consequences of declining world prices owing to overproduction caused by subsidies granted to farmers in the Unites States or in Europe.[4] In low-income countries where the formal sector of the economy is very small by definition, policy makers are also easily tempted to overrely on agricultural taxation as their means for financing development needs and for accommodating the desires of urban constituencies with strong political power (Bates 1981).

Clearly, development thinkers have too often neglected the agricultural sector. However, the temptation to correct such neglect by making agricultural development the ultimate goal of economic development would also be a mistake. For developing countries, the appropriate policy response to decades of failed agricultural transformation requires much more than channeling limited fiscal and administrative resources to the agriculture sector.

AVOIDING THE TRAP OF ROMANTICIZING RURAL POVERTY

What should be done in low-income countries to raise agricultural productivity and ignite sustained growth and structural transformation? Lessons from economic theory and from historical experiences (Alston and Pardey 2014; Lin 1992) suggest that development strategies should aim at stimulating agriculture but with the clear objective of quickly moving resources (especially surplus labor) out of there so that fast-growing industrial sectors with comparative advantage can use them for the benefit of the entire economy. No country can escape poverty by maintaining a substantial fraction of its labor force in underperforming sectors—and it should be acknowledged that because of its very nature, agriculture always remains less productive than industry (especially manufacturing) and modern services. Yet these lessons do not appear to be fully integrated into the new knowledge about development put forth by some leading development agencies and players. The need to improve agricultural productivity in rural farms across the developing world is too quickly translated into the adoption of policies aimed at keeping such farms small.

Raising agricultural productivity in small farms is indeed the most reliable pathway out of poverty. "The world's agriculture and food system is now outdated and inefficient," says Bill Gates (2012).

> Countries, food agencies, and donors aren't working together in a focused and coordinated way to provide the help small farmers need, when they need it. . . . According to estimates from our team at the foundation, it is possible for small farmers in South Asia and sub-Saharan Africa to double or almost triple their yields, respectively, in the next 20 years—while preserving the land for future generations. This is an ambitious goal. To meet it, farmers in both regions will have to increase productivity three to five times faster than they have been doing over the past 20 years.

Gates rightly observes that in order to meet any appropriately ambitious productivity target, one should take advantage of the digital revolution that is multiplying the rate of agricultural innovation. He points to important developments that can stimulate agriculture: from genomic science to information technology, new discoveries are indeed making it possible to solve old problems. Bringing today's breakthrough agricultural science and technology to poor farmers would generate many private and social benefits.

But such a strategy should not leave out the critical element of a viable policy framework: the need to facilitate industrial development, which can occur only with the development of nonfarm sectors that eventually absorb much of the resources currently allocated to agriculture. The high prevalence of labor in small agricultural farms has led some development institutions to conclude too optimistically that focusing on small farming could be a viable economic development strategy (Gates Foundation Africa Strategy). It is illusory to expect that the strengthening of micro farms that exploit small pieces of land across Africa or South Asia would constitute an effective approach to economic transformation and prosperity. While subsistence farming allows millions of poor people around the world to survive, its pervasiveness should not be celebrated as a worthwhile development objective. It actually reflects the failure of development thinking on how to generate shared growth in countries where large segments of the labor force find themselves trapped for centuries in low-productivity rural activities.

Because of the small size of their farms, the meager economic value of their land (often due to laws and regulations), the lack of transportation, the limited access to finance, and the deficit of knowledge (due to the absence of research and extension services), farmers in poor countries feel compelled to grow too many different crops, often in places where there are no irrigation systems. Marketing systems are nonexistent or fractured and ineffective. For sustained growth to occur in a manner that reduces poverty, most of the labor force in poor economies will eventually have to move out of agriculture and into industry (mainly manufacturing) and modern services. Otherwise the quest for prosperity may remain a mere slogan. It can therefore be said that excessive focus on small farming without a clear medium- and long-term exit strategy from agriculture poses the risk of relying on false development solutions that actually romanticize the fight against poverty.

Agriculture must be transformed from being a subsistence sector dominated by small farms (even with technology) to becoming large-scale, mechanized entities that use modern seeds and fertilizers and can access well-functioning national, regional, and international markets via global value chains. Small farms that rely on a large number of crops must be aggregated into cooperatives so that they can effectively respond to demand-side market signals on the types and quality of products that are economically viable. Governments, the private sector, and international development institutions should work together to build public investment for transportation and public goods institutions (research centers and marketing services), create the appropriate incentive systems, facilitate the insertion of farmers and cooperatives into global value chains, provide market information that is too costly for any single farmer to produce, and build the quality infrastructure necessary to ensure effective linkages with international markets. In addition, carefully designed land reforms are needed in most low-income countries (Deininger 2003; Deininger, Selod, and Burns 2011).

"Illusion is the first of all pleasures," famously said Voltaire. This may partly explain why some development thinkers who recommend that poor countries focus their development strategies on agricultural development (through support to small farms) forget to stress the ultimate goal of getting most of the labor force into higher-productivity industrial and modern services sectors. While the adoption of new crops and new technologies and the appropriate research and extension policy framework could help improve agricultural productivity, in the end, small farms should aim at becoming part of the larger groups of domestic and international groups that achieve economies of scale and participate effectively in global value chains. No matter how productive these small farms become, policy makers should not be under any illusion: a viable economic development strategy for any low-income economy requires that industrial development be its centerpiece. This is confirmed by the analyses of the main reasons for the decline in global poverty rates.

UNDERSTANDING THE DYNAMICS OF GLOBAL GROWTH AND ITS POTENTIAL DIVIDENDS

There is a new consensus on global poverty's broad empirical trends. For the world as a whole, poverty as a percentage of population has declined over the period 1980 to 2010 from just below 50 percent to 17.7 percent (table 5.1), and this decline has been monotonic over time (Ravallion and Chen 2012).

But the world is still a very unstable place, because the poverty story is incomplete: although many nations mirrored the global trend by seeing a steady decline over the thirty-year period (most notably the large middle-income economies of China, Brazil, India, Indonesia, and Mexico), for several nations, including Nigeria, Bangladesh, and Tanzania, poverty rose between 1980 and 1990. As noted by the World Bank's chief economist, "Global poverty dropped because China's and Mexico's poverty dropped very sharply during this period. The overall global poverty rate of 17.7 percent in 2010 hides the fact that in some countries, like Democratic Republic of Congo and Nigeria, it is extremely high, with a majority of people still living below the poverty line" (Basu 2013, 5).

Therefore tackling poverty remains a major global challenge; billions of people are still trapped in poverty not only in low-income countries but

	c. 1980	1990	2000	2010
Congo, Democratic Republic				87.7
Nigeria	53.9	61.9	63.1	54.4
Bangladesh	60.6	70.2	58.6	43.3
India	55.5	49.4		32.7
Ethiopia	66.2		60.5	30.7
Indonesia	62.8	54.3	47.7	18.1
China	84	60.2	35.6	11.8
Colombia		6.3	17.9	8.1
Brazil	13.6	17.2	11.8	6.1
Mexico	12.8	4	5.5	0.7

Source: World Bank (PovcalNet).

also in middle-income and even high-income countries (although relative poverty is typically the indicator used in the last group). Partly because of these general trends in many populous countries, the World Bank's Board of Governors[5] adopted in 2013 two overarching goals to guide its work in the decades ahead: first, to end extreme, chronic poverty in the world by 2030—extreme poverty defined as living on less than $1.25 (PPP-adjusted) per person per day; and second, to promote shared prosperity in every society, defined as an increase in the per capita income growth of the poorest 40 percent of people in each country.[6]

The goal of development is to help countries escape from low-income status and to help middle-income countries move to high-income status. Even in the poorest nations, farmers, workers, businesspeople, civil society, and government officials strive to reach that goal. Their commitment and energy should be enough to convince even skeptics that a world free of poverty is achievable. The often disappointing results feed cynicism and the self-fulfilling prophecy that some countries are destined to remain poor. Yet nothing could be further from the truth.

Moreover, even some countries that have achieved high growth rates, labor force participation, and employment are still confronted with poverty challenges. According to the International Labour Organization (ILO), worldwide working poverty dropped drastically over the 2000–2010 decade, but progress stalled in 2013. An estimated 375 million workers are still living on less than $1.25 a day, compared with 600 million in the early 2000s—a 12 percent drop per year on average. This shows that creating decent jobs is a pressing global development priority and should be at the heart of the development agenda as the international community adopts new development goals for post-2015. As noted by ILO director-general Guy Ryder, "overcoming employment vulnerability and informality are key to overcoming poverty in a sustainable way" (ILO 2014).

In searching for a strategy to achieve sustained and inclusive growth, of which employment generation is a crucial feature, policy makers in developing countries should start with lessons learned from successful experiences. Economic historians who have examined the evolution of growth performance since the beginning of time tend to divide it into three distinct periods: The first, which spanned most of human history up to the middle of the eighteenth century, was marked by static living standards, despite population growth—the so-called Malthusian conditions. The second, which lasted from about 1750 to the 1820s, was characterized by some improvement in living standards and changes in demographic trends (higher fertility rates and lower mortality rates). The third, observed initially in England at the end of the first quarter of the nineteenth century, has been that of modern economic growth (Cameron 1993). Deciphering the mystery of modern economic growth and explaining convergence and divergence have been major topics of research, especially since the 1950s. While much progress has been achieved on theoretical and empirical grounds, much remains to be understood on the policy front (Lin and Monga 2010).

Table 5.2 may be a good place to start making sense of the wheels of history—and to start deriving some of the first-order principles of success. It lists the economies that have recorded high growth rates for long periods and have succeeded in lifting their previously backward nations from low- to middle- or even high-income status.

These success stories are more than just stylized facts: these country cases—each with different histories and economic conditions but with many similar features—demonstrate that fast, sustained growth is possible in various country contexts and endowments. These "graduations" from low- to middle- and high-income economy status have brought enormous

Economy	Period of High Growth**	Per Capita Income at Beginning and in 2005	
Botswana	1960–2005	210	3,800
Brazil	1950–1980	960	4,000
China	1961–2005	105	1,400
Hong Kong-China*	1960–1997	3,100	29,900
Indonesia	1966–1997	200	900
Japan*	1950–1983	3,500	39,600
Korea, Rep. of*	1960–2001	1,100	13,200
Malaysia	1967–1997	790	4,400
Malta*	1963–1994	1,100	9,600
Oman	1960–1999	950	9,000
Singapore*	1967–2002	2,200	25,400
Taiwan-China*	1965–2002	1,500	16,400
Thailand	1960–1997	330	2,400

Source: World Bank, World Development Indicators.

*Economies that have reached industrialized countries' per capita income levels.

**Period in which GDP growth was 7 percent per year or more.

benefits to the world economy, and they are evidence of the potential that lifting the poor from their current status could contribute to global peace.

Economic progress by large economies has also shown that global growth need not be a zero-sum game, and that in fact there are global dividends to shared prosperity. The examples of remarkable economic successes listed in table 5.2 invalidate the widely held but inaccurate belief that countries compete in global markets the way corporations do—the underlying assumption being that there is a fixed stock of prosperity out there to be shared among nations, with the most aggressive ones gaining the largest portion. Criticizing the popular but misleading rhetoric of competitiveness, Paul Krugman (1996, 5) has rightly noted that the idea that a country's economic fortunes are largely determined by its success on world markets is a hypothesis, not a necessary truth; as a practical, empirical matter, that hypothesis is flatly wrong. That is, it is simply not the case that the world's leading nations are to any important degree in economic competition with each other, or that any of their major economic problems can be attributed to failures to compete on world markets. The growing obsession in most advanced nations with international competitiveness should be seen, not as a well-founded concern, but as a view held in the face of overwhelming contrary evidence.

Although performance on international trade is indeed a key component of economic performance for most countries—especially for developing economies whose domestic demand is limited owing to their low income—other factors such as the exchange rate also influence growth and living standards. In theory there could be situations where a country that is making steady progress on producing goods and services finds itself forced to continuously devalue its currency to maintain a competitive edge over others, which would eventually diminish the real income and living standards of its citizens (because the deteriorating terms of trade outweigh domestic growth). But economic history and empirical evidence presented by Krugman (1994) on the evolution of several major economies (United States, EU countries, and Japan) suggest that this has not been the case: "In each case, the growth rate of living standards essentially equals the growth rate of domestic productivity—not productivity relative to competitors, but simply domestic productivity. Even though world trade is larger than ever before, national living standards are overwhelmingly determined by domestic factors rather than by some competition for world markets." This is partly explained by the fact that exports still represent a small share of the value added in some of these advanced economies (most notably in the United States), implying that they produce goods and services predominantly for their own use.

Moreover, countries are not in competition with other economies in the same way that corporations are with one another. Unlike large economies that consume most of their own outputs, firms hardly sell their outputs to their own workers. And in contrast to corporations that generally compete at one another's expense, national economies are often one another's main export markets and main suppliers of imports. As a result, one country's excellent economic performance need not be at the expense of another. In fact, and this has been shown consistently throughout history, the economic success of one country generally has strong positive spillovers effects for its "competitors," as it enlarges their export markets and stimulates mutually profitable investment possibilities.

The global dividends from prosperity in developing countries are not just theoretical derivations from economic modeling. Consider China's emergence as the world's largest economy and its momentous growth performance, which some have described as a potential threat to global stability.[7] To the contrary, its spectacular growth over the past three decades has made China not only a driver for world development but also a stabilizing force in the world economy, as demonstrated by China's role during the East Asian financial crisis in the late 1990s and the global crisis in 2008.[8]

Speaking at the Asia-Pacific Economic Summit in 2014, President Barack Obama reminded the world that even the most dominant economy in the world still benefits enormously from sustained growth in developing countries. He noted that the existing trade and investment relationship benefits both China and the United States. China is the fastest-growing export market for the United States. Chinese direct investment in the United States rose sixfold in just the five-year period from 2008 to 2013. Chinese firms directly employ a rapidly growing number of Americans.

> And all these things mean jobs for the American people, and deepening these ties will mean more jobs and opportunity for both of our peoples. . . . [In 2013 alone], 1.8 million Chinese visitors to the United States contributed $21 billion to our economy and supported more than 100,000 American jobs. . . . Asia's largest export market is the United States—that benefits American consumers because it has led to more affordable goods and services. Six of America's top 10 export markets are APEC economies, and more than 60 percent of our exports—over $1 trillion worth of goods and services—are purchased by APEC economies. That supports millions of American jobs. So the work that APEC members have done together over the years has lowered tariffs, cut shipping costs, and made it cheaper, easier, and faster to do business—and that supports good jobs in all of our nations. (Obama 2014)

Today's rapidly evolving world economy is opening important opportunities not just for the two largest economies (the United States and China) but also for other high-, middle-, and low-income countries. In the aftermath of the recent global recession, R. B. Zoellick (2010) aptly described the new economic landscape as follows:

> If 1989 saw the end of the "Second World" with Communism's demise, then 2009 saw the end of what was known as the "Third World": We are now in a new, fast-evolving multipolar world economy—in which some developing countries are emerging as economic powers; others are moving toward becoming additional poles of growth; and some are struggling to attain their potential within this new system—where North and South, East and West, are now points on a compass, not economic destinies. . . . We are witnessing a move toward multiple poles of growth as middle classes grow in developing countries, billions of people join the world economy, and new patterns of integration combine regional intensification with global openness.

During the first decade of this century a burst of convergence occurred as developing countries grew substantially faster than high-income countries. With this superior growth, widespread across developing regions, the world has entered a new era, with emerging economies becoming new growth poles. In the 1980s and 1990s, among the top five contributors to global growth, all except China were G7 industrialized countries. But in 2000–2012 all except the United States were emerging economies—with China having become the top contributor.

Consistent with previous historical patterns, that shift in economic weight is likely to produce major benefits for the world economy, with positive effects for both high-income and developing countries. For high-income countries the growth of emerging economies will expand markets for their exports of capital goods and intermediate goods. For many developing countries that are still major producers of agricultural and natural resource commodities, higher consumption and production levels in the new growth poles will continue to support adequate prices for their commodity exports. In addition, firms and governments in emerging economies will provide funds for infrastructure and natural resource investment in developing countries.

These benefits are already happening—and are likely to continue into the future. Propelled by domestic demand for raw materials, Brazil has rapidly expanded investment and trade with Africa—with imports from the continent rising from $3 billion in 2000 to $18.5 billion in 2008.[9] Similarly, bilateral trade between China and Africa increased from $10 billion in 2000 to $91 billion in 2014, and China's investment in Africa jumped from $490 million in 2003 to $9.33 billion in 2009 (China Information Office of State Council 2010). Indeed, Chinese finance has a growing role in Africa, the developing region that faces the greatest constraints on access to finance (Wang 2009). Meanwhile, the Indian government—observing that five of the world's twelve fastest-growing economies are in sub-Saharan Africa, a continent richly endowed with natural resources—has announced plans to invest $1.5 trillion in African infrastructure development in the next decade.[10] More important than these beneficial trade and financial flows, the dynamic growth of the new poles will provide golden opportunities for industrialization in lower-income countries, an essential ingredient for growth and prosperity.

INCLUSIVE AND SUSTAINED GROWTH REQUIRES STRUCTURAL CHANGE

The realization that sustained growth is possible and has been achieved by countries of different sizes, economic structures, historical backgrounds, and geographic locations[11] leads to the next logical questions: What made it happen? What important principle did policy makers in successful economies understand that has eluded others? What forces, mechanisms, and institutions should be in place to foster sustained and inclusive growth? What main principles should govern economic policies and strategies to generate shared prosperity? And given that many growth episodes have occurred that could not be sustained, what sequencing problems must be integrated into an economic development strategy to make it viable?

The main answer to these questions lies in the simple but disciplined acknowledgment by successful policy makers that modern economic growth is a process of continuous structural changes in industry and technology and in political and socioeconomic institutions. This process did not appear until the eighteenth century—before that time every country in the world was poor and agrarian. But since then it has profoundly changed the world, especially successful high-income industrialized countries. The kind of structural transformation dynamics that brings about human well-being takes place only because of changes in technology, in comparative advantage, and in the global economy.

The definition by Simon Kuznets (1971) of a country's economic growth as "a long-term rise in capacity to supply increasingly diverse economic goods to its population, this growing capacity based on advancing technology and the institutional and ideological adjustments that it demands" helps us understand why. Although this definition reflects the world of the 1960s and 1970s that was dominated by closed economies and therefore predates some of the major features of globalization (that is, the role of trade with other nations as a major source of growth and the interlinkages that openness brings to any economy), it has four key components that are equally important and mutually reinforcing:

→ Growth is to be understood as the *cause* of the sustained rise in the supply of goods; thinking about it as such (and not just the *result* of the dynamics of higher levels of demand and supply) focuses on the sources of that process and on the respective and complementary roles of market mechanisms and state action that may be needed to facilitate it.

→ Growth should be the reflection of the diversification process; clearly, many economies have done well by relying for a long period on exploiting a single commodity or a small set of products. But they tend to be small, or they eventually manage to use the income derived from the initial products to develop a broader source of income.

→ Technological progress (through appropriation, imitation, or innovation) is the most sustainable source of long-term economic growth. Countries willing and able to continuously exploit technological advances must prepare their factor endowment (labor, capital) to do so through macroeconomic and sectoral policies that induce human and physical capital accumulation.

→ For technological progress to serve its purpose in the growth process, it must take place within an environment that is conducive to business development and innovation. This implies constant rethinking, validating, and updating of the prevailing intellectual frameworks, rules, and regulations that govern the business climate in the country.

In searching for the causes of structural change, successful policy makers have understood that the main engines are productivity growth and factor accumulation. They also have distinguished between "fundamental" (or first-order) conditions and "proximate" (second- or third-order) conditions. They have not treated proximate causes as ultimate causes. Long before Joseph Schumpeter and Robert Solow suggested that most growth comes from knowledge and innovation, successful policy makers realized that simple factor accumulation quickly leads to diminishing returns and certainly does not produce structural change. If the economy does not undergo the kind of structural transformation that creates business opportunities and increasingly large amounts of wealth, then simply accumulating human capital through education may result in more well-trained but unemployed workers. That was true during the Industrial Revolution and remains true today. A case in point is that of several North African countries, where education indicators improved considerably in the past decades, but structural change did not occur. The disappointing examples of countries like Tunisia, where a first-rate higher education system has not yielded enough benefits in sustained growth and employment generation, highlights that education is a proximate rather than a fundamental cause of structural change.

Structural change can then be analyzed from at least three perspectives: changes in sectoral contributions to growth and industrial structure, technological upgrading, and diversification.

Sectoral shifts. Shifting a poor economy's resources out of traditional agriculture and other low-productivity primary activities and expanding the "modern" sectors (including nontraditional agriculture) have always been at the core of the sustained productivity gains that characterize economic development. Economists have established at least since the early 1960s that manufacturing has always played a larger role in total output in richer countries, and that countries with higher incomes are typically those with a substantially bigger economic contribution from the transport and machinery sectors.

Margaret McMillan and Dani Rodrik (2011, 1) observe that "the countries that manage to pull out of poverty and get richer are those that are able to diversify away from agriculture and other traditional products. As labor and other resources move from agriculture into modern economic activities, overall productivity rises and incomes expand. The speed with which this structural transformation takes place is the key factor that differentiates successful countries from unsuccessful ones." In fact, as noted by a recent UNIDO report (2009), only in circumstances such as extraordinary abundance of land or resources have countries succeeded in developing without industrializing.

In addition to the generally much greater productivity in manufacturing than in traditional agriculture, the main reason for the growth in industrialization is that its potential is virtually unlimited, especially in an increasingly globalized world. As agricultural or purely extractive activities expand, they usually face shortages of land, water, or other resources. By contrast, manufacturing easily benefits from economies of scale and opportunities for further diversification and upgrading. Thanks to new inventions and technological development, and to changes in global trade rules, transport and unit costs of production have declined substantially during the past decades. Today almost any small country can access the world market, find a niche, and establish itself as a global manufacturing place. For example, Qiaotou and Yiwu, two once small Chinese villages, have become powerhouses, producing more than two-thirds of the world's buttons and zippers, respectively. As their income rose and capital accumulated, they continued diversifying and upgrading to other, more sophisticated products.

Production structure. Changing factor endowments (mainly physical and human capital) are an important first element of structural change. Their evolving dynamics contribute to shape the evolution of countries' productive structure—and economic potential—and affect aggregate economic performance. Recent empirical work has highlighted the relationship between the rate of GDP growth and the sector structure of the economy. GDP growth is often broken down into two components: one due to industry-level growth with a given industrial structure, and another due to changes in the relative importance of industries growing at different rates. This helps explain how firm dynamics contribute to these sectoral patterns through entry, exit, and reallocating resources across firms within sectors and across sectors (Haltiwanger et al. 2009, 2004). Because total factor productivity is the main driver of long-run growth, the analysis of firm-level data can shed light on the contributions of firm and industry dynamics to allocative efficiency, productivity, and growth and on what variations can be linked to the development level or the policy framework.

Looking at whether certain production bundles are preferable from the growth and development point of view, other studies have highlighted the existence of a "resource curse" in countries with rich natural resources, or they have advocated the desirability of high-tech goods and the advantages of high-value industries. The resource curse argument, which can be linked back to the so-called Prebisch-Singer hypothesis, is sometimes an overly broad generalization that is inconsistent with empirical evidence.[12] Throughout history, many natural-resource-rich countries such as the United States, the Scandinavian countries, and Australia have been able to diversify away from commodities and launch their industrialization process. As for the high-tech/high-value-added structural transformation strategy, it may not be optimal for poor countries. While the shift of resources (capital and labor) to industries with high value added per worker is an appealing formula for success, poor countries typically cannot achieve this quickly. The reason is that industries with high value added per worker are also those with high ratios of capital to labor—often in traditional heavy manufacturing.[13]

Export composition. Because many developing (and African) countries will have to rely on trade to sustain dynamic growth, the composition of the export basket is an important variable of structural change. The analysis of patterns of structural change also helps to assess the quality of different export bundles and to differentiate between high- and low-productivity goods, labor-intensive and capital-intensive goods, natural-resource-based goods, goods with greater potential for quality upgrading, and so on. It appears that *how* a country exports matters. One main observation from a recent study by Daniel Lederman and William Maloney (2011) is that externalities and rents are not associated with all goods equally; therefore government interventions are needed to encourage the development of certain goods more than the market naturally would. Under certain conditions, even service exports[14] can become a major engine of economic growth.

Technological upgrading and innovation are indispensable ingredients for long-run productivity growth. They generally involve externalities and coordination issues that if unaddressed often lead to too low a rate of technological upgrading and require some form of intervention. Globalization has enhanced developing countries' access to the flow of new ideas and new technologies, yet many African countries have not exploited the benefits of backwardness—often because of structural barriers such as poor education and infrastructure.

Kuznets (1966) pointed out the crucial role of structural transformation as the fundamental driver and result of sustained economic growth. Using a three-sector model, his work documented some important aspects of structural transformation and the emergence of "modern economic growth." It also highlighted the dynamics of institutions and infrastructures—an idea that can be traced back to Karl Marx. Kuznets observed in his Nobel Lecture that "advancing technology is the permissive source of economic growth, but it is only a potential, a necessary condition, in itself not sufficient. If technology is to be employed efficiently and widely, and, indeed, if its own progress is to be stimulated by such use, institutional and ideological adjustments must be made to effect the proper use of innovations generated by the advancing stock of human knowledge."

Economic theory has established that most increases in standard of living are related to acquiring knowledge—to "learning" (Joseph Schumpeter). Most increases in per capita income arise from advances in technology—about 70 percent of growth comes from sources other than factor accumulation. In developing countries, a substantial part of growth arises from closing the technology (or knowledge) gap between themselves and those at the forefront. And within any country, there is enormous opportunity for productivity improvement simply by closing the gap between best practices and average practices. If improvements in living standards come mainly from diffusing knowledge, learning strategies must be at the heart of the development strategies (Robert Solow).

In medium- and high-income countries in particular, a strong industrial sector creates more incentives for research and development and opens up opportunities for more resources for innovation, which in turn are better internalized by firms and even often shared among firms ("learning to learn and cross-border knowledge flows" as Stiglitz and Greenwald [2015] put it). Industrial development is also associated with higher levels of human capital formation, including public support for human capital accumulation. It also leads to the development of a robust financial sector. In sum, from a productivity perspective, the advantages of industrial development are numerous: high returns to scale, long-lived returns from continuity (learning to learn), and high rates of diffusion.

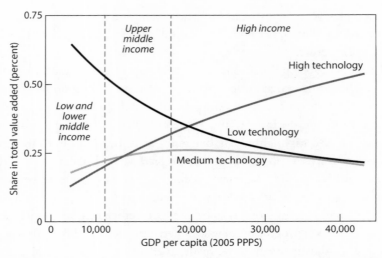

Figure 5.1. Changes in shares of manufacturing value added by income and technology group, 1963–2007. *Source*: UNIDO (2013, 61).

In low-income countries none of the Sustainable Development Goals (SDGs) adopted in September 2015 by the United Nations can be achieved without industrial development. Industrial development ensures that resources (labor, capital, knowledge) are transferred from low- to high-productivity sectors and geographical areas, including the migration of unskilled rural labor to unskilled labor-intensive industries, and labor productivity is increased substantially through learning, education, and workforce development.

Empirical analysis of the different types of technology in the industrial sector reveals a stylized fact that suggests the need for self-restraint, patience, and pragmatism in the design of a growth strategy: countries from all over the world generally exhibit a large share of low-tech industries (typically labor-intensive) at low levels of income. As GDP per capita increases, the share of low-tech industries declines rapidly while the shares of medium-tech (mainly capital-intensive and resource-processing industries) and high-tech (capital- and technology-intensive industries) increase.

Figure 5.1, from a UNIDO report, illustrates these fundamental patterns. The low-tech industries have the highest share of the manufacturing value added for low-income economies. But their contribution to growth declines with economic progress. Somewhere around a GDP per capita

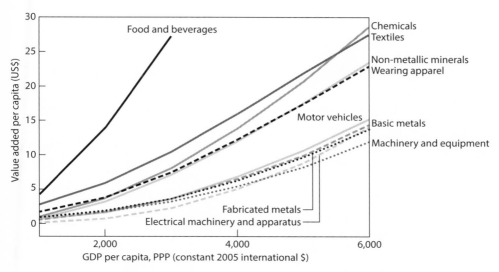

Figure 5.2. Change in value added per capita by income, low and lower-middle incomes, 1963–2007. *Source*: Haraguchi (2014).

of $20,000 only the share of high-tech industries increases to sustain economic growth.

Perhaps the most positive news from empirical research is that at low income levels, there are quite a few (mainly low- and medium-tech) industries that provide sources of growth. The analysis of ten industries at the two-digit level of International Standard Industrial Classification Revision (these industries typically account for more than 75 percent of value added and employment in manufacturing) shows that food and beverages, textiles, and wearing apparel provide the highest levels of value added for low-income countries (figure 5.2).

Economic diversification and agglomeration externalities. The study of economic diversification—another element of structural change that can be defined as the distribution of output, value added, and employment across industries—also provides important insights for economic development. Empirical research has often found that poor economies that are more diversified tend to have higher income levels per capita. Sectoral *diversification* in early development stages is generally accompanied by geographic *agglomeration*. In the words of I. Imbs and R. Wacziarg (2003, 2010), the range of industries expands and factors are allocated increasingly equally across sectors. At the same time, new sectors tend to localize in specific regions. Regions become more different. Such trends typically hold until countries reach an income level of approximately $9,000 per capita, after which more income per capita is then associated with increased specialization. In fact, sectoral concentration in later development stages is accompanied by geographic de-agglomeration. The range of activities produced across all regions is reduced, and the location of economic activities seems to matter much less. The location of production is of particular importance as it allows for (or impedes) agglomeration externalities, a key element for improving productivity and exploiting economies of scale.

These insights highlight the large scope of structural change that occurs in successful economies over time. They must be complemented with an examination of the dynamics of sectoral contributions to growth, the factors that help or hinder the reallocation of resources, and growth and employment generation.

STRUCTURAL CHANGE OCCURS MAINLY THROUGH INDUSTRIALIZATION

Industrialization is the main engine for structural change.[15] It provides the best opportunities for improving productivity, increasing output, and generating employment. On the whole, countries that have achieved sustained, inclusive growth over long periods, created enough full-time jobs to keep large fractions of their labor force employed, and moved from low- to middle- and even high-income status have been able to develop industries that are competitive domestically and internationally and have required these industries to be consistent with their comparative advantage (Lin and Monga 2011). Virtually no country in the world has been able to move from low- to middle- and high-income status without industrialization. It has played a key role in sustained growth acceleration processes that eventually transform economies from "poor" to "rich."

In the early phases of modern economic growth, which started with the Industrial Revolution, manufacturing played a larger role in successful countries' total output, and their higher incomes were associated with a substantially bigger role of the transport and machinery sectors. Manufacturing can reap economies of scale through geographic concentration. "This is most obvious at the plant level: the very idea of a plant is to bring

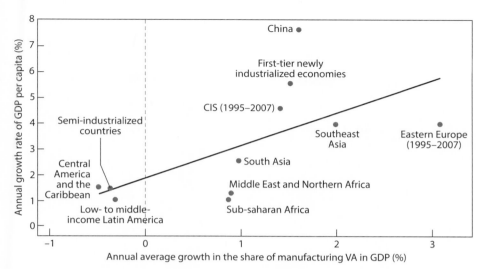

Figure 5.3. Manufacturing value added and economic growth, selected countries and regions, 1970–2007. *Source*: Alcorta (2014).

machinery and workers together in a single location. However, it also applies to the location of firms engaged in the same activity. By clustering together, similar firms reduce each other's costs" (UNIDO 2009, xv). Throughout the nineteenth and twentieth centuries, countries in North America, Western Europe, and Asia were able to transform their economies from agrarian to industrial, which included a rapidly growing services sector fueled in large part by the multiplier effect of manufacturing (figure 5.3). As a result, they built prosperous middle classes and raised their living standards.

Manufacturing still matters for employment generation. World manufacturing jobs increased from 262 million in 1970 to 471 million in 2009 and still represent 16.3 percent of global employment (UNIDO 2013). That positive trend has been steady in developing countries (figure 5.4).

Job creation in developing economies, preferably in the formal sector, is a precondition for achieving the Sustainable Development Goals. This requires integrating into the active labor force both skilled and unskilled or low-skilled people who are currently unemployed or underemployed. In low-income countries whose endowment structure is dominated by low-skilled labor, only inclusive sustainable industrialization provides

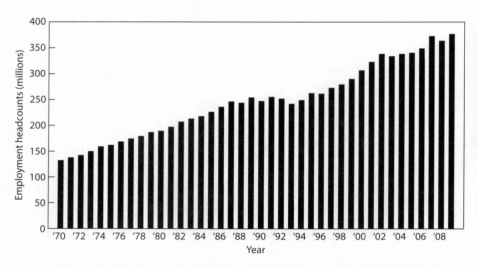

Figure 5.4. Manufacturing employment in developing countries, 1970–2009.
Source: Alcorta (2014).

employment. Employment creation is the single most important tool for eradicating poverty and helping people everywhere develop human capital and soft skills, which eventually give them the means for improving their health and productivity (World Bank 2012).

Decent employment also converts excluded women into empowered and active citizens. And it converts even the most unskilled people in the labor force into productive agents and taxpayers, which generates sustainable growth and allows governments to produce the financial resources needed for building infrastructure and providing public services and utilities. Inclusive and sustainable industrialization, which helps working families gain new and stable sources of income, is the most effective strategy to *end hunger and achieve food security and adequate nutrition for all*. It involves moving the labor force out of subsistence agriculture and low-productivity informal activities into more productive, value-added-generation activities, including in the agricultural sector.

Manufacturing can also provide equal opportunities to people across social groups and geographical areas and reduce inequality. It is the best way to *promote sustainable consumption and production patterns and build inclusive, safe, and sustainable cities and human settlements*. Given that economic growth cannot be sustained in developing countries without further and better integration into the world's economy and global value chains, inclusive sustainable industrialization is the appropriate platform for establishing mutually beneficial partnerships among low-, medium-, and high-income countries. It is the ideal framework for negotiating the optimal patterns and conditions for trade and for circulating private capital and aid flows. By creating the right incentives for designing and implementing profitable new models of cooperation and durable and productive business ventures, industrial development ensures that all parties have incentives to search for environmentally sensible deals. It can therefore help *address climate change and other environmental concerns while creating the optimal conditions for building peaceful and inclusive societies, rule of law, and effective and capable institutions.*

Empirical analyses confirm that manufacturing has evolved and changed the world economy's dynamics.[16] Profound changes in geopolitical relations among world nations, the widespread growth of digital information, the decline of transportation costs, the development of physical and financial infrastructure and computerized manufacturing technologies, and proliferating bilateral and multilateral trade agreements have contributed to the globalization of manufacturing. These developments have permitted the decentralization of supply chains into independent but coherent global networks that allow transnational firms to locate various parts of their businesses in different places around the world. The creative design of products, the sourcing of materials and components, and the manufacturing of products can now be done more cheaply and more efficiently from virtually any region of the planet. Final goods and services are customized and packaged to satisfy the needs of customers in faraway markets.

The globalization of manufacturing (figure 5.5) has thus allowed developed economies to benefit from lower-cost products, the lower cost driven by the lower production wages in developing countries such as China, India, Bangladesh, Costa Rica, Mexico, and Brazil that create jobs and learning opportunities in these formerly poor nations. The intensity of these exchanges has led to new forms of competition and codependency.

Technological developments and new sources of economic growth have generated skepticism about the economic virtues of manufacturing and have even led some researchers to question whether "manufacturing still matters" (Ghani and O'Connell 2014). Manufacturing's share of global value added has declined steadily over the past nearly thirty years as the

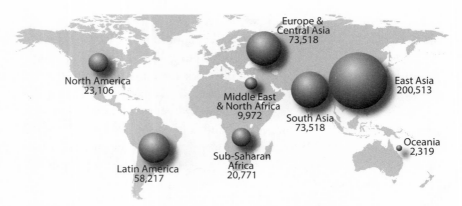

Figure 5.5. Global distribution of employment in manufacturing, 2009 (in thousands). *Source*: Alcorta (2014).

global value added of services has grown. In 1985 manufacturing's share of global value added was 35 percent; by the late 2000s it had declined to 27 percent. Services grew from 59 to 70 percent over the same period (UNIDO 2009). But these trends are mainly observed in high-income countries. They can be explained by several factors: productivity increases and rising living standards in advanced economies, which have pushed up wages and forced many industries to delocalize their production to lower-cost nations; the decrease in relative prices of consumption goods due to greater efficiency in the world economy and the simultaneous growth of the demand for services such as healthcare, security, or transportation; and, perhaps even more important, the multiplier effect of manufacturing on services jobs—the development of industries everywhere automatically generates a wide variety of new economic activities, from transportation to housing and from restaurants to entertainment.[17]

Concerns about the future of manufacturing as a viable source of economic growth have been investigated empirically by Ricardo Hausmann and colleagues (2011). They measure the sophistication of an economy based on how many products a country exports successfully and how many other countries also export those products. Looking at the composition and quantity of a nation's manufacturing, they observe that sophisticated economies export a large variety of "exclusive" goods that few other countries can produce. To do this, these economies have typically accumulated productive knowledge and developed manufacturing capabilities that others do not have. National income and economic sophistication ("economic complexity") tend to rise in tandem, and the linkage between manufacturing, economic complexity, and prosperity is highly predictive, with economic complexity being much better at explaining the variation in incomes across nations compared with any other leading indicators.

In other words, even basic manufacturing expertise and capabilities can gradually breed new knowledge and capabilities, and thus new more advanced products, provided that the right strategic and business decisions are made on industrial and technological upgrading. In the words of Hausmann and Hidalgo (2012, 13), economic development is "a social learning process, but one that is rife with pitfalls and dangers. Countries accumulate productive knowledge by developing the capacity to make a larger variety of products of increasing complexity. This process involves trial and error. It is a risky journey in search of the possible. Entrepreneurs, investors, and policy makers play a fundamental role in this economic exploration. Manufacturing, however, provides a ladder in which the rungs are more conveniently placed, making progress potentially easier."

Still, some valid questions remain about whether manufacturing as a long-term source of economic growth is a dying golden goose, especially for low-income countries that may not be well prepared to reap globalization's economic advantages. Several arguments can be made that question the viability of labor-intensive industries as a means of catching up in a world economy that is increasingly dominated by high-tech and sophisticated industries and innovative services. Although it is true that technological developments and the logic of mass production make it likely for an increasing share of goods to be produced more efficiently by machines, it is also certain that handmade labels will remain highly valuable features to customers of tradable goods around the world—just like the global rise of genetically modified food has not suppressed the large market for organic food. And some industries (most notably garments, footwear, and tourism) will remain labor intensive by their nature, despite technological progress.

Another concern about the size of manufacturing's potential benefits in developing countries has resurfaced recently in the economic literature in the form of export pessimism. It is based on the view that policies aiming to expand exports by developing countries will lead to a decline in their terms of trade because of an inability (due to weak demand created by the global recession) or unwillingness (expressed via new forms of protectionism) of developed countries to absorb these exports. Two reasons are often given to justify skepticism about the idea that today's poor economies can follow instead the export-led model that allowed many Asian countries to transform their economies. First, it is assumed that over the next decade the major international macroeconomic adjustment will consist of the reduction in excess demand by a few countries, notably the United States, and a concomitant increase in domestic absorption of GDP in a number of countries with excess savings, mainly in Asia. The argument here is twofold: it will be difficult for low-income countries to attract a substantial share of U.S. imports, which are projected to decline if rebalancing is to take place; and it has never been easy for poor countries to penetrate the Chinese and other Asian markets where the main policy priority is to increase domestic consumption. Second, it is often said the existence of very large and powerful industrial complexes benefiting from agglomeration economies, particularly in China, makes it difficult for new entrants to compete.

These arguments may not hold under close scrutiny. Even if the reduction of excess demand in large economies like the United States occurs, it is likely to be more than compensated for by the increase in excess demand in other industrialized and emerging economies, where rising income almost always changes saving and spending habits. Moreover, global imbalances may be less of a threat to the world economy than is often thought (Monga 2012), and they have been changing constantly. For much of the past few years, China was criticized for its contribution to global imbalances and a corresponding shortfall in global aggregate demand. It now appears that the surpluses of oil-exporting countries may actually be the main cause of the imbalances.[18] But there is no reason to assume that oil exporters will necessarily save most of their petrodollars, which would indeed reflect a permanent transfer of income from oil consumers to oil producers, with depressing implications for global demand.[19]

Although it seems likely that the rates of export growth that prevailed from 1960 to 2005 may not be sustained in the post–Great Recession era, it is highly unlikely that global trade volumes, which have increased constantly for more than half a century, will decline. Despite recurrent threats of protectionism, it is very likely that globalization will continue to shift an increasing part of manufacturing capacity from developed to emerging and from emerging to even low-income countries. In addition, substantial new markets will appear in the world economy—not least because large, new players such as China, India, and Brazil will find themselves sending the low-skilled manufacturing that made them successful to lower-income countries owing to the rising wages that are a result of their success. For low-income countries, including those in sub-Saharan Africa, it will always be possible to find a niche in which to achieve low costs and thus penetrate advanced markets. The challenge will be to identify the niche and to design pragmatic and targeted policies to exploit these opportunities (Page 2012).[20]

The other pessimistic suggestion that the mere existence of strong industrial complexes in Asia or elsewhere makes it difficult for new entrants to compete is true, but it is inconsistent with lessons from economic history. That same argument could have been made with regard to Japan in the 1950s and 1960s, or to dismiss industrialization attempts by other Asian countries in the 1970s and 1980s. The argument would have proven wrong because the great adventure of economic development has always been the story of the rise and fall of manufacturing powerhouses, once considered unshakable, that are eventually overtaken by new competition—the story of creative destruction. That mass production and close business links have already been established in most competitive and profitable industries simply makes it necessary for latecomers to find ways to use their low wages to compensate for the low efficiency that is due to the initial lack of networks and then gradually to integrate into such networks as their production base expands. The wage-productivity dynamic makes it difficult if not impossible for the successful Asian economies to permanently hold their comparative advantage in labor-intensive, low-skill manufacturing industries. This also opens up new manufacturing opportunities for lower-wage countries around the world.

The constant improvement of transportation and telecommunication services will continue to facilitate the distribution of production chains—even in the same industries—around the world. This will open up an infinite number of manufacturing opportunities for low-income countries, because locations need fewer "personbytes" in place than in the past. The various elements of the value chain (design, procurement, marketing, distribution, and manufacturing) need not occur in the same place, which means that places with few personbytes can more easily get their foot in the door and then add functions more gradually (Hausmann and Hidalgo 2012). Such changes will make the manufacturing space accessible to more countries, with the concomitant reduction of manufacturing jobs in advanced countries. Manufacturing will therefore provide more long-term economic benefits to African economies than other activities: it still generates economies of scale, sparks industrial and technological upgrading, fosters innovation, and has big multiplier effects.

CALIBRATING THE PACE OF THE TAKEOFF: THE BENEFITS OF DELAYED GRATIFICATION

In the early 1960s Stanford University psychology professor Walter Mischel fascinated the world with a simple exercise subsequently known as the "Marshmallow Test." In trying to understand achievement and what influences a child to reach his or her goals, he designed an experiment that yielded great insights on the benefits of delayed gratification and more generally on some of the conditions for success. Mischel gave children the choice between one reward (one marshmallow) that they could consume immediately and a larger reward (two marshmallows) for which they would have to wait alone for up to twenty minutes. Monitoring his cohort years later, he found that children who had waited for the second marshmallow generally fared better in life (Mischel 2014). Follow-up studies showed that a child's ability to delay eating the first treat predicted higher SAT scores (Lehrer 2009) and also a lower body mass index thirty years later (Schlam et al. 2013).

Some critics pointed out that his samples were too small or homogenous to support definitive scientific conclusions and that the Marshmallow Test actually measures trust in authority, not self-restraint and *sitzfleisch*, the ability to sit in a seat and reach a goal despite obstacles. Others wondered if the results showed that the children in a reliable environment (where they trusted that the delayed reward would actually materialize) were able to wait longer than children in an unreliable environment, and that the kids in the test were simply making a rational choice by assessing reliability.[21] Regardless of such criticism's validity, there is an interesting parallel with the story of successful economies: at low levels of development, self-restraint seems to be an important virtue. It pays off to resist the temptation of engaging in the most ambitious modernization strategies and instead calibrate the pace at which technologically advanced industries and sectors are selected.

Historical evidence shows that during the catch-up stage policy makers in successful countries may have been bold in their dreams and goals but were patient in adopting targets and implementing their strategies. They did not rush to replicate the economic strategies and industries that were in vogue in the most advanced economies. Instead they were patient—just like the wise children waiting for the marshmallows. They understood that the mechanisms and requirements for change differ in countries and depend on their level of development. They could see that while innovation in high-income countries amounts to invention, because their technology and industry are on the global forefront, in developing countries innovation at first amounts to imitation. A country with GDP per capita of $1,000 could get a lot of mileage from imitation. After a certain GDP per capita threshold is reached, innovation will become a central feature of growth strategy. Because the mechanism of innovation is different for countries at different levels of development, the educational requirements will also vary.

In their self-restraint, successful countries patiently used industrial policies to facilitate their industrial upgrading, and they targeted industries in dynamically growing countries with a similar endowment structure *but only* moderately higher per capita income. There is a long list of examples: Britain targeted the Netherlands' industries in the sixteenth and seventeenth centuries; Britain's per capita GDP was about 70 percent of that of the Netherlands. Germany, France, and the United States targeted Britain's industries in the late nineteenth century; their per capita incomes were about 60 to 75 percent of Britain's. During the Meiji Restoration Japan targeted Prussia's industries; its per capita GDP was about 40 percent of Prussia's. In the 1960s Japan targeted the industries of the United States; Japan's per capita GDP was about 40 percent of that of the United States. From the 1960s to the 1980s Korea, Taiwan-China, Hong Kong-China, and Singapore targeted Japan's industries; their per capita incomes were about 30 percent of Japan's. In the 1970s Mauritius targeted Hong Kong-China's textile and garment industries; per capita income in Mauritius was about 50 percent of Hong Kong-China's. In the 1980s Ireland targeted information, electronic, chemical, and pharmaceutical industries in the United States; Ireland's per capita income was about 45 percent of that of the United States. And in the 1990s Costa Rica targeted the memory chip packaging and testing industry; Costa Rica's per capita GDP was about 40 percent of Taiwan-China's, which was the main economy in this sector.

Why did these successful countries patiently target industries in dynamically growing economies with a similar endowment structure and somewhat

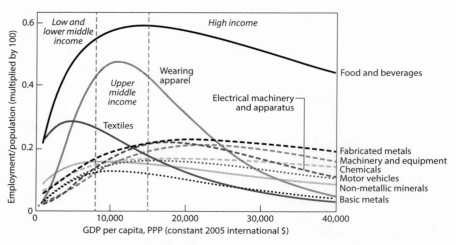

Figure 5.6. Changes in employment by income levels in various industries, 1963–2007.
Source: Haraguchi (2014).

higher income? There are several reasons. First, industrial upgrading is based on changes in comparative advantages due to changes in endowment structure, and countries that have a similar endowment structure should have similar comparative advantages. Second, the industries that sustain a dynamically growing economy should be consistent with that country's comparative advantages. Some of its industries will lose comparative advantage as the country grows and its endowment structure upgrades. Those "sunset" industries eventually become the latent comparative advantage, or the "sunrise" industries, of the latecomers. For countries with a similar endowment structure, the forerunners' successful and dynamic industrial development provides a blueprint for the latecomers' industrial policies. These patterns are most obvious on the employment front, where opportunities rise for the least advanced economies as the successful ones' GDP per capita increases. Manufacturing employment tends to increase rapidly at low- and lower-middle-income levels but declines at high-income levels (figure 5.6).

In contrast, policy makers in unsuccessful countries did not seem to have Marshmallow Test–type insights. They hastily tried to achieve greatness and gain instant economic gratification by launching the same advanced industries as those in the high-income industrialized countries. It was a fatal mistake. The old structuralist paradigm was very often a comparative-advantage-defying strategy, because it advised countries to give priority to the development of advanced countries' capital-intensive heavy industries even though capital in their economies was scarce. Such capital-intensive industries could not survive in an open, competitive market—unless the government was willing and able to grant them strong protection through large-scale subsidies or tax incentives—because they were in conflict with the comparative advantages determined by country endowment structure. In any case, these industries were subject to very high production costs compared with those in countries that developed similar industries but followed their comparative advantage.

Examples of such strategies include the ship construction industry launched in Indonesia in the 1960s at a time when the country's GDP per capita represented only 10 percent of that of its main competitor at the time, the Netherlands; or the attempt to build a car industry in the Democratic Republic of Congo (Zaire) in the 1970s when the country's GDP per capita was only 5 percent of that of the country with the leading manufacturer. The common denominator of these strategies was that the government targeted industries in countries whose per capita income was far higher than their own. Consequently, they were not able to produce these goods at a cost advantage and were therefore unable to compete in these industries. Table 5.3 gives examples of such countries and industries.

Another good illustration of trying to move too fast into industries that are inconsistent with an economy's comparative advantage is that of postindependence India. In 1958 its vision of a self-sufficient and self-reliant country motivated its political leadership to adopt a heavy-industrialization, import-substitution strategy. Large and costly investments in its steel industry; tertiary education in science, medicine, engineering, and management schools; a commitment to small and village enterprises and large, state-owned enterprises; and a large investment in agriculture to launch the Green Revolution that would fetch self-sufficiency in food were some of the hallmarks of India's development model. In retrospect, many of the investments, such as in education and agriculture, were prudent choices, but when combined with state-led heavy industrialization they constricted light manufacturing. India's choice of targeted industries in benchmark countries with GDP per capita often more than a thousand percent higher than its own was a comparative-advantage-defying strategy. For example, France, Germany, Netherlands, the United Kingdom, and the United States—countries that India emulated—had income levels that

TABLE 5.3. SELECTING THE WRONG INDUSTRIES: SOME EXAMPLES

Country	Industry	Time	Main Producer at Time	Real GDP (pc) Latecomer Country	Real GDP (pc) Leading Country	Income Ratio Follower versus Leader
Ethiopia	Beverages/Textile	1960s	USA	547	13,419	4%
Senegal	Trucks	1960s	USA	1,511	13,419	11%
Indonesia	Ships	1960s	Netherlands	983	9,798	10%
Turkey	Automobile Assembly	1950s	USA	2,093	10,897	19%
Egypt	Iron, Steel, Chemicals	1950s	USA	885	10,897	8%
Zambia	Automobile Assembly, Refrigerators, Air-Conditioning	1970s	USA	1,041	16,284	6%
DRC	Automobile Assembly, Textile	1970s	USA	761	16,284	5%

were between 950 and 1,500 percent higher. Even Japan, a relatively poor country at the time, had income levels that were 460 percent higher than India's (table 5.4).

Unsurprisingly, the choice of industries and benchmark countries was equally out of sync with India's level of development. At a stage when the country did not even have the industrial base for light manufacturing, a commitment to the heavy steel and engineering sectors (which also manufactured automobiles) necessitated high tariffs. The government sought to protect the industries with a complex web of industrial licensing requirements and a trade regime that was among the most restrictive in Asia. The economy's structure was virtually unchanged for several decades. The lack of structural transformation was mirrored in India's export basket, dominated for more than twenty-five years by resource-based low-tech exports.

Among the stylized facts that emerge from empirical observation, two stand out: First, the lack of economic convergence (neither absolute nor relative) among countries in the past two centuries appears to contrast with the rigid predictions of orthodox models of growth, which explicitly or

TABLE 5.4. RATIO OF FOREIGN TO INDIA'S PER CAPITA GDP IN 1958

	1958	1959	1960	1961	1962	1963	1964
India	*100*	*100*	*100*	*100*	*100*	*100*	*100*
China	96	96	88	73	73	76	79
Japan	460	496	529	584	630	658	690
France	958	973	982	1018	1064	1074	1074
Germany	941	1001	1023	1048	1084	1076	1074
United Kingdom	1113	1149	1148	1168	1169	1175	1165
Netherlands	1046	1079	1100	1081	1140	1134	1149
United States	1485	1566	1504	1503	1570	1572	1555
Total 12 Western Europe	959	999	1007	1040	1077	1084	1079
Total former USSR	528	512	524	540	546	512	541
World Average	364	373	368	373	384	382	381

Source: Maddison (2008).

implicitly set various structural prerequisites to economic prosperity (high savings, well-functioning institutions, good infrastructure indicators, strong human capital, excellent governance, and so on). This also invalidates the notion that all countries may eventually reach similar income levels by pursuing similar policy frameworks regardless of their initial economic structure. Second, international factors play a crucial role in the growth dynamics of the developing world—much more so than for high-income countries. This finding also weakens the traditional neoclassical emphasis on domestic policies and institutions as the primary determinants of economic performance (Ocampo, Rada, and Taylor 2009).

For policy makers in developing countries, the main lesson from economic history is perhaps the rejection of the "Sherlock Holmes syndrome," which consists of setting industrialized economies as model economies to be copied instantly and searching for the missing institutional and factor elements of growth to be developed hastily in an attempt to replicate the strategies in vogue elsewhere. Instead the focus should be on making the most of the existing assets and endowment structure of a country. For that to happen, pragmatism should be paramount in designing and implementing economic strategies. Regardless of whether they tried to address the fundamental causes or proximate causes of economic backwardness (as discussed), many past and existing policy prescriptions for poor countries have not taken into account that they will not be implemented in the context of a "first-best" world. Low-income countries are by definition in the "second-best," "third-best," or even "nth-best" world. While their policy makers should understand what an ideal, first-best world is, their strategy should be pragmatic and account for the political economy costs of working in suboptimal environments. Removing distortions in a second-best situation does not necessarily result in a Pareto improvement and convert a country into a first-best environment.

For poor countries, success requires moving away from adopting high-income model economies toward adopting the "flying-geese" strategy that has served well most of today's leading economies (Lin and Monga 2011; Lin 2011). All developing countries—regardless of their natural resources, location, or amount of capital—can break into global industrial markets and find their own niche or organize their economies to take advantage of the opportunities being vacated by middle-income countries that are forced out of their niche because of rising wages, rising productivity levels, and the need for industrial upgrading.

After rejecting the determinism of preconditions and mimicry in policy making, the question remains: what should be the practical blueprint for implementing such a strategy, especially in countries that have low physical and human capital indicators and lack the institutional arrangements and financial systems to support structural transformation? The next chapters address these issues, the need to set priorities, and how to identify policy instruments and the main pillars of a viable strategy for achieving prosperity.

APPENDIX 5.1: THE ANALYTICS OF INTERDEPENDENCE IN THE GLOBAL ECONOMY

The dynamic of the world economy is one of increasing interdependence among countries, and strong incentives to cooperate or collude even as they compete, rather than contemplating another "fight to death." Using the well-known Keynesian foreign trade multiplier, R. N. Cooper (1974) offered a useful mathematical exposition of the dynamics of mutual reliance. Célestin Monga (2012) uses a more explicit version of his model to provide the formal underpinnings for the discussion of U.S.-China external imbalances. Consider a two-country world where the macroeconomic linkages in each nation can be expressed as in equation 1,

$$(1a) \quad Y = C + I + G) + (X - M)$$

where (C) is consumption, (I) is investment, (G) is government spending, and $(X - M)$ is net exports.

$$(1b) \quad Y = C + X - M + Z$$

$$(2a \text{ and } 2b) \quad C = C(Y) \text{ and } C^* = C^*(Y^*)$$

$$(3a \text{ and } 3b) \quad M = M(Y) \text{ and } M^* = M^*(Y^*)$$

$$(4a \text{ and } 4b) \quad X = X(Y^*) = M^* \text{ and } X^* = X^*(Y) = M$$

where Y is the U.S. national income, that is, the total value of output produced for a given country and also the total value of incomes paid out (GNP), C is consumption, X is exports of goods and services, and Z is all other autonomous expenditures—all these variables in constant prices. The same relationships apply from the perspective of China, with an asterisk. Let us define the marginal propensities to import in the two countries as measures of interdependence. For the United States we have

$$(5a \text{ and } 5b) \quad m = \partial M / \partial Y \text{ and } m^* = \partial M^* / \partial Y^*$$

which is positive and less than unity. Using the marginal propensities to save as the unity minus the marginal propensity to consume,

$$(6a \text{ and } 6b) \quad s = 1 - \partial C / \partial Y \text{ and } s^* = 1 - \partial C^* / \partial Y^*$$

By combining all these terms for both countries and differentiating totally, we obtain the following system of simultaneous equations:

$$(7) \quad \begin{bmatrix} s+m & -m^* \\ -m & s^*+m^* \end{bmatrix} \begin{bmatrix} \frac{dY}{dY^*} \end{bmatrix} = \begin{bmatrix} \frac{dZ}{dZ^*} \end{bmatrix}$$

Solved as

$$(8) \begin{pmatrix} dY \\ dY^* \end{pmatrix} = \frac{1}{\Delta} \begin{bmatrix} s^* + m^* & m^* \\ m & s + m \end{bmatrix} \begin{pmatrix} dZ \\ dZ^* \end{pmatrix}$$

where Δ gives the well-known Keynesian foreign trade multipliers that allow for foreign repercussions, that is

$$(9) \quad \Delta = (s + m)(s^* + m^*) - mm^* = ss^* + sm^* + s^*m$$

Using m and m^* as measures of interdependence between the two countries, we can assess both the impact on world income and the impact on country income of an increased expenditure in the United States following Cooper's methodology. It can be shown that a proportionate change of x percent in both m and m^* affects interdependence in the two countries in the following ways:

For the United States,

$$(10) \quad \frac{\partial}{\partial x} \left(\frac{dY}{dZ} \right) = \frac{1}{\Delta^2} (-s^{*2}m) < 0$$

For China,

$$(11) \quad \frac{\partial}{\partial x} \left(\frac{dY^*}{dZ} \right) = \frac{1}{\Delta^2} (mms^*) > 0$$

Equations 10 and 11 tell a straightforward story: as the degree of interdependence between the United States and China rises, the impact of a given increase in expenditure on income in the United States declines while the impact on income in China rises. Incidentally, this may explain the perception of some politicians who opposed the 2008–09 fiscal stimulus packages in the United States, which they characterized as additional spending on larger volumes of Chinese imports.

Given that the marginal propensities to save differ in the two countries ($s \neq s^*$), interdependence highlights compositional effects on the aggregate world saving rate and hence on the total impact of world income. But even in the special situation where the marginal propensities to save would be strictly equal in the United States and China ($s = s^*$),

$$(12) \quad dY + dY^* = (1/s)dZ$$

implying that the change in total (world) income would not be affected by the values of m and m^*, and any gain in impact of increased expenditure on income in the United States as a result of changes in m and m^* would be offset by a proportionate reduction in China's income (and vice versa).[22]

6

The Art of Performing
Economic Miracles:
Implementation Guidelines

One of the most enduring pacts in modern political history happened almost by accident. It was sealed in 1978 on Maryland's Catoctin Mountain, where three world leaders met to find a way out of centuries of war and mistrust in the Middle East. At the invitation of then U.S. president Jimmy Carter, Prime Minister Menachem Begin of Israel and President Anwar Sadat of Egypt met in the secluded presidential retreat, Camp David, "hoping to find avenues to peace in their troubled part of the world." Serving as mediator, President Carter convinced his guests to stay until they had developed and agreed on a framework for peace.

Despite genuine efforts from all the leaders, the meeting did not go well. Age-old tragic battles over ancient land full of spiritual meaning and deep mistrust among the parties involved could not be overcome easily. The discussions between Sadat and Begin often escalated into heated arguments; Carter tried to referee but acknowledged that "the meeting was mean." Begin and Sadat were brutal with each other and often personal in their attacks. The result was stalemate and the leaders not speaking to each other. Several times they even broke off the talks. Initially scheduled for three days, the meeting lasted thirteen. The final day of talks was a flurry of writing and rewriting the agreement. Begin was strongly dissatisfied with the paragraph on Jerusalem and would not sign the final agreement. Nothing Carter could do, say, or even promise would move him. It was then concluded that the talks had failed and everyone packed to go back home.

At the very last hour, Carter decided to give Begin a series of pictures of the Camp David discussions to take home to each of his grandchildren in Israel. He wrote their names and a few nice words on the back of each picture. "I handed [Begin] the photographs. . . . [He] looked at each photograph individually, repeating the name of the grandchild I had written on it. His lips trembled, and tears welled up in his eyes. He told me a little about each child. . . . We were both emotional as we talked quietly for a few minutes about grandchildren and about war. . . . He said, 'I will accept the letter you have drafted on Jerusalem.'" (Carter 1982, 399) He did. On March 26, 1979, the Egyptian-Israeli Peace Treaty was signed at a grand ceremony on the South Lawn of the White House. The Camp David agreements sealed the peace between Egypt and Israel and laid strong foundations for subsequent efforts.

That story is often told by President Carter himself as he tries to shed light on the art of achieving success in the most unlikely circumstances. The story stresses the infinite power of human creativity and imagination in a world always full of possibilities and the need to have faith in opportunities inconsistent with previously known patterns. It is also an example of the unexpected phenomena that often result in nonlinear and irreversible dynamics (the "dissipative structures" studied by Ilya Prigogine).[1]

But from the perspective of economic development, the story of the Camp David agreements would be misleading if interpreted as evidence of the absolute dominance of randomness in the quest for success. True, economic miracles can occur in unpredictable ways. But economic success, which is about sustaining continuous improvements in productivity over the long run, cannot be attributed to chance and casualness. Important agreements do not materialize in a completely arbitrary manner. In the history of development, countries that have achieved sustained and inclusive growth and economic prosperity did not do so with the same kind of chance that brought Carter success at Camp David. Instead, they have deliberately designed and implemented strategies and partnership agreements based on careful analysis of their comparative advantages and their potential. As noted in previous chapters, they have always started with suboptimal conditions, poor business environments, and a lack of many policy ingredients too often listed as "prerequisites" for success in the development literature.

The art of performing economic miracles involves several important elements: First, economies must find the right entry points to spur competitive and profitable business ventures and ascertain the key elements and themes that will induce the virtuous circle of benefits for an increasingly large number of domestic constituencies and foreign partners. In the economic development realm this translates to identifying the industries and sectors in which a low-income country has comparative advantage and the potential to attract foreign investors in search of lower-cost locations, new products and services, or new markets. Second, economies must find ways and channels to connect small, context-specific ideas to a much larger narrative where they can become part of a more notable national and global story. This means connecting the infinitesimally small business opportunities found in poor countries to the global value chains that now dominate production and distribution networks across the planet. Third, economies must remove obstacles to growth in a realistic and sequential way and gradually overcome physical and capital deficits and institutional weaknesses. Fourth, they must use state resources parsimoniously to build foundations and infrastructure platforms for competitive industries and set up an affordable fiscal incentive package to encourage the development of trade and the connection between local firms and foreign investors.

These elements for success may sound abstract, but they actually provide a framework for achieving sustained growth, employment creation, and poverty reduction in poor business environments. This chapter applies them to real policy situations and offers a road map for implementing an economic development strategy that leaves little to randomness. Drawing from economic history and analysis, it explains why countries do not evolve from low- to medium- and high-income status as the result of chance. The chapter starts by explaining the importance of rational selection and the choice of policy domains that will give a poor economy the highest probability of developing dynamic business ventures. It then provides step-by-step guidelines for policy makers in poor countries struggling to make sense of the often conflicting economic advice they receive from many development institutions.

RATIONAL SELECTION: THE ESSENCE OF STRATEGY IS CHOOSING WHAT NOT TO DO

Most countries remain poor because they cannot find the right entry point—defined as the priority industries and activities on which they should focus their limited human, financial, and administrative resources—for igniting their development strategy. Unless one believes that political leaders in poor countries are generally sadistic psychopaths who enjoy seeing their countries fail and their people suffer from high unemployment, poverty, and social conflicts, one must acknowledge that development failures are mainly the consequences of intellectual and policy failures. Regardless of their political and ideological orientation, most political leaders—even the most brutal ones—tend to have two goals in mind: to stay in power and, if staying in power is a given, to achieve greatness through positive realizations for their people and their country so that they are remembered as positive historical figures. The best way to achieve both goals is to bring sustained and inclusive prosperity to their nations. But their quest for great political, economic, and social achievements is too often tainted by well-intended but disastrous choices—including selecting industries and sectors where the government should not invest. The failures often lead to a vicious cycle of policy choices that maintain the leaders' personal power at the cost of their people's well-being.

The results of such strategic mistakes typically are government involvement in economic activities not selected based on their economic viability and financial sustainability. They also include dispersing state resources into so many policy areas that their development impact is negligible. Moreover, such unfocused quests for sources of economic growth often lead to creating politically motivated initiatives, which subsequently become difficult to eliminate. Although the financial and economic returns of such initiatives are low or even negative, their political benefits to some constituencies are often substantial, which compounds the initial policy mistakes. For instance, a steel mill company that may have been established with government financing with the objective of spurring industrialization and modernization can quickly reveal itself to be a non-performing and nonviable venture. Yet because it has generated social and political enthusiasm and created a few costly employment opportunities in a particular geographic location, it also generates its own political constituencies and becomes difficult to abolish. Such "white elephants" are burdens on government finances and often the source of cronyism and corruption, as they can survive only with state protection and subsidies and special treatment from banks. But these are consequences, not the cause, of the initial failure to determine the right entry point for the country's growth strategy.

A case in point is that of Senegal, where policy makers decided a few months after independence in 1960, when the country had a GDP per capita of only $1,500, to start producing highly capital-intensive trucks, which they perceived as an important source of growth. Yet this was inconsistent with the country's endowment structure at the time, and it could not survive global competition, even with heavy subsidies from the government. Regardless, a few vocal Senegalese blue- and white-collar workers strongly opposed the decision to abandon the local production of trucks, even though it proved financially unsustainable. Similar struggles to find the right entry point have been observed across the developing world, often with difficult economic and political consequences. In the 1950s China chose the automobile industry as one of its main industrialization entry points. Although there might have been a strong political-economy rationale for selecting such a capital-intensive industry, there was no economic rationale, because China's GDP per capita was only 5 percent of that of the United States, then the leading country in the automobile industry. The industry choice was the wrong entry point and was therefore unsustainable. Likewise, Indonesian authorities thought they could launch a successful, state-owned shipbuilding company in the 1960s and successfully compete with the Netherlands, the dominant power in the industry at that time. Presidents Sukarno and Suharto had bold ambitions, hoping to build large ships and oil tankers. There again, the strategy was costly and largely ineffective for many decades. Even today, with a rich and long history in the shipbuilding industry, Indonesia still struggles to meet its targets. Local shipbuilders constantly need substantial financial incentives to survive, including tax allowances and government-paid import duties for component purchases.

Successful economic development typically starts with a realistic strategic vision. And there is no shortage of strategy documents in the world. In fact, the number of such documents that exist in the archives of government ministries and agencies seems to be inversely proportional to a country's GDP per capita. The low-income economies tend to have many failed strategies and misguided plans—often written by highly paid outside experts—which reflects their struggle to design and implement policies for shared prosperity. The proliferation of strategy documents and policy frameworks is evidence of serious implementation challenges and actually may be *the* main binding constraint to development performance. Solving this fundamental problem requires a change in development practitioners' mindset. Instead of looking at what low-income countries do not have and cannot do well, researchers and policy makers should look at what developing countries have and can do well and then work from that base to scale up.

The great Chinese philosopher Lao Tzu observed that "a journey of a thousand miles must begin with a single step." Economies that accumulate and integrate many small successes experience sustained and inclusive growth. This requires that countries make the best use of their limited resources. In sum, countries need to exploit their comparative advantage by using their endowments. One of the most powerful ideas in economics is that no matter how bad a country's situation, it always has a comparative advantage in some sectors or industries and can exploit the infinite opportunities offered by trade and globalization to ignite and sustain its quest for prosperity.

As noted in chapter 2, policy makers are often prescribed reform agendas that are too daunting and, in some political environments, too unrealistic to be implemented without serious macrofinancial risks or without jeopardizing political stability and social peace. Some binding constraints are politically too costly to remove all at once and for the whole country would require considerable funding. Take the case of infrastructure, for example. It is common sense to build infrastructure gradually, starting with locations where the expected economic payoff would be the largest. This is a realistic strategy that has indeed been implemented successfully around the world and throughout history. Yet political leaders facing political constraints or trying to appease constituents will often choose to spend a little money here and there to try to satisfy everyone, even though the result is poor-quality or insufficient and ultimately ineffective infrastructure.

Sectoral and institutional reforms also depend on available funding. By definition, poor countries do not have the financial and human resources and the capacity to deliver all they need in critical areas such as education and health. Ideally, geographical targeting and industry selection should precede spending decisions, but they are often either randomly done or politically motivated, the result of trying to accommodate too many constituencies at once.

Moreover, many national development strategies in these sectors and others, and even the policy advice from some development partners, are based on development paradigms that endorse ineffective growth models that have so far delivered few results. In particular, capital-intensive industries (especially in the mining sector) are still largely favored, even though they generate foreign exchange and fiscal revenues, while labor-intensive industries are neglected.

Developing countries should not allocate their limited government budgets and administrative capacity to generic, broad-based reforms or to "priority sectors," vaguely defined as "agriculture," "education," "infrastructure," or "private-sector development," but rather to some strategically targeted programs, reforms, and industries in which private firms can emerge and become competitive domestically and internationally. Policy makers need to go beyond the necessary blanket reforms ("maintaining a stable macroeconomic environment," "improving the business climate," "building infrastructure," "developing human capital," and so on) and direct reform efforts to the most binding constraints—those whose removal is key to the emergence of potentially competitive industries.

True, low-income countries are also those with the most daunting development challenges—from poor infrastructure to insufficient human capital, weak institutions, and bad governance. The main strategic questions facing their governments is how to optimize their limited human and financial resources to address these challenges, and how to find the right entry points for launching a sustained and inclusive growth strategy and a structural transformation process. Unfortunately, many low-income governments still mistakenly launch new industries without properly analyzing whether the targeted industries are consistent with their economy's comparative advantage, or they embrace too many politically difficult reforms and try to launch too many industries at the same time that are beyond their limited administrative and financial capacity. As a result, even when they manage to implement these reforms, achieve good macroeconomic performance, and improve some of their general business environment indicators, these economies still do not undergo the kind of structural transformation required to create employment and reduce poverty.

Tanzania, one of the best-performing economies in Africa, provides an illustration of the propensity to set a reform agenda that is too ambitious. The East African country once known to be one of the most rigid experiments in socialism now ranks among the top performers. It achieved an average annual growth rate of 7 percent from 1995 to 2014 thanks to political stability, persistent work on market reforms, sound macroeconomic policies, and expanding public and private investment. Yet despite high growth rates, Tanzania remains a low-income country with the prospect of meeting just half the Millennium Development Goals. Economic growth has been driven by mining, construction, communications, and the financial sector; manufacturing, transport, and tourism have also been influential. But structural transformation has been limited. Manufacturing shrank from 13 percent of GDP in the 1970s to less than 7 percent in 2014. Manufacturing's share of exports has been well below 15 percent (1995–2015), less than half of the 40 percent of most industrialized middle-income countries.

The absence of structural transformation is especially evident in Tanzania's labor market. Economic growth in recent years has taken place in capital- and skills-intensive sectors and has created few jobs. More than 70 percent of the labor force still works in traditional agriculture. Only 5 percent of new entrants to the labor market work in the formal and modern sectors. The household enterprise sector is Tanzania's fastest growing employment source.[2] Employment has grown too slowly to absorb the influx of young and educated workers, particularly in urban areas. Demographic trends make things even more challenging.[3]

The Tanzanian authorities now fully understand the importance of structural transformation and its opportunities for accelerated, inclusive growth. In the words of President Jakaya Mrisho Kikwete:

> This is envisaged to happen through the targeting of strategic priority interventions to move Tanzania to a higher growth trajectory coupled with modernisation and a shift from a subsistent agricultural-based to an industrial-based economy. Furthermore, this growth momentum needs to have broad sources in order to ensure that its benefits are broadly shared and reflected in improved quality of life for the majority of Tanzanians. Broad employment creation, particularly for the youth, is therefore [a] critical cross-cutting target of country's development plans. (POPC 2011, i)

But in trying to address these critical development problems, the government has adopted several overlapping and often conflicting strategy documents prescribing perhaps too many reforms in too many sectors. In 2000 it launched the Tanzania Development Vision 2025 (TDV 2025) with the goal of enhancing the transformation and diversification of the country's production structure and trade basket and fostering graduation to middle-income status. Following extensive consultations with various stakeholders, the government has outlined a path to reaching its targets through a series of three five-year development plans (FYDPs). The first FYDP (2011/12–2015/16) is tackling the main constraints to Tanzania's growth: infrastructure bottlenecks and weak human capital (ports, rural roads across the country, railways, skilled labor, information and communication technology, and so on). Once the most binding infrastructure constraints have been removed, it is expected that the Tanzanian economy will be well placed to develop its industrial sector. The second FYDP (2016/17–2020/21) will focus on transforming the country's resources: development of natural gas industries, agro-processing, and medium-technology industries. It is assumed that the rapid development of the country's industrial sector will then open up the economy to new foreign markets, and that a third FYDP (2021/22–2025/26) will focus on improving the competitiveness in all sectors, especially in manufacturing and services. The goal is to transform Tanzania into East Africa's manufacturing hub.

Adding to the already complicated strategy, the government has been preparing and adopting five-year national strategies for growth and reduction of poverty (known as MKUKUTA, its Kiswahili acronym) as part of Tanzania's efforts to deliver on its national Vision 2025. This is in addition to TDV 2025 and the FYDPs. The five-year strategy (2010/11–2014/15) adopted by the government in November 2010 (MKUKUTA II) sets the policy orientations toward these goals.[4] It builds on the preceding strategy document (MKUKUTA I) but focuses more explicitly on growth, productivity improvements through private-sector development, job creation, and infrastructure.

Just listing the various official strategy documents helps explain why the Tanzanian approach is likely to lead to disappointments. For a large country with a GDP per capita still well below $1,000 a year, it is unrealistic to rely on such a linear sequencing of action plans:

→ Some binding constraints are politically too costly to remove all at once and require extensive funding when the whole country is considered (infrastructure), yet political-economy constraints (winners and losers) are rarely assessed systematically.

→ Policy decisions sometimes depend on available funding (which explains why sectoral and geographical targeting is often either random or politically motivated).

→ Many national development strategies and even the policy advice from development institutions often leave little room for strategic selectivity—yet in all low-income countries, not everything can be done at once (capacity and financial constraints). In Tanzania, the dominant development paradigm endorses the existing, ineffective growth model. For instance, capital-intensive industries (mining) are often encouraged and favored even when they do not create many jobs, while labor-intensive industries are neglected.

What the Tanzanian authorities need is a series of quick wins, especially in employment creation. Given the country's low literacy rate and skilled-labor shortage, such quick wins can be generated only in labor-intensive industries and light manufacturing. Moreover, the comprehensive nature of the policy documents and reforms to be implemented in short periods represents a daunting policy agenda for any government—and even more so for the government of a low-income country. A clear sign of that nearly impossible challenge is that the Tanzanian authorities have identified twenty-five "cluster strategies" for increasing agricultural production. A list of "twenty-five priority areas for intervention" in just the agriculture sector raises administrative capacity issues, even if the necessary financial resources were available.

"The essence of strategy is choosing what not to do," Michael Porter once said. The proliferation of strategy documents and action plans inevitably leads to randomness in policy implementation. Policy makers should not leave economic development to chance or to generic, all-encompassing reform prescriptions. The primary goal of any development strategy in low-income countries such as Tanzania should be structural transformation, lifting the 70 to 90 percent of the people in low-productivity/subsistence activities that are too often only disguised unemployment into manufacturing. Few countries have been able to move from low- to middle- and high-income status without industrializing. Few countries in history—except a small sample of resource-rich nations—have been able to achieve sustained, inclusive growth without going through this transformation. But industrialization is not just about manufacturing, as discussed below. This has important policy implications well beyond manufacturing. The quest for industrialization should also be about services (education or health-sector strategies for instance) or agriculture.

The question then becomes: how does a government stimulate transformation? The answer is to develop a simple framework for finding the right entry point from which the quest for economic growth can be sustained. This stimulates the emergence of industries and sectors that are economically viable because they are suitable for the economy's endowment structure. The appropriate development strategy then focuses not on all possible sectors or needed reforms but only on those industries that can prosper, create employment, and ignite a virtuous circle of shared prosperity. The next section outlines a methodology for doing this.

FINDING THE RIGHT ENTRY POINTS: RATIONAL SELECTION AND IMPLEMENTATION

How do governments *actually* find that right entry point? How do they ensure that the priority industries and sectors in which they plan to devote most of their limited human, administrative, and financial resources are consistent with their comparative advantage and are viable as potential catalysts of the virtuous circle of industrial, technological, and institutional upgrading? Those are the most burning economic policy questions facing leaders around the world.

Many of the broad elements of development frameworks and reform plans that have been advocated in the past decades and that still appear in many official policy documents (macroeconomic stabilization, getting prices right, striving for efficiency in public management, competition, business environment improvement, and so on) are sensible, especially when considered individually, yet they yield few positive results when actually implemented. Their disappointing outcomes have led Michael Spence, the 2008 Growth Commission Report cochair, to wonder whether economists and policy makers have found the ingredients for growth but not the actual recipe. In fact, the disappointing results—and the many failed growth-strategy experiments—reflect fundamental problems with the design and sequencing of economic development strategies, which are likely to succeed only if they account for the economy's development level and the specific context and time.

Lin and Monga (2011) and Lin (2012a, b) suggest a practical six-step growth identification and facilitation framework (GIFF) to help policy makers in developing countries identify reliable growth paths and facilitate the emergence of employment-generating industries—the only viable way toward shared prosperity. The GIFF underlines the need to intervene selectively and to leverage financial and human resources for private investment toward the industries and sectors with revealed or latent comparative advantage.

Sector-targeted industrial policy has been taboo in mainstream academics and in the global development community after the failures of the import-substitution strategy in the 1960s and 1970s. Economic history shows that governments in almost all developing countries have attempted to play a leading role in selecting priority industries and have generally failed. For example, the former Soviet Union, Latin America, Africa, and Asia have all been marked by inefficient public investment and misguided government interventions that have resulted in many white elephants. These well-documented failures appear to be due mostly to governments' inability to align their efforts with their country's resource base and development level. Indeed, governments' propensity to be overly ambitious when selecting industries, leading to selections misaligned with available resources and skills, helps to explain why their attempts to "pick winners" often resulted in "picking losers."

But the dominant intellectual paradigm, which assumes that sustained growth and job creation in low-income countries can be achieved simply by promoting general, economy-wide improvements in the business environment, has also proven ineffective across the developing world. In fact, historical evidence shows that in countries that successfully transformed from an agrarian to a modern economy—including those in western Europe, North America, and, more recently, in East Asia—governments coordinated key investments by private firms that helped to launch specific, well-targeted new industries and often provided incentives to pioneering firms.

The GIFF's main rationale emerges from the observation that economic development and sustained growth result from continual industrial and technological change, a process that requires collaboration between the public and private sectors. The GIFF draws lessons from history and economic analysis. Its method for identifying new sectors is based on the comparative advantages theory. It recommends that low-income countries target tradable sectors in dynamically growing countries with similar endowment structures and 100–300 percent higher per capita GDP or with the same per capita GDP twenty years ago. This recommendation is based on the idea that a dynamically growing country's comparative advantages will necessarily change over time. Countries with a similar endowment structure will have a similar comparative advantage. A country growing dynamically for twenty years will lose comparative advantages in some of its tradable sectors. Those sectors will become the latent comparative advantage of countries with a similar endowment structure but with a lower income. In those sectors, the production factor costs in the lower-income country are generally lower than in the dynamically growing higher-income country.

Yet despite their latent comparative advantages in those sectors and industries, the firms in the lower-income country often cannot compete with the firms in the higher-income country, because the transaction costs they must support in their poor business environment are too high. After the government of the lower-income country identifies such potentially competitive industries and sectors, there are two key policy solutions. One is to help domestic firms outcompete firms in the dynamically growing higher-income country by removing the main binding constraints to their performance (the constraints causing high transaction costs). The other is to create particularly attractive business conditions (that is, by reducing transaction costs) to convince firms in the dynamically growing higher-income country to relocate their production to the lower-cost country.

The government should also pay attention to the development by private enterprises of new and competitive products and support the scaling up of successful private-sector innovations in new industries. In countries with a poor business environment, special economic zones or industrial parks can facilitate firm entry, foreign direct investment, and the formation of industrial clusters. Finally, the government might help pioneering firms in the new industries by offering tax incentives for a limited period, cofinancing investments, or providing access to land or foreign exchange.

The GIFF shifts the focus to manufacturing—especially to labor-intensive industries. The rationale for such a shift is that

> manufacturing is complex and its production processes increase demand for raw materials, energy, construction, and services from

a broad array of supplying industries in the economy. Additionally many functions previously done within manufacturing companies— from back-office and accounting to some types of logistics—are now contracted out to other service providers and hence not counted as part of the manufacturing sector itself. A measure of the breadth of the supply chain is the backward linkage in the input-output structure of the economy. For an industry with a larger backward linkage, growth in its output induces more production—both directly and indirectly—from other sectors. A mapping of relationships in the economy reveals that manufacturing has the highest backward linkage among the major sectors. As the demand for manufacturing grows, it in turn spurs the creation of jobs, investments and innovations elsewhere. (Manufacturing Institute 2012, 3)

Manufacturing provides more long-term economic benefits than do other activities. It generates economies of scale, sparks industrial and technological upgrading, fosters innovation, and has a large multiplier effect (which shows how much additional output is generated by a dollar's worth of final demand for each industry). Each factory requires accountants, marketing people, component suppliers, restaurants, and other services. Empirical studies show that one dollar in final sales of manufactured products supports $1.34 or more in output from other sectors of the economy, whereas a dollar invested in retail creates only about 50 cents of additional income (Manufacturing Institute 2012). Manufacturing always has the largest backward linkage or multiplier effect of all sectors.

Six specific steps allow for a straightforward GIFF implementation.

Step 1: Identifying Sectors with Latent Comparative Advantage

As noted earlier, the first step is for policy makers in a low-income economy to identify those tradable goods and services that have been produced for about twenty years in dynamically growing countries with endowment structures similar to theirs but with a per capita income that is about double. Comparator countries are selected using two criteria: first, an average growth rate of more than 6 percent annually in the past twenty years or so, and second, a per capita income that is roughly between 100 and 300 percent of the low-income country's or that was about at the same level twenty years earlier.

That exercise allows policy makers in the lower-income country to learn from the transformation experiences of comparator countries by examining their export and production structure. Using a simple methodology described in appendix 5.1, one can calculate export specialization indices (ESI) and analyze their revealed comparative advantage (RCA) to examine the export types where the lower-income and comparator countries have existing and latent comparative advantages.

Empirical analyses carried out in studies devoted to African countries show that among ninety-nine subsectors using the harmonized system commodity code (HS 2-digit code), they generally have *revealed comparative advantage* (RCA > 1) in the categories of food, beverages, and agricultural products and in light manufacturing goods such as goat skins and leather, paper, cotton, garments, and textiles and clothing (Monga and Mpango 2012; Dinh and Monga 2013; Dinh et al. 2011). But many of these subsectors in these African countries remain at the level of infant industries and have broken value chains. For example, there is a nascent garment sector in many African countries, but the textile sector is not well developed. Domestically produced fabrics are of poor quality and cannot be exported for more sophisticated textile production. These countries also appear to have *latent comparative advantage* in manufactured goods that require low technological sophistication levels.

These analyses can be complemented by examining existing products and sectors, with the consideration of the major constraints to and opportunities for their development. One can use the following criteria to filter down the list of ninety-nine sectors (using standard HS code 1–99):

→ Criterion 1: Production requires a low level of capital, and there is a substantial domestic or international market.

→ Criterion 2: Domestic production does not require a substantial power level (electricity) or high transport costs (that is, no short-term need for substantial improvements in the roads and railways to move raw materials and output).

→ Criterion 3: Production in comparator countries is done by small- and medium-sized enterprises, showing the potential for employment creation in the lower-income country.

→ Criterion 4: The factor endowment in the lower-income country is well suited for production—some supply chain elements are in place and the RCA or ESI indicate potential; and the labor skills requirements are either low or easily transferable.

From that screening exercise, the following industries and sectors satisfy all four criteria and tend to emerge as potentially competitive in low-income countries that have a large labor supply: agriculture and agribusiness; clothing/garment; assembly of basic electronics and motorcycles (and farm tractors); wood and wood products; light manufacturing related to fashion and tourism (handbags made of cotton and handicraft); hides, skins, and leather, as many developing countries are major livestock producers; and so on. Because there are thousands of products in these industries and sectors, the specific products to be encouraged will depend on decisions made by firms in a self-discovery process.

Step 2: Removing Constraints for Existing Firms

In all developing countries, official strategy documents have been designed to address broad constraints on the private sector. They typically offer comprehensive lists of reforms to be implemented by the authorities to foster economic activity in all sectors and industries. It is more realistic to identify specific reforms that would lift the burden on private firms in the most competitive industries. The second step in the GIFF approach involves identifying, from the industries on the recommended list from step 1, those that have attracted domestic private firms. It also involves focusing on the barriers that may be discouraging other private firms from entering competitive sectors; the major sources of the high transaction costs slowing down the development of private firms in these selected industries; and the constraints that private-sector firms face in upgrading their products' quality.

Studies of industrial development barriers in Africa highlight that the production of light manufacturing goods is composed of two distinct and underperforming segments separated physically as well as by quality, variety, and price (Dinh et al. 2011). One consists of many small firms operating mostly in the informal sector and offering a wide range of products. These goods are mostly characterized by lower quality, more limited variety, and lower prices than imports. They are not import substitutes and should be considered nontradables. The other segment is made up of some larger, formal-sector firms—many of them former state enterprises—that cater to niche (often protected) markets. "The goods they produce, including some exports and items for special orders placed by major domestic purchasers (often government agencies), are largely standardized, with an emphasis on stable quality but with little innovation in design. Many are produced on old equipment that is not being replaced because factories often operate below capacity. These two types of firms rarely interact with one another, whether through competition or subcontracting" (Dinh et al. 2011).

Industrial surveys and value-chain and empirical analyses show that firms in both segments tend to face many types of constraints (poor infrastructure, stringent and ineffective labor laws, a skilled labor shortage, limited access to land and credit, costly access to inputs, major trade logistics issues, corruption and poor governance, inadequate policies and incentives, and so on). But not all firms in all sectors experience these problems to the same extent. Even when they face similar issues, firms tend to handle them differently depending on their size or financial or capital structure. Some constraints critical for small firms are less important for large firms.

Likewise, certain constraints may prevent industrial development in a particular industry but not in another. In Tanzania, for instance, it has been observed that trade logistics issues (mainly the rules and regulations governing the import-export process) are quite important for large firms in industries such as textiles and apparels and wood products but obviously unimportant for small firms not involved in the tradable sector. By contrast, access to input industries is critical to small firms but much less so to large firms (see Table 3.4 in chapter 3).

For any government—especially in a developing country—sorting out the many constraints to firm development that emerge from all kinds of studies is a major challenge. Not all obstacles to firm performance have equal importance. In fact, some apparent issues identified in surveys and analyses as major obstacles to growth are often symptoms or consequences of other problems that may deserve more attention.

One way of sorting out the long obstacles list and setting priorities in a reform program is to sort the many impediments to sustained growth into one of two types of obstacles:

→ High factor costs (often due to bad policies and regulations implemented in the past and structural rigidities such as land policy)
→ High transaction costs (often due to bad infrastructure and poor governance)

Such simplification offers strong theoretical advantages because it uses simple Ricardian models based on international comparisons of unit labor costs to assess international competitiveness. The relative unit labor cost (comparative measure of the ratio of wages to productivity) is indeed an essential relative price in the Ricardian model of trade and as such provides a coherent basic framework for understanding the main macro- and microeconomic determinants of trade flows.[5] As noted by L. Edwards and S. S. Golub (2004, 1326), "in a world where capital is mobile and production is footloose between countries, it is the relative price of nontradable *inputs*, notably labor, rather than *outputs* that matters."

For policy makers in developing countries, it also has several practical advantages: First, it reduces the broad determinants of firm performance and growth to just two categories (competitiveness in factor costs and competitiveness in transaction costs). Second, it highlights that despite their poor business environments, almost all low-income countries still have lower factor costs than more advanced economies, opening a window of opportunity for smart, targeted reforms and policies with big potential payoffs. And finally, by forcing policy makers to focus their diagnosis and attention on just two broad categories of constraints, it allows them to focus on formulating policies that can actually be implemented in countries with low administrative capacities—most notably through building clusters and industrial parks, as discussed later.

Private-sector analysts, academic researchers, and policy makers could then carry out detailed value-chain studies (for products already produced locally) and feasibility studies (for products not yet produced locally), focusing specifically on the list from step 1. Such studies should do the following:

→ Examine global trends, market forces (productivity of the main producers and competition), and the development prospects in the world product market.
→ Review the structure of the country's product markets—including through a mapping of firms and their capabilities—to identify areas where the capacity of the private sector can be leveraged (such as good practice companies and industrial clusters, including informal ones) and where it needs to be built (for example, key missing links along industry value chains).

→ Assess the key features, strengths, and weaknesses of the country's existing supply chain for the product based on a benchmarking of key productivity and cost factors (for example, labor, capital, and inputs) against those in comparator countries.

→ Assess the overall economic efficiency of domestic production of the product in relation to world prices using alternative cost projection scenarios to establish current- and medium-term competitiveness.

→ Identify the *most binding constraints* to be lifted through government action or changes in policy if these potentially competitive industries are to be successful—that is, policy makers should be given a reform agenda that is realistic and manageable, not the usual "improve the business environment" recipe requiring hundreds of politically difficult reforms.

For governments with scarce resources and capacity and for political leaders with limited time in power (and in a developing world where 50 percent of the population is under thirty years old and unemployed), it is imperative to identify reforms to lift the burden on private firms in the potentially most competitive industries. Although the specific policy agenda would depend on a country's economic conditions, the following broad recommendations may be considered and adapted to prevailing economic circumstances.

Solve poor infrastructure issues. About 20 percent of firms in developing countries consider poor infrastructure (that is, inadequate and poor quality energy supplies, high utility prices, lack of railway transport, and so on) to negatively affect their business. The most popular recommendation to policy makers in low-income countries is to build infrastructure projects across their country and to encourage regional integration. African countries, for instance, are often encouraged to launch large regional infrastructure projects that are supposed to yield political and economic benefits mainly in cross-border economies of scale and the linkages of national markets. It is at best a costly and highly risky solution. In more than a half century of independence, it has proved to be a failed solution to the continent's infrastructure problems. Africa is the most fragmented continent on Earth, and its national economies are extremely small—even within large countries, many regions are often not connected. The continent's GDP is less than 2 percent of that of the world. That also implies a purchasing power of less than 2 percent of the global purchasing power. Compare that with 21 percent for the United States and 23 percent for Europe—a total of 44 percent, or the equivalent of twenty-two times Africa's share of the global economy. These numbers alone invalidate any infrastructure development strategy that would give priority to the regional integration of Africa's national economies. It would be very costly to build enough roads, ports, airports, and railways that link together fifty-five national economies that currently represent less than 2 percent of global market share.

What is needed in African and other low-income countries are instead carefully designed, targeted, and well-located infrastructure investments that allow their economies to spur the development of competitive industries. Such infrastructures would be most efficiently built in industrial parks for the industries and sectors selected in step 1 of the GIFF. That is the main lesson from economic history and most notably from China's success. When China started its spectacular growth (nearly 10 percent growth a year for three decades), its leaders were well aware that the country's infrastructure was poorer than Ethiopia's or even the Democratic Republic of Congo's today. They also realized that they did not have the financial resources and administrative capacity to build roads, highways, railways, ports, and airports in the entire country, or to foster regional interconnection with other (mainly poor) neighboring countries. The only sensible solution left was to set the correct priorities and to identify the geographic locations where high-quality infrastructure was necessary to support light manufacturing industries. Successful enterprises in these well-targeted industries, sectors, and locations quickly provided funding to support infrastructure projects in other parts of the country. As a result, China is well placed today to launch almost any regional integration infrastructure project its economy may need.

Simplify trade procedures, increase transparency and predictability of trade policies, and reduce the cost of satisfying border formalities. Most developing economies need to review their required import and export permits and licenses and reduce the costs of obtaining them, and they should implement standard border policies as well. In addition, there are specific issues that pertain to small cross-border traders that could be addressed to provide a clearer route to more effective formal trading arrangements. This is not necessarily an agenda of deregulation but rather one of delivering better regulation that allows government to achieve its public policy objectives but minimize the constraints to trade in doing so. This would require the involvement of traders, producers, and consumers in discussions about regulations that affect trade. On export bans the government could commit to precise notification procedures, both nationally and regionally, before restrictions on exports are implemented and make clear that bans will be implemented only if strategic reserves fall below a certain level (say a three-month supply).[6]

Solve credit and exchange rate issues. Access to stable financing at reasonable cost is an important prerequisite for firm performance and economic growth. At the microeconomic level, local manufacturers in potentially competitive industries still need to pay upfront in foreign currency for their imported equipment and inputs and to bear the often heavy costs of the exchange rate risk associated with a depreciating domestic currency. Hence they are hesitant to make the kind of large purchases that they would need to become viable producers on the global scene. Local banks in most developing countries do not grant preferential interest rates to large-scale investors, and the rates of interest are quite high (typically more than 20 percent).

The need to fund infrastructure projects is particularly important because their benefits to society as a whole are typically much larger than the private financial return is to the owner. Yet left alone, private investors would not necessarily finance them. Moreover, the process through which public infrastructure projects are selected and funding is allocated—especially in low-income countries—makes them subject to political pressure and elite capture. In these often authoritarian and unstable countries, the weak institutional framework, fuzzy budget rules, lack of transparency and accountability mechanisms, and need to accommodate political cronies at all government levels and beyond often lead to random and costly decision making.

At the macroeconomic level, overall investment and spending must be increased in all low-income countries to accelerate growth, create employment opportunities, and combat poverty. Although some developing countries' central banks have sometimes stimulated the economy through monetary policy—especially during the recent global downturn—by lowering interest rates and reserve requirements or purchasing government bonds held by financial institutions to make more resources available to the banking system (quantitative easing), most conceive their role as maintaining price stability, which they consider the best way to contribute to economic growth. But economic conditions in many developing countries remain slack, and high unemployment and underemployment persist. The consistently high capital flight from poor economies, a phenomenon also accompanied by a new buildup in external debt, reflects the existing challenges.[7]

In crisis situations where private-sector confidence and investors' willingness to take risk and to spend are low, the traditional Keynesian strategy consists of complementing loose monetary policy with higher public spending or lower taxes. Restoring aggregate demand through government action is then seen as the most effective way of replacing private spending that has not taken place. Most high-income countries have done just that to combat the 2008–09 global recession. But that strategy may well work for business cycles and fail when it comes to confronting growth and development structural issues of the types facing low-income countries. Moreover, the still dominant conventional wisdom—codified mainly in the old multiyear macroeconomic programs that poor countries used to negotiate under duress with the International Monetary Fund—is one that advocates "expansionary fiscal contraction."

Developing economies currently find themselves in a conundrum: aggregate demand is still too low, and there is no realistic expectation that it will increase sufficiently and rapidly enough to provide enough employment opportunities for poverty reduction. But it is financially, economically, and even politically impossible to increase government deficits—not least because of IMF program constraints. And even if central banks were willing and able to implement extraordinarily loose monetary policies, it would not be effective enough to produce high, sustained growth. What is therefore needed is a development financing strategy that sustains demand without creating unsustainable fiscal deficits.

A more viable solution to credit financing for economic development would be to strengthen development banks and public investment banks. Well-functioning development banks help countries meet two objectives simultaneously. They provide much-needed long-term financing to economies, contributing to expanding and modernizing infrastructure (energy, transportation, telecommunications, water supply), and they maintain sustainable fiscal balance. Reinforcing such banks' financial and economic role would not require developing country governments to substantially increase their borrowing. Rejuvenating public investment and development banks would stimulate confidence by supporting large-scale, regional investment projects and programs that create employment opportunities. But those investments would be made by the private sector or by some local governments, with the necessary funding borrowed or raised by the investment and development banks—not by central governments.[8]

Revitalizing these financial institutions would go a long way toward addressing the short-term market failures in private capital markets that currently exist and prevent poor economies from getting funding for their development projects. By making long-term finance available for sound investment, investment and development banks could support new export industries that reduce dependence on foreign borrowing to finance foreign products. Governments could use them to secure special credit lines and to provide incentives to commercial banks to offer in turn more favorable borrowing terms to firms in potentially competitive industries and sectors. This would also open up new possibilities for the development of new products and services by commercial banks (including insurance facilities against exchange rate risks).

Some researchers have argued that low investment has not been the major constraint on development in poor regions of the world; this is particularly so in Africa (Devarajan, Easterly, and Pack 2003). Africa's total investment rate has been below that of other developing countries, but public investment rates are often not that much lower. "Any statement about whether African investment was the source of poor performance would therefore have to analyze the composition of that investment—and whether more public investment, an instrument under government control, would have benefited the continent" (Devarajan, Easterly, and Pack 2003, 547). Although development and public investment banks have a poor track record across the developing world, it must be noted that these failures could again be traced to the blind pursuit of capital-intensive (modernization) projects that were not economically viable in the first place or were poorly managed and not upgraded to reflect changes in the economy's endowment structure.

Learning from past failures and successes, the new development finance institutions would operate on a "not-for-profit-maximizing" basis and borrow on the capital markets to finance economically viable projects in potentially competitive industries and sectors. They would offer partial or full guarantee of repayment of bonds issued by investment projects by bearing the risk and therefore reducing substantially the cost of funding. Newly revamped development finance institutions working with a rigorous, professional, and transparent operational framework would also issue their own long-term bonds with a modest premium over U.S. Treasury bills to raise money and finance large-scale projects directly. Good institutional and governance strategies would allow development and public investment banks to fund major infrastructure projects while consistently avoiding losses and maintaining a very low delinquency rate.[9]

Tackle unemployment, skills shortages, and other labor market issues. Unemployment and underemployment constitute perhaps the single most pressing economic issue facing policy makers around the world—especially those in developing economies. Investors also often point to skills shortages, weak human capital, and rigid labor laws as constraints to firm performance, again especially in low-income countries. Yet traditional, generic measures to address these problems are politically difficult to implement and often lead to disappointing results. Empirical analyses of the effectiveness of active labor market programs as remedies to unemployment or recipes for employment creation also rarely yield conclusive results (Betcherman, Olivas, and Dar 2004).

The GIFF suggests a three-pronged approach to tackling unemployment, underemployment, and other labor market rigidities. First, because of the difficulty of implementing labor market reforms for an entire country, which would have heavy short-term social costs, it recommends that the reforms be implemented initially in specific geographic zones. A special regime of labor laws and regulations could be granted to firms operating in industrial parks that allow more flexible hiring and firing practices and/or wage and benefit systems that will reduce their transaction costs.[10]

Second, governments, the private sector, and nongovernmental organizations should collaborate on the design and implementation of medium- and long-term workforce development plans for the selected industries. Most developing-country governments have shown commitment and have invested resources and efforts over the years to achieving quality education, considered the pillar of national development. Yet they still exhibit weak human development indicators and largely unsatisfactory education outcomes, indicating the need for a radical strategy change.

Performance and cost indicators in higher education are of particular concern in low-income regions of the world. In Africa, universities and colleges are understaffed, underfinanced, and in poor operating condition. The education quality is poor; the curricula are outdated, and graduates lack the basic skills needed to do their jobs. Despite their low revenue per capita, African countries have by and large managed to maintain a steady allocation of resources to higher education since the mid-1990s. On average, the continent has devoted 0.78 percent of its GDP to tertiary education, compared with 0.66 percent on average for other developing countries and 1.21 percent for OECD countries (Devarajan, Monga, and Zongo 2011). African governments also allocate about 20 percent of their current education spending to higher education, a rate higher than that of non-African developing countries (18 percent).

Because of demographic trends, the demand for higher education has been increasing faster than African governments' funding capacity. Although the quality of higher education is not a linear function of the resources available, there is some evidence that the decline in financing may have led to the deterioration of outcomes. Faced with economic crises and hard budget constraints—most notably in the 1980s and 1990s—many African governments reduced maintenance budgets and public wages, froze teaching staff recruitment and infrastructure investment, cut social aid and scholarships, and eliminated spending on books and equipment, all of which resulted in overcrowded lecture halls and excessive student-teacher ratios. Student protests and teacher strikes often prevented the curriculum's completion and weakened academic achievement. Limited funding and poor management are also associated with the sparse contributions to international academic research from researchers based in African colleges and universities. Inadequate funding also worsens the existing problems and diminishes the incentives for good faculty members to stay in the academic or research field when other employment is more profitable and more valued.

The financing gaps are likely to worsen in the future and create even more problems for Africa's higher education system. The ever-increasing number of college and university students (directly related to progress achieved in primary and secondary school enrollment) suggests that the current trends may be financially unsustainable. Given the currently narrow tax base and fiscal constraints of most African economies, and their dependence on foreign aid for much of their investment budgets, it is critical that the challenge of accommodating many students and providing them with a high-quality education be carefully analyzed.

The GIFF recommends that education and labor market reforms and resources be targeted to activities, programs, and projects that are economically viable. Governments should work with the private sector and the academic community to decide which type of education should be given priority and how to intervene in that sector to make success happen. To guide priorities in the education sector, some industries or lines of business should be identified—industries in which the country has clear or latent comparative advantage. In each selected priority industry (agribusiness, light manufacturing, tourism), the design and implementation of skills formation strategies and workforce development plans should provide a framework for firms, the government, and communities to work with one another.

These strategies and plans should include a holistic understanding of workforce issues and recognize that effective skills development can occur only when planned as part of the broader workforce and the future of the industry or community. They should identify issues common to an industry or community that are best addressed by their combined efforts or that cannot be addressed as an individual organization. All relevant stakeholders could then work together to analyze and address current and future workforce issues that may affect their future viability.

Developing countries should also focus their vocational training on industries in which their economies have clear or latent comparative advantage. Training could be provided both on the job (especially for agriculture/agribusiness, light manufacturing, and tourism) and in training schools. With the provision of knowledge and skills linked to acquiring the necessary job experience, trainees would be able to learn to cope with the job's constantly changing demands and to acquire precious "soft" skills. Government interventions would consist mainly of providing basic infrastructure, minimum regulations and quality assurance and connecting students to firms in various industries. The decisions made by individual companies as to their specific needs would make up both the aggregate demand and the aggregate supply of trainee vacancies.

Learning from other successful countries' experience, the policy makers and investors aim to develop the necessary workforce for the light manufacturing industry with strategies tailored to build human capital from specific groups:

→ For the existing workers, the focus could be to address shortfalls in skills as more experienced workers are taken by other sectors, particularly by the mining industry, and to provide pathways into manufacturing for people with skills in other sectors.
→ For new labor force entrants, the focus could be to improve the efficiency and effectiveness (retention) of pathways from high school to work—the type of basic assembly work in many light manufacturing activities that requires only high school-educated workers. By expanding pre-employment and prevocational places, the strategy would provide firms with work-ready new entrants and help them address the difficulty they face in attracting new entrants.
→ For women, whose contribution to effective poverty-reduction strategies in developing countries has been shown empirically (Strom 1989; Heath and Mobarak 2015), specific tasks and a more flexible and positive work environment should be created to attract them in large numbers.
→ For the many unemployed youth in geographic areas where light manufacturing industries are likely to build factories, the government and the private sector should actively seek to work with local communities and village networks to provide opportunities for training and employment for indigenous workers where expected demand for low-skilled labor will remain high.

Third, the GIFF calls for adjusting macroeconomic policies to proactively support employment creation in potentially competitive industries. Macroeconomic stability is of crucial importance, especially for developing economies that are small and most vulnerable to shocks. But the role of demand policies in the fight against unemployment should not be neglected, especially in developing countries with relatively good fundamentals. Output growth is the most important determinant of employment growth. Using fiscal and monetary policies whenever possible to support the economic recovery and sustain growth can help reduce uncertainty. It also makes firms more inclined to invest and recruit in economies where there is no lingering excess capacity.

There is generally little room for monetary policy, especially in countries where interest rates are already relatively low. But when the inflation threat is not too severe, central banks can resort to unconventional monetary policy tools to provide an enabling environment for business development. Monetary policy can also have large and long-lasting effects on real interest rates and, by implication, on output or unemployment. Furthermore, a sustained increase in real interest rates induced by monetary policy can affect not only the actual unemployment rate but also the natural rate: unemployment puts pressure on wages even when bargaining is only between employed workers and firms. Many unemployed college graduates throughout the developing world eventually give up their search or lose the skills gained from education. As a consequence, sustained high unemployment will lead to an increase in the natural rate itself. When monetary policy is able to affect real interest rates for a long period, it can also affect the natural rate of unemployment through capital accumulation. Real interest rates affect the cost of capital, the cost of capital affects capital accumulation, the capital stock affects the demand for labor, and the demand for labor affects unemployment.

Adopting a macroeconomic framework specifically geared toward employment creation and makes active labor market programs (ALMPs) much more likely to lead to positive results. In some countries there may be room for well-targeted fiscal measures that can increase economic output and job possibilities. Direct employment creation (that is, temporary jobs through public works), for example, would have a stabilizing effect in a climate of heightened sociopolitical tensions. Governments should refrain from hiring the unemployed directly but contract instead with private firms or nonprofit organizations to provide jobs. Vulnerable groups and people in the poorest regions and industries should be the targets of such measures.

In addition to providing much-needed income to people, typically the urban poor, well-targeted public works in infrastructure (new investment, repair, or maintenance) remove bottlenecks to growth and create the conditions for increased productivity. Accelerating the implementation of shovel-ready, labor-intensive, productive infrastructure projects should be a priority. Spending on productive infrastructure that removes bottlenecks on growth (with good rates of return) and spending on operations and maintenance can both boost demand and generate sources of growth in the longer run. Evidence from empirical work on Latin American and

Caribbean countries suggests that infrastructure investment can have a sizable impact on employment generation (Calderon and Servén 2011). It is true, however, that they may crowd out some private-sector jobs, especially if the targeting is ineffective. Salary levels should therefore be set carefully so that these programs are cost effective.

Wage subsidies can also be considered for industries that are clearly competitive but facing temporary shocks. They allow employers to keep employees on their payroll that they would otherwise lay off for economic reasons, and also to hire young workers or women by paying part of the salary for a given period. Wage subsidies allow such workers to acquire or develop important skills that eventually provide long-term employment. But because some employers may view subsidies simply as a temporary source of cheap labor, the risk of deadweight losses should also be considered. Governments should therefore be prudent in determining the subsidies' level and duration because extensive reliance on public-sector employment as a source of jobs and income often produces deep social and cultural consequences. Some regions can be caught in an equilibrium of dependency in which public-sector jobs become the only source of income, and opportunities for private-sector development do not materialize. This creates a vicious, self-fulfilling circle whereby entrepreneurship is discouraged while dependency on government for livelihood is enhanced. The end result is often the creation of powerful political constituencies of public-sector employees and unions who oppose labor market reforms.

Training programs to help new and laid off workers gain or regain skills could contribute to increased productivity if such programs are targeted to the neediest groups (youth, the disadvantaged, or women). Youth-oriented programs designed in close collaboration with private firms to assess demand for skills and to provide tailored training programs can yield good results. To ensure the maximum chance for success, they should be tailored to the business needs of the potentially competitive industries in each country.

Finally, job search assistance and employment services can help match jobs and job seekers. They are usually inexpensive and can reduce the length of unemployment. But they typically benefit only a small number of active job seekers. Promoting access to the information and communications technologies (ICT) sector could help remove supply- and demand-side constraints in the labor market. Young people are the biggest consumers of technology, which they can use to enhance their skills, seize opportunities, and connect to a global audience. Well-targeted policy measures to provide disadvantaged groups with access to ICT (IT alphabetization, investments to create ICT communal areas for rural youth and women, and so on) could foster the emergence of new economic activities and generate employment.

It should be acknowledged that many jobs in the labor-intensive industries generated in low-income countries through the GIFF will be low-wage opportunities, at least in the short term. But that is where all successful economies start. As their competitive firms improve their productivity and their industries grow over time, wages will increase, and policy makers will have to carefully anticipate the changes in their endowment structure and adopt new industrial-upgrading strategies. Unfortunately the notion that economic prosperity often starts with humble social and economic benefits is not understood by those who simply oppose world trade, capitalism, and globalization. And when a country like Bangladesh makes headlines for a tragedy such as that of Rana Plaza in April 2013, where poorly constructed and unregulated buildings hosting garment workers collapsed, killing more than 1,100 people and injuring 2,500, the understandable public outrage prompts some political leaders to give up on a strategy that has generally served the country well. In the tragedy's aftermath it was easily forgotten that the garment industry in Bangladesh employed in 2013 about 3.5 million people, mainly young women, and more than four-fifths of its $20 billion production went to Western markets (80 percent of exports), which was important for foreign exchange and government revenue. The pay at factories is generally much better than other industries, and, despite difficult work conditions and poor job security, sewing is less arduous than alternative employment, such as agricultural labor, construction work, cleaning homes, and shipbreaking. What Bangladesh, and many other countries that were able to ignite growth through developing labor-intensive industries, subsequently failed to do was to constantly monitor labor and construction laws to make necessary changes and to develop in parallel a viable strategy for industrial upgrading and diversification.

In an article provocatively titled "In Praise of Cheap Labor: Bad Jobs at Bad Wages Are Better than No Jobs at All" (1997), Paul Krugman, a Nobel laureate with impeccable credentials as a progressive economist, shocked many opponents of capitalism and globalization. He told the story of a large Manila garbage dump known as Smokey Mountain in which several thousand men, women, and children lived voluntarily, "enduring the stench, the flies, and the toxic waste in order to make a living combing the garbage for scrap metal and other recyclables . . . because the $10 or so a squatter family could clear in a day was better than the alternatives." He argued that while wages and working conditions in the third world's new export industries are appalling, they are a big improvement over the previous, less visible rural poverty. It is true indeed that in low-income countries where competitive new export industries have emerged, even at low wages there has been measurable improvement in the lives of the poor. This is because such growing industries can recruit workers only if they offer a somewhat higher wage than those workers could get elsewhere. In addition, the growth of manufacturing always has a ripple effect throughout the economy. Eventually, "the pool of unemployed urban dwellers always anxious for work shrinks, so factories start to compete with each other for workers, and urban wages also begin to rise. Where the process has gone on long enough—say, in South Korea or Taiwan-China—average wages start to approach what an American teenager can earn at McDonald's. And eventually people are no longer eager to live on garbage dumps."

Step 3: Seek Foreign Direct Investment or Facilitate New Firm Incubation Programs

The GIFF's third step consists of adopting nondistortive policy measures through which a state can support the establishment or development of competitive industries (identified in step 1) that may be completely new to domestic firms. This is particularly important in low-income countries where local entrepreneurs have difficulty connecting to supply chains and other business networks from which they could derive managerial expertise and learning and financing opportunities and gain international buyers' trust with their ability to deliver quality products on time.

To help address some of these coordination and externalities problems, the government could encourage firms in the target countries (where they are losing competitiveness mostly because of rising wages) to invest in these industries, because those firms are motivated by reduced labor costs to relocate their production to lower-income countries. The government could also set up incubation programs to assist private domestic firms' entry into these industries.

Neoclassical and endogenous growth models provide the main theoretical frameworks for understanding how foreign direct investment (FDI)[11] and international trade offer powerful channels for transmitting knowledge, ideas, and new technologies from advanced or middle-income economies to lower-income economies (Romer 1986; Lucas 1988; Barro and Sala-i-Martin 1995). FDI provides long-term capital and induces industrial upgrading and the adoption of new technology and innovation in host countries, stimulating economic growth.

In addition, FDI often stimulates fixed investment and exports and therefore boosts economic growth through increased aggregate demand. In the medium and long term, FDI contributes to transforming the industrial structure of the host economy and the commodity composition of its exports, typically toward producing more value-added goods and services. It has been observed that the presence in an economy of foreign firms with their superior technology and management skills generally forces domestic firms to more intense competition, leading to improved performance and more research and development (R&D) spending. That process tends to enhance the marginal productivity of the capital stock in the host economies and thereby promotes growth (Wang and Blomström 1992).

It has been observed that foreign firms' higher efficiency may help lower prices and hence increase consumers surplus (Lahiri and Ono 1998). FDI can also encourage the development of "agglomeration economies" by establishing clusters and networks of industries that are both collaborative and competitive (Krugman 1991). Ultimately, perhaps, FDI's most important benefit is that it raises employment in host countries by creating new jobs either directly or using local inputs and by generating the demand for additional services linked to the primary activities that have attracted external capital (thus indirectly creating more employment).

These benefits explain why all countries are now designing strategies to attract FDI. This includes the United States, which has traditionally not felt the need to advocate for FDI at the federal government level, leaving that responsibility to state and local officials. President Barack Obama himself recently promised to become more personally involved in attracting foreign investors to the United States; he proposed new steps to make the U.S. government more receptive to inward investment. Speaking to a gathering of 1,200 foreign investors at a Washington conference, the president said:

> Officials at the highest levels, up to and including me, are going to do even more to make the case for investing in America. As a country, we don't always make our case in a coordinated way that links our teams overseas to the right senior officials in Washington. And we're going to change that, make our advocacy more efficient, more effective, more connected so that businesses who are making decisions about where to invest are getting timely answers and know that they're going to have all the help that they need. . . . Think about it: globalization and technology means you can go just about anywhere. But there are a whole lot of reasons you ought to come here. (Politi 2013)

The president then touted his country's low energy costs, strong intellectual property protections, rule of law, and worker productivity.[12]

Obama instructed high-ranking officials in the Departments of State and Commerce to make attracting FDI one of their "core priorities," putting it as high on their agenda as export promotion. New global teams led by U.S. ambassadors in thirty-two key countries were charged with encouraging foreign investment in the United States, and a "coordinated process" has been set up to connect prospective investors with senior U.S. officials—and in "high-priority cases" all the way up to the president. This is a major shift for the United States. The White House director of the Council of Economic Advisers provided the following justification: "It's not a level playing field for a mayor of one of our cities to have to compete against a prime minister or head of state of a major industrial power when we are competing for the location of a new service center or manufacturing plant" (quoted in Politi 2013).

Developing countries need FDI even more, because it supplies much more than just capital. It also provides best-practice managerial know-how and opens up access to new technologies and international networks of suppliers and buyers. Since the mid-1990s the FDI volume in developing economies has become greater than that of official development assistance. It has been the dominant form of capital flow in the global economy, even for developing countries. Although other forms of capital flows (portfolio flows and private loans)[13] have been associated with economic crises in Latin America and Southeast Asia, FDI is considered less prone to crisis because direct investors typically take a longer-term perspective in their search for profitability. Direct investors are therefore more reliable development partners when engaging in a host country.[14]

Empirical studies tend to confirm most of the predictions from neoclassical and endogenous growth theories (Nath 2009; Saint-Paul 1992; UNCTAD 1992). But from a policy perspective the most relevant question is: what should a developing country do to attract growth-enhancing FDI? On that important topic, even the most carefully done empirical research has offered policy recommendations that simply reflect the traditional agenda for "improving the business environment." For instance, Asiedu (2006) shows that countries endowed with natural resources or with large markets will attract more FDI. Countries with good infrastructure, an educated labor force, macroeconomic stability, openness to external financial flows, an efficient legal system, less corruption, and political stability will also attract FDI. But such results may not be practical enough for developing countries that do not yet have adequate enough infrastructure and human capital to attract foreign investors.

The GIFF posits that economic research should provide more focused policy recommendations to help developing countries with insufficient physical and human capital, and even very poor governance environments, to also attract FDI. In such countries, the secret for success is again to identify the specific sectors and industries in which targeted economic reforms and actions by policy makers are most likely to yield the highest payoffs—both in FDI and in growth. New research shows that countries can indeed selectively attract FDI to specific sectors of their economy and be quite successful in channeling to those sectors financial resources that sustain growth and employment. The World Bank Census of Investment Promotion Agencies, which covers more than a hundred countries, notes that sector targeting is considered best practice by investment promotion professionals, because efforts concentrated on a few priority sectors are likely to lead to greater FDI flows than nontargeted, across-the-board attempts (Loewendahl 2001; Proksch 2004). A study based on difference-in-differences analysis by Harding and Javorcik (2011) shows that targeting of a particular sector by a national investment promotion agency leads to more than doubling of FDI inflows into the sector.[15] The exported products from sectors prioritized in national efforts to attract FDI have 11 percent higher unit values than other sectors (Harding and Javorcik 2012, 20).

For developing countries using the GIFF to identify their industries and sectors with the most competitive potential, the main questions are therefore what activities should be promoted to attract FDI, and what government policies should be in place to ensure the maximum likelihood of success. By definition, low labor costs are the most important factor from which to elaborate an economic development strategy in labor-intensive economies. Many low-income countries—especially in Africa—currently have very competitive labor costs that could overcompensate the costs arising from poor logistics, infrastructure, and business environment and help them attract companies based even in other developing counties where some industries are facing wage increases, which makes them less competitive and forces investors to consider relocation opportunities. At the development strategy's beginning, governments might have to encourage foreign firms to invest in their country. Once these foreign firms are established in sectors consistent with the economy's comparative advantages, local workers will gain training, and some of them will eventually be able to become managers either in these foreign corporations or in their own ventures. Workers will quickly become familiar with the technology and will be able to consistently deliver high-quality goods and services. They would know where to buy the intermediate products that are not available domestically and establish contacts with international buyers. The capital investment required to start such firms may not be too high, which makes the process easy to start if the government acts as a facilitator. To show its commitment to attracting investment, the government could set up a few well-located industrial parks (building factory shells, ensuring that they have adequate infrastructure, electricity, and telecommunications) and provide incentives for foreign firms to start their operations.

There are many historical and ongoing examples of such ventures that have proved to be major win-win opportunities for both developing countries and foreign investors. Perhaps the most spectacular example in modern times occurred in mainland China, which has been successful in mobilizing inward FDI. Most of the growth of China's exports can be attributed to foreign-invested enterprises, and per capita income growth in those regions of China where FDI is concentrated has been substantially higher than in other regions (Wei 1996). When market institutions were not fully in place in 1980s and 1990s, China experimented with opening up to foreign investment in selected coastal cities and in special economic zones and industrial parks with a focus on attracting export-oriented manufacturing FDI. Exports, measured in current U.S. dollars, grew at a 15.5 percent annual rate from 1978 to 2001 before China joined the World Trade Organization and further increased to 18.2 percent annually in 2001–2014. Meanwhile, the share of manufacturing products in exports increased from 49.7 percent in 1980 to 95.2 percent in 2014, making China the "factory of the world" (data from China's National Bureau of Statistics).[16]

Similar to Japan's policy after World War II, Korea's policy on FDI relied on extensive restrictions on capital inflows, reserved sectors, and ownership restrictions. Initially Korea preferred heavy foreign borrowing over substantial FDI inflows (Read 2002). It promoted technology transfer through licensing and other technical agreements. These provided a means, as in the case of Japan, for Korea to acquire important technology it could modify and use to promote domestic economic growth. It also encouraged targeted R&D to modify and develop new indigenous technologies and increased the likelihood of positive domestic technological spillover effects. This inward-looking strategy toward FDI was subsequently changed as a mature Korean economy has opened itself to both the emergence of new domestic firms and the entry of foreign multinational corporations. Initially the great bulk of FDI inflows came from Japan, which was responsible for almost 50 percent of all inflows until 1989. In recent decades the United States and the Netherlands have been responsible for between 30 and 50 percent of inflows, with a strong combined showing from elsewhere in Europe (France, Germany, and the UK).

Taiwan-China followed in Korea's footsteps. Its initial stance toward FDI was to attract export-oriented investment based on the competitiveness of its highly educated and productive labor force. FDI in Taiwan-China up until the mid-1970s was mainly in basic labor-intensive manufacturing, textiles, and clothing. Subsequently there was a marked shift into the chemical and electronic sectors, from the 1970s onward, and more recently FDI has flowed into the nontraditional food, metals, and machinery sectors. As the economy successfully grew and rapidly achieved structural transformation, the country modified this objective to focus on attracting

FDI in increasingly technology-intensive areas and to encourage or promote domestic technological spillovers (Read 2002).

Several other countries around the world have successfully followed the
same path. Bangladesh imitated China's strategy in attracting FDI to set up
labor-intensive industries in which its economy could prosper.[17] It started
in 1980 with a Korean firm that trained 160 workers in the garment industry. Only two years later, those workers were able to set up their own
shops. At present the garment sector in Bangladesh employs three million
workers. In an approach similar to the GIFF's, Rhee (1990) identifies the
major elements that have contributed to Bangladesh's resounding success
with garment exports. He sketches a catalyst model for initiating development in an outward-oriented direction, based on the pioneering efforts of
foreign and local catalysts. His model features mechanisms for transmitting throughout the entire economy the development initiated by catalysts.
It also offers a framework for sequencing realistic policy reforms, starting
from equal-footing export incentives (that is, equal footing with foreign
competitors), parallel to increasing industrial competence gained through
world market competition initiated and transmitted throughout the economy by the catalysts.

In the 1970s manufacturers from Hong Kong-China and Taiwan-
China invested in large ventures to produce quota-free garments in
Mauritius, thanks to proactive government policy to attract FDI in that
sector. This development allowed the local textile industry to improve
its infrastructure and become more competitive. They set up industrial
parks to circumvent some of the most challenging bottlenecks to firm
growth (most notably some rigidities in labor laws). The firm owners at
the beginning were from either Taiwan-China or Hong Kong-China. But
things changed quickly as local people became increasingly involved in
and knowledgeable of the industry. It is now estimated that more than
70 percent of the firms in the garment and textile industries are owned
by local people. Eventually the Hong Kong-China manufacturers left
Mauritius, moving their production facilities to lower-cost China. This
was a big challenge for the local textile industry but also an opportunity
for industrial upgrading. Prior to 2000 Mauritius was basically a "sewing"
country. This has now changed. Spinning has become important in the
production processes, and knitting is now the primary technology for fab-
ric formation. The country's factories produce more than 90 percent of all

required yarns, mainly cotton. Because of the ongoing "verticalization" of the industry, some big companies have spinning, knitting, finishing, and garment-manufacturing divisions. A small island nation, Mauritius offers high productivity and high-quality textile products supported by sophisticated business and trade organizations.

The recent development of labor-intensive industries in Ethiopia is perhaps the best illustration of operationalizing the GIFF. The country's success in attracting FDI and facilitating the creation of new firms that employ numerous local workers and export light manufacturing leather goods has sparked a lot of interest. To understand that achievement's significance, it must be noted that in 2012 Ethiopia was not considered a "good" place to invest at all. That year the country was ranked 125th in the *Doing Business Report* by the World Bank. In 2013 it dropped to 127th. Despite an average growth of 11 percent in Ethiopia's economy for nearly a decade, more than double the rate for sub-Saharan Africa, it was still not perceived as a place that could attract long-term private investment. Virtually no one believed that Ethiopia could be home to manufactured goods the country could successfully export to the global market.

Development experts and researchers tended to focus on its communist past and epic famines that sparked global appeals for help, its poor governance record, its macroeconomic policy inconsistencies, its lack of infrastructure, and its large (and potentially angry) population of almost ninety million, most with little education and low skills. Yet the Ethiopian authorities understood that they should use the discretionary power and limited resources of the government to set up industrial parks and provide infrastructure within these parks. That strategy has proved a very effective way of attracting investors from more advanced developing economies such as China who are forced to search for opportunities to relocate their labor-intensive activities that are no longer competitive at their current higher wage rates. Creating industrial parks with infrastructure good enough to give confidence to external investors is a critical aspect of the strategy. China and other countries followed a similar strategy of creating "islands of excellence" within which their private sectors did not face the overwhelming issues of poor business environments associated with developing economies. These well-designed industrial parks quickly became not only small shelters of excellent governance for potentially competitive firms but also powerful platforms from which backward and forward linkages could develop between local and external firms, as well as successful boosters for export-growth strategies. That strategy brought the foreign exchange and government revenues necessary to support public investment in other industries and government activities.

Following the GIFF, the late Prime Minister Meles Zenawi found the right entry point for the Ethiopian economy—light manufacturing in sectors with comparative advantage—and personally convinced foreign investors to relocate their increasingly uncompetitive activities from higher wage places like China to East Africa. Thanks to the prime minister's leadership and vision, Huajian, one of China's largest shoe exporters and the company that makes women's shoes for major Western brands such as Guess, Tommy Hilfiger, Naturalizer, and Clarks and employed 25,000 workers in mainland China, opened its first factory in a purpose-built industrial zone on the outskirts of Addis Ababa in January 2012. The Ethiopian venture started with just two production lines, an initial investment of less than $5 million, and about 600 workers. The firm was able to quickly employ 2,000 workers, and its exports grew fast. In just two years, about 4,000 new jobs were created. Huajian also signed an agreement with the China-Africa Development Fund, a private equity fund owned by the China Development Bank, to channel tens of millions of dollars of investments during a ten-year period into shoemaking clusters in Ethiopia. The government stepped in with the right approach to build a new industrial park in the Bole Lemi area in three phases. The first phase was financed by the government and was aimed at setting up twenty-two factory units to attract even more FDI. In 2013 eight factory units were built and fourteen others were quickly completed. Within three months all twenty-two units were leased out to export-oriented companies from Turkey, Korea, Taiwan-China, China, and Bangladesh. Hence one successful initial story was multiplied twenty-two times.

The Huajian story has convinced even the most skeptical investors that it is possible to build a vibrant manufacturing industry in Ethiopia. Until 2012 few international buyers had the confidence to place manufacturing orders with firms based in Ethiopia or anywhere else in Africa, because they needed not only competitive prices but also impeccable quality standards and reliable on-time deliveries. But times have changed: some major retail companies in the fashion industry (H&M, Tesco, and others) have now set up representative offices in Ethiopia to place orders and source products.

Although the Huajian project is an ongoing experience, engineering new business ventures and generating employment through a proactive government strategy to attract FDI, it can be said that it has sparked a new phase in Ethiopia's economic development. Its most important contribution to the country's future success may not even be the thousands of new jobs but the symbolic and powerful effect of its success on changing people's mind-set about the possibility of a poor African economy converting itself into a global manufacturing base. The Huajian story has made Ethiopia a credible destination for FDI.[18]

Inspired by Ethiopia's success, President Paul Kagame actively promoted Rwanda as a destination for export-oriented FDIs in light manufacturing. In response to the president's invitation, C&H Garments, a firm founded by Helen Hai, who was the manager of Huajian in Ethiopia, set up an operation in Kigali's special economic zone in February 2015, initially with 200 workers and expanding to 500 workers by July. Because of Rwanda's logistical and distance challenges, the firm has chosen to specialize in T-shirts and protective clothing, which are easy to transport, have a standard design, and can have a relatively long delivery lead time. The firm started to export in August, six months after setting up, and expected to expand to 1,000 workers by March 2016.

If Ethiopia and Rwanda, both landlocked countries with poor infrastructure, can competitively develop labor-intensive, light manufacturing products for global markets by using their comparative advantages in labor supply, other countries in Africa and across the developing world can adopt a similar approach to development and enjoy similar success. It is therefore an intellectual and even moral victory not just over poverty but also over the myth of an unshakable past, on the pessimistic notion that a poor infrastructure and bad business environment are a "death sentence" for any developing economy.

Step 4: Scale Up Self-Discovery by Private Firms

The GIFF highlights the key economic role that the government must play to tackle the coordination and externalities issues that no single firm can successfully address. But it also acknowledges the critical pioneering initiatives that the private sector constantly takes on to ignite and sustain the dynamics of economic growth. The GIFF is therefore a practical and realistic framework for implementing public-private partnerships in a manner that allows for continuous industrial upgrading for the most viable sectors. Owing to rapid changes in technology, some new opportunities might not have existed twenty years ago in dynamically growing countries. A good example is the information-processing service that started in India in the 1980s. Every country may also have some unique endowments that are valuable in the market but unavailable in other countries. The production of mangoes in Mali, discussed in the introductory chapter of this book, is a good example. Step 4 recommends that the government pay attention to spontaneous self-discovery by private enterprises and support scaling up successful private innovations in new industries.

This is a particularly delicate endeavor that requires adopting a transparent institutional setup to select industries, sectors, or firms to be supported and clear criteria for government support (means, duration, and monitoring). The government should not fall into the trap of past industrial policies that often consisted of granting subsidies and protection to nonviable firms and industries. Such policies often led to economic distortions and pervasive rent seeking and state capture by a few business leaders with good political connections. Although identifying potentially successful ventures will always involve trial and error, it is possible to mitigate that risk by ensuring that all decisions are the responsibility of an independent committee working under transparent rules. It should include policy makers, private-sector representatives, business experts, and academics. Using publicly discussed selection criteria, such a committee would be more likely to identify industries, firms, projects, or programs consistent with comparative advantage and could therefore be viable in open, competitive markets.

It is well known that several Asian countries—most notably Japan, Korea, Taiwan-China, and China—successfully followed that approach to develop competitive industries and firms (Scitovsky 1985; Wade 1990). The many episodes of failures observed in other developing countries did not invalidate the strategy. Yet those examples are often downplayed in mainstream economics and presented by some authors as simply evidence of a form of "Asian exceptionalism"—a code phrase for politely implying that the authoritarian Asian regimes are unique because they could run their economies with an "efficient" brutality that ensures discipline and high likelihood of success.

But the truth is that all developed economies in the world try to do exactly the same thing, irrespective of the ideological claims of the political party in power. The European Commission, the world's largest club of high-income countries, has been pursuing an integrated industrial policy approach since its creation. Its approach is outlined in the Industrial Policy Communications of 2010 and 2012.[19] The commission has constantly issued growth-enhancing recommendations to its member states. In many official documents, it has set out key priorities for industrial policy and specific actions to scale up self-discovery by private firms in the priority industries and sectors or to foster technological upgrading.

In the United Kingdom for instance, private-sector firms and government have joined forces to foster technological upgrading in several well-targeted industries. One of them, which they identified as the foundation for a competitive economy, is the rail supply chain.[20] Government experts and private-sector representatives worked together within a Rail Supply Group to set the strategic vision for strengthening the country's rail supply chain and to provide leadership, direction, and support so that the rail industry can grow employment and market share and make a substantial contribution to the UK economy. Cochaired by the business secretary, transport secretary, and a high-level industry executive, the group brings together private-sector representatives from across the rail industry and UK government leaders. It seeks to help British manufacturers take full advantage of the anticipated growth in domestic and international rail. Its vision statement, outlining how the industry will meet the demands of tomorrow's railways, create more employment, and boost UK exports, also sets out an ambitious view of the future where, by 2025, the industry will do the following:

→ More than double export volumes
→ Attract the very best UK talent to create a sustainable skills base and to develop new technologies
→ Harness the energy, drive, and innovation of SMEs to meet the global railway market's needs
→ Be a global leader in high-speed rail
→ Have an entrepreneurial supply chain that constantly innovates to meet customer needs from urban to intercity networks

Speaking at the program's official launch, the business secretary (from a proudly conservative government) declared:

Britain's valuable train supply chain is renowned for excellence in an array of disciplines from train design to signal solutions. We are committed to keeping the industry on track as a global leader which is why we are creating a unique partnership through the Rail Supply Group. The group will work together to future proof this valuable sector through a long-term Rail Supply Chain Industrial Strategy—creating more jobs and ensuring the UK can capture a share of the global rail market, worth £150 billion [about $186 billion] per year. (Government of United Kingdom 2014).

This announcement was just one more example of government support for the rail supply industry after the "Accelerating Innovation in Rail" collaboration between rail companies and Innovate UK. The Rail Supply Group awards financial support to businesses innovating in technologies that can address future challenges and customer needs in UK and international rail markets, laying the tracks for long-term growth.

Another example of the same type of public-private partnership aimed at boosting new industries' development is the Technology Demonstration Program, announced in September 2013 by the Canadian Ministry of Industry as a centerpiece of the government's Economic Action Plan. The program funds large-scale technology demonstration projects that typically require integrating several different technologies and coordinating many partners' activities. Demonstration activities involve moving new technologies out of the laboratory and testing them in real-world settings to ensure they fulfill their intended use in a safe and efficient manner. Companies often find it difficult to finance this step in the technology development process, which limits the speed and scale with which innovation is advanced.

The selection process is simple, transparent, and competitive. It starts every year with an initial call for project proposals, with statements of interest in the new program. Projects must be led by an original equipment manufacturer. Lead companies must bring together small and medium-sized Canadian-based companies to promote the development of supply chains as well as accredited Canadian universities and colleges or their affiliated research institutes to promote knowledge transfer. Approved projects are announced a few months later. The Technology Demonstration Program covers up to 50 percent of eligible project costs, including equipment located in broadly accessible hubs to fuel innovation.[21]

"Canada's aerospace and defence industries make important contributions to our economy, support high-skilled jobs across the country, and are leading investors in research and development," said the minister of industry at the event opening. "Our government is proud to launch this new program that will support large-scale technology demonstration projects with strong commercialization potential and that will promote cross-industry collaboration" (Government of Canada 2013). Jim Quick, president and CEO of the Aerospace Industries Association of Canada, offered the economic rationale for such support to private firms by the Canadian government: "Technology demonstration is a vital part of bringing innovation to market, but it is very complex and involves high levels of risk. The program announced today will help our companies to develop and produce the kinds of cutting-edge products that are at the heart of what makes Canadian aerospace companies the best in the world." Tim Page, president of the Canadian Association of Defence and Security Industries, concurred: "We believe that this program will help to create knowledge-based jobs in the defence and security sector and strengthen the ability of Canadian industry to support Canada's Armed Forces with world-class capability across the land, sea, and air domains. It will also contribute to greater Canadian success in export markets around the world."

Confronted with issues of coordination and externalities,[22] start-up firms in low-income countries face larger obstacles to success than those in advanced economies even when they have strong competitive potential. Developing-country governments should therefore learn from the experiences of countries such as the United Kingdom and Canada when designing and implementing transparent criteria for setting up a framework for public-private partnerships to encourage self-discovery.

Step 5: Transform SEZs and EPZs into Industrial Clusters

After identifying potentially competitive industries and designing viable strategies for removing obstacles to their development and to building public-private partnerships, policy makers face the challenge of concretely and quickly addressing certain cross-cutting issues (such as poor infrastructure, poor governance, rigid labor laws, and costly skilled labor for small market size) to attract domestic and foreign investors. Solving acute infrastructure problems is particularly important but typically requires substantial financial resources (as discussed in chapter 2).

Traditional development policy prescriptions provide that governments implement nationwide reforms that would lead to improvement in the business environment. In many countries, one of the publicized economic events of the year is the release of the *Doing Business Report*, which attempts to provide objective measures of business regulations and their enforcement across a large sample of economies and selected cities at the subnational and regional level. "By gathering and analyzing comprehensive quantitative data to compare business regulation environments across economies and over time, *Doing Business* encourages economies to compete towards more efficient regulation; offers measurable benchmarks for reform; and serves as a resource for academics, journalists, private sector researchers and others interested in the business climate of each economy."[23] The Doing Business project also offers detailed subnational reports, which exhaustively cover business regulation and reform in different cities and regions within a nation. These reports provide data on the ease of doing business, rank each location, and recommend reforms to improve performance in each of the indicator areas. Cities can compare their business regulations with other cities in an economy or region and with the economies that *are* ranked.

Although the Doing Business project is undoubtedly a very rich and useful information source for all policy makers concerned about binding constraints on economic growth, it remains unfocused and cannot be used as a formula for action. It randomly grants importance to all alleged obstacles to firm growth and productivity. It gives equal merit to "objective" problems subjectively identified and reported, often mixing up causal factors and policy consequences. Moreover, it always recommends lengthy lists of reforms to be carried out without clear criteria for prioritization. It is therefore not surprising that the report's annual release always generates controversies, because the top-performing economies in the world in recent decades tend to rank poorly.

What, then, should be done to effectively solve major issues such as the infrastructure deficit? Infrastructure development and maintenance are by definition highly capital intensive and quite costly. Building high-quality roads, ports, airports, railways, and electricity, water, and telecommunications systems across an entire country is also politically difficult, especially in countries with insufficient administrative capacity. The GIFF recommends a realistic strategy—one that political leaders would be more willing to spend their political capital on—which is to devote substantial financial and administrative resources to quickly implementing reforms in policy and geographic areas where visible, quick wins can be achieved. Observable positive results in generating new businesses and jobs would then provide the political and policy space to gradually implement even the most difficult reforms.

"A journey of a thousand miles begins with a single step," said Chinese philosopher Lao Tzu, stressing the importance of pragmatism when embarking upon a challenging and long endeavor. Great achievements often begin with very humble beginnings. Low-income countries facing a wide range of difficult infrastructure and other economy-wide constraints can gradually address them by creating well-targeted special economic zones (SEZs),[24] especially industrial parks. SEZs have often been used effectively by some latecomers (such as Ireland, Korea, Mauritius, Taiwan-China, and China) to emulate leading countries and even catch up with them in the race to economic prosperity.

The well-known rationale for SEZs in developing countries is to provide special policy incentives and infrastructure in a circumscribed geographic location to firms that can attract foreign direct investment, create jobs, develop and diversify exports (even when economy-wide business environment problems and protective barriers are not yet resolved), increase foreign exchange earnings, and serve as "experimental laboratories" for new pricing, financial, or labor policies. Policy incentives in SEZs typically include import and export duty exemptions, streamlined customs and administrative controls and procedures, facilitated access to foreign exchange, and relatively low income-tax rates. Export-oriented SEZs are intended to "convey 'free trade status' to export manufacturers, enabling them to compete in global markets and counterbalance the anti-export bias of trade policies" (FIAS 2008, 12). For instance, several African countries that successfully established export-processing zones have benefited by gaining entry to the African Growth and Opportunity Act (AGOA) market in the United States.[25]

SEZs specifically designed as industrial parks and export-processing zones also have the benefit of encouraging industrial clustering. They are more likely to produce increasing returns (economics of agglomeration) arising from localizing industries. These increasing returns, mainly in the form of localized external economies, allow for large-scale production. That process is sustained by the agglomeration effects observed in nineteenth-century England and described by Alfred Marshall: information spillovers, specialized suppliers, and deep labor markets (geographical concentration of the skilled or unskilled workers needed by the various industries).[26] In sum, industrial parks and export-processing zones can generate direct benefits from export growth and export diversification, employment and income generation, foreign direct investment, foreign exchange and government earnings, and indirect benefits such as technology transfer, skills upgrading, and knowledge spillovers that eventually translate into productivity increases across the entire economy.

It must be noted, however, that creating an SEZ is not in itself a panacea to solve the infrastructure deficit in a developing country. There have been many examples of disappointing experiments across the developing world.[27] In many countries, the benefit-cost ratio for setting up and running SEZs has been disappointing. Personal income tax on employment, permit fees and services charges, sale and rental fees on public land to developers, import duties and taxes on products from the zones sold to the domestic customs territories, concession fees for facilities such as ports or power plants, and corporate income tax (when assessed) totaled only negligible amounts. In the meantime, import duties and charges lost from the smuggling opportunities created by SEZs, tax revenue forgone from firms relocating from the domestic customs territory into the zones, public investment for (often untargeted) infrastructure, and recurrent expenditures (mainly the wage bill of public-sector workers needed to run and regulate the zones) often represent substantial costs to governments.

The reasons for such failures are discussed in the next chapter. Suffice it to note here that among the factors often listed in the economic and business literature (from poor institutional design and management of the initial concept to ineffective macro- and microeconomic policies), the most important ones are the lack of clear criteria for industry selection, which has often led developing countries to launch SEZs that do not promote potentially competitive industries; the ineffective choice of location, which can lead to additional costs for firms; and governments' inability to provide the supporting investment and accompanying policies to facilitate economic takeoff and linkages to the domestic economy. The GIFF recommends that careful consideration be given to the provision of basic infrastructure and policies necessary for the success of SEZs.

Step 6: Provide Limited Subsidies to Compensate for Externalities

Step 6 of the GIFF recommends that governments be willing to compensate pioneer firms in competitive industries with time-limited tax incentives, cofinancing of and direct credit for investments, or access to foreign exchange. This type of policy prescription often generates controversy, even though all successful countries in the world—at all development levels—continually use such measures. So let us explain the rationale for it and how it can be done without resulting in state capture and corruption.

The question often raised by state intervention skeptics is: why should governments consider granting small and time-limited subsidies to private firms already engaged in competitive industries? It is a legitimate question. There are several reasons for governments to provide financial support to firms operating in industries of latent comparative advantage. First, almost everywhere in the world access to finance can be an impediment to firm growth, especially for new ventures offering products and services that require substantial initial investment. This is even more the case for developing economies whose factor endowments must quickly change to reflect an increasing share of capital relative to labor. As discussed in previous chapters, the factor endowment—defined as the relative composition of natural resources, labor, human capital, and physical capital—reflects an economy's development level, and sustained growth is both the cause and the result of steady changes in the economy's endowment structure. For the economy to evolve from low- to middle- and high-income status, firms' nature, size, organization, and operations must constantly adjust to the economic and business conditions. This happens only when governments provide the necessary hard and soft infrastructures and coordinate their improvements (Lin 2012a).

Developing-country firms have unique characteristics and specific needs that require particular types of public policy support. They operate in economies where capital is scarce relative to labor and/or natural resources. Their production activities should be labor-intensive or resource-intensive and rely on conventional, mature technologies for manufacturing "mature," well-established products. Except in the mining and some agro-processing industries, their production generally has limited economies of scale. Firm sizes are usually relatively small, often with informal market transactions and limited to local markets with familiar customers.

Developing-country firms also differ from firms in developed countries in other ways, such as size distributions, ownership, financing patterns, and institutional constraints (Ayyagari, Demirgüç-Kunt, and Maksimovic 2012). Bank finance is the largest firms' major source of external funding. They have a high proportion of net fixed assets to total assets and use little long-term debt financing.[28] Many of these large firms also have access to foreign capital, bringing them various benefits (reduced cost of capital, an increased shareholder base, greater liquidity, enhanced prestige, and so on). But the majority of firms in developing countries are small in size. In fact, informal firms and household enterprises typically account for up to half of all economic activity according to some estimates and for more than 70 percent of employment.[29] Their productivity is extremely low. They are typically run by less educated managers, do not export, do not have large customers, and do not rely on external finance (La Porta, Lopez-de-Silanies, and Shleifer 2008). Informal financing typically relies on relationships based on trust and reputation but has been shown to be associated with lower firm growth and increased firm illegality (for example, tax evasion) than formal finance (Ayyagari, Demirgüç-Kunt, and Maksimovic 2010).

A second reason for governments to provide financial support is that all firms—even those operating in industries consistent with the country's comparative advantage—face coordination and externalities problems. Such problems occur in a variety of ways, each of which is central to the economic development process: investment, innovation, labor training, and so on.[30] Pioneer firms may fail owing to the lack of adequate infrastructure needed for the new industry to succeed, because they have difficulty finding and retaining the specialized skilled workers to operate their equipment or because they are too small and therefore excluded from the suppliers' networks where complementary inputs can be purchased at competitive costs.

If left completely to chance or to the private sector's supposed risk-taking propensity, industrial upgrading is likely to be a completely random and costly trial-and-error discovery exercise. For instance, pioneer firms may need information about their industries. Such information has the same properties as public goods: The costs of collecting and processing information are substantial; however, once the information is generated the marginal cost of allowing one more firm to share the information is almost zero. Therefore there are few incentives for one firm to bear that cost alone, especially in a competitive, open environment. The government can play a facilitating role by investing in information collection and processing and making information about the relevant new industries freely available to firms. The same is true for recruiting highly specialized workers for equipment maintenance or repair. It may be too costly for one firm but would be financially easier to do if several firms—even competitors—were willing to share such expert resources. There again a government team playing its facilitating role could help mobilize expert resources, at least for infant industries.

Technological innovation and industrial upgrading also involve changes in capital and skills requirements for firms, as well as changes in their market scope and infrastructure needs due to the evolving nature of production embodied in the process. Individual firms are not capable of internalizing these provisions or of deploying the kind of coordination efforts among firms in different sectors to meet these increasing demands. Even when some large single companies are willing to finance the construction of a national road or a power network, coordination and various forms of financial support by the public sector are always needed to ensure consistency and efficiency and to prevent the forming of natural monopolies when the national economy grows. For instance, it has been observed that the development of export agriculture and the agribusiness industry always depends on government financial and logistical support. In countries that have been successful in exporting cut flowers, for example, firms have benefited from many forms of government support, such as the construction of cooling facilities near airports, subsidized low-cost storage facilities for cargo freight at airports, and flight schedules that suit the needs of foreign markets and are secured through the government's soft power. In potentially competitive industries that require substantial initial investment, having government guarantees also helps local firms attract external partners.

To avoid rent seeking and the risk of political capture, financial incentives provided by the government should be limited both in duration and in cost and should not be in the form of monopoly rent, high tariffs on imports, or other distortions. In addition, the process of allocating and removing financial incentives among firms and industries should be fully transparent and contestable. Countries that have successfully managed such processes have generally relied on interministerial committees or independent panels comprising public and private sector representatives and some outside experts (mainly from academia). The list of projects submitted for consideration is then reviewed and validated by respected experts following an open and transparent process with clear selection, performance, and monitoring criteria.

In advanced economies already on the global technology and industrial frontier, firms are mostly formal and have access to formal financing. They also rely on creative destruction or the invention of new technology and products for achieving technological innovation and industrial upgrading. Even those firms often benefit from strong government support because they are engaged in the upgrading process and need to undertake risky R&D activities that generate nonrival, public knowledge (which benefits other firms in the economy). Governments provide subsidies for firms' R&D, funding for basic research in universities, patents for new inventions, and preferential taxes and defense and other government procurements.[31] Developing economies—especially low-income countries—cannot and need not devote as many resources to R&D as high-income countries because their distance from the technological frontier gives them enough room to achieve sustained growth through imitation (producing mature goods and services at lower costs) and integration into global value chains.

* * *

In sum, it can be said today that any developing country—even those with poor infrastructure and a weak business environment—can start on a path to dynamic structural transformation and growth. Any country in the world, regardless of its current conditions, can experience economic miracles. How? Not by chance and randomness, as one could describe President Carter's experience in the Camp David agreements but instead by facilitating technological innovation and development for industries in which it has a comparative advantage. The only condition is for policy makers to adopt and carefully follow the approach outlined in this chapter. Sometimes the results materialize so quickly that they surpass expectations.

Take China: at the time of its transition to a market economy in 1979, the country's per capita income was less than one-third of that of the sub-Saharan countries. Its business environment was poor, its infrastructure was very bad, and it lacked the capacity to take advantage of its cheap labor market to produce goods for export. To overcome these obstacles, the Chinese government—at all levels and in all regions—encouraged foreign investment in special economic zones and industrial parks. This enabled China to rapidly develop labor-intensive light manufacturing and become the world's factory.

In 1979, when its economic transformation began, China's official goal was to quadruple GDP growth in twenty years; its goal for its annual average growth rate was 7.2 percent. No one believed China could achieve these goals, because of its poor business environment, its communist past, and its perceived bad governance. Its exports were extremely low. Most people were living in deep poverty. Many observers, including in China, thought that realizing a 7.2 percent annual growth rate for twenty years straight was impossible. They saw it as a political slogan. Looking at China today, we see that the miracle has happened. The average growth rate was 9.8 percent for several decades, exceeding the 7.2 percent target by 2.6 percentage points. It lasted not only for twenty years but for thirty-five consecutive years. China has become a middle-high-income country. It is likely that it will become a high-income country by 2020.

With the right policies and the right strategies, prosperity can occur in a generation. One economic concept played a central role in China's success: the special economic zones and industrial parks. Since then some developing countries have tried unsuccessfully to develop these zones. Given their importance, we devote the next chapter to the analysis of the conditions needed to design and implement successful special economic zones and industrial parks.

7

Reaping the Dividends of Globalization: A Winning Road Map

One day in 1946 in Argentina, shortly after a president had come to power in a military coup, a representative of the new government went to the prestigious Buenos Aires Library to inform one of its staffers that his tenure was over. The staffer in question had written some fictional short stories and had contributed to a literary journal and was thus perceived in some political circles as a nuisance. His dismissal was conceived with some humor: he was "promoted" to inspector of rabbits and poultry of public markets. When he asked why, the response was straightforward: his humiliating new assignment was justified because of his (perceived) political opinions. He immediately resigned from the inspector position and found himself with no other career choice than to search for his true calling.

He had previously been an unsuccessful poet and writer, and he was shy and not considered articulate—not even by his own mother. He was also rapidly becoming blind. Regardless, some of his friends helped him find a job as a literature professor, which eventually led to invitations to teach, write, and lecture in some of the most prestigious venues and academic institutions in the world. He had carefully reflected on what he knew best and on what he could do better than almost anyone else. He prepared his public appearances meticulously and delivered them to make the maximum impact. And he realized that his escape route from failure was to look for intellectual and professional opportunities well beyond his country's boundaries. He had no choice but to try to sell his skills on the global labor market.

To his surprise and to the amazement of his family, friends, and adversaries alike, his search for a new career and life strategy was a success. His literary, oratory, and teaching skills quickly received recognition beyond the Argentinian market. His talents and services were in high demand in North America, Europe, and Asia. He became so good at his new occupation that he rapidly established himself as one of the most sought-after international lecturers in the world. He mesmerized global audiences in sold-out lectures across the globe. He wrote many books that became instant classics, earned him many prestigious literary prizes, and cemented his place as the master of the modern short story and one of the twentieth century's finest writers. Thanks to his dismissal from the library, Jorge Luis Borges—yes, it was him—went from a complete unknown to one of the most towering figures in literary history. Losing his obscure assistant job turned out to be a major career blessing and source of revenue and fame— and eventually, after the military dictator was overthrown in 1955, he was even appointed director of the Buenos Aires Library.

Borges's success story is a metaphor for the potential benefits that a crisis can bring to one's life—and to economic policy making—and for why developing countries should never shy away from global trade. When hit suddenly by a negative shock that forced him to change his life trajectory, Borges had to do some soul searching and reallocate his (intellectual) resources to activities that he knew he could perform best. He found the right entry point for his work and focused on services that could quickly generate the highest payoffs. Because of his country's political circumstances and the absence of a national market for his services, he was also forced to "think global" and to connect to international markets and networks where his expertise was not only most needed but also most highly rewarded. Perhaps unwittingly, he traded his skills on the international market, found a gratifying niche for his talents, and rapidly gained from it. Also, it is very likely that Argentina eventually reaped some balance-of-payments gains from his economic success abroad.

What Borges did was to identify and tap into his latent comparative advantage and exploit the opportunities beyond his nation's borders. The major crisis that could have ended his career forced him to see opportunities beyond his traditional horizon. His story also provides a metaphor for any low-income country that has been facing economic shocks. The 2008–09 financial and economic crisis should have been a similar moment of truth. Not for soul searching—the general recipe for success is readily available—but for redefining a country's economic strategy and focusing its resources in activities where it has comparative advantage.

This chapter outlines a road map for doing just that. It starts by discussing long-term trends and fundamental issues in global trade—because trade is the main source of growth for low-income countries that have limited domestic demand. In recent years the story of global trade has often been presented by some economists and development experts as a cause for concern—concerns that the export-led growth model that made possible the so-called Asian Miracle is no longer available for poor countries in Africa or South Asia. Statistics appear to show a turning tide: the value of world merchandise exports rose from \$2.03 trillion in 1980 to \$18.26 trillion in 2011, equivalent to 7.3 percent growth per year on average in current dollar terms (WTO trade statistics). But in 2012–2014, world trade growth averaged only 2.2 percent, well below the average for the proceeding 20-year period. This has raised the question whether the same shaping factors that have given rise to today's global trade system are likely to continue in the medium and long term. Development economists' fear is palpable. They wonder whether transport and communication costs will maintain their dramatic, linear decline from continued incremental technological improvement or the introduction of entirely new technologies. They also debate whether the marginal improvements observed in recent decades will diminish in the future, making declining transport and communications costs a less salient shaping factor for world trade—even leading to a slowing of trade growth.

Such questions are the reaction to the analysis of fundamental changes in global trade patterns, showing that developing countries can still gain from a much larger world economy, but they must confront the new barriers to trade and organize their economies to enter global value chains. As Jawaharlal Nehru, India's first prime minister, famously said, "Every little thing counts in a crisis." The current global economic crisis provides a unique opportunity for developing economies to also carefully review their strategies, policies, and instruments for reaping new benefits from an increasingly interlinked world economy. The second part of this chapter outlines the benefits of clusters, discusses what is wrong with the current institutions for fostering trade (most notably the special economic zones), and presents guiding principles for building and running them effectively.

GLOBAL TRADE TRENDS AND PATTERNS:
NOTHING TO FEAR BUT FEAR ITSELF

An important new narrative in the economic discourse on global growth tells the story of a deep decline in global trade with potentially catastrophic consequences for the world economy. In the words of Gavyn Davies, "world trade has lost its mojo," and global trends support his observation. From 1990 to 2008 global real GDP expanded at a 3.2 percent annual rate, while world trade volume grew at 6.0 percent. Since 2008, however, world trade has grown slightly slower than GDP, so the share of exports in GDP has actually fallen after a twenty-five-year uptrend (Davies 2013). The first reason many researchers provide for this trend is that protectionism has been on the rise (Evenett 2013). This raises fears of a repeat of the protectionist disaster in the 1930s and has led to the logical conclusion that multilateral negotiations on trade barriers should be revived and made the centerpiece of the world's economic agenda.

Another, even more disturbing suggestion is the idea that the export-led growth model, allowing many previously poor countries such as Korea and China to lift large parts of their populations out of poverty and become dominant global economies in the past few decades, may have run its course. In the words of Howard Pack (2010):

> The earlier experience is likely to be difficult to replicate. First, the generation of huge industrial complexes benefitting from agglomeration economies, particularly in China, makes it difficult for new entrants to compete. Second, over the next decade the major international macroeconomic adjustment will consist of the reduction in excess demand by a few countries, notably the United States and a concomitant increase in domestic absorption of GDP in a number of surplus countries mainly in Asia. To achieve a share of (relatively) contracting U.S. imports will not be easy nor will it be easy for non-Asian emerging markets to penetrate the Chinese and other Asian markets as they redirect their own production toward domestic uses.

These are valid concerns because they reflect the recent trends and changing patterns of global trade. But the facts and figures on which they are based can be analyzed differently. It would be unfair to compare the new trade skeptics' views to the export pessimism of the early structuralists in the 1950s. But their thesis is somewhat reminiscent of Raul Prebisch (1950) and Hans Singer (1950), who interpreted the international trade slump in the Great Depression as a sign that developing countries would not be able to gain from opening their economies. They believed that the decline in the terms of trade against the export of primary commodities was a secular and almost irreversible phenomenon, and that any attempt to boost developing countries' exports would simply result in the transfer of income from resource-intensive poor countries to capital-intensive rich countries. In Latin America, where such views were most influential, political leaders and social elites chose to adopt inward-looking economic policies not based on their economies' comparative advantage, which eventually proved to be a misguided strategy.

The kind of trade skepticism expressed today by leading economists is not based on the principles of early structuralism. But they use analogous reasoning. Let us review their arguments. First, the initial proposition that global trade must always expand at a much higher pace than global output and that anything less would be detrimental to global economic prospects is not supported by historical evidence. While trade has grown faster than output since 1950, up through about 1970 that only represented a return to levels of trade relative to output that prevailed before World War I (Krugman 2013). One should not set the almost exponential rate of trade expansion after 1970 to be the norm. It reflects the profound changes in the global economic environment, the declining costs of trade among nations, new technological developments, and the understanding that the rules governing commercial and financial transactions among firms in nations across the world should be amended to benefit all. In addition, business cycles tend to produce large fluctuations in trade, much bigger in percentage terms than the changes in GDP.

Over the long term, the trade-GDP relationship is usually not a static one. Douglas Irwin (2002) examined the statistical relationship between world trade and world income (GDP) over three different epochs: the pre–World War I era (1870–1913), the interwar era (1920–1938), and the post–World War II era (1950–2000). He found that trade grew slightly more rapidly than income in the late nineteenth century, with little structural change in the trade-income relationship. His study also showed that in the interwar and postwar periods, the trade-income relationship can

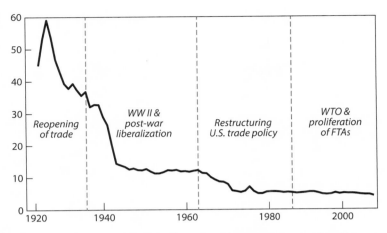

Figure 7.1. U.S. trade-weighted tariffs on dutiable imports (percent) and historical periods, 1930–2008. *Source*: USITC staff compilation from U.S. Department of Commerce statistics.

be divided into different periods owing to structural breaks, but since the mid-1980s trade has been more responsive to income than in any other period under consideration. It is therefore not too surprising or even a major concern that world trade volume has been virtually stagnant in recent years—or even on a declining trend. Irwin's study also highlighted that the trade policy regime differed in each period, from the bilateral treaty network in the late nineteenth century to interwar protectionism to postwar liberalization under the General Agreement on Tariffs and Trade (GATT) and the World Trade Organization (WTO). The commodity composition of trade has also shifted from primary commodities to manufactured goods over the past century, but the results cannot directly determine the reasons for the increased sensitivity of trade to income.

Is protectionism the culprit for the recent decline in global trade? That contention too is not supported by the facts. As noted by Paul Krugman (2013), the rapid trade growth since World War II was driven by major waves of trade liberalization, which took place in advanced economies until about 1980 (figure 7.1) and in developing economies since then (figure 7.2), and by the almost linear decline of trade barriers over the course of the twentieth century.[1]

Now, skeptics could argue that there has been a reversal of the declining trend in average tariffs after the Great Recession of 2008, which in

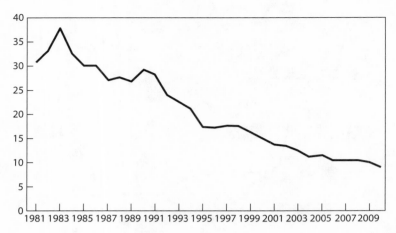

Figure 7.2. Evolution of average tariffs in developing countries, 1980–2009 (in percent).

their view is the reason world trade grew by less than 3.0 percent in 2012 and 2013, compared with the precrisis average of 7.1 percent (1987–2007). C. Constantinescu, A. Mattoo, and M. Ruta (2015) have examined whether the slower growth in trade reflects simply the sluggishness of GDP or there is a deeper structural shift in the relationship between trade and GDP. They find that the long-term elasticity of trade with respect to income was 1.3 between 1970 and 1985, rose to 2.2 in the period 1986–2000, but reverted back to 1.3 in the 2000s. Looking specifically at the 2000s, they find that a 1 percent increase in income was associated with a 1.5 percent increase in trade from 2001 to 2007 and a 0.7 percent increase from 2008 to 2013. This suggests that that the change in the trade-income relationship cannot be entirely attributed to the financial crisis. But it cannot be inferred from these numbers that protectionism is the culprit. In fact, their empirical analysis shows that the changing structure of global trade and aggregate demand accounts for much more than any resurgence of protectionism.[2]

The main reasons for the declining trends in tariffs are the successful outcomes of multilateral negotiations pursued under the GATT after World War II—including the Uruguay Round, completed in 1994—and the granting of special preferences by industrialized countries to developing countries for their exports.[3]

But tariffs are only part of the story of global trade flows and patterns. Many other important factors determine the flow of trade among countries. Firms involved in international trade are also and increasingly confronted with nontariff measures (NTMs) that can seriously restrict their business transactions through important changes in the quantities of goods and services traded, or their prices. NTMs represent a wide range of regulations and requirements other than customs tariffs, which all countries apply to exports and imports of goods and services. They include customs procedures, technical regulations, conformity assessments, and so on.[4] They vary across products and countries and are often changed quickly and unilaterally by national governments and other sovereign entities. Their purpose is generally not to impose new forms of protectionism but to ensure public health and safety, environmental standards, compliance with various standards, or even some broad ethical values that authorities in each country may subjectively determine.

For instance, in many industries, compliance with international standards has become a critical criterion for firm performance in global markets. Goods exported from developing countries are often rejected at their destination country's border on quality or sanitary grounds. In the case of perishable foods, entire consignments are destroyed at the point of entry—after the producers have already incurred substantial production and transportation costs. In other instances, these undesirable consignments must be shipped back to their place of origin. Such rejections not only cause major financial losses for the producers, but they can also damage their home country's reputation and discourage business initiatives in other potentially competitive and profitable sectors. The rejection problem illustrates the limitations of the Doing Business prescriptions in developing countries: no amount of procedural changes or streamlining of documentation can overcome such situations.

Empirical studies based on various methodologies have estimated the negative impact of NTMs on trade, focusing on "direct" and "indirect" approaches.[5] José de Sousa, Thierry Mayer, and Soledad Zignago (2012) have provided evidence that the difference between de jure protection (tariffs) and de facto protection (the tariff equivalent of crossing borders) is almost always much greater for developing countries, leading to the conclusion that most trade costs—other than those associated with geographical distance—are associated with NTMs. In most countries, few individual firms (especially small and medium-sized enterprises) involved in international trade can comply with NTMs.

One obvious solution is to ensure that firms in developing countries can produce better-quality goods and services, which have been inspected, tested, and certified—through an internationally recognized accredited body—before they are shipped overseas. Although such a requirement may appear to burden production costs and slow down business processes, the savings will ultimately far outweigh the initial costs. Conformity assessment certificates will facilitate and expedite the transit process, and goods and services that go through such a rigorous process will pass through borders more quickly because the risk of rejection will be minimized.[6] Another solution, not exclusive of the first one, is to develop special zones where such problems are most efficiently handled. This is discussed below.

Despite the NTMs, the general, long-term trend of global trade is still a very positive one for developing countries. Moreover, the declining general trend in average tariffs around the world is unlikely to be rolled back given the structural changes declining tariffs have induced in the global production system and the enormous win-win opportunities they have created for advanced and developing economies. The best indicator of that evolution is that many goods are manufactured now in several countries at the same time. Global trade is therefore no longer a series of transactions between countries producing individual goods and services within their national boundaries and exchanging them in international markets. It is often about collaboration and partnerships, even in an intensively more competitive world. Manufacturing is increasingly a network of global supply chains in which the various production stages take place in the most cost-efficient locations—regardless of where they are in the world (Baldwin 2011).

Perhaps nothing better illustrates the changes in recent years in world trade than a disaggregated picture of an aircraft, revealing the distribution of productive knowledge among nations and the need for cooperation. As shown in figure 7.3, the Boeing 787 aircraft, one of America's more visible industrial flagship products and a major symbol of modern times, is actually the work of a very large number of firms from many different countries. Years ago the management team at Boeing adopted a business model aimed at cutting costs and reducing its employee count by outsourcing the design and manufacture of 787 parts all over the planet. The rationale was to avoid "betting the company" on 787 development and instead to convince

Global Partners by Country

United States	Japan	Canada	United Kingdom	Australia
Boeing	Kawasaki	Boeing	Messier-Dowty	Boeing
Spirit	Mitsubishi	Messier-Dowty	Rolls-Royce	
Vought	Fuji			
GE				
Goodrich	**Korea**			
	KAL-ASD			
France	**Sweden**			
Latecoere	Saab			
Italy				
Alenia				

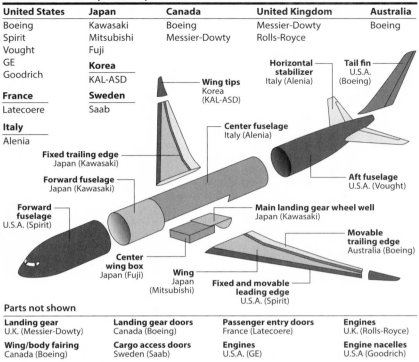

Wing tips
Korea
(KAL-ASD)

Horizontal
stabilizer
Italy (Alenia)

Tail fin
U.S.A.
(Boeing)

Center fuselage
Italy (Alenia)

Fixed trailing edge
Japan (Kawasaki)

Forward fuselage
Japan (Kawasaki)

Aft fuselage
U.S.A. (Vought)

Forward
fuselage
U.S.A. (Spirit)

Main landing gear wheel well
Japan (Kawasaki)

Movable
trailing edge
Australia (Boeing)

Center
wing box
Japan (Fuji)

Wing
Japan
(Mitsubishi)

Fixed and movable
leading edge
U.S.A. (Spirit)

Parts not shown

Landing gear	Landing gear doors	Passenger entry doors	Engines
U.K. (Messier-Dowty)	Canada (Boeing)	France (Latecoere)	U.K. (Rolls-Royce)
Wing/body fairing	**Cargo access doors**	**Engines**	**Engine nacelles**
Canada (Boeing)	Sweden (Saab)	U.S.A. (GE)	U.S.A (Goodrich)

Figure 7.3. Partners across the globe are bringing the 787 together.

suppliers from various countries—including firms that were competitors to Boeing—to spend hundreds of millions of their own dollars to design and produce the parts. Even within the United States, the company managed to obtain substantial fiscal advantages from states and local governments that were interested in its potential for employment creation. Just to secure the final assembly jobs, the state of Washington granted Boeing a tax break so massive that the WTO deemed it an illegal subsidy (Groves 2013).

The Boeing production strategy has led to some controversial financial results.[7] But it was successful in bringing together an unlikely coalition of firms in a carefully choreographed industrial ballet—one that illustrates well some of the major trends in today's global economy. One of the engines of the 787 aircraft is produced in California, the other in the United Kingdom; the wing tips are from Korea; the movable trailing edge from

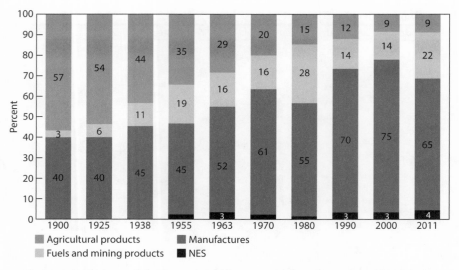

Figure 7.4. 100 years of changes and opportunities: product shares in world merchandise exports, 1900–2011 (percent). *Source*: WTO (2014, 54). NES ("not elsewhere specified") is used (a) for low-value trade and (b) if the trading party designation was unknown to the country or if an error was made in the partner assignment.

Australia; the horizontal stabilizer of the tail from Italy; the cargo access doors from Sweden; the forward fuselage from Japan; the passenger entry door from France; and so on. That example is just one illustration of the importance and dominance of global value chains in the world economy today and in the decades ahead.

The profound changes that have occurred in the composition of global trade in the past decades confirm the emergence of new patterns. Up to the end of World War II, commercial exchanges among nations were largely dominated by the exchange of raw materials and agricultural products for manufactured goods. Since 1945 manufactured goods or the components of manufactured goods have become the main features of trade, with their value increasing from 40 percent of world trade in 1900 to 75 percent in 2000, while agriculture's relative share of world trade has steadily declined (figure 7.4). That change also reflects the shift from a world where trade took place between national economies selling nationally produced goods to an era of international exchange of goods often coproduced by competing national economies. Such an evolution leaves less room for high-impact protectionist policies.

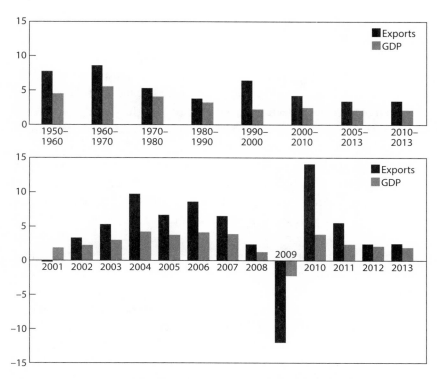

Figure 7.5. Volume of world merchandise exports and GDP (percentage change), 1950–2013. *Source*: WTO (2014).

If protectionism is not really a threat for world trade, what about the problem of global imbalances and the need for macroeconomic adjustment in advanced economies, said to limit the volume of exports that developing countries can expect in the future? That line of argument deserves scrutiny, too. Pack (2010), one of its main proponents, writes: "This is not to say that world exports will be absolutely stagnant, simply that rates of growth that prevailed from the 1960s to 2007 are extremely unlikely to continue. Realistically domestic markets will prove critical over the next decade."

In fact, the actual size of the recent decline in global trade should be put in perspective: international trade has grown dramatically over the past three decades. According to WTO statistics, the value of world merchandise exports rose from $2.03 trillion in 1980 to $18.26 trillion in 2011, which is equivalent to 7.3 per cent growth per year on average in current dollar terms (figure 7.5). "Commercial services trade recorded even faster growth over the same period, advancing from US$ 367 billion in 1980 to US$ 4.17 trillion in 2011, or 8.2 per cent per year. When considered in volume terms (i.e., accounting for changes in prices and exchange rates), world merchandise trade recorded a more than four-fold increase between 1980 and 2011" (WTO 2014, 55). The arithmetic logic mitigates the negative implications of a small decline in global trade. In other words, a reduction in a pie that had grown much bigger in size over decades sheds light on the fundamental observation that things may not be as bad as they appear.

Moreover, the world trading system has become more balanced, a positive development for global economic stability. Between 1980 and 2011 developing economies raised their share in world exports from 34 percent to 47 percent and their share in world imports from 29 percent to 42 percent (UNCTAD 2013).

It should also be noted that the world has entered a new era, with emerging economies becoming new growth poles. In the 1980s and 1990s, among the top five contributors to global growth all except China were G7 industrialized countries. But in 2000–2009 all except the United States were emerging economies—with China having become the top contributor. The trend has been reinforced in the aftermath of the 2007–2009 global crisis. The recovery was characterized by a two-speed pattern, with developing countries as a group growing more than twice as fast as high-income countries. That shift in economic weight is likely to produce major benefits for the world economy, with positive effects for both high-income and developing countries. For high-income countries, the growth of emerging economies will expand markets for their exports of capital goods and intermediate goods. For many developing countries that are still major producers of agricultural and natural resource commodities, greater consumption and production in the new growth poles will continue to support adequate prices for their commodity exports. And, thanks to the enormous benefits reaped from several decades of successful performance in trade, firms and governments in emerging economies are well positioned to provide funds for infrastructure and natural resource investment in developing countries.

The broader argument about global imbalances made by trade skeptics also deserves critical assessment. First, many believe that global imbalances, driven by an undervalued renminbi, were a major cause of the 2007–2009 global crisis (Bernanke 2007a, b). But it has become clear that the cause was the loose monetary policy introduced in 2001 by the U.S. Federal Reserve

Bank in response to the bursting of the dotcom bubble, magnified by financial deregulation and innovations in financial instruments, resulting in a boom in the U.S. housing market (Lin 2012a, b). The imbalance was caused by the large current account deficits in the United States and western Europe, except Germany, on the one hand, and the current account surpluses accumulated by oil-exporting countries, China, and Japan, on the other.[8]

Second, although size is always an important issue to consider, one should not forget that the real issue with large current account deficits is their sustainability, that is, whether they will be met by sufficient, timely, and affordable foreign capital inflows. Célestin Monga (2012) suggests that these deficits mainly reflect the general equilibrium interaction between many macroeconomic variables (national rates of saving and investment, fiscal, monetary and exchange rate policies, patterns of growth, and international trade, and so on). Moreover these variables themselves reflect the prevailing deeper macropolitical and sociocultural choices, which must be taken into consideration in the analysis of current account deficits. Philip Lane and Gian Maria Milesi-Ferretti (2014) have documented the substantial narrowing of current account global imbalances following the financial crisis of 2008, with projections suggesting a further compression in current account imbalances in the medium term.

Finally, Pack's pessimism about the ability of small, poor economies of Africa and South Asia to outcompete large manufacturing groups may not fully take into account the importance of new developments in global trade, and the increasing dominance of global value chains (GVCs), which have become powerful vehicles to link small and large firms from around the world. In fact, economic history shows that the small size of an economy has really never been a binding constraint to growth and success. Small economies such as Luxemburg, Switzerland, and Singapore have been able to position themselves well on the global scene by developing competitive industries and sometimes exploiting linkages with some of their bigger and more successful neighbors. Following the flying-geese model, others such as Taiwan-China or Mauritius have created domestic firms that link up with foreign firms and are able to access supplier networks, technology, and knowledge. As discussed in chapter 5, rising wages in large, middle-income countries such as China provide even greater opportunities for today's lower-income economies where labor-intensive activities can be developed in many industries.

Perhaps a more credible and more immediate threat to industrial development in low-income countries that have to rely primarily on low-skilled labor is that of technology—and its corollary, the risk that many of the jobs being performed in light manufacturing industries will soon be carried out more efficiently and cheaply by machines and robots (Brynjolfsson and McAfee 2012). It is true that throughout history, breakthrough technologies with major economic impact have been accompanied by stagnant or even declining wages for some workers along with rising inequality. That was certainly the case during the Industrial Revolution. The threat is often perceived to be even more daunting today given the wide scope and rapid pace of changes that information technology brings to industrial production and managerial processes (many white-collar jobs are being automated, just like blue-collar ones).

But studies devoted to the impact of technology on low-wage workers show that fears are often exaggerated. Looking at the impact of adopting transformative new equipment in the textile industry in the United States in the nineteenth century, James Bessen (2015a) notes that most gains from this new technology took a long time to materialize and required the skills and knowledge of many people—including factory workers with little education who were considered unskilled.

> Although the early mill workers had little formal schooling, they learned skills on the job, skills that were critical to keeping the strange, new, expensive machines running efficiently. Their skills were narrow compared to those of traditional craftsmen but valuable nonetheless. These skills eventually allowed factory weavers to earn far more than earlier artisan weavers; steel workers with narrow skills earned more than craft ironworkers with broad skills; typographers on the new Linotype machines earned more than the hand compositors they replaced. Moreover, employers paid these workers well at a time when unions had little power. Technical skills learned through experience allowed blue-collar workers with little education to enter the middle class.

Similar slow patterns of change were observed with the advent of steam engines, factory electrification, and petroleum refining (Bessen 2015b). The obvious policy lesson is for firms and governments to adopt the appropriate modernization strategies to mitigate the short-term negative impacts of automation and new technologies on low-skilled workers, by providing strong incentives for learning on the job.

But while the short-run effects of technology may apply to workers with few skills and in industries that require routine and arduous efforts, it should be stressed that the relationship between job growth and productivity is not unidimensional. Beyond the first-order effects of automation where the machine replaces workers in some industries, there are also important second-order effects. Firms using new technology may save money, which flows back into the economy either through lower prices for their goods and services, higher wages for the remaining workers, or higher profits. Thanks to these three channels, the money saved in the use of new technologies eventually gets spent, creating new demand that leads other companies to hire more workers. In the longer run, the net effect of technological change is always positive for wages and for aggregate employment (Atkinson and Ezell 2012). This is also the conclusion of a comprehensive report by the Organization for Economic Cooperation and Development (1994, 33) reviewing several empirical studies on the subject: "Historically, the income-generating effects of new technologies have proved more powerful than the labor-displacing effects: technological progress has been accompanied not only by higher output and productivity, but also by higher overall employment."

Technology and products may change very fast. But the nature of production activity will not change at the same pace unless workers have the skills to adapt. Furthermore, it is quite conceivable that even in industries that are more prone to automation, some segments of the value chain may remain labor intensive or require the kind of human touch that gives special value to the goods and services. This is true not only for textiles, garments, and footwear but also for capital-intensive industries such as the automobile industry. The new Rolls-Royce Dawn unveiled in September 2015 as the most technologically advanced luxury cabriolet ever produced displays under the company logo: "Hand Built in Goodwood, England."[9] It has been known for decades that machines and robots are excellent at assembling parts into final products, including in the automobile industry. But increasingly firms in all industries advertise the value that handicraft and direct, tedious human involvement bring to their goods and services.

For developing countries, international trade used to generate important benefits through various preference schemes. Under the U.S. Generalized System of Preferences (GSP),[10] they had access to the markets of rich economies where they could export their goods (typically commodities) with fewer constraints, including reduced tariff rates and less restrictive quotas. Although the GSP also includes rules of origin as the criteria needed to determine the national source of traded products, which sometimes reduced the effectiveness of preferences, the system generally has worked well and has often provided preferential duty-free entry for various products from designated beneficiary countries and territories. In addition to the GSP, other preference schemes, such as the European Union's Lomé and Cotonou Agreements, the Caribbean Basin Initiative, the Andean Trade Promotion Act, and the United States' African Growth and Opportunity Act, were adopted to facilitate participation by developing economies in the international trading system.

The benefits of trade preferences typically accrue through several channels: first, there is the transfer of rents to developing countries (tariff revenue or quota rents that would normally be received by the developed importer country are instead gained by recipient, developing countries). The preference margin is therefore transferred to producers in exporting countries. Second, there is the potential for a substantial export supply response, which can generate foreign exchange revenue and create employment in developing countries. Although agricultural and natural resource–based exports can generate rents from trade preferences, they eventually face limitations due to land availability. By contrast, manufacturing exports generally provide much greater potential: they do not face the constraints of market size or domestic endowments and can therefore be expanded virtually without running into diminishing returns to scale. Therefore trade preferences can stimulate production and exports if they are designed to allow import of complementary inputs and to facilitate connecting domestic firms operating in competitive industries to international production and trade networks.

Thanks to the considerable changes that have occurred in the organization and structure of global trade in recent decades, trade preferences can indeed contribute to boost the economic performance of developing countries—provided that they are used to promote manufacturing and develop industries and sectors that are economically viable. As noted by Paul Collier and Anthony Venables 2007, 4),

> modern sector production is [no longer] simply a matter of transforming primary factors into final output. It requires primary factors and many other complementary inputs, ranging from specialist skills and knowledge to component parts. These are frequently supplied by many different countries, with design, engineering, marketing, and component production occurring in different places—a process known as fragmentation of production. Furthermore, productivity in these different activities is not exogenously fixed. They are shaped by learning and by complementarities with other activities. These processes often give rise to increasing returns to scale, and imply that clusters are more productive than is dispersed activity.

The emergence of intrafirm trade as the primary vehicle for international trade raises new analytical questions for economists, but it mainly offers new opportunities for policy makers across the planet. Each country actually imports intermediate products—whether goods or services—to which they add value before reexporting them or using them domestically, whether for consumption or for incorporation in new productive processes. Pascal Lamy (2013), the former director-general of the World Trade Organization, often stressed the common benefits of the new trade landscape:

> We may still think in terms of Ricardo's world of trade between nations, but in reality most trade now takes place *within* globe-spanning multinational companies and their suppliers. The results of this "trade in tasks" are all around us. With value chains, it is no longer necessary to be competitive in producing a particular product or service; it is enough to be competitive in delivering a particular task. The growing weight of services in the business portfolios of countries and the increase in the reach of technology and transportation are fast narrowing the distances between and to markets and creating new opportunities for all countries (developed or developing) to grow through trade.

He also observed that only two decades ago, 60 percent of world trade was between developed countries (North–North), 30 percent was between developed and developing countries (North–South), and 10 percent was South–South. By 2020 it is expected that world trade will be split equally three ways, so the relative weight of North–North trade will have been halved in just thirty years or so.

International production fragmentation, taking place in GVCs, has indeed generated new and stronger incentives for economies at different development levels to cooperate.[11] By unbundling the value chains, it also generates win-win opportunities for all parties involved. Because the different stages involved in producing a particular final good are performed in different countries, specific tasks can be outsourced and undertaken separately, simultaneously, or consecutively in different countries. Whether these new production processes occur within a single multinational firm or through several production networks of supplier firms does not really matter. Advanced-economy firms can take advantage of the factor price and productivity differences and focus on the high-skilled/capital-intensive aspects of production while firms in developing countries can concentrate on the labor-intensive activities in which they have comparative advantage.

In fact, GVCs are typically organized around a dominant or lead firm located in an advanced economy and rely on a dense network of suppliers from across the globe. Participating firms may simply supply intermediate goods that are put together in the lead firm's home country. They may also put together the final good with the role of the lead firm centered in activities such as research and innovation, product design, advertising, and distribution. GVCs are therefore potentially powerful vehicles for structural transformation in developing countries. First, these countries no longer need to build entire industries from scratch to industrialize and assert themselves as credible competitors in world markets—they can simply specialize in activities that they do best and at the lowest cost (Baldwin 2012).

Second, GVCs allow even the poorest countries with the worst business environments to be associated with high-quality manufactured goods and to learn through cooperation with partner firms in advanced economies. As noted by Neil Foster-McGregor and colleagues (2015):

Through participation in GVCs, and the exposure to international markets and foreign competitors, the potential for technology transfer and spillover effects arises. Such effects can take a number of forms, for example by providing access to best practice management and business methods, through the use of high-quality and high-tech intermediates, through developed country intellectual property and trademarks, through lead firm knowledge and technology sharing, through skills demand and upgrading, and through learning from customers. Such effects can impact upon local firms not engaged in GVCs as well as those that are involved in GVCs, with the development of a part of a GVC in a country potentially also leading to spin-off firms and industries.

It is therefore important for developing-country policy makers to recognize that their domestic firms that are connected to GVCs can learn and access supplier and financial networks. Governments that are able to build the right institutions to foster firm participation in GVCs (mainly special economic zones and industrial parks) and adopt the appropriate policies to make them work properly can actually shift resources out of traditional agriculture and other low-productivity primary activities into industry to boost productivity.[12] In doing so, they could increase the part of the working population engaged in manufacturing, an essential feature of sustainable and inclusive growth.

The advent and dominance of GVCs also has substantial macroeconomic implications. In a world economy with integrated production networks and businesses collaborating across boundaries—including firms from "competing" countries—domestic firms must purchase goods and services abroad and use them as intermediate inputs in their own production, which is then sold on world markets. Likewise, their export products are used as contributing inputs to producing final goods and services in other countries, which are also traded in international markets. Such patterns of industrial interdependency change some of the fundamentals of macroeconomic policy. The quantity, quality, and cost of imports become as important for developing and developed countries as those of exports.

Policy makers should be aware that imports have become direct contributors to economic growth and employment generation. Lamy (2013) stresses that point:

One lesson is that to be able to export, you must know how to import. When an industry's competitiveness relies on the cost effectiveness of the components and intermediate goods and services making up the production chain, strong performance in all segments of the value chain is essential. Indeed, there is a positive correlation between the buoyancy of a country's exports and its integration in value chains through imports of intermediate goods. Importing competitive components where necessary enables developed-country firms to generate margins for investing in those segments where their real comparative advantages lie. Far from killing jobs, this enables Europe, the United States, and Japan to maintain industrial activities linked in particular to research and development, industrial engineering, and high value-added services. These are the activities that can and will generate the best-paid jobs.

It follows that in some instances exchange rate policies such as competitive devaluation, typically used to reduce imports and boost exports, may have adverse effects on domestic firms and burden their production costs. This would penalize their competitiveness, with potential consequences on foreign exchange, export and fiscal revenues, and economic growth.

The increasing dominance of GVCs and the opportunities they provide for developing countries are not just a matter of conjecture. There is now ample empirical evidence to document their role as new anchors of global trade and potential vehicles for rapid growth. Statisticians have to redesign national accounting systems in each country in a value chain to capture the industrial interactions between the different countries and world regions. Such tedious work necessitates constructing a large international input-output matrix, which contains all interindustry trade that precedes production and consumption of a final good or service. It also requires properly harmonizing each of the trading partners' national accounts and detailed analyses of how the traded goods and services are used, that is, either for consumption or investment purposes or for further use in a new production process.

The empirical analyses that must be carried out to measure the various trade flows into and out of GVCs are challenging because they require detailed data across countries and industries. Any country involved in GVCs produces goods and services using both imported inputs as intermediates (imported value added) and its own domestic value added. A straightforward approach often used by trade economists starts with the observation that Country A's exports (or final demand) can be divided into two components: one capturing domestically produced value added and the other capturing the imported value added from other countries that is incorporated into Country A's exports (final demand). A complete analysis of GVCs should also account for the fact that a country's exports need not constitute final goods only and can be used as inputs into other countries' production (and exports).

To measure Country A's participation in GVCs, one should therefore think of at least two main components:

→ The share of foreign value added (FVA) used in its own exports and calculated as a percentage of Country A's total exports (this is the indicator of how much Country A is involved in *downstream* production in GVCs because it measures its use of foreign inputs in the processing of export products)

→ The share of Country A's domestic value added (DVX) that is absorbed as intermediate inputs into the value added exported by all other countries in the world, calculated as a percentage of Country A's total exports (this is the indicator of how much Country A is involved in *upstream* production in GVCs because it measures its inputs—value added—into other countries' production and export of goods and services)

Thus GVC participation combines the FVA and DVX measures by summing up the foreign value added used in a country's own exports and the value added supplied to other countries' exports and taking the sum as a ratio to gross exports (figure 7.6).[13]

Using that calculation framework, Neil Foster-McGregor and colleagues (2015) shed light on participation in GVCs by world region for 1995, 2000, 2005, and 2010.[14] Their empirical analyses highlight several interesting facts. First, they confirm that GVC participation has been increasing over time in most regions of the world, with the share of exports that are part of a multistage process increasing from around 41 percent in 1995 to just almost 50 percent in 2010. The only exceptions are Central America and the Caribbean, where GVC participation has tended to decline somewhat (figure 7.7).

Foreign value added in own exports

Other countries	Country A
Export intermediate inputs to Country A for the production of its goods and services	*Produces goods and services using both its own value added and imported inputs (foreign value added)*

A. Own value added created locally: **$80 million**

B. Imported intermediate inputs (value added): **$20 million**

C. Total exports of Country A: **$100 million**

In this case FVA of Country A is 20% (*B/C*)

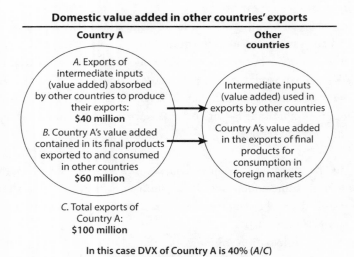

Domestic value added in other countries' exports

Country A	Other countries

A. Exports of intermediate inputs (value added) absorbed by other countries to produce their exports: **$40 million**

Intermediate inputs (value added) used in exports by other countries

B. Country A's value added contained in its final products exported to and consumed in other countries **$60 million**

Country A's value added in the exports of final products for consumption in foreign markets

C. Total exports of Country A: **$100 million**

In this case DVX of Country A is 40% (*A/C*)

Figure 7.6. Measuring GVC participation as FVA + DVX. *Source*: Authors.

Advanced countries—the EU member states in particular—are heavily integrated in GVCs, which is not surprising. The intense GVC participation of East and Southeast Asia and to a lesser extent West Asia is also in line with expectations. Perhaps the most encouraging evidence that even low-income countries can perform well in global trade is African economies'

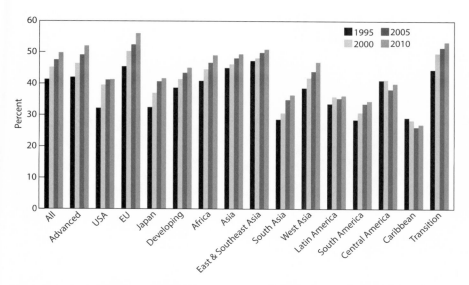

Figure 7.7. Participation in global value chains by region, 1995–2010.
Source: Foster-McGregor, Kaulich, and Stehrer (2015).

rising participation in GVCs. In fact, Africa has some of the highest rates of GVC participation, matching the levels found in Asia. In 1995 Africa's GVC participation was about the average for all regions (about 41 percent), though its involvement is mainly in upstream production (that is, providing inputs to other countries) rather than downstream production (processing for exports). The growth rate of GVC participation between 1995 and 2010 in Africa has also been similar to that for all countries, with GVC participation increasing by 19.9 percent for Africa and 20.5 percent for all countries over the period 1995–2010.

Perhaps the most encouraging news for developing countries is the story derived from the empirical analyses of GVCs by sectoral category (figure 7.8). High-tech sectors represent, on average, 58 percent of GVCs' participation in all countries, with the numbers being larger for developed countries (62 percent) as well as Central America (69 percent). Asia's contribution of high-tech sectors to GVCs is around the average, though contributions in South and West Asia lag behind those for East and Southeast Asia. Most striking is Africa's sectoral contribution, which seems quite balanced, with the primary sector's share at 26 percent, two services categories (high- and low-tech) at around 20 percent each, and the two manufacturing

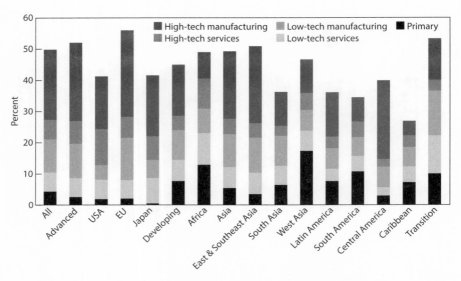

Figure 7.8. GVC participation by region and by sector category, 2010. *Source:* Foster-McGregor, Kaulich, and Stehrer (2015).

categories (high- and low-tech) at around 17 percent each. But Africa's contribution of manufacturing goods and services to GVCs (33 percent) lags behind that of all other regions, with the average for all countries being 66 percent—West Asia and the Caribbean are the only other regions with shares below 40 percent.

Skeptics of this overall positive story could still observe that even involving its firms in GVCs does not guarantee that a poor economy will eventually grow at sustained high rates. They would point to the experiences of countries such as Bangladesh that have done quite well in developing labor-intensive industries (textiles and garment) but seem trapped in low value-added segments of the GVC, where there is little possibility for innovation or technology transfer. It is true that the world economy has witnessed many growth-acceleration episodes that did not lead to convergence between low- and high-income countries. Ricardo Hausmann, Lant Pritchett, and Dani Rodrik (2005) identify eighty such growth-acceleration episodes since the 1950s, which they find to be "highly unpredictable." They conclude pessimistically that the vast majority of these accelerations are unrelated to standard determinants in the growth literature and that most instances of economic reform do not produce growth acceleration.

It is indeed possible that an economic development strategy can initially succeed—even foster the emergence of competitive firms, generate employment, and contribute to a country's growth—but eventually fail because it was not designed to sustain continuous industrial and technological upgrading. This raises the broader problem of the validity of the economic development strategy in question, which must evolve to reflect the economy's changing endowment structure and constantly adjust to its institutional and factor requirements. Countries that have succeeded in boosting production and in developing trade as a steady and reliable source of economic growth have often built clusters of firms for their most competitive industries. They have generally done so by ensuring that the government allows domestic and foreign investors to establish strong partnerships and nurture firms that can succeed in international markets.

HOW TO BOOST PRODUCTION AND TRADE? BEYOND A RANDOM THEORY OF CLUSTERS

The wisdom inherent in the well-known saying "one hand cannot tie a bundle" is generally offered as justification for unity and collaboration within social groups. Surprisingly, it appears to be valid also in the realm of business, even when capitalist principles and war-sounding mottos such as "survival of the fittest" are prevalent. For firms competing not only to gain bigger market shares but also to push one another out of business, the benefits of collaborating with the enemy often outweigh the costs. This was made obvious by Paul Krugman's (1991) seminal work on the geography of trade, which suggested that clustering—the phenomenon of firms in the same industry (or in neighboring industries) gathering in the same geographic location—was a very common pattern of economic activity.[15] With the growth of global trade and the changes that have occurred in recent decades in the ways in which goods and services are produced and exchanged among economies, the importance of clusters is now widely accepted: they offer opportunities for firms to benefit from increasing returns to scale and external economies of scale.[16]

Marshall (1890) offered a first compelling theoretical rationale explaining and justifying that phenomenon. His insights have sparked a rich economic literature looking at clusters mainly through the prism of increasing returns to scale, or economies of scale, which convert increased levels of output into downward-sloping average costs curves. These insights were derived from Marshall's industrial district analysis, which showed that economies of scale may even be "external," emerging from outside the firm because of asset sharing, such as the provision of specific goods and services by specialized suppliers or the emergence of a localized labor pool due to the concentration of production. Also, the very proximity of firms working on similar products or competing closely against one another eventually yields collective benefits in new research, managerial, and organizational practices (Griliches 1979). Such learning dynamics and spillovers increase the stock of knowledge available for individual firms.

By building factories or offices next to those of their competitors, firms can benefit from some critical aspects of their production, including tapping into the neighborhood's pool of expertise and skilled workers, accessing a larger network of component suppliers, and learning from one another (even simply through the informal channels of gossiping or closely monitoring best business practices). Moreover, as clusters attract more firms, a network of specialist input suppliers develops and markets for intermediate goods expand, opening up new activities, and transport and infrastructure support tends to improve along with the local labor market. The combined spillover effects of firms setting up next to one another generally outweigh the cost of competition among them. It has been shown empirically that productivity is higher in areas of dense economic activity (Duranton and Puga 2005), and analyses focusing on cities have noted that, over a wide range of city sizes, each doubling of size raises productivity by 3 to 8 percent (Rosenthal and Strange 2005). Most of these insights have been known intuitively for centuries. In eighteenth-century England industrial districts (clusters) were common. Adam Smith described them in his works. The town of Staffordshire was the location of many potteries, and that region is still known today as "The Potteries." The town of Nottingham was home to many lace-makers, and so on. Since French economist François Perroux suggested the notion of growth poles in 1949, countries as different as Austria, Belgium, Bolivia, France, Great Britain, Italy, Peru, Spain, the United States, and Venezuela have adopted and attempted various interpretations of it (Perroux 1955; Darwent 1969; Christofakis and Papadaskalopoulos 2011).

Today's best-known clusters include Silicon Valley in the San Francisco Bay Area (California), where many firms have gathered to produce some of the most innovative, life-changing technologies in use around the world, and Hollywood (California) and Bollywood (Mumbai) where the film industry cohabits, competes, and collaborates. It may seem counterintuitive that highly competitive firms would be willing and even eager to locate their headquarters and operational units close to one another and thus expose their business strategies and trade secrets to spying risks. It generally turns out that the potential costs of such risks are outweighed by their benefits. By working close to one another, firms in almost all industries realize that they have unparalleled access to financiers, the best experts in the business, and a culture of innovation and risk taking. It has been observed that "new information technology and Internet firms continue to gather there in spite of the high prices of local property and the danger of earthquakes. Ironically, they find that much of the most valuable information that they obtain comes not electronically but from face-to-face meetings" (Hindle 2008, 36).

The success of clusters has led to a broad consensus among economists on the importance of policies that facilitate their development. The implications of industrial policy, the welfare gains from trade, and all the Marshallian externalities for the patterns of international trade have been studied extensively, most notably by Krugman (1991, 1995, 2008), Paul and Siegel (1999), Rodriguez-Clare (2005), Aghion (2009), and Harrison and Rodriguez-Clare (2010). The topic is particularly important in an increasingly globalized world economy. Recent work based on quantitative analysis that looks at whether Marshallian externalities lead to additional gains from trade indicates that they do lead to gains, and that the externalities increase overall gains from trade by around 50 percent (Lyn and Rodriguez-Clare 2011).

In recent decades analyses of the Marshallian externalities have been enriched by the experiences of developing economies that found clusters to be the optimal tool for circumventing some of the structural issues they face. The infrastructure and human capital deficits, the rigid labor laws and regulations, and the weak governance that afflicts low-income economies and reflects their low capacity and limited resources can be effectively addressed within the circumscribed and more easily managed cluster (Ayele et al. 2010).

But there are still unanswered questions. Is the clustering of firms in a particular location a phenomenon that occurs randomly as one of the many enigmas of economic development? Or are there government policies that can be implemented to establish clusters and then foster dynamics that create viable, competitive firms in which workers (unskilled or educated) are given incentives and opportunities to acquire the skills that help them prepare for the constantly changing demands of the global economy? The answers to these questions concerning the causes and optimal conditions for the emergence of clusters have remained a mystery, even for economic theorists who have focused their efforts on the topic.

Theories of agglomeration and clusters proposed by various authors since Adam Smith and Alfred Marshall generally have suggested that successful clusters emerge randomly, according to some spontaneous generation process. As a result, such theories have had a limited role in government policies to create clusters from scratch. Michael Porter (1998) observed that in today's world of global competition, rapid transport, and high-speed telecommunications, location should no longer be a source of competitive advantage. Yet he pointed to puzzling cases such as the flower-growing industry in the Netherlands, which could not have been an obvious first choice for anyone starting a flower-growing business today except that the business is already there. The cluster granted new entrants with strong competitive advantage that consisted of the sophisticated Dutch flower auctions, the flower-growers' associations, and the country's advanced research centers. Porter did not explain the genesis of clusters, but his analysis was consistent with the random theory that they emerge in unpredictable ways.

For several decades the emergence of clusters was explained in the economic literature simply as illustrating "the economics of QWERTY." It was based primarily on the work of Paul David (1985), who chronicled the QWERTY keyboard's rise to dominance. Although it was not the most efficient layout in terms of finger movement, it forced typists to work slowly and mitigated the risk of mistakes caused by the jamming keys of the early machines. With innovation and technical progress, the jamming problem was subsequently corrected, but a path had already been set, and manufacturers and typists were accustomed to the bizarre keyboard layout. In sum, a historical accident had set the stage for a long-lasting technical standard and the development of keyboards.

The theoretical lesson derived from this story was straightforward:

A *path-dependent* sequence of economic changes is one in which important influences upon the eventual outcome can be exerted by temporally remote events, including happenings dominated by chance elements rather than systematic forces. Stochastic processes like that do not converge automatically to a fixed-point distribution of outcomes, and are called *non-ergodic*. In such circumstances "historical accidents" can neither be ignored, nor neatly quarantined for the purpose of economic analysis; the dynamic process itself takes on an *essentially historical* character. (David 1985, 332)

David tried not to draw definitive conclusions about economic phenomena from his investigation of the origins of the QWERTY keyboards. He wrote: "Standing alone, my story will be simply illustrative and does not establish how much of the world works this way. That is an open empirical issue and I would be presumptuous to claim to have settled it, or to instruct you in what to do about it" (332). However, his main conclusion that "it is sometimes not possible to uncover the logic (or illogic) of the world around us except by understanding how it got that way" led some economic theorists to assert that clusters are always random phenomena.

Arguing that the QWERTY keyboard was "not just a cute piece of trivia" but "a symbol for a new view about how the economy works" and "a parable that opens our eyes to a whole different way of thinking about economics," Krugman (1994, 223) hailed it as evidence that neither the market nor the government can manufacture good economic outcomes. He wrote: "That different way of thinking rejects the idea that markets invariably lead the economy to a unique best solution; instead, it asserts that the outcome of market competition often depends crucially on historical accident. . . . And this conclusion is fraught with political implications, because a sophisticated government may try to make sure that the accidents of history run the way it wants." He then went on to compare the randomness of QWERTY emergence and dominance to that of the film industry in Hollywood or the concentration of banking and financial institutions in New York.

Krugman's use of the QWERTY story may just have been a rhetorical device to make the broader and theoretically valid points about the importance of clusters once they have been created and are functioning well. But his skepticism about the effectiveness of government policy agendas designed to facilitate the emergence of clusters implied that he adhered to the random theories, which have dominated the literature since Smith and Marshall. While it is true that historic clusters such as Silicon Valley or

Hollywood may have been random phenomena, the notion that governments should refrain from getting involved in the emergence of clusters has been proved to be inaccurate. As shown by Xiaobo Zhang, Jin Yang, and Thomas Reardon (2015), several developing countries have actually been successful in using smart government policies to deliberately create successful clusters in places where nothing existed before.

Alfred Marshall observed that many of Britain's successful industries in the late nineteenth century were concentrated in specific industrial districts: cotton around Manchester, ironworking in Birmingham, cutlery in Sheffield, and so on. Subsequent theories of agglomeration and clustering have explained well the underlying reasons for success and highlighted their perceived unpredictability. But the more recent successes of some developing countries that defied geographic randomness and that engineered clusters in specific locations provide useful lessons for policy making.

"Look down at the shirt you're wearing. Chances are the buttons came from Qiaotou. The small Chinese town, with about 200 factories and 20,000 migrant workers, produces 60 percent of the world's supply" (Lim 2006).[17] It all started in the early 1980s when Qiaotou in the remote Zhejiang Province was a poor small town with unproductive paddy fields and dusty roads, no infrastructure, and no capital. Two village brothers started buying buttons from Hubei Province and selling them to local garment manufacturers. They quickly became successful and inspired a large number of other merchants. Everything changed in the 1990s when entrepreneurs from Qiaotou visited Italy to convince button producers that they could import equipment and start low-end manufacturing in China using Italian designs and material. "Faced with rising costs, exhaustion of raw materials, and competition from emerging economies, Italian button producers saw outsourcing of the low end activities to Chinese manufacturers as the right solution to remain in business" (Rasiah, Kong, and Vinanchiarachi 2012, 32). They saw win-win opportunities in relocating button production to a place where production costs would make the industry more competitive.

In just two decades Qiaotou converted itself into a manufacturing powerhouse, with hundreds of family-run new firms so competitive that they put out of business some of the established European firms that had been producing buttons for centuries. The low-investment, labor-intensive industry was perfectly suited for Qiaotou and consistent with the country's comparative advantage at that time. The Chinese government worked closely with local communities and business associations to complement the development of the button industry. In recent years, despite the normal challenges associated with rapid industrial development, Qiaotou has also become the world capital for other industries, such as zipper manufacturing. In other industries in China, local governments were even more proactive with creating clusters; they provided targeted infrastructures and specific incentives for the private sector and facilitated the creation of cooperatives so that small local entrepreneurs could have a voice and have their interests preserved (Zhang et al. 2015; Dinh et al. 2013).

More recently, the magic of government-engineered or government-supported clustering has been observed well beyond the traditional Marshallian externalities. In trying to determine why agricultural production in China has increased steadily despite small landholdings, a high degree of land fragmentation, and rising labor costs, Zhang and colleagues (2015) find that the main explanation may lie in new clustering strategies. Confronted with unsustainable labor costs, farmers organized themselves not just to act as single small-producer households but to cooperate (while still competing against one another) to share the main element of their cost structure. They outsourced some power-intensive stages of production, such as harvesting, to specialized mechanization service providers, which are often clustered in a few counties and travel throughout the country to harvest crops at very competitive prices. Through such an arrangement, smallholder farmers could stay viable in agricultural production. Again, local and central governments intervened proactively to facilitate the development of such activities with agricultural clusters.[18]

Stories of successful government-engineered clusters have been recorded from well beyond China. The Penang electrical-electronic cluster, one of the largest of several major clusters of this type in East Asia, also resulted not from random theory but from smart, activist government policy. It is another successful case of "artificial agglomeration." In 1972 Malaysian authorities decided to create an export-processing zone (EPZ) where the country could develop its electric and electronic industry. Although it was a case of learning by doing, the project took shape through several industrial master plans, each including a series of policies to attract foreign direct investment. The second of such plans (1996) was specifically designed to strengthen linkages and complementarities between foreign investors and local firms.

As a result, the electrical-electronic industry has been a major source of manufacturing value added, employment, and exports in Malaysia for several decades.

In Penang, excellent basic infrastructure—good transport services, power supply, water supply, and telecommunications—was combined with superior supply of social services, such as public health facilities and schools to make the region attractive to skilled workers and managers. Institutional reforms were also introduced to improve the performance of the security and customs within the EPZ. Drawn by these investments and financial incentives, Japanese, European, and giant North American firms such as Hitachi, Sony, Siemens, Advanced Micro Devices, Hewlett Packard, Intel, National Semiconductor, and Seagate moved to Penang. The agglomeration of these flagship firms helped stimulate the development of local supplier firms." (UNIDO 2009, 34)

Similar successes in creating new clusters were observed in countries as different as Mauritius (Lall and Wignaraja 1998), Costa Rica (Ciravegna 2011), and the United Arab Emirates (Ketels 2009).

The main lesson from these experiments in "artificial agglomeration" and from the fragmentation of global value chains is that the old theories of clusters as random phenomena may be obsolete. It is actually possible for a developing economy to create a successful strategy that facilitates its engagement with the international trading system. But few policy makers in these developing countries have managed to take full advantage of the new opportunities offered by changes in trade patterns and the evolving global economy. One of the main reasons for this lack of initiative is that the traditional policy advice given to developing countries by most mainstream economists and development institutions has been to stick to minimalist government intervention and adopt "neutral," "horizontal" economic strategies. This includes implementing prudent macroeconomic policies and improving the business environment through broad microeconomic and institutional reforms without giving special consideration to particular industries. The value of such advice is questionable. Evaluation studies often show that such generic prescriptions have rarely yielded sustained and inclusive growth. In fact, many of the success stories in economic development (most notably China, Brazil, and Vietnam in recent years) are countries where policy makers did not follow that advice, often simply because it would have required the abrupt removal of all the distortions that stifled the economy in the first place, with the high risk of creating social and political disruptions.

Economic development requires uninterrupted and coordinated upgrading of physical and human capital and institutions. For poor economies with limited financial resources and administrative capacity, it is therefore essential that economic policies be geared toward the changing patterns of industrial structure and technology diffusion and choosing production bundles and modernization and innovation strategies that are consistent with their comparative advantage and development level (Lin 2012a, b). At lower incomes, the main economic policy challenge is therefore to break into global industrial markets and find their niches or to organize their economies to take advantage of the opportunities being vacated by middle-income countries that are forced out of these niches because of rising wages, rising productivity, and the need for industrial upgrading. Despite the recent declines in global trade, the opportunities to attract foreign capital in potentially competitive industries, to create employment, and to develop production and exports have never been so numerous for developing countries. Clusters in well-targeted industries are viable if not essential policy tools to circumvent the well-known constraints on growth in developing economies (weak governance, infrastructure bottlenecks, and insufficient human capital).

The real questions then become: Why have only a few developing country's governments been able to successfully facilitate the formation of such clusters? Why have the main instruments used to build clusters (SEZs) often failed to yield positive economic results? What are the guiding principles for success?

WHY SPECIAL ECONOMIC ZONES OFTEN FAIL TO GENERATE VIABLE CLUSTERS

Certain ideas are unlucky. Despite their potentially great value, they are too often associated with past failed experiments and doubt. Or they are casually discussed in public policy debates mainly with skepticism. Even when they are put to good use and lead to success, these cases are quickly dismissed as anomalies and exceptions that confirm the rule. Consider SEZs (broadly defined as administratively separated areas where investors may run their business activity based on specific preferential conditions such as tax and tariff incentives, streamlined customs procedures, and less regulation), often seen as the best modern institutions to generate industrial clusters.

The well-known rationale for SEZs is to provide special policy incentives and infrastructure in a circumscribed geographic location to firms that can attract foreign direct investment, create employment, develop and diversify exports (even when economy-wide business environment problems and protective barriers are not yet resolved) and foreign exchange earnings, and serve as "experimental laboratories" for new pricing, labor, financial, or labor policies. The ultimate expectation is that the knowledge spillovers of these experiments eventually translate into private-sector development, sustained growth, productivity increases, and other financial and economic benefits for the entire economy.

The most popular form of SEZs are export-processing zones, which typically operate under a few basic principles: allowing investors to import and export free of duties and exchange controls; streamlining customs and administrative controls and procedures; facilitating licensing and other regulatory processes; and freeing firms from obligations to pay corporate taxes, value-added taxes, or other local taxes (Farole 2011). To ensure effective monitoring of their activities, export-processing zones are often fenced-in estates with customs controls at the entrances, and sales are typically restricted to export markets. Export-oriented SEZs are generally intended to "convey 'free trade status' to export manufacturers, enabling them to compete in global markets and counterbalance the anti-export bias of trade policies" (FIAS 2008, 12).

SEZs and export-processing zones have been around for a while. It is believed that they were initiated in ancient Phoenicia as basic free-trade zones. In recent times their track record is stellar: they were a central pillar of China's growth strategy, which allowed the most populous nation on earth to lift out of poverty about 700 million people in a rather short period of time (1979–2015). An SEZ was established in 1937 in New York. Another one was created in 1942 in Puerto Rico. Iceland and Taiwan-China also established SEZs in 1960. In 1959 one was set up at Shannon Airport in Ireland. SEZs were used effectively by some latecomers such as Korea and Taiwan-China to build clusters, emulate the economic development strategies of leader countries, and even catch up with them in the race to economic prosperity. Some developing countries in other parts of the world have been quite successful in establishing various types of well-functioning SEZs to boost their export and growth strategies, which allowed them to generate much-needed employment and also spark their industrial upgrading process. Well-known cases are those of Costa Rica, Honduras, El Salvador, Bangladesh, Vietnam, and Mauritius.

The best SEZ success story—at least in recent memory—occurred when Deng Xiaoping's China embraced them in the 1980s, using them, for instance, to convert a poor, sleepy fishing village such as Shenzhen with no natural resources and no infrastructure into one of the world's premier export powerhouses, with a 10.7 million population and a $24,000 per capita GDP in 2014.[19] In fact, various types of SEZs and industrial clusters initiated by the government have been the main laboratories and engines of China's remarkable economic development.[20]

Such success stories cannot go unnoticed. Developing countries in various parts of the world have used SEZs as the main instrument to attract FDI and transform their economies. Thomas Farole (2011) notes that SEZs have allowed the Dominican Republic to create more than 100,000 manufacturing jobs and shift dramatically away from reliance on agriculture. Qatar has launched SEZs to diversify its economy from a hydrocarbon-led economy—which made it one of the richest in the world but is subject to volatile global oil prices—to a knowledge-based economy. Ethiopia has followed the same path, mainly to address its logistics woes (infrastructure) and to experiment with new models of governance that give more flexibility to investors and allow them to recruit workers for light manufacturing industries in which the country has comparative advantage. Advanced industrialized economies are also using various forms of SEZs at the federal, state, and local levels to attract investors, stimulate economic activity, and create employment.

Yet there has been widespread skepticism about the potential economic value of SEZs in developing economies, and understandably so. Although the general recipe of such zones has long been understood by economists and policy makers, few countries have actually managed to design and make good use of policy frameworks and instruments to achieve their development goals. In fact, most countries that have tried to replicate this strategy have not gained the expected benefits. Globally there are now about 4,500 such special zones, with few actually delivering the expected results. In most countries, the benefit-cost ratio for setting up and running SEZs has been disappointing. Personal income tax on employment, permit fees and services charges, sale and rental fees on public land to developers, import duties and taxes on products from the zones sold to the domestic customs territories, concession fees for facilities such as ports or power plants, and corporate income tax (when assessed) totaled only negligible amounts. In the meantime, import duties and charges lost from the smuggling opportunities created by SEZs, tax revenue forgone from firms relocating from the domestic customs territory into the zones, and public investment for (often untargeted) infrastructure and recurrent expenditures (mainly the wage bill of public-sector workers needed to run and regulate the zones) often represented substantial costs to governments. Even in China, some of these initiatives failed to attract competitive industries and generate employment, requiring the authorities to reengineer them (Chenggang 2011, Zhang 2012). Over the decades, many SEZs have indeed failed and were simply abandoned by policy makers who did not know how to make them function properly. As a result, SEZs are often dismissed in mainstream economic circles as mere illusions, or worse, a "Chinese" affair—with the usual and not-so-subliminal tone of political and ideological disdain.

Nothing could be further from the truth. First, as the historical record clearly shows that China did not invent SEZs. In fact, when Deng Xiaoping became China's leader in 1978, he actively sought new ideas and useful policies wherever he could. Brushing aside the ideological battles of the past, he famously commented, "Who cares if a cat is black or white, as long as it catches the mice." In 1980 a younger reformist, engineer Jiang Zemin (president of China, 1993–2002), and a group of other Chinese officials were sent around the world to study how SEZs worked. When they reached Ireland, they experienced a revelation:

> The delegation was introduced to the world's first duty free shop, an airport-focused infrastructure, and a special zone of low tax and free trade. They welcomed the pragmatic approach of Shannon Development. Unlike all the other countries [Jiang] Zemin visited—most of which had a stake in the cold war—Ireland was not touting an ideological agenda. The officials in Shannon were focused on jobs

creation, practical education and transfer of skills, and facilitation of each new company's needs. This was a cat that could catch mice. After touring various economic zones around the world, the Shannon model and that of Singapore were the only two that the Chinese decided to follow. (Quigley 2012).

More important, SEZs have become the most effective channel for attracting FDI and for building the kinds of clusters or industrial districts that allow large or small economies to take advantage of the new patterns of global trade. If fragmentation (as highlighted above) is indeed the "new normal" in global exchanges for the foreseeable future, then even countries with poor infrastructure, limited human capital, or weak governance can find pragmatic solutions to position their economies as credible business environments for global supply chains. Successful SEZs are not only zones of excellence where such problems can be addressed but also essential places where business linkages can be built between domestic firms (small and large) in various sectors and international firms.

Economists' and policy makers' reasons for why most SEZs fail range widely—each makes sense individually but they are overwhelming and confusing when lumped together. They include generic opposition to the very idea of SEZs, that is, of "government bureaucrats in business"—a view primarily based on ideological grounds (World Bank 1995): the suggestion that they are "political priorities" that often lead to creating so-called white elephants (Economist 2015); problems of poor governance; lack of institutional framework and political commitment; weak implementation capacity; and improper monitoring and evaluation mechanisms (Zeng 2012).

These explanations for the high failure rates of SEZs tend to merge the causes of the problem with the symptoms or consequences. Although many types of mistakes can explain the inability of policymakers in developing countries to replicate the success of SEZs recorded in China and in a small number of other countries, the fundamental problem has often been one of strategic selection. The first-order condition for building a viable SEZ is to choose the "right" industries—not necessarily the most "modern" or the most attractive ones. The industries with economic viability potential are those that reflect the economy's comparative advantage, not the political ambitions of the leaders, so that they can develop into industries with competitive advantages quickly. As noted by Farole (2011): "Increasingly it is not the existence of a special-economic-zone regime, a compelling master plan, or even a fully built-out infrastructure that will make the difference in attracting investment, creating jobs, and generating spillovers to the local economy. Rather, it is the relevance of the special-economic-zone programmes in the specific context in which they are introduced, and the effectiveness with which they are designed, implemented, and managed on an ongoing basis that will determine success or failure."

In retrospect, the main reason for the weak performance of SEZs appears to be the belief that they should emerge randomly (just like QWERTY keyboards). Most SEZs do not live up to the expectations of policy makers because of poor targeting of appropriate industries or their generic nature, which makes them too broad to attract enough competitive firms. Many developing-country policy makers who have attempted to create SEZs did not properly reflect on the conditions needed for success in an increasingly globalized world and on how best to exploit the comparative advantage of their economies. Poor countries typically face two broad types of constraints that impede private-sector development: high factor costs (for skilled labor and capital) and high transaction costs (mainly due to poor infrastructure, unfriendly business environment, and weak administrative capacity), which are often compounded by political capture and rent seeking.

Thanks to globalization and free movement of labor and capital, high factor costs have generally declined in recent decades, even in remote places. In 2015 a country like Bolivia that needs highly trained engineers could attract large numbers of them from Mexico or Spain at costs lower than in 1970. Likewise, Sri Lanka can attract private capital from Qatar or Malaysia (countries with well-endowed sovereign wealth funds) much more easily today than three decades ago. But the best way for most low-income countries to circumvent the high factor cost constraint and launch a development strategy with the highest likelihood of success is to formulate economic development strategies that aim at using their only competitive factor costs (low-skilled labor and land). Factor costs can indeed be lowered if economic development strategies are consistent with a country's comparative advantage and the abundant factors (unskilled labor, land, or natural resources) are used extensively. The first constraint is therefore removed when the industries selected for and attracted into SEZs are primarily those making good use of low-skill labor.

To circumvent the second constraint, developing countries can build SEZs as zones of excellence, where the pervasive infrastructure problems, unfriendly business environment, and poor governance and administrative capacity can be addressed effectively. It is indeed much easier even for a government with very limited financial resources and administrative capacity to deliver first-rate infrastructure and to combat red tape and corruption within the geographic boundaries of an SEZ than across the entire country.

But for this second set of constraints to be removed and for SEZs to function effectively, the firms operating in these zones of excellence must be economically viable in the first place, and the conditions and the policy incentives must be appropriate for them to cooperate *and* compete. Therefore SEZs are best conceived initially as industrial parks ("specialized" SEZs) in which the government only has to provide the same kind of infrastructure to all firms. Generic SEZs that attract firms from different industries need different kinds of infrastructure, requiring extensive government financing and making the sustainability of the SEZs much more challenging.

Because the industries attracted to the SEZs have often defied the country's comparative advantage, they are not viable without a strong set of protection policies. In most instances, policy makers either have identified the industries they favor for personal and political reasons or have not actively attempted to identify the industries that may be most suited to their country's endowment structure (e.g., labor-intensive industries). They have assumed that foreign firms willing to join an SEZ or EPZ would create employment, which would be better than nothing. One consequence of the absence of identification strategies has been the random emergence of small single firms from very different types of industries. But given the limitations of state budgets and weaknesses of public investment programs, few governments can provide them the industry-specific infrastructure support they need.

The choice of the location for SEZs has not always been optimal. Although some zones are built in port cities that are already growth poles or near transport hubs, others are created as isolated geographic zones or in remote areas, not on the basis of an economic rationale but as a way of appeasing political constituencies. This has resulted in increased production and transaction costs for the few firms willing to build factories there. Reducing transaction costs has not been part of the strategic focus. Because of the randomness in industry selection and the limited government financial resources, even basic utilities and services are sometimes not made available in many of these zones. Governments have not proactively played their indispensable facilitating role. They have not provided basic industry-specific infrastructure and often wait (in vain) for qualifying firms to finance investment in electricity, water, or telecommunication within the zone. They have not coordinated the design and implementation of the investment needed and used collectively by firms in their industries (storage facilities, for example).

Another major problem has been the limited volume of business transactions generated by SEZs. The likelihood that a small number of firms specializing in many different industries within the same SEZ can generate the critical mass of business transactions necessary for Marshallian externalities to materialize and make firms in that location credible partners in global markets is generally low. In today's global economy, the firms that are able to negotiate the lowest prices for their inputs and intermediate goods and services from their suppliers are typically those that are part of a network—by buying in large quantities, they are better positioned to obtain the best unit costs. SEZs that host many different industries are therefore at a disadvantage when placing single-firm orders for inputs and intermediary goods and services. In other words, even an SEZ that hosts industries that are economically viable (and consistent with the economy's comparative advantage) can still fail if it is trying to develop too many different activities and sectors at the same time and therefore not attracting enough market power for its firms—such SEZs are in fact spread too thin. In sum, the removal of the second constraint—high transaction costs—necessitates the development of SEZs that create clusters of large numbers of firms in industries where economies of scale, intraindustry knowledge spillovers, and other agglomeration effects can be realized. Governments in many developing countries have simply created generic SEZs with broad fiscal incentives across industries and firms and have failed to facilitate the process of industrial agglomeration, which requires the provision of industry-specific infrastructures and managing the coordination and externalities issues that always arise in collective-action situations (Lin 2012a, b).

Another first-order, strategic mistake that often leads to the failure of many SEZs across the developing world is the inability of their promoters (governments or private-sector actors) to establish effective linkages between these zones of excellence and the rest of the domestic economy. They do not consider the political economy issues that are always at the heart of the development process. By its very nature, a gradual economic development strategy based on strategic selectivity and geographical targeting of the most promising growth potential necessarily creates groups of winners and losers, at least in the short term. It is essential to deliver quick wins (time and results) and to establish backward and forward linkages that mitigate the risks of social tensions.[21] In some countries the local business community perceives SEZs suspiciously as geographic enclaves and closed "special clubs" where opaque business practices take place, often involving foreign firms and a few rich business leaders who are well connected to the ruling political class. In India, for instance, a country where federal and state laws and regulations often overlap, it has been reported that subsidies and tax incentives have been abused in SEZs and that land acquisition for zones has often led to protests. According to Arpita Mukherjee:

> Land taken under the SEZ policy is sometimes misused. States have their own SEZ act, which sometimes differs from the central act. Multi-layered government and multiple policies create scope for corruption. Too many SEZs have been awarded and government continues to award SEZs in spite of the fact that existing ones are not performing. Corruption can be addressed . . . through more stringent evaluation of feasibility of project proposals and online application and approval systems. Also, project evaluations should be independent of the government. (Mukherjee, quoted by Gray 2013)

It should be noted that in almost all poor countries, corruption is likely to be a pervasive problem, not only in SEZs but also across the entire economic spectrum. It is a stylized fact that has been observed across time in all regions of the world (Lin and Monga 2012). The reason is the high costs of running a well-staffed, well-equipped, and well-functioning national judicial system are often beyond what the public sector in a low-income country can afford. The problem is compounded in some countries where corruption is embedded in societal, economic, and power relations and virtually all state institutions, including the judicial system, are caught in the low-equilibrium dynamics of what Richard Joseph (2014) called "prebendal politics." If that is the case, and if virtually all governments in the world—including those in high-income and democratic countries—must constantly combat corruption, then the issue at hand has little to do with the existence of SEZs but rather involves the policies adopted to mitigate the risks. The challenge then is to understand which policy circumstances provide the best incentives for successful anticorruption mechanisms and for good governance in general.

Countries that successfully limit the prevalence of corruption in SEZs are generally those that lift trade restrictions, price controls, and multiple exchange rates, which A. O. Krueger (1974) has identified as some of the main causes of the problem. However, because these well-functioning SEZs have been designed to support well-targeted industries with competitive potential, there is no need for governments to provide protection or subsidies. Thus the risks of state capture and rent seeking are minimal. In that context, the sustainability of SEZs is determined by comparative advantage and the economic viability of the firms they host. Government intervention and public policies are indeed in place to support these SEZ firms, but they are carefully targeted incentives (of limited amount and time) and are allocated in a transparent manner to compensate for the externality generated by pioneer firms. The only beneficiaries are firms that will be viable in open, competitive markets. The investment and survival of such SEZ firms do not depend on protection, large budgetary subsidies, or direct resource allocations through measures such as monopoly rent, high tariffs, quota restrictions, or subsidized credits. In the absence of large rents embedded in generic SEZs that try to attract all kinds of firms from all industries, there will not be distortions that easily become the targets of political capture. In sum, the likelihood of the pervasive governance problems observed in many SEZs would be much reduced by government facilitating the development of new industries that are consistent with the country's changing comparative advantage determined by the change in its endowment structure.

SEZs also fail because of poor institutional organization and ineffective management. But while such reasons are certainly valid, they are less important than the first-order problems discussed earlier. And often these second-stage issues are consequences of the strategic mistakes committed in launching SEZs for industries that defy comparative advantage. In some instances, government policies to support the newly created SEZs were either insufficient or inappropriate. Other failed experiments involve SEZs that were exclusively developed, regulated, and operated by governments or public entities. Beyond the obvious issues of expertise and capacity, their institutional arrangements often led to conflict-of-interest situations, with regulatory agencies also engaged in zone development activity, especially when public zones compete with private firms outside the zone.

Investment climate surveys also indicate that SEZ managers in many countries did not realize that successful integration into the world economy increasingly requires behind-border measures that fall under the heading of trade facilitation. Too often they did not alleviate the burden of red tape, nor did they provide services such as customs and port efficiency. In some countries, it often took more than a year for a foreign firm to obtain necessary permits to operate. They also had to deal with heavy and complex bureaucratic rules and procedures, a very high cost of infrastructure (communications, energy, water), and constraining labor regulations. In addition, they had to commit their companies to unrealistic employment creation goals and high requirements for initial investment. In other places, qualifying firms that managed to join SEZs still had serious difficulties accessing foreign exchange and other financial services.

In sum, the belief in allowing clusters to emerge randomly generally led to disappointing results. Because of their poor design, ineffective management, and misguided policies, most SEZs did not attract enough firms in competitive industries. Moreover, their firms did not generate enough backward linkages and subcontracting business relationships with local enterprises. Too often local firms either had no interest in supplying cluster-based firms in the zones or failed to meet world market standards for quality, price, and delivery times. SEZ-based firms themselves tended to use domestic factors and inputs only to a limited extent and condemned themselves to remaining in small enclaves in poor economies. Given the often inappropriate strategic focus of these zones (where a few firms often benefited from lucrative special deals with influential politicians and could afford to produce the wrong goods in otherwise uncompetitive factories), their status as enclaves of foreign corporations with limited interactions with the local private sector exacerbated the economy-wide distortions. The disconnect with the domestic private sector worsened local business people's perception of them. In some cases, the poor logistics and weak supply chain (both a reflection of limited clustering) led these firms to rely heavily on imports (with industries such as electronics or even apparel often showing imports ratios well over 60 percent). In such situations, currency devaluations compounded the distortion of net exports. Eventually they faced high transaction costs. Despite the benefits of distortive protection by governments, they failed to yield enough business volume to be credible entities.

Basketball Hall of Famer Michael Jordan, whom many consider the greatest player ever, is often quoted as saying, "I've failed over and over and over again in my life and that is why I succeed." Perseverance and drawing the right lessons from failed experiences are certainly keys to success. However, promoters of SEZs need not experience several rounds of painful and costly failures before getting it right. The world has recorded enough success stories in different country contexts to allow development economists to derive broad, useful guidelines for success.

BUILDING SUCCESSFUL SEZS AND INDUSTRIAL PARKS: A FEW GUIDING PRINCIPLES

To maximize the chances of success of SEZs (making them the main vehicles for the journey toward industrial and technological upgrading, sustainable growth, and employment), developing countries should be more selective in the choice of industries developed, ensure that they are equipped with the infrastructure needed by potentially competitive firms, remove the distortions and inefficiencies that have characterized many of them in the past, and adopt a policy and institutional framework that provides the right incentives for growth and for linkages to the domestic economy. Instead of creating generic, broad-purpose SEZs, they should consider building zones with specialized facilities that are configured to the needs of specific industries and sectors—cluster-based industrial parks (CBIPs). How they are developed will depend on the industries to be promoted, all of which should be consistent with the country's revealed or latent comparative advantage.[22] With their specialized facilities customized to the unique needs of target industries, they may be airport-based zones to support air-based activities (fruits and vegetables or cut-flower exports for instance), agriprocessing zones, or even simply financial services zones aimed at promoting off-shore activities.

Good General Principles

The industries in CBIPs should be carefully selected and consistent with each country's revealed or latent comparative advantage to ensure that they make the best possible use of the abundant factor (typically low-skilled labor) and can become competitive in international markets without excessive forms of government protection. At least in their initial phase, they should host labor-intensive, assembly-oriented activities such as textiles, apparel, and footwear, and electrical and electronic goods. Within such industries, the scope of activities should be expanded to include not only manufacturing and processing but also commercial and professional services such as warehousing or transshipment.

All investors (foreign and local) should be treated equally. Appropriate legislation, rules, and regulation should therefore be in force to reduce the probability of distortions in incentives. Moreover, there should be a unique set of fiscal incentives for all promoted industries, regardless of their location (within the zone or outside). Never before have political leaders around the world been confronted with the difficult sociopolitical challenges posed by increasingly large, demanding, and often educated crowds. In fact, it has become very costly to remain in power without delivering tangible results, especially on the employment front. With the emergence of a new, more pragmatic leadership in developing countries, policy makers are much more likely to respond to electoral politics and be more accountable for their economic policy choices.

Deliberate efforts should be made to integrate CBIPs into national economies, not just because exporting firms operating in well-protected SEZs are better accepted politically and socially when they establish business linkages with the local private sector but also because they are more effective at building the foundations of sustained and inclusive growth when they proactively give a stake to domestic firms (especially small and medium-sized enterprises) in their activities. There is nothing worse for a potentially successful SEZ that has attracted private firms with strong competitive potential than to be (mis-)perceived as a domestic enclave for shady business ventures between corrupt politicians and foreign industrialists. Building economic and social connections with a local network of small firms and other actors (such as academic institutions) can help reduce the suspicion and resentment often faced by foreign investors arriving in developing countries.

To preempt the inevitable domestic criticism, social fears, and other political economy issues, CBIPs should strive to generate quick wins soon after they have been established.[23] This is done most effectively when the newly created zones rapidly create manufacturing jobs and absorb sizable segments of the low-skill labor force. Their promoters should encourage linkages between CBIPs-based firms and local firms so that the zones can serve as examples for success and as catalysts to broader reforms and work with local authorities and business associations to comply with ILO labor standards. It is indeed important to communicate the message that for most people in the labor force in poor countries, the alternative to employment in such CBIPs would be low-productivity, low-income informal activities, underemployment in urban areas, unprofitable and highly risky agricultural work in rural areas, unemployment, and the perpetual trap of poverty. Even with minimal formal education, many unskilled workers could still be employed in CBIPs that specialize in basic assembly operations. In the medium and long run, the strategic focus of CBIPs should be to improve the economy's endowment structure by moving toward higher-value activities but at a realistic pace. This can be achieved only by promoting skills development for the workforce and setting industrial and technological upgrading as the ultimate goal of the firms hosted in CBIPs.

Effective Institutional Arrangements

An important question is the distribution of roles between the public and private sectors in the design, ownership, and management of CBIPs. CBIPs that are privately owned, managed, and operated should be encouraged. But they could start as public-private partnerships, with public provision of off-site infrastructure such as roads and public-private funding of on-site facilities. Governments can provide direct financial support or guarantees to build infrastructure and facilities in the zone. Private-sector participation can take many different forms: basic partnership with shared risks and rewards with governments; concession agreements; or "build-own-operate," "build-operate-transfer," or "build-own-operate-transfer" arrangements (FIAS 2008). Successful models of CBIPs include a variety of contract types, often with public-private partnerships that evolve over time. A model that has been popular recently involves "equity-shifting" arrangements, which allow a private contract manager of a government zone to exercise a purchase option once predefined performance levels have been reached.

Even well-designed CBIPs can succeed only if they are backed by strong political commitment from the highest government levels to improve the business environment and quickly remove all obstacles to implementation. A good institutional framework for preparation could be an interministerial committee headed by a political "champion" who has the credibility and power to make things happen. That champion should also be the main interface between CBIPs developers and firms and all government entities. He or she should be able to respond quickly and effectively to the requests from the business community. But the champion should be insulated from political pressures to please any domestic political constituency.

Land, Facilities, and Services

Building clusters is less challenging when governments are willing to find land parcels and secure titles for lease to private zone developers. In many poor countries, the legal framework allows for an enduring influence of state bureaucracy on land distribution and land rights. Governments are reluctant to hand over the power of land distribution, and state control is legitimized as historically and socially fair. Such control opens the potential for rent seeking and bureaucratic arbitrariness. State ownership, and especially the power to redistribute land plots, makes citizens and business people vulnerable to arbitrary actions of local bureaucrats who decide to whom access to land is granted. CBIPs represent a good opportunity for implementing land reforms gradually, in a way that can generate quick wins for all stakeholders and improve their collective welfare. Even countries such as Ethiopia or Tanzania, with a long history of strong resistance to land privatization and property rights for individual plot holders, are considering changes in their land tenure policy—a sign of progress and the recognition that it may be the most viable alternative.

To expand the range of facilities and amenities available within CBIPs, public and private partners should consider not only industry-specific factories and infrastructure but also a wide array of services such as high-speed telecommunications and Internet services, common bonded warehouse facilities, training facilities, maintenance and repair centers, product exhibition areas, on-site customs clearance and trade logistics facilities, on-site housing, and on-site banking, medical clinics, shopping centers, and childcare facilities. Developing a cluster zone as an integrated industrial, commercial, residential, and recreational entity—not as a stand-alone—allows developers to diversify their potential sources of revenue and offset the potential low profitability of certain activities with higher margins in others. In many well-managed private zones in East Asia, as much as half of total annual revenue is derived from business support services and other sources of income.

Solving the Infrastructure Problem

Poor infrastructure (inadequate and poor-quality energy supplies, high utility prices, lack of railway transport) negatively affects business. To alleviate the problem, policy makers in low-income countries are typically recommended simply to build infrastructure projects, preferably across the country and across borders. Yet large regional infrastructure projects that are supposed to yield cross-border economies of scale and link national markets often end up being costly, risky, and ineffective. The needs are enormous, and no country may ever be able to safely assert that the quantity and quality of its infrastructure is appropriate to sustain high rates of economic growth for a long period of time. It is and will remain a constant problem to be addressed in both rich and poor economies.[24]

Infrastructure projects are perhaps the most profitable investments any society can make. When they are productive they contribute to and sustain a country's economic growth and therefore provide the financial resources to do everything else. But many policy makers do not find the right strategy to tackle the problem. Either they try to do too much at the same time and end up not actually doing much, or they give priority to the wrong industries and sectors and devote their limited financial, administrative, and human resources to activities that are not competitive enough and cannot generate enough payoff to sustain the development process.

The problem of infrastructure finance is therefore one of market failures, government failures, and donor failures:

→ *Market failures* stem from the fact that infrastructures are generally public goods. Once they are built, the marginal costs of additional consumers tend to decline toward zero. But the challenge is obviously to find the financing to invest in the heavy part. Private investors need to recover their fixed and sunk costs and make profits. If their perspective is that there is no market or credible and stable stream of revenue in a strong legal and regulatory framework, investors will obviously not get involved—even when they are granted monopolistic rights. From the perspective of the private sector, where the focus is normally on profitability and money, there is also a deficit of wisdom and innovation. Some private investors are concerned that infrastructure projects tend to offer lower-than-average return. Others are hesitant to invest in them because the existing asset classes do not provide the structure needed for these projects to compete with traditional equity or debt.

→ *Government failures* are the consequences of selecting priority industries and sectors, even on the basis of traditional rate-of-return analyses, that often lead to disappointing results. The infrastructure projects that are selected do not yield expected results because of their inappropriate location, poor design, and so on. Moreover, infrastructure decisions are often political in nature and involve parliamentary processes that do not necessarily follow technical analyses and transparent processes.

→ *Donor failures* are due to the ineffective policy advice given by external development institutions that too often conform to dominant intellectual paradigms without seriously accounting for both market and government failures and the constraints they pose in countries with limited financial resources and administrative capacity.

These problems can be addressed effectively in countries where governments have the credibility to commit to long-term institutional and regulatory arrangements and most effectively with the involvement of international partners and development finance institutions. In an ideal world, advanced economies would be willing and even eager to transfer trillions of dollars to developing countries for infrastructure finance. This would create a global win-win, because these rich economies would benefit even more from such bold ventures. But that first-best solution would not be politically easy to carry out—even though during the Great Recession of 2008 all advanced economies could mobilize a large amount of fiscal stimulus to stimulate their domestic demand, often with limited results.

No developing nation will ever have the financial resources and administrative capacity to build roads, highways, railways, seaports, and airports across its entire territory or to foster regional interconnection with other (mainly poor) neighboring countries. The only sensible solution left is to set the correct priorities and to identify the geographic locations where high-quality infrastructure is necessary to support export-oriented light manufacturing industries for the global market. That second-best but still optimal solution is a carefully designed strategy that locates infrastructure investments primarily in and around industrial parks that connect domestic firms to foreign firms and domestic economies to GVCs.

The provision of industry-specific, on-site infrastructure is indeed an important determinant of transaction costs and competitiveness in CBIPs. It helps attract firms and facilitate the clustering and the development of subcontracting relationships among them. Policy makers should work closely with private-sector operators to fully equip and service CBIPs with purpose-built facilities, which can then be put up for sale or lease. Private zone developers should be allowed to supply utilities services (water, power, sewerage, and telecommunications) to cluster-based firms.

Over several decades the ownership and financing of many infrastructure assets have been transferred to the private sector. A new model of privately owned and privately financed infrastructure utilities has emerged, with the government mainly playing the role of regulator. But the privatization model cannot cover all infrastructure categories, especially those that are circumscribed to small geographic areas covered by CBIPs. There is a need for project-specific institutional arrangements such as public-private partnerships and private finance initiatives. Developing countries can profit from the low interest rates across the world's capital markets and find ways of bridging the gap between the relatively low cost of debt for existing regulated assets and the high cost of new projects.

In view of capital and regulatory constraints on banks in the wake of the financial crisis, capital markets are an increasingly important source of finance for infrastructure projects. Justin Yifu Lin, Kevin Lu, and Cledan Mandri-Perrott (2015) have proposed new financial instruments that could help channel FDI into infrastructure, including in CBIPs located in developing economies. Specifically, they recommend creating an asset class called "buy-and-hold equity," which is between traditional equity and debt and held for fifteen years or longer. It would offer returns close to those of equity investments but with some of the risk offset by its long-term nature. The private sector would bring in infrastructure investment expertise, while sovereign funds and international financial institutions would provide the capital and stability. The platform would focus on projects with defined cash flows and contractual terms (which could include associated risk-mitigation strategies) guaranteed for twenty to thirty years.

Another viable solution to credit financing for infrastructure and economic development is strengthening public investment banks—providing long-term financing while maintaining sustainable fiscal balance and avoiding undue strains on the borrowing capacity of central government (Aryeetey 2015; Monga 2012). Such development finance institutions can borrow on the capital markets to finance economically viable projects in competitive industries and sectors. They could offer partial or full guarantee of repayment on bonds issued by project initiators by bearing the risk and therefore substantially reducing the cost of funding. The Korea Development Bank and Development Bank of Japan offer good models of institutional and governance setups that allow them to fund major infrastructure projects while consistently avoiding losses and maintaining a tight hold on credit risk.

Mitigating the Risks of Corruption and Rent Seeking

Political economy concerns often identified in the theoretical literature on clusters are legitimate only for the traditional type of SEZs and EPZs that host firms in industries that defy comparative advantage. Firms in these industries are not viable in an open, competitive market. Their existence and continuous operation often depend on large subsidies and protection, which create opportunities for rent seeking and corruption and make it difficult for the government to abandon interventions and exit from distortions. CBIPs should promote a completely different development model: the industries that are consistent with an economy's latent comparative advantage. Firms are viable once the constraints to their entry and operation are removed. Government incentives provided to the first movers must be transparent, targeted, temporary, and small solely to compensate for their information externality. In that context, the issues of pervasive rent seeking and the persistence of government intervention beyond its initial timetable can be mitigated. Selecting labor-intensive industries with economies of scale (so that there are incentives for foreign investors to localize in lower-wage countries) and potential for upgrading (to open up future possibilities for domestic value-added creation) would generate the kind of quick wins that policy makers need to build their own domestic political capital and to pursue reforms.

Not all developing countries are confronted with the kind of poor incentive systems and extreme rigidity in labor market rules that either stimulates rent seeking or impedes the effective development of special zones such as CBIPs. In some of them minimum wage and other labor law rigidities are actually much less binding in practice than they appear on the books. In such countries (especially those where basic transportation, energy, and telecommunication infrastructure could be improved quickly), CBIPs could be much bolder in their design and implementation and become "freeports." Instead of being mainly export drivers, they could be large platforms for private investment and catalysts for knowledge spillovers throughout the entire national economy and beyond and could even serve as a basis for regional hubs in specific industries. CBIPs that are selected on the basis of their economic rationale and not for political considerations can then cover much larger areas. These would therefore allow greater flexibility to firms in their choice of plant location and opportunities for interfirm linkages. They would allow full access to the domestic markets on a duty-paid basis—that is, lift the traditional requirement of exporting 80 percent or more of the production and allow instead unrestricted sale to domestic consumers as long as all applicable import taxes and other duties are paid. They would also enable firms to engage in any legal economic activity they deem profitable, including manufacturing, warehousing, and transshipment. Registered firms or individuals could be offered duty-free privileges to introduce all types of merchandise, which can then be sold at the retail or wholesale level or even consumed within the zone area.

Developing country policy makers should also learn from best practices in Ireland, Taiwan-China, and Korea and allow duty-free access to inputs for local firms, as is the case for CBIP-based firms. Domestic producers, especially small and medium-sized enterprises, could then benefit from tax credits and rebates on duties paid on imported goods and services used in products sold to CBIP-based firms. Local suppliers could import intermediary products and components using letters of credit initiated by CBIP-based firms. The latter could also provide domestic firms with technical assistance or financing arrangements as part of subcontracting arrangements. Such policy measures aimed at fostering backward linkages would eventually help diffuse political opposition to CBIPs.

Governments should also work closely with firms in competitive industries to support training and apprenticeship for workers, promote study tours and personnel exchanges, and implement programs tailored for purchasing and technical managers of export-oriented firms based in CBIPs to help their local suppliers achieve high-quality standards and meet the required delivery times. By bringing local business leaders into the picture and creating the conditions for them to fully share the success of CBIPs, governments will foster job generation and weaken domestic sociopolitical resistance to the new policy (including from trade unions).

Finally, governments should make clear their political commitment to potential foreign investors to convince them that all constraints on businesses in CBIPs will be removed quickly. Personal engagement by presidents, prime ministers, and other high-level government officials will be needed to convey the message that once the policy is adopted, there will be no reversal. Well-organized and well-targeted (to specific industries) visits to countries where potential investors are located (China, Thailand, India, Brazil, Qatar, and so on) would help overcome skepticism and give credibility to the new policy.

* * *

The Great Recession, which plunged the world economy into turmoil in 2008–09, and its lasting negative impact on global trade and employment have also provided new opportunities for developing countries to address some of the difficult challenges they face—especially in the domain of infrastructure. Just as Jorge Luis Borges was forced to explore his true self and find a new calling, eventually making him not only Argentina's most famous writer but also one of the greatest of the modern era, developing countries can seize this moment to reassess their economic strategies and reposition themselves to take full advantage of the infinite possibilities offered by the new world.

Foreign direct investment has been the main engine of economic growth for centuries, stimulating industrial, technological, and institutional upgrading and fostering knowledge transfer and learning opportunities. It is therefore the main ingredient for igniting and sustaining the dynamics of change that allow societies to combat poverty and achieve shared prosperity. FDI is at its best when it focuses initially on infrastructure financing in select industries and geographic locations with big potential for positive spillovers. Paradoxically, the still sluggish state of the world economy actually offers new avenues for growth to developing countries. In recent years, the cost of building infrastructure and launching economically viable new projects and programs has been much cheaper, thanks to excess capacity in advanced economies (especially in the construction sector) and to record low interest rates.

Development experts and policy makers should find innovative ways of channeling the surplus savings from rich countries where there is excess capacity and fewer investment opportunities to developing countries where there is an urgent need for profitable ventures. This could be achieved through a new global pact between advanced and developing countries, the development of new instruments for infrastructure finance, and the rediscovery of the almost magical virtues of well-conceived, well-designed, well-managed industrial clusters.

To maximize the impact of infrastructure investment, industrial parks should be considered the most effective way of developing clusters. They can yield the clear benefits that are exemplified in economic theory dating back to Alfred Marshall. Marshall showed that concentrating production in a particular geographic area brings major external benefits for firms in that location through knowledge spillovers, labor pooling, and close proximity of specialized suppliers. Beyond his theoretical arguments are crucial and practical ones. Industrial parks provide great opportunities for building islands of excellence, even in economies afflicted with many other problems. A country with a poor business environment can still develop industrial parks and clusters with high-quality infrastructure and excellent governance and chart its path toward economic prosperity and social peace.

APPENDIX 7.1: GVC PARTICIPATION: SECTOR GROUPINGS

TABLE A7.1. EORA SECTORS

Sector Number	Short Name	Type
1	Agriculture	Primary
2	Fishing	Primary
3	Mining and quarrying	Primary
4	Food and beverages	Low-tech manufacturing
5	Textiles and apparel	Low-tech manufacturing
6	Wood and paper	Low-tech manufacturing
7	Petroleum and chemicals	High-tech manufacturing
8	Metal products	Low-tech manufacturing
9	Electrical and machinery	High-tech manufacturing
10	Transport equipment	High-tech manufacturing
11	Other manufacturing	Low-tech manufacturing
12	Recycling	Low-tech manufacturing
13	Electricity, gas, and water	Low-tech services
14	Construction	Low-tech services
15	Maintenance and repairs	Low-tech services
16	Wholesale trade	Low-tech services
17	Retail trade	Low-tech services
18	Hotels and restaurants	Low-tech services
19	Transport	Low-tech services
20	Post and telecommunications	High-tech services
21	Financial intermediation	High-tech services
22	Public administration	High-tech services
23	Education, health, and other services	High-tech services
24	Private households	Low-tech services
25	Others	Low-tech services

Conclusion: Making the Most of Existing Circumstances

The story of *The Conference of the Birds* [1177 (1984)] by the twelfth-century Persian poet Farid Attar sums up well the main argument made in this book and may also shed additional light on the policy framework laid out in previous pages. Thousands of birds decide to find their ideal king, the Simurgh. On learning that in order to find him they must embark upon a long and perilous journey, many of the birds start expressing concerns and reservations. With great diplomatic skills and eloquence, the hoopoe, who leads the search for the leader, convinces them to rise up to the challenge. Using witty parables to calm their fears, the hoopoe exhorts them to fly to the mystical island home of King Simurgh the wise.

But the trip is not an easy one. Along the way, individual birds confront difficult situations and obstacles: the hawk, seeking to arrive first, becomes lost; the parrot wears her heavy jewelry, which eventually weighs her down; the duck is lazy; the finch is too fearful of storm to fly. Some birds give up, some decide to return, some make excuses to get away, and some even die on the way. Their wise guide, the hoopoe, keeps encouraging them to be patient, humble, and brave as they learn from their own mistakes and overcome fears during their flight.

Only thirty birds eventually make it through the whole journey—a journey marked by learning and wisdom, frustration and joy. Having reached their destination, the residence of the Simurgh, all they find is a lake. The King of Simurgh bird is not there. All they can see in the lake is a reflection of themselves! The thirty birds in the search for spiritual truth then realize the moral of the story: the king is actually in each one of them—and there is no need to look for him elsewhere. In Farsi (the Persian language in which the story was written), *si* means thirty and *murgh* means bird. In his story, Attar named the king "Simurgh."

The Conference of the Birds is indeed about the quest for the truth, which is often hidden in plain sight for everyone to see. It is also a story of persistence and hope in overcoming mistakes, fear, impatience, greed, and skepticism. It is a useful metaphor to summarize the critique of development economics made in this book: too often researchers and policy makers have engaged in perilous quests for perfection, which they felt was a prerequisite for low-income countries to ignite and sustain their growth process. Despite disagreements among various schools of thought, development economists have tended to start their assessment of country circumstances by considering that high-income economies were the absolute model that all poor economies should resemble, and by identifying the long lists of "missing ingredients" that would be needed *before* the quest for prosperity could be credibly pursued. Whether they defined themselves as early structuralists, neoclassical economists, or as post–Washington Consensus proponents of randomization techniques, many development experts have implicitly or explicitly embarked on a quest for the Simurgh whose intellectual and policy prescriptions would be necessary as *preconditions* for economic success. This book suggests a radically different approach to economic development: taking into accounts lessons from history and policy, it posits that the recipes for success must be found in each country in its current state of development, regardless of country circumstances. It also argues that the lengthy list of preconditions and the challenging quest for a Simurgh of prosperity are misguided.

* * *

Despite a steady decline in global poverty over recent decades—mainly due to progress in a very small number of large countries such as China— tackling poverty remains a major global challenge. With billions around the world still trapped in economic and social misery, there is broad consensus at the international level that global peace and security will remain fragile for the foreseeable future. Such considerations were on the minds of world leaders when they gathered in New York in September 2015 to adopt ambitious Sustainable Development Goals to be reached by the international community by 2030. But reducing poverty and climbing the ladder to prosperity aren't easy: From 1950 to 2008 only twenty-eight economies in the world reduced their gaps with the United States by 10 percent or more. Among those twenty-eight economies, only twelve were non-European and non–oil exporters. Such a small number is sobering: it means that most countries on the planet have been trapped in middle-income or low-income status. Development economists must find a way to help them improve their performance so that the global human dream of "a world free of poverty" can be realized and they can close the gap with the high-income countries.

This book has taken stock of lessons from development thinking and experience and identified the main reasons why past intellectual and policy frameworks failed to yield the expected results. It has also offered a pragmatic blueprint for allowing low-income countries to ignite and sustain economic growth without preconditions.

WHAT WENT WRONG? PAST INTELLECTUAL AND POLICY MISTAKES

Some eight decades of research in economic development have generated invaluable knowledge. However, much research still remains to be done on the specific policy levers that low-income countries facing difficult circumstances (by definition) can use to boost growth and structural transformation. It was therefore necessary to understand what went wrong in development thinking and development policy despite the compendium of analytical and policy work done since World War II.

The first wave of development economics, which emerged as a new subdiscipline of modern economics after World War II, was heavily influenced by structuralism. Emphasizing the importance of structural change, it attributed the lack thereof to market failures and proposed government interventions to correct them, most notably via import substitution strategies, many of which failed. Early structuralists were right to try to close the structural gaps between low-income and high-income countries. But they identified the wrong causes of the problem. They attributed to market rigidities the low-income countries' inability to establish high-income countries' advanced industries. Based on this assumption, they advocated inward-looking policies to build industries that in fact defied their comparative advantages, and firms in those industries were not viable in open, competitive environments. While subsidies and protection allowed some countries to achieve high investment-led growth for a period of time, that strategy came with costly distortions and was not sustainable in the medium to long term. Certainly the approach could not help them converge to high-income country levels.

By the 1970s a second wave of thinking led to a gradual shift to free-market policies, which culminated in the Washington Consensus. It expected spontaneous structural change to occur as long as markets remained free. Its policy framework consisted mainly of getting prices right through liberalization and privatization, ensuring macroeconomic stability, and improving governance. Its results were at best controversial, and some have even characterized the 1980s and 1990s as developing countries' "lost decades."

The Washington Consensus shifted the policy pendulum toward market fundamentalism. By focusing obsessively on government failures and ignoring the structural issues, its advocates assumed that free markets will automatically create spontaneous forces to correct structural differences among countries. Yet market failures from externality generated by first movers and coordination of required improvement in hard and soft infrastructure are inherent in the process of structural change. Without the government's facilitation, the spontaneous process that ignites the change either is too slow or never even happens in a country. Unfortunately, the Washington Consensus neglected this. It also neglected many existing distortions in a developing country that are second-best arrangements to protect nonviable firms in structuralism's priority sectors in the country. Without addressing the firms' viability, the attempt to eliminate those distortions could cause their collapse, large-scale unemployment, and social and political instability. For fear of such dire consequences, many governments reintroduced disguised protections and subsidies that were even less efficient than the old subsidies and protections.

To spark a process of structural transformation, low-income countries need technological improvements in agriculture and the development of low-skilled and labor-intensive manufacturing sectors. Given their low level of domestic savings and weak or nonexistent linkage to global production networks and distribution chains, it would be desirable to bring in foreign direct investment. However, the investment climate and business environment in such countries are weak. In such situations, proponents of the Washington Consensus looked at low-income countries through the lenses of a first-best world and recommended immediate removal of various distortions to improve the business and investment environment (the assumption being that FDI will flow in spontaneously if the business environment is improved). Their proposed policies generally led to disappointment, and for good reasons: First, it may take decades for the improvement of the business environment to reach the ideal level. Second, even after such hard-earned improvements, FDI may not flow in spontaneously. Countries such as Tunisia or Botswana ranked among the best of developing countries on the Doing Business indicators. Yet they did not attract substantial amounts of FDI to ignite and sustain their structural change process.

Because developing countries were not able to close the gap with high-income countries, and because of persistent poverty, the international donor community shifted its efforts to humanitarian projects such as investing directly in education and health for poor people. But service delivery remained disappointing in most countries. This led to a new focus on improving project performance, which researchers at MIT's Poverty Action Lab have pioneered with randomized controlled experiments. This has been the third main wave of development thinking. Commenting on the evolution of development thinking from early structuralism/ Washington Consensus to project- or sector-based approaches, Michael Woolcock (2012) has written about a shift from "Big Development" to "Small Development." While it is clearly important to understand the determinants of project performance, it is questionable whether that is really the route to economic prosperity. After all, the only twelve economies that were able to close the gap with the United States by 10 percent or more did not start their development journey with micro projects but with big ideas.

WHERE DO WE GO FROM HERE?
REHABILITATING PRAGMATISM

To refocus economic development thinking and practice on the main lessons learned from various experiments of structural transformation throughout the world, and to draw policy principles and frameworks that poor countries can use to fight poverty—regardless of their economic circumstances—one must first highlight some key principles that are too often overlooked. Modern economic growth is a process of continuous structural change. Many past development thinkers failed to deliver results because they got either the nature or causes of modern economic growth wrong. First, in searching for the causes of structural change, it is essential to start by distinguishing between "fundamental" causes and "proximate" causes. For example, innovation is a fundamental cause of structural change while education is only a proximate cause. A proximate cause should not be treated as the ultimate cause. If this distinction is not made theoretically and also at the policy level, one cannot understand why North African countries (and some sub-Saharan nations) were able to improve education quite substantially without experiencing structural change. This example reveals education to be a proximate rather than an ultimate cause.

Second, in disentangling fundamental versus proximate causes, it is also important to bear in mind that the mechanisms and requirements for change differ in countries depending on their level of development. For example, while innovation in high-income countries amounts to invention as their technology and industry are on the global frontier, in developing countries it can be imitation. Because the mechanism of innovation is different for countries at different levels of development, the educational requirements also vary.

Third, pragmatism is paramount. Regardless of whether they tried to address fundamental causes or proximate causes, many past and existing policy prescriptions for poor countries overlook that they will not be implemented in the context of a first-best world. In fact, by definition, all developing countries are in the second-best, third-best, or nth-best world. While it is important to keep in mind a good understanding of what an ideal, first-best world would look like for these countries, it is even more critical that the policy recommendations suggested to them be helpful, implementable, and pragmatic. Economic theorists generally agree that removing distortions in a second-best situation does not necessarily result in a Pareto improvement. Yet development economists tend to overlook the implication of this basic insight and too often recommend "big-bang" approaches to economic reforms as a strategy for converting bad country environments into first-best environments.[1]

The goals of development are to help countries get out of the low-income trap and for middle-income countries to proceed further to high-income status. To achieve these goals, development experts often used high-income countries as a reference point and naturally observed what developing countries did not have or could not do well. The intentions may have been noble, but to this day the results all too often remain unsatisfactory. Development practitioners must avoid this mindset. Instead of looking at what their developing-country clients do not have and cannot do well, they should look at what they have now, can do well, and can scale up.

Structural transformation generally begins with agricultural transformation and the need to raise productivity of rural workers. But ultimately, poor countries must implement policies that move their resources (including their workforce) from agriculture into industry and modern services, where productivity levels are much higher. Many developing-country leaders have become aware that, if they are to achieve and maintain a robust growth rate, they must move away from agriculture, the dominant sector, toward industrial upgrading and technological innovation, often by imitating economies just a few rungs up the economic ladder. In low-income countries of Africa and South Asia, the agriculture sector is important and should not be neglected by policy makers, but that alone would not be sufficient to move their economies onto a path toward middle-income and finally to high-income status.

A dynamic economic process is the integration and accumulation of many small successes, and such successes can be had only when countries do well with what they have at any given point in their history. Poor countries must exploit their comparative advantage by using their endowments. One of the most powerful ideas in economics is that no matter how bad a situation a country is in at any time, it always has a comparative advantage in some sectors or industries. It is therefore critical for policy makers in developing countries to start their transformation strategies by making the most of the existing economic conditions—instead of trying desperately to replicate and mimic the economic and financial institutions of high-income economies, even when they are not yet needed and cannot be sustained at low levels of development.

THE ADVANTAGES OF BACKWARDNESS IN A CHANGING GLOBAL LANDSCAPE

Economic development strategies and policy instruments should reflect the reality that even countries with poor business environments can succeed. In an ever more globalized world, all poor countries, regardless of their constraints (infrastructure gaps, weak human capital, etc.), can find a niche to stimulate trade and generate sustained and inclusive growth, provided that they design and implement pragmatic strategies that focus on the development of competitive industries that are consistent with their comparative advantage. This can be done even more easily today than was possible in the 1980s when China entered the global scene. Things have changed dramatically in the past decade: new empirical research (World Economic Forum 2013) shows that tariff reductions and market access have become much less relevant for economic growth than was the case a generation ago. Trade is no longer about manufacturing a product in one country and selling it elsewhere but about cooperating across boundaries and time zones to minimize production costs and maximize market coverage.

Global value chains are therefore the dominant framework for trade. Estimates suggest that reducing supply-chain barriers could increase global GDP up to six times more than removing all import tariffs. Simulations indicate that improvements on just two key bottlenecks to supply chains (border administration and transport and communications infrastructure) to all countries' performance only halfway to that of Singapore would yield an increase of $2.7 trillion (4.7 percent) in global GDP and $1.6 trillion (14.5 percent) in global exports. These staggering numbers compare with much smaller gains from complete worldwide tariff elimination, which would only lead to $400 billion (0.7 percent) in global GDP and $1.1 trillion (10.1 percent) in global exports. Global trade and value chains operating around the planet open up new opportunities to poor countries, just like the "graduation" of large manufacturing centers like China, which relinquishes low-skilled employment to poorer economies.

Developing countries can reap substantial economic benefits from their status as latecomers. They can exploit their low factor costs to promote successful labor-intensive industries in which they have comparative advantage. Even in their generally poor business environments, they can also lower the cost of doing business by building a series of strategically located clusters and industrial parks and attracting foreign direct investment, which also brings the positive externalities of technology transfer, managerial best practices, new knowledge, state-of-the-art learning, and access to large global markets. Such a two-pronged approach could facilitate the dynamic development of competitive private firms in well-selected regions and industries, provide employment for a labor force with low skills, and rapidly increase fiscal revenues. Such a pragmatic economic development strategy would generate a steadily growing trend in government revenues as well as foreign exchange and allow for the improvement of infrastructure in other regions. Eventually it would also create the conditions for prosperity and social peace. To be successful, this strategy obviously requires strong collaborative work between the state and the private sector in the identification of new sectors or lines of business and prioritization of infrastructure investment.

Clusters, industrial parks and export-processing zones, and active FDI promotions are pragmatic instruments for circumventing infrastructure and human capital deficits, as well as governance problems that are pervasive in low-income countries. They are also useful bridges to connect poor countries to global value chains. They constitute essential pillars of the strategy for exploiting comparative advantage. They have been widely used by successful East Asian economies and have recently served a good purpose in countries such as Vietnam, Cambodia, Bangladesh, Mauritius, Ethiopia, and Rwanda. This strategy is in fact better than the conventional development strategy, which intended to support domestic firms to enter domestic markets and then gradually international markets.

Why are well-designed, well-equipped, and well-managed industrial parks and export-processing zones so important? First, infrastructure in a poor country is almost always poor. The required improvement in infrastructure to reach the domestic market is much larger than to reach international markets. The reason is that in order to reach international markets, a poor country government only needs to build the road linking the export-processing zone to the port, whereas the reach of its own domestic market typically requires the construction of many more roads across the nation. Yet the domestic market of a poor economy is, by definition, only a tiny fraction of the global market. For example, the combined GDP of all fifty-four African countries represents about 2 percent of the global GDP, while Europe alone accounts for 23 percent, and the United States 21 percent. The return on investment for the infrastructure linking national economies to the global market is much higher than for the domestic market. This is also the reason that many ambitious programs for domestic and regional integration yielded few economic results and never took off.

It should be acknowledged that the quality of goods produced by domestic firms in poor countries is generally inferior to that of imported goods, because domestic producers typically lack good intermediate products, cutting-edge know-how, best-practice processes, high-level skilled workers and managerial expertise, and so on, which are all hard to develop by domestic firms themselves. With the liberalization of trade in the 1980s and 1990s, many domestic manufacturers could not face competition and were wiped out. Early deindustrialization became a trend in most developing countries (as documented by Rodrik 2016). However, when developing-country governments leverage export-processing zones to attract the relocation of export-processing light manufacturing from more advanced economies with rising wages, as the East Asian tiger did in the 1960s and China did in the 1980s, they can leap into the global market immediately. By attracting foreign direct investment and foreign firms in export-processing zones, poor countries can improve their trade logistics, benefit from knowledge transfer (with new skills and management expertise being transferred to local entrepreneurs), and make their local firms gradually competitive in domestic and global markets. This is what happened not only in East Asian economies but also in Bangladesh and Mauritius.

Even when their development strategy is successful, policy makers in developing countries should not forget the quintessential dynamics that propel economies from low- to medium- and high-income status; that is, the need to continuously pursue industrial, technological, and institutional upgrading in a manner that is consistent with changes in the comparative advantage. Failing to do so leads to countries being stuck for too long in low value-added industrial activities (e.g., Bangladesh) or in the so-called middle-income trap. Structural transformation is a continuous process that becomes harder as economies get closer to the technological frontier, where marginal income gains require new inventions. But before they reach that higher hurdle, all developing countries can reap enormous gains in growth simply by implementing carefully designed growth strategies that allow them to compete with more advanced economies with similar endowment structures.

The pragmatic approach of giving targeted industries a good enough business environment in some enclaves of excellence (industrial parks and export-processing zones) has allowed a number of developing countries to grow dynamically in spite of the poor overall business environment in their countries. Brazil, China, India, Indonesia, Vietnam, and Ethiopia are good examples. They certainly still face some major economic challenges. But their general economic performance in recent decades illustrates the wisdom in Attar's *The Conference of the Birds*:

> The Truth we seek is like a shoreless sea,
> Of which your paradise is but a drop.
> This ocean can be yours; why should you stop
> Beguiled by dreams of evanescent dew?
> The secrets of the sun are yours, but you
> Content yourself with motes trapped in its beams.

Notes

INTRODUCTION: THE ART OF ENGINEERING
PROSPERITY IN UNLIKELY PLACES

1. The term *hysteresis* originates from the physical sciences and generally refers to situations where equilibrium is path-dependent. In economics it is often used more loosely mainly to describe situations where actual unemployment affects equilibrium unemployment for a long time, i. e., historical rates of unemployment are likely to influence the current and future rates of unemployment. See Blanchard and Summers (1987). We use the term to refer to situations where short-term shocks and effects manifest themselves in long-term problems that inhibit economic performance and make it difficult to return to precrisis trends.
2. From the end of World War II to the Great Recession of 2008, only thirty-one economies have been able to reduce the income gap with the United States. And even among that group, only about a dozen non-Western countries have managed to successfully reduce that gap. See Lin and Rosenblatt (2012).
3. A new industry in an economy is said to have latent comparative advantage if its factor costs of production are lower than the factors of production in other countries. Such an industry generally uses the economy's relatively abundant factors as its main input. An efficient market is required because only with an efficient market will the relative factor prices reflect the relative abundances of different factors in the endowments and determine in which industries the economy has latent comparative advantages.
4. For an industry to be competitive in the world, its total costs, including factor costs and transaction costs, need to be comparatively low in the world. Reducing transaction costs requires improving general and industry-specific infrastructure, labor skills, financial services, regulations, logistics, and so on, which are mostly beyond the capacity of any individual firm. Successful economic development requires enabling the state to coordinate and provide those improvements that will facilitate the economy's upgrading to industries in which it has latent comparative advantages.
5. Some big farmers use desalinated water in drip irrigation systems, which help reduce water waste. But because the desalination process is expensive, others use brackish water found more than 2,200 feet below the ground's surface to water their crops and grapevines.
6. According to Sangho, Labaste, and Ravry (2011), exporters provide support services to farmers such as helping to manage their plantations, working to reduce fruit

flies, and implementing certification or traceability programs on the plantation. In return, exporters purchase farmers' final product—often without a contract. "The trust established by these interactions allows exporters to obtain a higher-quality product, because farmers are more willing to respect phytosanitary controls when provided assistance. In fact, trust among all actors in the mango value chain has increased over time."

7. Donald Rumsfeld, press conference, Washington, DC, February 12, 2002.

8. Causal analysis and causal reasoning have preoccupied philosophers and economists at least since David Hume. See Hoover (2001) for an excellent assessment of the big ideas on these topics.

9. Making a similar point about literary theory, Kavanagh (1989) notes that the word "limit" should be understood in this context in its mathematical sense, designating a frontier beyond which a change occurs, a border beyond which one thing becomes another.

CHAPTER 1: THE TYRANNY OF LITANIES

1. Annual spending from aid institutions devoted to infrastructure rose from $8 billion to only $11 billion between 2005–2007 and 2008–2011 (Wignaraja 2013).

2. The American Society of Civil Engineers, which issues a yearly report card for infrastructure in the United States, gave the country a D+ in 2013 and estimated that it needs $3.6 trillion in investments for improvement by 2020. Germany, a country that consistently ranks at the top in investor surveys for the quality of its infrastructure, also faces big challenges. A study carried out by McKinsey & Company in 2013 estimated that it needs to invest $69 billion in its roads to meet expected demand in the coming years. A government-appointed commission recently concurred, concluding that the country needs to spend $9.7 billion a year, for the next fifteen years—roughly 70 percent more than it spends now—just to get existing infrastructure back to normal standards (Daley 2013).

3. See chapter 7.

4. See OECD (2001) and Liu and Greaker (2009).

5. Human capital stocks are measured indirectly (as residuals) or directly. The indirect method typically consists of estimating the national wealth from the inputs (natural resource stocks, human capital stock, physical capital stocks, and financial assets) used to produce net national income. By calculating the streams of income from the other wealth components, one can deduct the value of the human capital stock as a residual or the unexplained part of net national income. A similar residual approach based on national accounts calculates human capital as the difference between total wealth and the sum of the tangible components of wealth (i.e., produced capital and natural capital). This indirect residual approach is increasingly seen as unsatisfactory because it cannot explain why and how human capital evolves, and thus it offers little information for policy making. In addition, indirect

measures of human capital are subject to many measurement errors in all the terms entering the accounting identities.

6. Obama's remarks were delivered at Fudan University in China, November 16, 2009.

7. International surveys of student abilities (PISA for fifteen-year-old students, PIRLS and TIMMS for fourth- and eighth-grade students) always reveal wide differences across (and within) countries in the actual skills of individuals with similar formal education.

8. Nobel Prize–winning economist Gunnar Myrdal (1968) published a pessimistic account of the economic future of Asia. Two years earlier, Chenery and Strout (1966) had released in the *American Economic Review* a forecast of global growth that did not did even include Hong Kong-China and Singapore, which were considered too insignificant. Yet their study heralded a great economic future in the medium term for Sri Lanka and India. By 1980—less than fifteen years later—the city-state of Singapore, with its 2.5 million inhabitants, exported more than India and its 700 million people at the time.

9. There is a more systematic way of telling the same story, which economists favor because it relies on algebra. Popular models of determinants of growth developed for small open economies by Dornbusch (1988) would apply well to most developing economies. The standard of living (SL) is defined as the purchasing power of the income produced by an hour of work. Labor productivity is defined as the amount of output per hour worked (α). With the price of domestic output denoted as P and the consumer price index denoted as Q, the purchasing power of an hour of work is $SL = \alpha P/Q$. The consumer price index is a function of domestic prices and import prices. Assuming that it is an exponentially weighted average, $Q = P^{1-b} \times (P^*)^b$ where $1-b$ is the share of domestic goods in spending. Substituting in the previous equation yields $SL = \alpha(P/P^*)^b$. This formula shows there are two ways of increasing the standard of living. The first is to improve labor productivity (a higher output per hour increases consumption, regardless of whether the increase is traded abroad or consumed domestically). The second is through better terms of trade, because an increase in the prices at which any country sells its products, relative to those it buys as imports (P/P^*), raises its real income.

10. 2014 African Transformation Report, 83.

11. Such dynamics may have profound influence on the demand for different categories of workers and their earnings. Goldin and Katz (2008) observed that in the United States the earnings of skilled workers relative to less skilled workers followed a U-shaped pattern over the twentieth century, declining during the first half of the century and increasing in the second half.

CHAPTER 2: UNPLEASANT TRUTHS ABOUT INSTITUTIONAL AND FINANCIAL DEVELOPMENT

1. The number of sovereign nations that are United Nations member states has grown from 51 in 1945 to 193 in 2014.

2. http://www.transparency.org/news_room/faq/corruption_faq.
3. U.S. Department of Justice (2006). A total of 23,550 people were charged and 20,513 were convicted.
4. T. Allen-Mills, "Congo Leader's £169,000 Hotel Bill," *Sunday Times*, February 12, 2006.
5. Ibid.
6. This is a much broader definition than the one typically used in the literature, which usually refers to only one dimension of the problem: the relative importance of financial markets and financial intermediaries. The notion of financial structure can be examined from various angles. For instance, to examine the channels of financial intermediation, the relative importance of financial markets and financial intermediaries will be the focus. In terms of long-term or short-term financing, the composition of monetary markets and capital markets is important. For the discussion of government regulation, the distinction and composition of formal finance and informal finance are relevant. In the banking sector, one may want to analyze the distribution of big banks and small banks. See Lin (2009) for discussion.
7. Some authors downplay the importance of distinguishing the financial system as bank-based or market-based and argue that banks and markets provide complementary services. See Merton (1995) and Merton and Bodies (2005).

CHAPTER 3: THE ECONOMICS OF CHANCE: POLICY PRESCRIPTIONS AS LAUNDRY LISTS

1. One important issue not often discussed about the economics of colonialism is that of "periodization," the optimal or relevant sequencing of time and periods of analysis. Although the conventional wisdom among Western historians is to distinguish between traditional time categories like Antiquity, the Middle Ages, the Enlightenment, and so on, some African historians question what they consider to be an ideologically designed sequencing of events. Instead, Daniel Amara Cissé (1988), for instance, suggests using a completely different and longer time frame (starting from the Neolithic) to assess performance over time.
2. Using records of the Chamber of Commerce and Colonial Office papers, Williams Hynes (1979) showed the heavy pressure brought to bear on various British governments by merchants and manufacturers to convince them to extend British influence in various parts of Africa and Southeast Asia. As a result of the decline in traditional outlets for British goods and the rise of protectionism in world markets, the interest in African markets grew sharply between 1880 and 1995, shaping the pattern of British involvement in West Africa. French authorities were even more direct in putting forward an economic rationale for their involvement in African colonies (Manning 1988). They decided to build railroads and motor roads, introduced their currency, imposed a monetary union among territories under French rule in 1939 (Monga 1997), and made labor more mobile through the end of slavery and peacekeeping. Jean Suret-Canale (1971) showed that the authoritarian and

oppressive administrative system put in place by the French government served to force Africans into the colonial economy, compelling local producers to supply primary products for the profit of a French commercial oligarchy. Jacques Marseille (1984) made the same point, stressing however, the divergence of views between politicians and businessmen in France toward the colonial period's end.

3. The so-called Augmented Washington Consensus added the following ten items to the previous list of policy prescriptions: anticorruption, social safety nets, corporate governance, flexible labor markets, targeted poverty reduction, "prudent" capital-account opening, financial codes and standards, World Trade Organization agreements, nonintermediate exchange rate regimes, and independent central banks/inflation targeting. See Rodrik (2002) and Fischer (2012).

4. Examples of works relying on this approach include Acemoglu and Zilibotti (2001) on technological adoption and human capital, and Banerjee and Newman (2004) on trade and financial development.

5. For instance, the World Bank supports investment climate reform with sector investment loans and development policy loans with substantial elements covering regulation and competition; trade facilitation and market access; support for small and medium-size enterprises; and tax administration reform. Beyond lending, the bank's Investment Climate Advisory Services unit offers client governments a range of advisory services to assist them in improving the investment climate for domestic and foreign investors. It helps promote investment, strengthen fair competition, and implement reforms that reduce unnecessary costs and risks faced by firms. Investment Climate reform work focuses on several dimensions: insolvency, business taxation, business regulation, trade logistics, industry-based programs, public-private dialogue, alternative dispute resolution, investment policy and promotion, and the development of special economic zones. Technical assistance is also provided through loan products and analytic and advisory services that conduct economic and sector analyses. The Multilateral Investment Guarantee Agency supports foreign direct investment in emerging markets through political risk insurance.

6. Other popular benchmarking tools include Investing across Borders, which compares regulation of foreign direct investment around the world. It presents quantitative indicators on economies' laws, regulations, and practices affecting how foreign companies invest across sectors, start businesses, access industrial land, and arbitrate commercial disputes; and Global Investment Promotion Best Practices, which surveys the ability of government-mandated investment promotion intermediaries to promote foreign direct investment by meeting prospective foreign investors' needs for country and sector information.

7. Equation 1 contains a strong restriction: δ_m is assumed to be the same across all firms. This implies that there is homogeneity in the behavior of firms on their reaction to policy variables. This crude assumption is not fully satisfactory. A fully fleshed out econometric model would have to go beyond such uniform reactions and introduce heterogeneity in the δ coefficients. See Bourguignon (2006).

8. The analysis of light manufacturing's potential in Tanzania, part of a larger project covering China, Vietnam, Zambia, Tanzania, and Ethiopia, draws on several analytical tools: World Bank Enterprise Surveys; qualitative interviews with about 300 enterprises (both formal and informal of all sizes) in all five countries; quantitative interviews with representatives of some 1,400 enterprises (of all sizes, both formal and informal) in all five countries; in-depth interviews with about 300 formal medium enterprises that were focused on the value chain in all five countries; and a study of the impact of Kaizen managerial training among owners of small and medium enterprises. For a detailed discussion, see Dinh and others (2012).

9. We acknowledge insightful discussions with and suggestions from L. Alan Winters on this topic.

10. See World Bank (2005). The evolution of knowledge and policies at the IMF on the validity of traditional macroeconomic frameworks and policies has also been remarkable. See Blanchard (2009) and Blanchard and others (2010, 2013).

CHAPTER 4: THE MECHANICS OF FAILURE AND THE SECRETS OF SUCCESS

1. We use here a slightly modified summary version offered by Dornbusch (1990a).

2. The order of the equations has been changed here to facilitate the model's presentation.

3. The Commonwealth of Independent States (CIS) was formed in 1991 and consisted of ten former Soviet Republics: Armenia, Belarus, Kazakhstan, Kyrgyzstan, Moldova, Russia, Tajikistan, Turkmenistan, Ukraine, and Uzbekistan.

4. Since this regression is based on a rather small data sample and there were few controls, the results are only indicative. The Doing Business data suffer from a lack of variance over time—although the aggregate rankings did change over time, individual categories (time to get a building permit, number of procedures to register a business, and so on) sometimes did not change during the period. There are also some methodological limitations in their computation: changes in individual categories were not weighted by the changes in the variance, leading to some bias in the data. How much this affects our results is open to debate, but we believe it is minimal.

5. As noted by Devarajan (2011), the infrastructure constraint is not just a lack of hardware. "A lot has to do with regulation. It is widely said Africa lacks competitiveness, as there are many land-locked countries that have to ship goods through ports and on poor-quality roads, increasing costs. But we conducted a study of four major road transport corridors in Africa and found the pure vehicle operating costs were no higher than in France. The transport prices, however, were the highest in the world, the difference being the profit margins accruing to the trucking companies. These profit margins are over 100 percent in Central Africa where they are the highest. This is because of a lack of competition, with 50-year-old regulations prohibiting

entry into the trucking industry. Rwanda, however, deregulated its trucking industry, and transport prices fell by 75 percent in real terms."

6. In 2013 GDP per capita in Qatar, Luxemburg, and Singapore was $146,000, $90,000, and $79,000, respectively, while it was only $750, $650, and $600 in Malawi, the DRC, and the Central African Republic.

7. In November 1998, as part of the legislation authorizing about $18 billion in additional funding by the United States for the International Monetary Fund, Congress established the International Financial Institution Advisory Commission, chaired by Allan Meltzer, to consider the future roles of seven international financial institutions: the World Bank Group, the World Trade Organization, the Asian Development Bank, the African Development Bank, the International Monetary Fund, the Inter-American Development Bank, and the Bank for International Settlements. The commission did not call for eliminating one or more of these institutions. Nor did it decide to merge institutions into a larger, multipurpose agency. A large majority of its members agreed that the institutions should continue if properly reformed to become more effective, eliminate overlap and conflict, increase transparency and accountability, and return to or assume specific functions. The Meltzer Report is online at http://www.house.gov/jec/imf/meltzer.htm.

8. Short-term effects of aid may indeed differ sharply from long-term effects. Michael Clemens et al. (2012) divide aid into three categories: (1) emergency and humanitarian assistance, often negatively correlated with growth because transfers typically occur in desperate country situations; (2) aid to build social capital (health, democracy, education, environment), which affects growth only in the long term and therefore does not appear in cross-country analyses whose time horizon is often short; and (3) aid directed to productive sectors (budget, infrastructure, and balance-of-payments support). By disaggregating official development assistance (ODA) flows among these various categories of assistance, they find that the third category, accounting for about half of aid flows, has a positive causal relationship with growth over a four-year period, with diminishing returns.

9. "Addiction" was initially used in medicine as a pharmacology term to describe the use of a drug in sufficient quantity to cause tolerance, thereby creating a situation in which given higher dosages of the drug must be used to produce an identical effect as time passes. Pharmacologists consider such addiction to be a disease state. Some psychiatrists tend to refer to the disease state as dependence. Other physicians also consider it a disease as addicted individuals tend to continue to use a given drug despite their own best interest. Nowadays medical research makes a theoretical distinction between *physical dependence* (characterized by symptoms of withdrawal) and *psychological dependence* (or simply *addiction*, defined as uncontrolled, compulsive use) (American Psychiatric Association, 2000).

10. *Afrobarometer Briefing Paper* no. 1, online at www.afrobarometer.org. The surveys were conducted in mid-2001. The findings for each country are based on nationally representative samples—usually 1,200 respondents.

11. See IMF (2001); World Bank (2005); Koeberle et al. (2005); Polak (1991).
12. L. Gbagbo, interview with Senegal Television, February 24, 2006.
13. The World Bank considers "conditions" to be prior actions preceding board presentation, or required for effectiveness and tranche release. They are set out in the legal agreements signed with recipient countries. "Benchmarks" are policy measures listed in board documents to serve as monitoring indicators of progress on reforms. They are not legally binding but constitute the basis for the subjective assessment made by the bank on whether to proceed with preparing new loans. The IMF distinguishes "performance criteria," conditions that must be met for its financing to continue, unless its board grants a waiver, from "structural benchmarks," used to map out a series of steps toward a policy result. Failure to achieve them would not by itself interrupt IMF financing.
14. Despite being the most commonly used indicator, aid as a share of GNI or GDP is only one of the three ways often used to measure aid flows. The two others are ODA flows in U.S. dollars (nominal or real terms), and aid per capita (Radelet 2006). Each of these measures is useful but could be misleading if analyzed in isolation. Moreover, they all give different results when analyzed over only short periods.
15. As a robustness check, we also used the net ODA received (percent of central government expense); the results are consistent with those reported here.
16. Using a Tobit specification does not alter our main results.

CHAPTER 5: AMBITIOUS PRAGMATISM: FIRST-ORDER ECONOMIC PRINCIPLES

1. It was not until 1982 that the World Bank devoted its first, full-fledged *World Development Report*, its annual flagship publication, to agriculture. See World Bank (1982). See also World Bank (2008) for an updated assessment and stocktaking of the role of agriculture in development. It must be noted, however, that other, less influential international development institutions such as the Food and Agriculture Organization (FAO) and the International Fund for Agricultural Development (IFAD) of the United Nations and some bilateral aid organizations—most notably the US Agency for International Development (USAID) and the Agence Française de Développement—consistently advocated an important role for agriculture in development strategies.
2. In situations where agricultural output does not grow rapidly enough to compensate for increasing demands, it is possible that rising prices allow farmers to gain a bigger share of consumers' expenditures. But in market systems these are anomalies, as these higher prices of agricultural products do not reflect economic growth.
3. Timmer (1988) notes that this second phase has been the focus of dual economy models of development.
4. Export subsidies allowed U.S. and EU exporters to capture market share around the world, put downward pressure on the level of world market prices, and compete unfairly with local producers in many developing countries (Action Aid 2011; Oxfam 2002, 2004; Matthews 2015).

5. The World Bank defines itself as being "like a cooperative, made up of 188 member countries. These member countries, or shareholders, are represented by a board of governors, who are the ultimate policymakers at the World Bank. Generally, the governors are member countries' ministers of finance or ministers of development." They meet once a year at the annual meetings of the Boards of Governors of the World Bank Group and the International Monetary Fund.

6. "Since the aim is to end *chronic* poverty and since frictional poverty—stemming from unexpected economic fluctuations in poor countries, political conflict, and war— cannot as yet be brought to an end, the first goal is formalized as a target of bringing the number of people living below this 'poverty line' to less than 3 percent of the world's population." (Basu 2013, 4). Besides the fact that the $1.25-a-day yardstick can be considered quite a low threshold, the use of a money metric measure of poverty does not do justice to the well-acknowledged multidimensional nature of the problem: improving people's lives requires much more than income but also better health, nutrition, and education, stronger individual rights, and so on (Sen 1982).

7. U.S. senator Max Baucus said that "China's competitive challenge makes Americans nervous. From Wall Street to Main Street, Americans are nervous about China's effect on the American economy, American jobs, on the American way of life" (Statement during the Senate Committee on Finance hearing on U.S.-China Relations, June 23, 2005). See also Roy (1996) and Ravenhill (2006) among others.

8. Monga (2012) offers a simple model that explains the mutually beneficial economic relationships generated by two competing economies that trade intensively with each other. See appendix to this chapter.

9. See Lapper (2010). In Mozambique, for example, Brazilian companies are working to develop coal reserves, build a power station, and construct rail and port infrastructure to bring the coal to export markets. In Angola a Brazilian firm has become the largest private-sector employer, with involvement in food and ethanol production, offices, factories, and supermarkets.

10. Statement by Indian minister of commerce and industry Anand Sharma, reported by *Leadership* (Abuja, Nigeria), January 15, 2010.

11. The concept of "economic structure" refers to "the composition of production activities, the associated patterns of specialization in international trade, the technological capabilities of the economy, including the educational level of the labor force, the structure of ownership of factors of production, the nature and development of basic state institutions, and the degree of development and constraints under which certain markets operate (the absence of certain segments of the financial market or the presence of a large underemployed labor force, for example)" (Ocampo, Rada, and Taylor 2009, 7).

12. For an assessment and literature review, see Ross (1999). The Prebisch-Singer hypothesis suggests negative long-run trends in commodity prices. Cuddington, Ludema, and Jayasuriya (2002) assess it by considering trend and difference stationary models with up to two possible break points at unknown dates. They show that rather than a downward trend, real primary prices over the last century have

experienced one or more abrupt shifts, or "structural breaks," downward. The preponderance of evidence points to a single break in 1921, with *no* trend, positive or negative, before or since.

13. It is important to note that in national income accounting, the value added by a firm is the value of its production minus the value of intermediate goods (purchases from other firms) used up. The sum of value added in the economy is equal to its national product.

14. Historically, services were produced for domestic consumption. In a globalized world, they are gradually becoming tradable. Mishra, Lundstrom, and Anand (2011) construct an index of "service export sophistication" to document this new trend. Panel data estimations show that their index is a robust predictor for low- and middle-income country growth rates.

15. This section draws on Monga (2013b).

16. Recent empirical studies show that manufacturing has been a key factor in the prosperity of nations, with more than 70 percent of the income variations of 128 nations explained by differences in manufactured product export data alone (Hausmann et al. 2011).

17. A study by the U.S. Department of Commerce, Bureau of Economic Analysis, shows that manufacturing has a higher multiplier effect on the U.S. economy than any other sector. It generates $1.40 in additional value added in other sectors for every $1.00 in manufacturing value added (World Economic Forum 2012).

18. The largest counterpart to the U.S. current-account deficit is the combined surplus of oil-exporting economies, which have experienced big windfalls from high oil prices. The IMF projects they will run a record surplus of $740 billion in 2012, most of which will come from the Middle East. That would dwarf China's expected surplus of $180 billion. Since 2000 the cumulative surpluses of oil exporters have come to more than $4 trillion, twice as much as that of China.

19. It is generally estimated that after the oil-price shocks in the 1970s, about 70 percent of the increase in export revenues was spent on imports of goods and services.

20. Lin and Monga (2011) offer a menu of policy options that all low-income countries could choose from to exploit the benefits of backwardness, including those countries with low technology and physical and human capital.

21. Mischel (2014) has responded convincingly to his critics.

22. Cooper (1974) offers an elegant generalization of these results to a three-country dynamic by adding some additional complexities to the basic structure of the system of simultaneous equations in (6).

CHAPTER 6: THE ART OF PERFORMING ECONOMIC MIRACLES: IMPLEMENTATION GUIDELINES

1. Prigogine, who studied the problem of time in physics and chemistry, argued that nonequilibrium may become a source of order and that irreversible processes may lead to a new type of dynamic states of matter, which he called "dissipative

structures" (Prigogine 1977). His theory has led to a burgeoning field of research on dissipative structures in the social sciences. See, for instance, Schieve and Allen (2014) and Monga (1996).

2. Integrated Labor Force Survey data show that employment in household enterprises grew 13 percent over 2000–2006, higher than the change in the overall labor force and faster than the growth of wage employment in both nonagricultural and agricultural sectors.

3. Tanzania's population, around 44 million in 2010, has doubled since 1985. It is projected to nearly double to 81 million in 2030. The working-age population was estimated at 24 million in 2010 and will be a rising share of the population in the next twenty years. With population growth projected to be 2.2 percent a year in the next twenty-five years, the Tanzanian private sector faces the challenge of creating employment opportunities to absorb the youth bulge. About two-thirds of the country's population is under the age of twenty-four and is underemployed—including those with college and university degrees. Tanzania will have to generate about 800,000 jobs annually to accommodate the high rate of population growth.

4. Concurrently, the Revolutionary Government of Zanzibar finalized the Zanzibar strategy for growth and reduction of poverty (Kiswahili acronym MKUZA II), covering the same period.

5. See Dornbusch, Fischer, and Samuelson (1977) for the general formulation, and Monga (2013) for an extension of the model in developing economies that use labor arbitrage to industrialize.

6. As a first step, some development institutions have proposed a basic charter of rights and obligations for small traders in Africa that could be clearly posted at all border posts. The concept of the charter was endorsed by the African Union trade ministers in November 2011.

7. Many poor countries obtained debt reduction through the Highly Indebted Poor Countries (HIPC), Enhanced HIPC, and Multilateral Debt Relief Initiatives in the 1990s and 2000s. These various debt relief operations cost over $100 billion (Giugale and Thomas 2014). To qualify for partial debt cancellation, countries had to fulfill four requirements: produce a periodic "Poverty Reduction Strategy Paper" using templates provided by foreign donors; stick to macroeconomic stabilization plans mainly designed by the IMF; reject nonconcessional borrowing; and devote all their savings in debt payments to social programs. Not surprisingly, most of these countries were able to improve their social and poverty indicators but did not manage to invest in productive industries and sectors. As a result, they failed to reap the macroeconomic benefits (that is, higher growth rates, increased fiscal revenue and reserves) that could have been expected. Some of them are now being lured into contracting new debt from Paris and non–Paris Club lenders, often on nonconcessional terms, which may lead yet again to unsustainable indebtedness levels.

8. In the case of the African Investment Bank (AIB) created by the African Union in 2009 but never made functional, Monga (2012) estimates that an initial capital endowment of at least $50 billion would be required to make it credible. The bank

would then be able to raise a sizable multiple of that for its operations. The countries of the European Union initially contributed $50 billion in capital to the European Investment Bank, which borrowed an additional $420 billion and is therefore able to finance investments worth more than $470 billion (Skidelsky and Martin 2011). Although the EU has an economy almost ten times the size of the economies of Africa ($16 trillion in 2010), the same principle would work for the AIB if the institution is credibly set up and managed.

9. Besides the European Investment Bank, the list of well-known cases includes the German Kreditanstalt für Wiederafbau (KfW), the Korea Development Bank, and the Development Bank of Japan.

10. Mauritius is one of the first countries in modern times to successfully adopt export-processing zones with labor law flexibility that allows firms to dismiss workers and set wage rates. See Rhee and Belot (1990).

11. FDI is defined as the net inflows of investment to acquire a lasting management interest (10 percent or more of voting stock) in an enterprise operating in an economy other than that of the investor. The World Bank calculates FDI as the sum of equity capital, reinvestment of earnings, other long-term capital, and short-term capital as shown in the balance of payments. Data for all countries in the world are available at http://data.worldbank.org/indicator/BX.KLT.DINV.CD.WD.

12. The United States has been the world's largest recipient of FDI for most of the past decade. In 2012 foreign affiliates' net U.S. assets totaled $3.9 trillion. For 2012 FDI inflows totaled $166 billion. These financial inflows benefit the U.S. economy in various ways. In 2011 value added by majority-owned U.S. affiliates of foreign companies accounted for 4.7 percent of total U.S. private output. These firms employed 5.6 million people in the United States, or 4.1 percent of private-sector employment. About one-third of jobs at U.S. affiliates are in the manufacturing sector. These affiliates account for 9.6 percent of U.S. private investment and 15.9 percent of U.S. private research and development spending. Employment at U.S. affiliates was more stable than overall private-sector employment. As a result, U.S. affiliates' share of U.S. manufacturing employment rose from 14.8 percent in 2007 to 17.8 percent in 2011. Compensation at U.S. affiliates has been consistently higher than the U.S. average over time, and the differential holds for both manufacturing and nonmanufacturing jobs. See White House (2013).

13. International capital flows can be categorized based on the types of investors, because changes in the incentives facing different types of investors are the major determinants of the behavior of flows during a crisis. An alternative is categorization based on maturity, which leads empirical researchers to divide private loans into two categories: short-term and long-term loans. Portfolio debt flows are also sometimes included in these categories based on their maturity, whereas portfolio equity flows become a separate category. FDI typically grants foreign firms a controlling stake in the local firm. It includes equity capital, reinvested earnings, and financial transactions between parent and host enterprises. Portfolio equity investment generally refers to purchases of a local firm's securities without a controlling stake. It includes

shares, stock participations, and similar vehicles that usually denote ownership of equity. Debt flows include bonds, debentures, notes, and money market or negotiable debt instruments. As noted by Thorbecke and Salike (2013, 4), "Capital and particularly financial flows tend to be highly volatile and reversible. The degree of volatility depends upon the type of capital flow. In particular, short-term financing is considered the most volatile. Bank credits, portfolio flows, and financial derivatives are highly volatile. FDI is less volatile, making it more valuable for developing economies. This stability especially applies to equity capital flows, the largest of the three components of FDI."

14. Sula and Willett (2009) investigate whether some types of capital flows are more likely to reverse than others during currency crises. Several previous statistical testing exercises had yielded conflicting results on this issue. Sula and Willett argue that the problem with the earlier studies is that the degree of variability of capital flows during normal or inflow periods may give little clue as to their behavior during crises, and it is the latter that is most important for policy. Using data for thirty-five emerging economies from 1990 through 2003, their analysis confirms that direct investment is the most stable category but finds that, contrary to much popular analysis, private loans on average are as reversible as portfolio flows.

15. Based on empirical analysis using four-digit-level trade data from 105 countries over the period 1984–2000, the paper shows there is a positive effect of FDI on unit value of exports in developing countries. That is, there is a positive relationship between FDI and export quality, and the effect is economically meaningful. The evidence for high-income countries is ambiguous.

16. Attracted by the country's investment opportunities and by its sheer size and growing domestic market, thousands of multinational corporations also brought large inflows of FDI into China, mainly in the form of greenfield investment—by contrast to inward FDI in advanced economies generally by takeover of existing enterprises rather than by new establishment (Graham and Wada 2001).

17. See Adhikary (2011) for an empirical analysis of the impact of FDI on economic growth in Bangladesh.

18. Addis Ababa's Bole International Airport has witnessed a rapid growth in passengers from 900,000 in 2000 to more than seven million in 2014. Ethiopia earned about $3.2 billion from aviation-related services in 2014, four times more than from agricultural production of cereals. The country also increased traditional coffee exports by 45 percent between 2006 and 2014. The economic success has allowed the government to embark on ambitious new infrastructure projects, likely to continue boosting future growth. One of the biggest projects is the Grand Ethiopian Renaissance Dam on the Nile River, expected to cost $4.2 billion and to produce 6,000 megawatts of electricity, making it Africa's largest hydroelectric power plant and giving Ethiopia the capacity to be a major electricity exporter to neighboring countries.

19. See COM (2012) 582, "A Stronger European Industry for Growth and Economic Recovery" of 10.10.2012, and COM (2010) 614, "An Integrated Industrial Policy for the Globalisation Era Putting Competitiveness and Sustainability at Centre

Stage" of 28.10.2010. The commission has also announced that several current member states, including France, Spain, Germany, and the UK, have also defined industrial policies or strategies at national and regional levels in recent years.

20. The British rail industry contributes £9.3 billion (about $12 billion) a year to the UK economy and employs more than 200,000 people. See http://www.railsupplygroup.org.

21. For more information on the Canadian Technology Demonstration Program, see http://ito.ic.gc.ca/eic/site/ito-oti.nsf/eng/Home.

22. See the discussion under step 6.

23. See http://www.doingbusiness.org/about-us.

24. A special economic zone is a geographical area that offers investors more liberal economic laws than the country's typical laws. It is an economic development tool to promote rapid economic growth by using fiscal and business incentives to attract investment, technology, and knowledge. The zone is supposed to act as a magnet for investment in desirable activities in specially designated areas by providing quality infrastructure, attractive fiscal packages, business support services, cluster formation, and minimal regulation.

25. The African Growth and Opportunity Act is U.S. legislation that liberalizes market access to the United States for forty eligible sub-Saharan African countries. The act originally covered the eight-year period from October 2000 to September 2008, but amendments further extended it to 2015. AGOA builds on existing U.S. trade programs by expanding the duty-free benefits previously available only under the Generalized System of Preferences (GSP). Duty-free access to the U.S. market under the combined AGOA/GSP program stood at 6,421 product tariff lines in November 2016, including the roughly 1,800 product tariff lines that were added to the GSP by the AGOA legislation. Notably, these include items such as apparel and footwear, wine, certain motor vehicle components, a variety of agricultural products, chemicals, and steel.

26. These lessons from economic history and analysis go back to Marshall's *Principles of Economics* (1880), especially chapter 10 on "the concentration of specialized industries in particular localities." He provided the examples of the Sheffield cutlery industry and the Staffordshire pottery industry.

27. In 2008 it was estimated that sub-Saharan Africa alone had 114 zones, of which 65 were private (FIAS 2008, 18). At the same time there were already about 3,000 zones in 135 countries worldwide, accounting for some sixty-eight million direct jobs and more than $500 billion of direct trade-related value added.

28. This can be attributed to weak property rights and enforcement that reduces the value of collateral of firm assets and leads to lower investment in intangible assets (Claessens and Laeven 2003).

29. Informal employment is very diverse, from daily agriculture workers to street vendors, undeclared work, nonregistered self-employment, and many other forms. There are different informality levels, from workers without labor rights to workers with a contract but unpaid overtime work. In addition, there is a difference within

informal employment between wage workers and workers in self-employment. Recent work by Fox and Sohnesen (2012) highlights that most African firms are household enterprises and micro enterprises (informal nonfarm enterprises that are unincorporated and owned by households).

30. Cooper (1999) offers an overview of mathematical treatment of game-theoretic models of coordination.

31. In his industrial policy document titled "A Blueprint for an America Built to Last" (2012), President Barack Obama proposes a wide range of measures to support private firms and encourage manufacturing. They include lowering tax rates for companies that manufacture and create jobs in the United States; helping start-ups and small businesses succeed and create jobs by reforming regulations and expanding tax relief; helping spur innovation by investing in research and development; providing new incentives for manufacturers to upgrade equipment and eliminate wasted energy in their facilities, and so on.

CHAPTER 7: REAPING THE DIVIDENDS OF GLOBALIZATION: A WINNING ROAD MAP

1. UNCTAD (2013, 55) defines trade barriers as including all costs of getting a good to the final consumer other than the cost of producing the good itself: transportation costs (both freight costs and time costs), policy barriers (tariffs and nontariff barriers), and internal trade and transaction costs (including domestic information costs, contract enforcement costs, legal and regulatory costs, local distribution, customs clearance procedures, administrative red tape, and so on).

2. According to Constantinescu, Mattoo, and Ruta (2015), the explanation for the lower responsiveness of trade to income lies primarily in changes in international vertical specialization, most notably in the United States and China. For example, they note that Chinese exporters are now using more domestically produced inputs than imported inputs; the share of Chinese imports of parts and components in total exports has decreased from 60 percent in the mid-1990s to 35 percent today.

3. In 2015 it was estimated that manufacturing exports from developing economies faced a mean theoretical ad valorem tariff of only 0.63 percent in developed countries, while those from least developed countries (LDCs) faced an average tariff of 0.15 percent. Agricultural exports from developing countries and LDCs were subject to average tariff rates of 7.42 percent and 2.21 percent, respectively (ITC 2015, 1).

4. The UNCTAD classification of NTMs encompasses sixteen chapters (A to P), and each chapter is divided into groups with a depth of up to three levels.

5. Direct approaches attempt to collect information on measures of the NTMs (for example, customs procedures). This information is then introduced into gravity equations, which explain bilateral trade using a series of country characteristics, various trade cost factors, and the available information on NTMs. An assessment of the trade impact of these measures on quantities, price, or price-cost margins is then carried out. Indirect approaches use benchmarks such as traded quantities or prices

and estimate NTM ad valorem equivalents from the deviation between observed trade and the benchmark. A typical benchmark is trade within the border of the national economy (intranational trade), normally not subjected to or impeded by borders, foreign exchange issues, or the types of communications problems encountered when goods and services are exported. Trade among regions and cities of the same country is also normally subject to the same regulations, which provide an adequate basis for comparison with external trade. See Fontagné and Mitaritonna (2013), Cadot and Gourdon (2012), or Disdier, Fontagné, and Mimouni (2008).

6. International public institutions such as the United Nations Industrial Development Organization, the International Trade Centre, and the World Bank have launched effective programs of trade capacity building and trade facilitation to help firms in developing countries address NTMs.

7. It was subsequently reported that the outsourcing experiment has been too costly to Boeing. According to a "conservative" estimate by the *Seattle Times*, the cost of developing the 787 and rebuilding already-assembled but unusable jets may have amounted to $32 billion. The *Wall Street Journal* has also estimated that Boeing will have to deliver 1,100 of the 787s before the program will return a profit—at that time it had delivered fewer than 100. The more than three-year delay in the 787's rollout also weakened its competitive position versus Airbus because it substantially delayed Boeing's entire jet development schedule, including its next major aircraft program, the 777X.

8. While the focus has been on the United States and China, the global macroeconomic imbalances involved many other emerging economies, including oil-exporting Gulf countries. See Lane and Milesi-Ferretti (2014).

9. The press release for the car reads: "In common with the entire Rolls-Royce family of fine motor cars, the new Dawn is at the very vanguard of automotive design and technology. Dawn presents drivers with a suite of discreet technologies that ensure their leisure time in the car is a super-luxurious effortless experience."

10. In July 2015 the U.S. Congress adopted an act to extend the GSP program, which had expired July 31, 2013, until December 31, 2017. The U.S. Congress first enacted the GSP in the Trade Act of 1974, which authorized the granting of duty-free treatment to specified goods from designated lesser-developed countries called "Beneficiary Developing Countries" (BDCs). There are currently 122 designated beneficiary countries and territories. Eligible articles from BDCs may be entered duty-free provided that 35 percent of the value of the article originates from one of the BDCs. The program promotes economic development by eliminating duties on up to 5,000 types of products when imported from one of the BDCs. Since its inception, GSP legislation has always included a sunset component, and the issue of lapse has been a major source of uncertainty for developing country exporters and U.S. importers.

11. The term "fragmentation" was originally proposed by Jones and Kierzkowski (1990). A GVC "describes a full range of activities undertaken to bring a product or service from its conception to its end use and how these activities are distributed over geographic space and across international borders" (DFAIT 2011, 86). Amador and Di

Mauro (2015) note that the economic literature has used a wide range of terminologies to describe the same phenomenon, including "vertical specialization," "outsourcing," "offshoring," "multistage production," "intraproduct specialization," and so on.

12. Policies to build successful SEZs and industrial parks are discussed in the final section of this chapter.

13. In the example described in figure 7.6, Country A's total exports amount to $100 million, of which its own value added (created by its own firms within its national borders) is $80 million and the imported intermediate input (value added) is $20 million. Hence FVA in Country A's export is 20 percent. Calculating its domestic value added in global exports by other countries follows a similar logic: Country A's total exports of $100 million can also be broken down from the perspective of the value of its intermediate inputs used in exports by other countries of $40 million, and the valued added in its own exports of final products for consumption in foreign markets is $60 million. DVX is therefore 40 percent.

14. The data used to construct the indicators of GVC participation come from UNCTAD's Eora database. It provides multiregion input-output tables at the world level, with international input-output tables reported for 187 countries over the period 1970–2011. The database reports information on between 25 and 500 industries, depending on the country. Foster-McGregor, Kaulich, and Stehrer (2015) use the twenty-five-sector database over the period 1995–2010, with data on basic prices, which reports consistent data at this level of aggregation for all 187 countries. See appendix 7.1 for the description of the twenty-five Eora sector groupings.

15. Krugman (1991) used a modified Gini coefficient to show that several traditional industries display a higher spatial concentration than even high-tech industries, which were thought to be the real engines of clustering. Porter (1988) defines a cluster as "a geographic concentration of interconnected companies and institutions in a particular field." Swann, Prevezer and Stout (1998) offer a similar definition: "a large group of firms in related industries at a particular location," which is echoed by Bresnahan, Gambardella, and Saxenian (2001): "a spatial and sectoral concentrations of firms."

16. Increasing returns to scale typically refer to gains due to declining costs, which tend to fall with longer production runs. They are therefore internal to the firm. External returns to scale are typically the location gains from the presence of other firms in the same industry or related activities. For instance, technological or managerial externalities may occur as firms learn from one another by observing and borrowing best-practice techniques or organizational processes.

17. One reporter has commented that Qiaotou is "located slap-bang in the middle of nowhere" and "is the sort of place you might drive through without noticing. It is too small to be marked on most Western maps of China, too insignificant to merit a mention in newspapers, and so little-known that few outside the local county have heard its name" (Watts 2005).

18. For instance, in Peixian County, Jiangsu Province, one of the first and largest cross-regional mechanization service clusters, the government built infrastructure to

connect the townships to the national transportation network. "Peixian Bureau of Agricultural Mechanization (PBAM) selected directors from 18 agricultural mechanization service stations dispersed in different townships in the county and organized a study tour to Weifang of Shandong province to learn about their mechanization experience.... After returning home from the tour, PBAM organized free demonstration and training sessions for farmers and technicians at the township agricultural mechanization service stations. After completing training, PBAM issued a certificate allowing the trainees to drive trucks and combines to provide harvesting services. In addition, PBAM gathered harvest information nationwide, printed a pocketsize harvest calendar covering major cropping areas, and distributed them to potential machinery operators for free" (Zhang, Yang, and Reardon 2015, 15).

19. *Bulletin of Shenzhen's National Economy and Social Development in 2015*, http://www.sztj.gov.cn/xxgk/tjsj/tjgb/201504/t20150424_2862885.htm.

20. Zeng (2010) estimated that as of 2007, SEZs (including all types of industrial parks and zones) accounted for about 22 percent of national GDP, about 46 percent of FDI, and about 60 percent of exports and generated in excess of thirty million jobs. In addition, fifty-four high-tech industrial development zones (HIDZ) hosted about half of China's national high-tech firms and science and technology incubators. They registered some 50,000 invention patents in total, more than 70 percent of which were registered by domestic firms. They also hosted 1.2 million R&D personnel (18.5 percent of HIDZ employees) and accounted for 33 percent of the country's high-tech output. In just their first fifteen years of existence, HIDZs accounted for half of China's high-tech gross industrial output and one-third of China's high-tech exports. In addition, similar institutions called Economic and Technological Development Zones (ETDZs) were also responsible for another one-third of China's high-tech industrial output and exports.

21. Backward linkages can be defined as the various channels through which money, goods, services, and information flow between a firm and its suppliers and create a network of interdependence and mutually beneficial business opportunities. Such linkages exist when the development of an industry stimulates the growth of the industries that supply it. For example, growth of the leather industry may encourage the development of the livestock industry, which will lead to higher incomes for farmers and will create a greater demand for goods and services in the rural areas. Some authors distinguish between direct backward linkages and indirect linkages; a typical example is that of the auto industry, which has a direct backward linkage to the steel industry and an indirect backward linkage to the coal and iron industries (since coal and iron are inputs to steel production). Forward linkages are similar connections between a firm and its customers. They emerge when the growth of an industry leads to the development of the industries that use its output as input, or when the output of an industry helps stimulate activities in another industry. For example, through a forward linkage the development of the mining industry in a remote location can help build a network of rural roads needed to transport mining products.

22. CBIPs should not try to promote static comparative advantage. They should support industrial diversification and upgrading. But their goals should not be too ambitious, as is often the case in countries where policy makers advocate the promotion of *dynamic* comparative advantage. The nuance here is important. Theories of dynamic comparative advantage typically attempt to help firms enter industries that are a country's *future* comparative advantage. Because of endowment constraints in the African context, firms in those industries would not yet be viable in a competitive market even if the government helped them with the coordination and externality compensation. By contrast, CBIPs should aim at helping firms enter industries with *latent* comparative advantage. Under that scenario, firms would be *immediately* viable and require no subsidies or protection once the government provides coordination and externality compensation.

23. It is estimated that SEZs in sub-Saharan Africa generally contribute nearly 50 percent of exports. It can be inferred from their impact on diversifying the region's export base that they also contribute to skill upgrading.

24. According to the Africa Infrastructure Country Diagnostic (AICD), part of the African Development Bank group, the infrastructure needs of sub-Saharan Africa exceed $93 billion annually over the next ten years. To date less than half that amount is being provided, leaving a financing gap of more than $50 billion.

CONCLUSION: MAKING THE MOST OF EXISTING CIRCUMSTANCES

1. See Lin (2012b) for a discussion of "big-bang" versus "gradualist" approaches to economic reforms.

References

Abramoff, Jack. 2011. *Capitol Punishment: The Hard Truth about Washington*. Long Beach, CA: WND Books.

Acemoglu, Daron, and Fabrizio Zilibotti. 2001. "Productivity Differences." *Quarterly Journal of Economics* 116 (2): 563–606.

ActionAid, 2011. *Milking the Poor: How EU Subsidies Hurt Dairy Producers in Bangladesh*. Copenhagen.

ADB/ADBI (Asian Development Bank and Asian Development Bank Institute). 2009. *Infrastructure for a Seamless Asia*. Tokyo: ADB/ADBI. http://www.adbi.org/files/2009.08.31.book.infrastructure.seamless.asia.pdf.

Addison, T., and L. Demery. 1985. "Macroeconomic Stabilization, Income Distribution, and Poverty: A Preliminary Survey." ODI Working Paper no. 15. London: Overseas Development Institute, February.

Adhikary, B. K. 2011. "FDI, Trade Openness, Capital Formation, and Economic Growth in Bangladesh: A Linkage Analysis." *International Journal of Business Management* 6 (1) (January): 16–28.

Aghion, P. 2009. "Some Thoughts on Industrial Policy and Growth." Working Paper no. 2009–09. Paris: OFCE-Sciences Po.

Akamatsu, K. 1962. "A Historical Pattern of Economic Growth in Developing Countries." *The Developing Economies* (Tokyo). Supplement issue no. 1:3–25.

Akinola, G. A. 1997. "Colonialism and Imperialism: The African Experience." In *Encyclopedia of Africa South of the Sahara*. Edited by John Middleton. 4 vols. New York: Charles Scribner's Sons, 321–28.

Alcorta, L., 2014. "Patterns of Industrialization," Lecture at Peking University National School of Development. Beijing, China.

Allen-Mills, Tony. 2008. "Congo Sapped of Riches as Denis Menaces Boulevard St. Germain." *The Australian*, June 17 2008. http://www.theaustralian.com.au/archive/lifestyle/congo-sapped-of-riches/news-story/919967909b5cd9b3412d52a77804f51c

Alston, J. M., and P. G. Pardey. 2014. "Agriculture in the Global Economy." *Journal of Economic Perspectives* 28 (1) (Winter): 121–46.

Amador, J., and F. di Mauro. 2015. "Introduction." In *The Age of Global Value Chains: Maps and Policy Issues*. Edited by J. Amador and F. di Mauro. London: CEPR Press.

American Psychiatric Association. 2000. *Diagnostic and Statistical Manual of Mental Disorders*. 4th edition, text revision (DSM-IV-TR). Washington, DC.

Anderson, K., and Y. Hayami, with associates. 1986. *The Political Economy of Agricultural Protection: East Asia in International Perspective*. London: Allen and Unwin.

Andres, L., D. Biller, and M. Herrera Dappe. 2013. *Reducing Poverty by Closing South Asia's Infrastructure Gap*. Washington, DC: World Bank.

Arndt, C., S. Jones, and F. Tarp. 2015. "Assessing Foreign Aid's Long-Run Contribution to Growth and Development." *World Development* 69 (May): 6–18.

Aryeetey, E. 2015. "African Development Banks: Lessons for Development Economics." In *The Oxford Handbook of Africa and Economics*. Vol. 2: *Policies and Practices*. Edited by C. Monga and J. Y. Lin. New York: Oxford University Press, 663–79.

Aschauer, D. 1989. "Is Public Expenditure Productive?" *Journal of Monetary Economics* 23:177–200.

Asiedu, E. 2006. "Foreign Direct Investment in Africa: The Role of Natural Resources, Market Size, Government Policy, Institutions and Political Instability." *World Economy* 29 (1) (January): 63–77.

Atkinson, R. D., and S. J. Ezell. 2012. *Innovation Economics: The Race for Global Advantage*. New Haven, CT: Yale University Press.

Attar, Farid al-Din Attar. [1177] 1984. *The Conference of the Birds*. Edited and translated by Afkham Darbandi and Dick Davis. New York: Penguin Classics.

Auerbach, Jonathan D. 1987. "Turning Sand into Land. Desert Farms in Israel Grow Lush Crops from Sand and Salty Water." *Christian Science Monitor*, May 19.

Austen, Ralph. 1987. *African Economic History*. London and Portsmouth, NH: James Currey and Heinemann.

Austin, Gareth. 2010. "African Economic Development and Colonial Legacies." *International Development Policy/Revue internationale de politique de développement*. http://poldev.revues.org/78; DOI:10.4000/poldev.78.

———. 2015. "The Economics of Colonialism." In *The Oxford Handbook of Africa and Economics*. Vol. 1: *Context and Concepts*. Edited by C. Monga and J. Y. Lin. New York: Oxford University Press.

Ayele, G., L. Moorman, K. Wamisho, and X. Zhang. 2010. "Infrastructure and Cluster Development: A Case Study of Handloom Weavers in Ethiopia." IFPRI Discussion Paper no. 00980. Washington, DC: IFPRI.

Ayyagari, Meghana, Asli Demirgüç-Kunt, and Vojislav Maksimovic. 2008. "How Important Are Financing Constraints? The Role of Finance in the Business Environment." *World Bank Economic Review* 22 (3): 483–516.

———. 2010. "Are Innovating Firms Victims or Perpetrators? Tax Evasion, Bribe Payments, and the Role of External Finance in Developing Countries." Policy Research Working Paper no. 5389. Washington, DC: World Bank.

———. 2012. "Financing of Firms in Developing Countries: Lessons from Research." Policy Research Working Paper no. 6036. Washington, DC: World Bank.

Baldwin, Richard E. 2011. "Trade and Industrialisation after Globalisation's Second Unbundling: How Building and Joining a Supply Chain Are Different and Why It Matters." In *Globalization in an Age of Crisis: Multilateral Economic Cooperation in the Twenty-First Century*. Edited by R. C. Feenstra and A. M. Taylor. Cambridge, MA, National Bureau of Economic Research.

———. 2012. "Global Supply Chains: Why They Emerged, Why They Matter, and Where They Are Going." CEPR Discussion Paper no. 9103. London: Centre for Economic Policy Research.

Banerjee, Abhijit, and Esther Duflo. 2005. "Growth Theory through the Lens of Development Economics." In *Handbook of Economic Growth*. Edited by P. Aghion and P. Durlauf. Vol. 1a. Amsterdam: Elsevier.

Banerjee, Abhijit V., and Andrew F. Newman. 2004. "Notes for Credit, Growth and Trade Policy." Unpublished manuscript. Cambridge, MA: Massachusetts Institute of Technology.

Barro, Robert J. 1991. "Economic Growth in a Cross Section of Countries." *Quarterly Journal of Economics* 106:407–43.

Barro, R. J., and X. Sala-i-Martin. 1995. "Capital Mobility in Neoclassical Models of Growth." *American Economic Review* 85:103–15.

Basu, K. 2013. "Shared Prosperity and the Mitigation of Poverty: In Practice and in Precept." Policy Research Working Paper no. 6700. Washington, DC: World Bank.

Bates, R. H. 1981. *Markets and States in Tropical Africa: The Political Basis of Agricultural Policies*. Berkeley: University of California Press.

Bauer, P. T. 1976. *Dissent on Development*. London: Weidenfeld and Nicolson.

Beck, T., Asli Demirgüç-Kunt, and Ross Levine. 2007. "Bank Concentration and Fragility: Impact and Mechanics." In *The Risks of Financial Institutions*. Edited by Mark Carey and René M. Stulz. Chicago: Chicago University Press, 193–231.

Becker, Gary S. 1964. *Human Capital: A Theoretical and Empirical Analysis, with Special Reference to Education*. New York: National Bureau of Economic Research.

———. 1968. "Crime and Punishment: An Economic Approach." *Journal of Political Economy* 76 (92) (March–April): 169–217.

Becker. Gary S. 2008. "Human Capital." In *The Concise Encyclopedia of Economics*. Edited by David R. Henderson. Liberty Fund, Library of Economics and Liberty. http://www.econlib.org/library/Enc/HumanCapital.html.

Ben-David, Dan. 1998. "Convergence Clubs and Subsistence Economies." *Journal of Development Economics* 55 (February): 153–69.

Bernanke, B. S. 2007a. "Global Imbalances: Links to Economic and Financial Stability." Speech at the Banque de France Financial Stability Review. February 18.

———. 2007b. "Global Imbalances: Recent Developments and Prospects." Bundesbank lecture. Berlin, Germany, September 11.

Bertola, Giuseppe, and Paolo Sestito. 2011. "A Comparative Perspective on Italy's Human Capital Accumulation." Quaderni di Storia Economica (Economic History Working Papers) 6 (October). Rome: Banca d'Italia.

Bessen, J. 2015a. "How Technology Has Affected Wages for the Last 200 Years." *Harvard Business Review*, April 29.

———. 2015b. *Learning by Doing: The Real Connection between Innovation, Wages, and Wealth*. New Haven, CT: Yale University Press.

Betcherman, Gordon, Karina Olivas, and Amit Dar. 2004. "Impacts of Active Labor Market Programs: New Evidence from Evaluations with Particular Attention to Developing and Transition Countries." Social Protection Discussion Paper Series no. 0402. Washington, DC: World Bank.

Blanchard, O. J. 2009. "The State of Macro." *Annual Review of Economics* 1 (May): 209–28.

Blanchard, Olivier, Giovanni Dell'Ariccia, and Paolo Mauro. 2010. "Rethinking Macroeconomic Policy." *Journal of Money, Credit, and Banking* 42 (supplement): 199–215.

———. 2013. "Rethinking Macroeconomic Policy II: Getting Granular." IMF Staff Discussion Note 13/03. Washington, DC.

Blanchard, Olivier J., and Lawrence H. Summers. 1987. "Hysteresis in Unemployment." *European Economic Review* 31 (1/2): 288–95.

Bold, Tessa, Bernard Gauthier, Ottar Maestad, Jakob Svensson, and Waly Wane. 2012. *Leakage of Public Resources and Student Performance in Tanzania*. Montreal: HEC.

Bourguignon, François. 2006. "Economic Growth: Heterogeneity and Firm-Level Disaggregation." PREM lecture (May). Washington, DC: World Bank.

Boycko, M., A. Shleifer, and R. Vishny. 1995. *Privatizing Russia*. Cambridge, MA: MIT Press.

Bratton, M. G. Lambright, and R. Sentamu. 2000. "Democracy and Economy in Uganda: A Public Opinion Perspective." *Afrobarometer Paper* no. 4 (December).

Bresnahan T., A. Gambardella, and A. Saxenian. 2001. "'Old Economy' Inputs for 'New Economy' Outcomes: Cluster Formation in the New Silicon Valleys." *Industrial and Corporate Change* 4:835–60.

Brynjolfsson, E., and A. McAfee. 2012. *Race against the Machine: How the Digital Revolution Is Accelerating Innovation, Driving Productivity, and Irreversibly Transforming Employment and the Economy*. Lexington, MA: Digital Frontier Press.

Burnside, C., and D. Dollar. 2000. "Aid, Policies, and Growth." *American Economic Review* 90 (4) (September): 847–68.

Busso, Matias, Lucia Madrigal, and Carmen Pagés. 2012. "Productivity and Resource Misallocation in Latin America." IDB Working Papers Series no. 306. Washington, DC: Inter-American Development Bank.

Cadot, O., and J. Gourdon. 2012. "Assessing the Price-Raising Effect of Non-Tariff Measures in Africa." Working Papers 2012–16. Paris: CEPII Research Center.

Calderón, César, and Luis Servén. 2011. "Infrastructure in Latin America." In *Handbook of Latin American Economies*. Edited by José Antonio Ocampo and Jaime Ros. Oxford: Oxford University Press.

Cameron, R. 1993. *A Concise Economic History of the World*. 2nd ed. Oxford: Oxford University Press.

Canning, D. 1999. "The Contribution of Infrastructure to Aggregate Output." Policy Research Working Paper no. 2246. Washington, DC: World Bank.

Caro, Robert. 1982–2012. *The Years of Lyndon Johnson*. 4 vols. New York: Alfred A. Knopf.

Carter, J. 1982. *Keeping Faith: Memoirs of a President*. New York: Bantam Books.

Cartwright, Nancy, and Jeremy Hardie. 2012. *Evidence-Based Policy: A Practical Guide to Doing It Better*. New York: Oxford University Press.

Castberg, A. D. 1999. "Corruption in Japan and the US." http://www.unafei.or.jp /english/pdf/PDF_rms/no56/56-33.pdf.

Cecchetti, Stephen G., and Enisse Kharroubi. 2012. "Reassessing the Impact of Finance on Growth." BIS Working Papers no. 381 (July). Basel, Switzerland: Bank for International Settlements.

Chan, Vei-Lin. 2000. "Foreign Direct Investment and Economic Growth in Taiwan's Manufacturing Industries." In *The Role of Foreign Direct Investment in East Asian Economic Development*. Edited by Takatoshi Ito and Anne O. Krueger. Chicago: Chicago University Press, 249–66.

Chandra, Vandana, Justin Yifu Lin, and Yan Wang. 2013. "Leading Dragon Phenomenon: New Opportunities for Catch-up in Low-Income Countries." *Asian Development Review* 30 (1): 52–84.

Chang, Ha-Joon. 2007. *Bad Samaritans: The Myth of Free Trade and the Secret History of Capitalism*. London: Bloomsbury Press.

Chenery, Hollis B., and Allan M. Strout. 1966. "Foreign Assistance and Economic Development." *American Economic Review* 56 (September): 679–733.

Chenery, H. B., and M. Syrquin. 1975. *Patterns of Economic Growth*. London: Oxford University Press.

Chenggang, X. 2011. "The Fundamental Institutions of China's Reforms and Development." *Journal of Economic Literature* 49 (4): 1076–1151.

China Information Office of State Council. 2010. "White Paper on China-Africa Economic and Trade Cooperation." September 23. http://news.xinhuanet.com /english2010/china/2010-12/23/c_13661632.htm.

Christiaensen, L., L. Demery, and S. Paternostro. 2002. *Growth, Distribution and Poverty in Africa: Messages from the 1990s*. Washington, DC: World Bank.

Christofakis, M., and A. Papadaskalopoulos. 2011. "The Growth Poles Strategy in Regional Planning: The Recent Experience of Greece." *Theoretical and Empirical Researches in Urban Management* 6 (2) (May): 5–20.

Chuhan-Pole, Punam, and Mwanka Angwafo, eds. 2011. *Yes Africa Can: Success Stories from a Dynamic Continent*. Washington DC: World Bank.

Ciravegna, L. 2011. "FDI, Social Ties and Technological Learning in New Silicon Valley Clones. Evidence from the Costa Rican ICT Cluster." *Journal of Development Studies* 47 (8): 1178–98.

Cissé, Daniel Amara. 1988. *Histoire économique de l'Afrique noire*. Abidjan and Paris: Presses Universitaires et Scolaires d'Afrique and L'Harmattan.

Claessens, Stijn, and Luc Laeven. 2004. "What Drives Bank Competition? Some International Evidence." *Journal of Money, Credit and Banking* 36 (3) (June): 563–83.

Clark, C. 1940 [1957]. *The Conditions of Economic Progress*. 3rd ed. London: Macmillan.

Clemens, M., S. Radelet, R. R. Bhavnani, and S. Bazzi. 2012. "Counting Chickens When They Hatch: The Short-Term Effect of Aid on Growth." *Economic Journal* 122 (561): 590–617.

Collier, P. 1999. "Aid 'Dependency': A Critique." *Journal of African Economies* 8 (4): 528–45.

Collier, P., P. Guillaumont, S. Guillaumont, and J. W. Gunning. 1997. "Redesigning Conditionality." *World Development* 25 (9): 1399–1407.

Collier, P., and A. J. Venables. 2007. "Trade Preferences and Manufacturing Export Response; Lessons from Theory and Policy." Unpublished manuscript, University of Oxford, London School of Economics, and CEPR.

Commission on Growth and Development. 2008. *The Growth Report: Strategies for Sustained Growth and Inclusive Development*. Washington, DC: World Bank.

Constantinescu, C., A. Mattoo, and M. Ruta. 2015. "The Global Trade Slowdown: Cyclical or Structural?" IMF Working Paper WP/15/6 (January). Washington, DC: IMF.

Cooper, Frederick. 1997. "Colonialism and Imperialism: An Overview." In *Encyclopedia of Africa South of the Sahara*. Edited by John Middleton. New York: Charles Scribner's Sons, 316–21.

Cooper, R. N. 1974. "Economic Mobility and National Economic Policy." *Wicksell Lectures 1973*. Uppsala, Sweden: Almqvist & Wiksell.

Cooper, Russell W. 1999. *Coordination Games: Complementarities and Macroeconomics*. Cambridge: Cambridge University Press.

Cuddington, John T., Rodney Ludema, and Shamila A. Jayasuriya, 2002. "Prebisch-Singer Redux." Working Paper no. 15857, United States International Trade Commission, Office of Economics.

Daley, Suzanne. 2013. "Germany, Austerity's Champion, Faces Some Big Repair Bills." *Washington Post*, November 20.

Darwent, D. 1969. "Growth Poles and Growth Centers in Regional Planning—a Review." *Environment and Planning* 1:5–32.

David, P. A. 1985. "Clio and the Economics of QWERTY." Papers and Proceedings of the Ninety-Seventh Annual Meeting of the American Economic Association. *American Economic Review* 75 (2): 332–37.

Davies, G. 2013. "Why World Trade Growth Has Lost Its Mojo." *Financial Times*, September 29.

De Sousa, J., Thierry Mayer, and Soledad Zignago. 2012. "Market Access in Global and Regional Trade." *Regional Science and Urban Economics* (November): 1037–52.

Deininger, K. 2003. *Land Policies for Growth and Poverty Reduction: Key Issues and Challenges Ahead*. Washington, DC: World Bank.

Deininger, K., H. Selod, and A. Burns. 2011. The Land Governance Assessment Framework: Identifying and Monitoring Good Practice in the Land Sector. Washington, DC: World Bank.

Demirgüç-Kunt, A., and R. Levine. 2001. *Financial Structures and Economic Growth: A Cross-Country Comparison of Banks, Markets, and Development*. Cambridge, MA: MIT Press.

Demirgüç-Kunt, Asli, and Leora Klapper. 2012. *Financial Inclusion in Africa: An Overview*. Washington, DC: World Bank.

Dervis, K. 1981. "Comments on Taylor." In *Economic Stabilization in Developing Countries*. Edited by W. R. Cline and S. Weintraub. Washington, DC: Brookings Institution, 503–6.

Dethier, Jean-Jacques. 2015. "Infrastructure in Africa." In *The Oxford Handbook of Africa and Economics*. Vol. 2: *Policies and Practices*. Edited by C. Monga and J. Y. Lin. Oxford: Oxford University Press.

Devarajan, S. 2012. "In Defense of Industrial Policy." *Africa Can End Poverty*. http://blogs.worldbank.org/africacan/in-defense-of-industrial-policy.

———. 2011. "OBG Talks to Shanta Devarajan, Chief Economist for Africa, World Bank." *OxfordBusinessGroup.com*. http://www.oxfordbusinessgroup.com/interview/obg-talks-shanta-devarajan-chief-economist-africa-world-bank.

Devarajan, S., C. Monga, and T. Zongo. 2011. "Making Higher Education Finance Work for Africa." *Journal of African Economies* 20 (3): iii133–iii154.

Devarajan, Shanta, William Easterly, and Howard Pack. 2003. "Low Investment Is Not the Constraint on African Development." *Economic Development and Cultural Change* 51 (3) (April): 547–71.

DFAIT. 2011. "The Evolution of Global Value Chains." In *Canada's State of Trade: Trade and Investment Update—2011*. Ottawa: Department of Foreign Affairs and International Trade, 85–101.

Dinh, Hinh T., Vincent Palmade, Vandana Chandra, and Frances Cossar. 2011. *Light Manufacturing in Africa*. Vol. 2. Washington, DC: World Bank.

Dinh, Hinh T., and George R. G. Clarke, eds. 2012. *Performance of Manufacturing Firms in Africa: An Empirical Analysis*. Washington, DC: World Bank.

Dinh, Hinh T., and Célestin Monga. 2013. *Light Manufacturing in Tanzania: A Reform Agenda for Job Creation and Prosperity*. Washington, DC: World Bank.

Dinh, Hinh T., Thomas G. Rawski, Ali Zafar, Lihong Wang, and Eleonora Mavroeid. 2013. *Tales from the Development Frontier: How China and Other Countries Harness Light Manufacturing to Create Jobs and Prosperity*. Washington, DC: World Bank.

Disdier, A.-C., L. Fontagné, and M. Mimouni. 2008. "The Impact of Regulations on Agricultural Trade: Evidence from the SPS and TBT Agreements." *American Journal of Agricultural Economics* 90 (2): 336–50.

Dornbusch, Rudiger, and Sebastian Edwards. 1989. *Macroeconomic Populism in Latin America*. Chicago: University of Chicago Press.

Dornbusch, Rudiger. 1988. "Balance of Payment Issues." In *Open Economy: Tools for Policymakers in Developing Countries*. Edited by Rudiger Dornbusch and F. Leslie C. H. Helmers. New York: Oxford University Press.

———. 1990a. "From Stabilization to Growth." Working Paper no. 3302. Cambridge, MA: NBER.

———. 1990b. "Policies to Move from Stabilization to Growth." CEPR Discussion Paper no. 458 (September). London: Center for Economic Policy Research.

———. 1991. "Policies to Move from Stabilization to Growth." In *Proceedings of the World Bank Annual Conference on Development Economics 1990*. Edited by Stanley Fischer, Dennis de Tray, and Shekhar Shah. Washington, DC: World Bank, 19–48.

Dornbusch, R., S. Fischer, and P. A. Samuelson. 1977. "Comparative Advantage, Trade and Payments in a Ricardian Model with a Continuum of Goods." *American Economic Review* 65 (5): 823–39.

Duranton, G., and D. Puga. 2005. "Micro-Foundations of Urban Agglomeration Economies." In *Handbook of Urban and Regional Economics*. Edited by V. Henderson and J. Thisse. Vol. 4. Amsterdam: North Holland.

Easterly, William. 2001. *The Elusive Quest for Growth: Economists' Adventures and Misadventures in the Tropics*. Cambridge, MA, MIT Press.

———. 2002. *The Cartel of Good Intentions: Bureaucracy versus Markets in Foreign Aid*. Washington, DC: Center for Global Development.

———. 2003. "Can Foreign Aid Buy Growth?" *Journal of Economic Perspectives* 17 (3): 23–48.

———. 2006. *The White Man's Burden: Why the West's Efforts to Aid the Rest Have Done So Much Ill and So Little Good*. New York: Penguin Press.

———. 2009. "The Cartel of Good Intentions." *Foreign Policy*, November 11.

Economist. 2015. "Special Economic Zones: Political Priority, Economic Gamble. Free Trade Zones Are More Popular than Ever—with Politicians, if Not Economists." April 4.

Edwards, L., and S. S. Golub. 2004. "South Africa's International Cost Competitiveness and Exports in Manufacturing." *World Development* 32 (8): 1323–39.

Ela, J.-M. 1990a. *Ma foi d'Africain*. Paris: Karthala.

———. 1990b. *Quand l'Etat pénètre en brousse: les ripostes paysannes à la crise*. Paris: Karthala.

Elster, J., and J. Roemer, eds. 1991. *Interpersonal Comparisons of Well-Being*. New York: Cambridge University Press.

Etounga-Manguelle, Daniel. 1991. *L'Afrique a-t-elle besoin d'un programme d'ajustement culturel?* Ivry-sur-Seine: Nouvelles du Sud.

———. 2000. "Does Africa Needs a Cultural Adjustment Program?" In *Culture Matters: How Values Shape Human Progress*. Edited by L. Harrison and S. Huntington. New York: Basic Books.

European Commission, 2010. *Communication from the Commission to the European Parliament, the Council, the European Economic and Social Committee, and the Committee of the Regions: An Integrated Industrial Policy for the Globalisation Era—Putting Competitiveness and Sustainability at Centre Stage*, Brussels, October 28.

European Commission, 2012. *Communication from the Commission to the European Parliament, the Council, the European Economic and Social Committee, and the*

Committee of the Regions: A Stronger European Industry for Growth and Economic Recovery, Brussels, October 10.

Evenett, S. J. 2013. "Five More Years of the G20 Standstill on Protectionism?" *Voxeu. org*, September 3. http://www.voxeu.org/article/five-more-years-g20-standstill -protectionism.

Executive Office of the President. 2011. *Recent Examples of the Economic Benefits from Investing in Infrastructure*. Washington, DC: White House, November.

Farole, T. 2011. "Special Economic Zones: What Have We Learned?" *Voxeu.org*, September 28. http://www.voxeu.org/article/special-economic-zones-what-have-we -learned.

FIAS. 2008. *Special Economic Zones: Performance, Lessons Learned, and Implications for Zone Development*. Washington, DC: IFC-World Bank.

Fieldhouse, D. K. 1981. *Colonialism: An Introduction*. London: Weidenfeld and Nicolson.

FIFA. 2007. "El Flaco Menotti Raised Argentina's Game." http://www.fifa.com/news/y =2007/m=4/news=flaco-menotti-raised-argentina-game-510452.html.

Fischer, Stanley. 2012. "The Washington Consensus." In *Global Economics in Extraordinary Times: Essays in Honor of John Williamson*. Edited by C. Fred Bergsten and C. Randall Henning. Washington, DC: Peterson Institute for International Economics.

FitzGerald, Valpy. 2006. "Financial Development and Economic Growth: A Critical View." Background paper for *World Economic and Social Survey 2006*. http:// www.un.org/en/development/desa/policy/wess/wess_bg_papers/bp_wess2006 _fitzgerald.pdf.

Fontagné, L., and C. C. Mitaritonna. 2013. "Assessing Barriers to Trade in the Distribution and Telecom Sectors in Emerging Countries." *World Trade Review* 12 (1) (January): 57–78.

Foster, V., and C. Briceño-Garmendia. 2010. *Africa's Infrastructure. A Time for Transformation*. Paris and Washington, DC: Agence Française de Développement and World Bank.

Foster-McGregor, N., F. Kaulich, and R. Stehrer. 2015. "Global Value Chains in Africa." Background paper for *UNIDO Industrial Development Report 2016*. Vienna.

Fox, Louise, and Thomas Pave Sohnesen. 2012. "Household Enterprises in Sub-Saharan Africa: Why They Matter for Growth, Jobs, and Livelihoods." Policy Research Working Paper no. 6184. Washington, DC: World Bank.

Galbraith, J. K. 1977. *The Age of Uncertainty*. Episode 1: "The Prophets and Promise of Classical Capitalism." Television series coproduced by BBC, CBC, KCET, and OECA.

Gates, B., 2012. Remarks at the International Fund for Agricultural Development Governing Council, February 23. http://www.gatesfoundation.org/media-center /speeches/2012/02/bill-gates-ifad.

Gates Foundation. *Africa Strategy*.

Gerschenkron, A. 1962. *Economic Backwardness in Historical Perspective: A Book of Essays*. Cambridge, MA: Belknap Press of Harvard University Press.

Ghani, E., and S. D. O'Connell. 2014. "Can Service Be a Growth Escalator in Low Income Countries?" Policy Research Working Paper no. 6971. Washington, DC: World Bank.

Giugale, M., and M. R. Thomas. 2014. "African Debt and Debt Relief." In *The Oxford Handbook of Africa and Economics*. Vol. 2: *Policies and Practices*. Edited by C. Monga and J. Y. Lin. New York: Oxford University Press.

Glaeser, E. L. and C. Goldin, eds. 2006. *Corruption and Reform: Lessons from America's Economic History*. Chicago: University of Chicago Press.

Glaeser, E. L., and R. Sacks. 2004. "Corruption in America." Discussion Paper no. 2043. Cambridge, MA: Harvard Institute of Economic Research.

Global Entrepreneurship Monitor. 2012. *Sub-Saharan African Regional Report*.

Goldin, Claudia. 2001. "The Human Capital Century and American Leadership: Virtues of the Past." *Journal of Economic History* 61 (2) (February): 263–92.

Goldin, Claudia, and Lawrence Katz. 2008. *The Race between Education and Technology*. Cambridge, MA: Harvard University Press.

Goldsmith, R. 1969. *Financial Structure and Development*. New Haven, CT: Yale University Press.

Government of Canada. 2013. "Harper Government Launches Key Aerospace and Defence Program." Press release. Ottawa: Minister of Industry, September 4.

Government of United Kingdom. 2014. "Industry and Government Join Forces to Launch New Vision for UK Rail Supply Chain." Press release.

Graham, E. M., and E. Wada. 2001. "Foreign Direct Investment in China: Effects on Growth and Economic Performance." In *Achieving High Growth: Experience of Transitional Economies in East Asia*. Edited by P. Drysdale. New York: Oxford University Press.

Gray, Jules. 2013. "Special Economic Zones: Spurring Urban Regeneration." *World Finance*, August 15. http://www.worldfinance.com/infrastructure-investment /government-policy/special-economic-zones-spurring-urban-regeneration.

Greenwald, Bruce, and Joseph E. Stiglitz. 2013. "Industrial Policies, the Creation of a Learning Society, and Economic Development." In *The Industrial Policy Revolution I—The Role of Government Beyond Ideology*. Edited by Joseph E. Stiglitz and Justin Yifu Lin. New York: Palgrave Macmillan, 43–71.

Griliches, Zvi. 1970. "Notes on the Role of Education in Production Functions and Growth Accounting." In *Education, Income, and Human Capital*. Edited by W. L. Hansen. Studies in Income and Wealth 35. New York: National Bureau of Economic Research.

———. 1979. "Issues in Assessing the Contribution of R&D to Productivity Growth." *Bell Journal of Economics* 10:92–116.

Grossman, S. J., and O. D. Hart. 1982. "Corporate Financial Structure and Managerial Incentives." In *The Economics of Information and Uncertainty*. Edited by John J. McCall. Chicago: University of Chicago Press, 107–40.

Groves, D. 2013. "Washington State Is the Clear Choice for Building the 777X." *The Stand*, October 31. http://www.thestand.org/2013/10/washington-the-clear -choice-for-the-777x/.

Gullick, Sidney. 1903. *Evolution of the Japanese*. New York: Fleming H. Revell.

Haltiwanger, J. C., E. Bartelsman, and S. Scarpetta. 2009. "Measuring and Analyzing Cross Country Differences in Firm Dynamics." In *Producer Dynamics: New Evidence from Micro Data*. Edited by Timothy Dunne, Bradford Jensen, and Mark J. Roberts. Chicago: NBER/University of Chicago Press.

Haltiwanger, J. C., M. Eslava, A. Kugler, and M. Kugler. 2004. "The Effect of Structural Reforms on Productivity and Profitability Enhancing Reallocation: Evidence from Colombia." *Journal of Development Economics* 75 (December): 333–71.

Hansen, H., and F. Tarp. 2001. "Aid and Growth Regressions." *Journal of Development Economics* 64 (2) (April): 547–70.

Haraguchi, N. 2014. "Patterns of Industrialization and Effects of Country-Specific Conditions." Presentation at the Meeting of the IPD/JICA Task Force on Industrial Policy and Transformation. Dead Sea, Jordan, June 5–6.

Harding, T., and B. S. Javorcik. 2011. "FDI and Export Upgrading." Discussion Papers Series no. 526 (January). Oxford University, Department of Economics.

———. 2012. "Foreign Direct Investment and Export Upgrading." *Review of Economics and Statistics* 94 (4) (November): 964–80.

Harrison, A., and A. Rodríguez-Clare. 2010. "Trade, Foreign Investment, and Industrial Policy for Developing Countries." In *Handbook of Economic Growth*. Edited by D. Rodrik. Vol. 5. Amsterdam: North-Holland, 4039–213.

Harrison, Ann E., Justin Yifu Lin, and Lixin Colin Xu. 2014. "Explaining Africa's (Dis) advantage." *World Development* 63 (C): 59–77.

Hausmann, R., and C. Hidalgo. 2012. "Economic Complexity and the Future of Manufacturing." *The Future of Manufacturing: Opportunities to Drive Economic Growth*. Cologne/Geneva: World Economic Forum, April 13.

Hausmann, R., C. Hidalgo, S. Bustos, M. Coscia, S. Chung, J. Jimenez, A. Simoes, and M. A. Yıldırım. 2011. *Atlas of Economic Complexity: Mapping Paths to Prosperity*. Cambridge, MA: Harvard Center for International Development.

Hausmann, R., L. Pritchett, and D. Rodrik. 2005. "Growth Accelerations." *Journal of Economic Growth* 10 (4): 303–29.

Hausmann, R., D. Rodrik, and A. Velasco, 2008. "Growth Diagnostics." In *The Washington Consensus Reconsidered: Towards a New Global Governance*. Edited by N. Serra and J. E. Stiglitz. New York: Oxford University Press, 324–54.

Heath, R., and A. M. Mobarak, 2015. "Manufacturing Growth and the Lives of Bangladeshi Women." *Journal of Development Economics* 115 (July): 1–15.

Heckman, James J. 2003. "China's Investment in Human Capital." *Economic Development and Cultural Change* 51 (4): 795–804.

Herfkens, E. 1999. "Aid Works—Let's Prove It!" *Journal of African Economies* 8 (4): 481–86.

Hindle, T. 2008. "Guide to Management Ideas and Gurus." *Economist*.

Hobson, John Atkinson. [1902] 1988. *Imperialism: A Study*. London: Unwin Hyman.

Hodgskin, T. 1820. *Travels in the North of Germany: Describing the Present State of the Social and Political Institutions, the Agriculture, Manufactures, Commerce, Education,*

Arts and Manners in that Country, Particularly in the Kingdom of Hannover. Vol. 1. Edinburgh: Archibald.

Hofstede, Geert, and Michael Harris Bond. 1988. "The Confucius Connection: From Cultural Roots to Economic Growth." *Organizational Dynamics* 16 (4) (Spring): 5–21.

Hoover, Kevin D. 2001. *Causality in Macroeconomics.* New York: Cambridge University Press.

Hopkins, A. G. 1973. *An Economic History of West Africa.* London: Longman.

Huntington, S. P. 1968. *Political Order in Changing Societies.* New Haven, CT: Yale University Press.

———. 2000. "Foreword." In *Culture Matters: How Values Shape Human Progress.* Edited by L. Harrison and S. Huntington. New York: Basic Books.

Hynes, Williams G. 1979. *The Economics of Empire: Britain, Africa, and the New Imperialism, 1870–95.* London: Longman.

ILO (International Labour Organization). 2014. *Global Employment Trends 2014: Risk of a Jobless Recovery?* Geneva.

Imai, Katsushi S., Raghav Gaiha, Abdilahi Ali, and Nidhi Kaicker. 2012. *Remittances, Growth and Poverty: New Evidence from Asian Countries.* Occasional Papers no. 15. Rome: IFAD.

Imbs, J., and R. Wacziarg. 2003. "Stages of Diversification." *American Economic Review* 93 (1): 63–86.

———. 2010. "The Process of Economic Integration." Paper presented at the World Bank Seminar on Structural Transformation. Washington, DC, October 19.

IMF (International Monetary Fund). 2001. *Conditionality in Fund-Supported Programs—Overview.* Washington, DC, February.

Irwin, D. A. 2002. "Long-Run Trends in World Trade and Income." *World Trade Review* 1 (1) (March): 89–100.

ITC (International Trade Centre). 2015. *The Invisible Barriers to Trade: How Businesses Experience Non-Tariff Measures.* Technical Paper no. MAR-15–326.E. Geneva: ITC.

James, John T. 2013. "A New, Evidence-Based Estimate of Patient Harms Associated with Hospital Care." *Journal of Patient Safety* 9 (3): 122–28.

Jayaratne, J., and John Wolken. 1999. "How Important Are Small Banks to Small Business Lending? New Evidence from a Survey of Small Firms." *Journal of Banking and Finance* 23:427–58.

Jemio M., Luis Carlos, Fernando Candia C., and José Luis Evia V. 2009. "Reforms and Counter-Reforms in Bolivia." IDB Working Papers. Washington, DC: Inter-American Development Bank.

Johnson, D. T. 2001. "Bureaucratic Corruption in Japan." JPRI Working Paper no. 76. San Francisco: Japan Policy Research Institute, University of San Francisco Center for the Pacific Rim.

Johnston, D. G. 1970. "Agriculture and Structural Transformation in Developing Countries: A Survey of Research." *Journal of Economic Literature* 3:369–404.

———. 1973. *World Agriculture in Disarray.* New York: St. Martin Press.

Jones, R. W., and H. Kierzkowski. 1990. "The Role of Services in Production and International Trade: A Theoretical Framework." In *The Political Economy of International Trade*. Edited by R. W. Jones and A. Krueger. Oxford: Basil Blackwell, 31–48.

Joseph, R. A. 1998. "Class, State and Prebendal Politics in Nigeria." In *Africa: Dilemmas of Development and Change*. Edited by P. Lewis. Boulder, CO: Westview Press.

———. 2014. *Democracy and Prebendal Politics in Nigeria: The Rise and Fall of the Second Republic*. New York: Cambridge University Press.

Ju, J., J. Y. Lin, and Y. Wang. 2015. "Endowment Structures, Industrial Dynamics, and Economic Growth." *Journal of Monetary Economics* 76:244–63.

Juma, Calestous. 2012. "Poor Infrastructure Is Africa's Soft Underbelly." *Forbes Magazine,* October 25.

Kabou, Axelle. 1991. *Et si L'Afrique Refusait le Développement?* Paris: L'Harmattan.

Kavanagh, Thomas M. 1989. "Introduction." In *The Limits of Theory*. Edited by T. M. Kavanagh. Stanford, CA: Stanford University Press, 1–22.

Keefer, P., and S. Knack. 1997. "Why Don't Poor Countries Catch Up? A Cross-National Test of an Institutional Explanation." *Economic Inquiry* 35 (July): 590–602.

Ketels, C.H.M. 2009. *Clusters and Dubai's Competitiveness*. Dubai: Dubai Economic Council.

Khan, M., and M. D. Knight. 1985. *Fund-Supported Adjustment Programs and Economic Growth*. Occasional Paper no. 41. Washington, DC: IMF.

Killick, T. 1997. "Principals, Agents, and the Failings of Conditionality." *Journal of International Development* 9 (4): 483–95.

Kissinger, H. 2000. "Foreword." In *From Third World to First—The Singapore Story: 1965–2000*. Singapore: Singapore Press Holdings and Time Editions, 8–16.

Knack, S. 2007. "Measuring Corruption: A Critique of Indicators in Eastern Europe and Central Asia." *Journal of Public Policy* 27 (3) (December): 255–91.

Koeberle, S., H. Bedoya, P. Silarsky, and G. Verheyen, eds. 2005. *Conditionality Revisited: Concepts, Experiences, and Lessons*. Washington, DC: World Bank.

Koojaroenprasit, S. 2010. "The Impact of Foreign Direct Investment on Economic Growth: A Case Study of South Korea." *International Journal of Business and Social Science* 3 (21): 8–19.

Krieger, Murray. 1976. *Theory of Criticism: A Tradition and Its Systems*. Baltimore: Johns Hopkins University Press.

Krueger, A. O. 1974. "The Political Economy of the Rent-Seeking Society." *American Economic Review* 64 (June): 291–303.

Krugman, Paul. 1991. *Geography and Trade*. Cambridge, MA: MIT Press.

———. 1994a. "Competitiveness: A Dangerous Obsession." *Foreign Affairs* (March–April): 28–44.

———. 1994b. *Peddling Prosperity: Economic Sense and Nonsense in the Age of Diminished Expectations*. New York: Norton.

———. 1995. "Increasing Returns, Imperfect Competition, and the Positive Theory of International Trade." In *Handbook of International Economics*. Edited by G. M. Grossman and K. Rogoff. Vol. 3. Amsterdam: North-Holland.

———. 1996. *Pop Internationalism*. Cambridge, MA: MIT Press.

———. 1997. "In Praise of Cheap Wages: Bad Jobs at Bad Wages Are Better than No Jobs at All." *Slate.com*, March.

———. 2008. "The Increasing Returns Revolution in Trade and Geography." Nobel Prize lecture. Oslo, December 8.

———. 2013. "Should Slowing Trade Growth Worry Us?" *New York Times*, September 30.

Kuper, S. 2006. *Soccer against the Enemy: How the World's Most Popular Sport Starts and Fuels Revolutions and Keep Dictators in Power*. New York: Nation Books.

Kuznets, S. 1966. *Modern Economic Growth: Rate, Structure and Spread*. New Haven, CT: Yale University Press.

———. 1971. *Modern Economic Growth: Findings and Reflections*. Nobel Prize lecture. Oslo, December 11.

La Porta, R., F. Lopez-de-Silanies, and A. Shleifer. 2008. "The Unofficial Economy and Economic Development." *Brookings Papers on Economic Activity*, Economic Studies Program. Brookings Institution 39 (2): 275–363.

Lahiri, S., and Y. Ono. 1998. "Foreign Direct Investment, Local Content Requirement and Profit Taxation." *Economic Journal* 108:444–57.

Lall, S., and G. Wignaraja. 1998. *Mauritius: Dynamising Export Competitiveness*. London: Commonwealth Secretariat.

Lamy, P. 2013. "Global Value Chains, Interdependence, and the Future of Trade." *Voxeu.org*, December 18. http://www.voxeu.org/article/global-value-chains-interdependence-and-future-trade.

Lancaster, C. 1999. "Aid Effectiveness in Africa: the Unfinished Agenda." *Journal of African Economies* 8 (4): 487–503.

Lane, P. R., and G. M. Milesi-Ferretti. 2014. "Global Imbalances and External Adjustment after the Crisis." IMF Working Paper no. 14/151. Washington, DC: IMF, August.

Lapper, R. 2010. "Brazil Accelerates Investment in Africa." *Financial Times*, February 9.

Lederman, D., and W. F. Maloney. 2011. *Does What You Export Matter? In Search of Empirical Guidance for Industrial Policies*. Washington, DC: World Bank.

Leff, N. 1964. "Economic Development through Bureaucratic Corruption." *American Behavioral Scientist* 8 (3): 8–14.

Lehrer, J. 2009. "Don't! The Secret of Self-Control." *New Yorker*, May 18.

Leibenstein, H. 1957. *Economic Backwardness and Economic Growth: Studies in the Theory of Economic Development*. New York: Wiley.

Letz, K. 2007. *The Luxembourg Economy—an Eventful History*. http://www.luxembourg.public.lu/en/publications/k/letz-economie-histoire/letz-economie-histoire-2007-EN.pdf.

Lewis, W. A. 1954. "Economic Development with Unlimited Supplies of Labor." *Manchester School of Economic and Social Studies* 22:139–91.

Li, Haizheng, Barbara M. Fraumeni, Zhiqiang Liu, and Xiaojun Wang. 2009. "Human Capital in China." NBER Working Paper no. 15500 (November).

Lien, D-H. D. 1986. "A Note on Competitive Bribery Games." *Economics Letters* 22:337–41.

Lim, L. 2006. "Chinese 'Button Town' Struggles with Success." *National Public Radio Morning Edition*, August 22.

Lin, Justin Yifu. 1992. "Rural Reforms and Agricultural Growth in China." *American Economic Review* 82 (1) (March): 34–51.

———. 2009. *Economic Development and Transition: Thought, Strategy, and Viability.* Cambridge: Cambridge University Press.

———. 2011. "From Flying Geese to Leading Dragons: New Opportunities and Strategies for Structural Transformation in Developing Countries." WIDER lecture 15. Helsinki: UNU-WIDER, May 4.

———. 2012a. *New Structural Economics: A Framework for Rethinking Development and Policy.* Washington, DC: World Bank.

———. 2012b. *The Quest for Prosperity: How Developing Economies Can Take Off.* Princeton, NJ: Princeton University Press.

———. 2012c. "From Flying Geese to Leading Dragons: New Opportunities and Strategies for Structural Transformation in Developing Countries." *Global Policy* 3 (4): 397–409.

———. 2014. "China's Rise and Structural Transformation in Africa: Ideas and Opportunities." In *Oxford Handbook of Africa and Economics.* Vol. 2: *Policies and Practices.* Edited by C. Monga and J. Y. Lin. New York: Oxford University Press.

Lin, J. Y., K. Lu, and C. Mandri-Perrott. 2015. "New Equities for Infrastructure Investment." *Project Syndicate*, March 4.

Lin, J. Y., and C. Monga. 2010. "The Growth Report and New Structural Economics." Policy Research Working Papers no. 5336. Washington, DC: World Bank. http://dx.doi.org/10.1596/1813–9450–5336.

———. 2011. "Growth Identification and Facilitation: The Role of the State in the Dynamics of Structural Change." *Development Policy Review* 29 (3): 259–310.

———. 2012. "Solving the Mystery of African Governance." *New Political Economy* 17 (5): 659–66.

———. 2013. "Comparative Advantage: The Silver Bullet of Industrial Policy." In *The Industrial Policy Revolution.* Vol. 1: *The Role of Government Beyond Ideology.* Edited by Joseph E. Stiglitz and Justin Yifu Lin. New York: Palgrave MacMillan, 19–39.

———. 2014. "The Evolving Paradigms of Structural Change." In *International Development: Ideas, Experience, and Prospects.* Edited by Bruce Currie-Alder, Ravi Kanbur, David M. Malone, and Rohinton Medhora. New York: Oxford University Press.

Lin, J. Y., and D. Rosenblatt. 2012. "Shifting Patterns of Economic Growth and Rethinking Development." *Journal of Economic Policy Reform* 13 (3): 1–24.

Lin, J. Y., and G. Tan. 1999. "Policy Burdens, Accountability, and Soft Budget Constraints." *American Economic Review* 89 (2): 426–31.

Lin, J. Y., X. Sun, and Y. Jiang. 2013. "Endowment, Industrial Structure and Appropriate Financial Structure: A New Structural Economics Perspective." *Journal of Economic Policy Reform* 16 (2): 1–14.

Liu, Gang, and Mads Greaker. 2009. *Measuring the Stock of Human Capital for Norway: A Lifetime Labour Income Approach*. Statistics Norway. http://www.ssb.no/a /english/publikasjoner/pdf/doc_200912_en/doc_200912_en.pdf.

Lizondo, S., and P. Montiel. 1989. "Contractionary Devaluation in Developing Countries: An Analytical Overview." *IMF Staff Papers* 36 (1).

Loewendahl, H. 2001. "A Framework for FDI Promotion." *Transnational Corporations* 10 (1): 1–42.

Lucas, R. E. 1988. "On the Mechanics of Economic Development." *Journal of Monetary Economics* 22 (1): 3–42.

Lui, F. T. 1985. "An Equilibrium Queuing Model of Bribery." *Journal of Political Economy* 93 (August): 760–81.

Lyn, G., and A. Rodriguez-Clare. 2011. "Marshallian Externalities, Comparative Advantage, and International Trade." Unpublished manuscript. University of California Berkeley. http://emlab.berkeley.edu/~arodeml/Papers/LR_Marshallian _Externalities_Trade.pdf.

Maddison, Angus. 2001. *The World Economy: A Millennial Perspective*. Paris: OECD.

Maddison, Angus, 2008. Historical Statistics of the World Economy, 1–2008 AD, available online at www.ggdc.net/maddison/historical_statistics/horizontal-file _02–2010.xls

Mankiw, N. Gregorey, David Romer, and D. N. Weil. 1992. "A Contribution to the Empirics of Economic Growth." *Quarterly Journal of Economics* 107 (2): 407–37.

Manning, Patrick. 1988. *Francophone Sub-Saharan Africa, 1880–1985*. New York: Cambridge University Press.

Manski, Charles F. 2013. *Public Policy in an Uncertain World: Analysis and Decisions*. Cambridge, MA: Harvard University Press.

Manufacturing Institute, 2012. *Facts about Manufacturing*. Washington, DC.

Marseille, Jacques. 1984. *Empire colonial et capitalisme français: histoire d'un divorce*. Paris: Albin Michel.

Marshall, A. 1890. *Principles of Economics*. London: Macmillan.

Matthews, Alan. 2015. "The EU Has Finally Agreed to Eliminate Export Subsidies . . . Three Cheers!" *CAPReform*.

Mauro, P. 1995. "Corruption and Growth." *Quarterly Journal of Economics* 110 (August): 681–712.

Mayer, Colin. 1990. "Financial Systems, Corporate Finance, and Economic Development." In *Asymmetric Information, Corporate Finance, and Investment*. Edited by R. Glenn Hubbard. Chicago: University of Chicago Press, 307–27.

McKinnon, R. 1973. *Money and Capital in Economic Development*. Washington, DC: Brookings Institution.

McMillan, M., and D. Rodrik. 2011. "Globalization, Structural Change and Productivity Growth." Unpublished manuscript. February.

Merton, Robert C. 1995. "Financial Innovation and the Management and Regulation of Financial Institutions." *Journal of Banking and Finance* 19 (3–4): 461–81.

Merton, R.C., and Z. Bodie, 1995. "A Framework for Analyzing the Financial System," in: D.B. Crane et al. (eds.), *The Global Financial System: A Functional Perspective*, Boston, Harvard Business School Press.

Messer, Ellen. 2000. "Potatoes (White)." In *The Cambridge World History of Food*. Edited by Kenneth F. Kiple and Kiemhild Conee Ornelas. Vol. 1. New York: Cambridge University Press, 187–201.

Miller, G. E. 2009. "Kicking the Old Habits: How the World Cup Memories of Argentina's 1978 National Team Are Crossing Cultural Divides and Scoring in the Field of Reconciliation." PhD dissertation, Vanderbilt University.

Mischel. W. 2014. *The Marshmallow Test: Mastering Self-Control*. Boston: Little, Brown.

Mishra, Saurabh, Susanna Lundstrom, and Rahul Anand, 2011. "Service Export Sophistication and Economic Growth." Policy Research Working Paper 5606. Washington, DC: World Bank.

Mitchell, R. H. 1996. *Political Bribery in Japan*. Honolulu: University of Hawai'i Press.

Mkandawire, T. 2014. "The Spread of Economic Doctrines and Policymaking in Postcolonial Africa." *African Studies Review* 57 (1): 171–98.

Mkandawire, T., and A. Olukoshi, eds. 1995. *Between Liberalisation and Oppression: The Politics of Structural Adjustment in Africa*. Dakar: Codesria.

Mkandawire, T., and C. Soludo. 1999. *Our Continent, Our Future: African Perspectives on Structural Adjustment*. Dakar: Codesria.

———, eds. 2003. *African Voices on Structural Adjustment*. Dakar: Codesria.

Mogae, F. G. 2009. "Democracy in Africa: What Africa Expects from the Obama Administration." Schomburg International Update lecture. New York Public Library, Schomburg Center for Research in Black Culture, September 23.

Monga, Celestín. 1996. *The Anthropology of Anger: Civil Society and Democracy in Africa*. Boulder, CO: Lynne Rienner.

———. 1997. *L'argent des autres: Banques et petites entreprises en Afrique—le cas du Cameroun*. Paris: LGDJ.

———. 2006. "Commodities, Mercedes-Benz, and Adjustment: An Episode in West African History." In *Themes in West Africa's History*. Edited by E. K. Akyeampong. Oxford: James Currey, 227–64.

———. 2012a. "The Hegelian Dialectics of Global Imbalances." *Journal of Philosophical Economics* 6 (1) (Autumn): 1–52.

———. 2012b. "Shifting Gears: Igniting Structural Transformation in Africa." *Journal of African Economies* 21 (supplement 2): ii19–ii54.

———. 2013a. "Governance and Economic Growth in Africa: Rethinking the Conventional Paradigm." *Africa Plus* (July). http://africaplus.wordpress.com/2013/07/03/governance-and-economic-growth-in-africa-rethinking-the-conventional-paradigm/.

———. 2013b. "Winning the Jackpot: Job Dividends in a Multipolar World." In *The Industrial Policy Revolution II: Africa in the 21st Century*. Edited by J. E. Stiglitz, J. Y. Lin, and E. Patel. New York: Palgrave Macmillan, 135–72.

———. 2014a. *Aid Addiction: Symptoms, Side Effects, and Possible Cures*. Washington, DC: World Bank.

———. 2015. "Measuring Democracy: An Economic Approach." In *The Oxford Handbook of Africa and Economics*. Vol. 1: *Context and Concepts*. Edited by C. Monga and J. Y. Lin. New York: Oxford University Press, 427–51.

Monga, C., and J. Y. Lin. 2015. "Introduction: Africa's Evolving Economic Policy Frameworks." In *The Oxford Handbook of Africa and Economics*. Vol. 2: *Policies and Practices*. Edited by C. Monga and J. Y. Lin. New York: Oxford University Press, 1–20.

Monga, C., and P. Mpango. 2012. "Creating New Jobs in Tanzania: A Growth Identification and Facilitation Approach." Unpublished manuscript. Washington, DC: World Bank.

Morales, Evo. 2006. Inaugural speech, January 22. La Paz.

Murphy, K. M., A. Shleifer, and R. W. Vishny. 1993. "Why Is Rent-Seeking So Costly to Growth?" *American Economic Review Papers and Proceedings* 83 (May): 409–14.

Mussa, M., and M. Savastano. 2000. "The IMF Approach to Economic Stabilization." In *NBER Macroeconomics Annual 1999*. Edited by B. S. Bernanke and J. J. Rotemberg. Cambridge, MA: MIT Press, 79–128.

Myrdal, Gunnar. 1968. *Asian Drama: An Inquiry into the Poverty of Nations*. New York: Pantheon.

Naipaul, V. S. 2010. *The Masque of Africa: Glimpses of African Belief*. New York: Knopf.

Nath, H. K. 2009. "Trade, Foreign Direct Investment, and Growth." *Comparative Economic Studies* 51:20–50.

Nelson, R. R., and E. Phelps. 1966. "Investment in Humans, Technological Diffusion and Economic Growth." *American Economic Review* 61 (2): 69–75.

Nunn, Nathan. 2008. "The Long Term Effects of Africa's Slave Trades." *Quarterly Journal of Economics* 123 (1) (February): 139–76.

Nurkse, Ragnar. 1953. *Problems of Capital Formation in Underdeveloped Countries*. Oxford: Basil Blackwell.

Obama, B. 2014. Remarks at APEC CEO Summit. Beijing, November 10.

Ocampo, J. A., C. Rada, and L. Taylor. 2009. *Growth and Policy in Developing Countries: A Structuralist Approach*. New York: Columbia University Press.

Ocampo, Jose Antonio. 2005. *Beyond Reforms: Structural Dynamics and Macroeconomic Vulnerability*. Stanford, CA, and Washington, DC: Stanford University Press and World Bank.

OECD (Organization for Economic Cooperation and Development). 2010. *Review of Agricultural Policies: Israel*. Paris: OECD.

———. 1994. *Technology, Productivity and Job Creation—Best Policy Practices*. Paris: OECD.

———. 2001. *The Well-being of Nations: The Role of Human and Social Capital*. Paris: OECD.

Oqubay, A. 2015. *Made in Africa: Industrial Policy in Africa*. Oxford: Oxford University Press.

Oxfam. 2002. "Stop the Dumping! How EU Agricultural Subsidies Are Damaging Livelihoods in the Developing World."

———. 2004. "Dumping on the World: How EU Sugar Policies Hurt Poor Countries."

Pack, H. 2010. "Sectoral Upgrading a Half Century Later—2010 Is Not 1960." *Let's Talk Development*. World Bank blog, November 1. http://blogs.worldbank.org/developmenttalk/sectoral-upgrading-a-half-century-later-2010-is-not-1960.

Page, J. 2012. "Can Africa Industrialise?" *Journal of African Economies* 21 (2): ii86–ii124.

Pagés, Carmen, ed. 2010. *The Age of Productivity: Transforming Economies from the Bottom Up*. Washington, DC: Inter-American Development Bank.

Parente, S. L., and E.C. Prescott. 2002. *Barriers to Riches*. Cambridge, MA: MIT Press.

Paul, C. J., and D. S. Siegel. 1999. "Scale Economies and Industry Agglomeration Externalities: A Dynamic Cost Function Approach." *American Economic Review* 89: 272–90.

Perroux, F. 1955. "Note sur les notion de pole de croissance." *Economie Appliquée* 7 (1–2): 307–20.

Petersen, M. A., and Raghuram G. Rajan. 1995. "The Effect of Credit Market Competition on Firm-Creditor Relationships." *Quarterly Journal of Economics* 110:407–43.

Poirson, H. 1998. "Economic Security, Private Investment, and Growth in Developing Countries." IMF Working Paper no. 98/4. Washington, DC: International Monetary Fund.

Polak, J. J. 1991. "The Changing Nature of IMF Conditionality." *Essays in International Finance* 184. Princeton, NJ: Princeton University.

Politi, J. 2013. "Barack Obama Unveils Plans to Attract Foreign Investment." *Financial Times*, October 31.

POPC (President's Office Planning Commission). 2011. *The Tanzania Five Year Development Plan 2011/12–2015/16: Unleashing Latent Growth Potentials*. Dar-es-Salaam.

Popov, Vladimir. 2007. "Shock Therapy versus Gradualism Reconsidered: Lessons from Transition Economies after 15 Years of Reforms." *Comparative Economic Studies* 49 (1): 1–31.

Porter, M. 1998. "Clusters and the New Economics of Competition." *Harvard Business Review* 20 (November–December): 77–90.

Powell, Andrew. 2013. *Rethinking Reforms: How Latin America and the Caribbean Can Escape Suppressed World Growth*. Washington, DC: Inter-American Development Bank.

Prebisch, R. 1950. *The Economic Development of Latin America and its Principal Problems*. New York: United Nations. Reprinted in *Economic Bulletin for Latin America* 7 (1) (February 1962): 1–22.

Premchand, A. 1993. *Public Expenditure Management*. Washington, DC: International Monetary Fund.

Prigogine, I. 1977. "Time, Structure, and Fluctuations." Nobel Prize lecture, December 8. Stockholm.

Pritchett, Lant. 2001. "Where Has All the Education Gone?" *World Bank Economic Review* 15 (3): 367–91.

Pritchett, L., 2006. "The Quest Continues," *Finance and Development*, vol. 43, no. 1.

Proksch, M. 2004. "Selected Issues on Promotion and Attraction of Foreign Direct Investment in Least Developed Countries and Economies in Transition." *Investment Promotion and Enterprise Development Bulletin for Asia and the Pacific* 2:1–17. United Nations Publications.

Quigley, P. 2012. "Why Do China's Leaders Love Visiting Shannon?" *Business ETC—Economy, Technology, and Companies*, February 23. http://businessetc.thejournal.ie /why-do-chinas-leaders-love-visiting-shannon-363579-Feb2012/.

Radelet, S. 2006. "A Primer on Foreign Aid." Working Paper no. 92. Washington, DC: Center for Global Development.

Rajan, R. G. 1992. "Insiders and Outsiders: The Choice between Informed and Arm's Length Debt." *Journal of Finance* 47:1367–1400.

Rajan, R. G., and Luigi Zingales. 2003. "The Great Reversals: The Politics of Financial Development in the Twentieth Century." *Journal of Financial Economics* 69:5–50.

Rasiah, R., Xin-Xin Kong, and Jebamalai Vinanchiarachi. 2012. "Moving Up in the Global Value Chain in Button Manufacturing in China." In *Innovation and Learning Experiences in Rapidly Developing East Asia*. Edited by Rajah Rasiah, Thiruchelvam Kanagasundram, and Keun Lee. London: Routledge, 27–40.

Ravallion, Martin, and Chen, Shaohua. 2012. "Absolute Poverty Measures for the Developing World." In *Measuring the Real Size of the World Economy—The Framework, Methodology, and Results of the International Comparison Program (ICP)*. Washington, DC: World Bank.

Ravenhill, J. 2006. "Is China an Economic Threat to South Asia?" *Asian Survey* 46 (5): 653–74.

Read, R. 2002. "Foreign Direct Investment & the Growth of Taiwan & Korea." Paper presented at the IBRG FDI: Country Case Studies Conference, Grange-over-Sands, September 13–14.

Restuccia, D., and R. Rogerson. 2008. "Policy Distortions and Aggregate Productivity with Heterogeneous Establishments." *Review of Economic Dynamics* 11 (4): 707–20.

Rhee, Y. W. 1990. "The Catalyst Model of Development: Lessons from Bangladesh's Success with Garment Exports." *World Development* 18 (2) (February): 333–46.

Rhee, Y. W., and T. Belot. 1990. "Export Catalysts in Low-Income Countries: A Review of Eleven Success Stories." World Bank Discussion Papers no. 72. Washington, DC: World Bank.

Ricardo, David, 1817. "On the Principles of Political Economy and Taxation." In *The Works and Correspondence of David Ricardo*. Edited by Piero Sraffa with the collaboration of M. H. Dobb. 11 vols. Cambridge: Cambridge University Press, 1951–1973.

Rodriguez-Clare, A. 2005. "Clusters and Comparative Advantage: Implications for Industrial Policy." Working Paper no. 523. Washington, DC: Inter-American Development Bank.

Rodrik, Dani. 2002. "After Neoliberalism, What?" Paper presented at the Alternatives to Neoliberalism Conference, May 23–24, Washington, DC. http://www.new-rules .org/storage/documents/afterneolib/rodrik.pdf.

———. 2006. "Goodbye Washington Consensus, Hello Washington Confusion? A Review of the World Bank's *Economic Growth in the 1990s: Learning from a Decade of Reform.*" *Journal of Economic Literature* 44 (December): 973–87.

———. 2012. "Why We Learn Nothing from Regressing Economic Growth on Policies." *Seoul Journal of Economics* 25 (2): 137–51.

———. 2016. "Premature Deindustrialization," *Journal of Economic Growth* 21 (1): 1–33.

Romer, P. M. 1986. "Increasing Returns and Long-Run Growth." *Journal of Political Economy* 95 (5): 1002–37.

———. 1994. "New Goods, Old Theory, and the Welfare Costs of Trade Restrictions." *Journal of Development Economics* 43 (February): 5–38.

Rose-Ackerman, S. 1975. "The Economics of Corruption." *Journal of Public Economics* 4 (February): 187–203.

Rosenstein-Rodan, P. 1943. "Problems of Industrialization of Eastern and Southeastern Europe." *Economic Journal* 111 (210–211) (June–September): 202–11.

Rosenthal, S. S., and W. C. Strange. 2005. "Evidence on the Nature and Sources of Agglomeration Economies." In *Handbook of Urban and Regional Economics*. Edited by V. Henderson and J. Thisse. Vol. 4. Amsterdam: North-Holland.

Ross, Michael L. 1999. "The Political Economy of the Resource Curse." *World Politics* 51 (2): 297–322.

Roy, D. 1996. "The 'China Threat' Issue: Major Arguments." *Asian Survey* 36 (8) (August): 758–71.

Russell, John. 1828. *A Tour in Germany*. Vol. 1. Edinburgh: Archibald Constable.

Sachs, Jeffrey D. 2005. *The End of Poverty: Economic Possibilities for Our Time*. New York: Penguin Press.

———. 2014. "The Case for Aid." *Foreign Policy*, January 21. http://foreignpolicy.com /2014/01/21/the-case-for-aid/.

Said, Edward W. 1978. *Orientalism*. New York: Pantheon.

Saint-Paul, G. 1992. "Technological Choice, Financial Markets, and Economic Development." *European Economic Review* 36 (4): 763–81.

Sanchez-Robles, B. 1998. "Infrastructure Investment and Growth: Some Empirical Evidence." *Contemporary Economic Policy* 16:98–108.

Sangho, Yéyandé, Patrick Labaste, and Christophe Ravry. 2011. "Growing Mali's Mango Exports: Linking Farmers to Market through Innovations in the Value Chain." In *Yes Africa Can: Success Stories from a Dynamic Continent*. Edited by Punam Chuhan-Pole and Mwanka Angwafo. Washington, DC: World Bank, 167–83.

Sarkozy, Nicolas. 2007. Speech at the Cheikh Anta Diop University of Dakar. Senegal, July 26.

Schieve, W. C., and P. M. Allen, eds. 2014. *Self-Organization and Dissipative Structures: Applications in the Physical and Social Sciences*. Austin: University of Texas Press.

Schlam, T. R., N. L. Wilson, Y. Shoda, W. Mischel, and O. Ayduk. 2013. "Preschoolers' Delay of Gratification Predicts Their Body Mass 30 Years Later." *Journal of Pediatrics* 162 (1) (January): 90–93.

Schultz, Theodore W. 1960. "Capital Formation by Education." *Journal of Political Economy* 68:571–83.

———. 1961. "Investment in Human Capital." *American Economic Review* 51 (1): 1–17.

Scitovsky, T. 1985. "Economic Development in Taiwan and South Korea, 1965–1981." *Food Research Institute Studies* 19 (3): 215–64.

Sen, Amartya K. 1977. "Rational Fools: A Critique of the Behavioral Foundations of Economic Theory." *Philosophy & Public Affairs* 6 (4) (Summer): 317–44.

———. 1982. *Poverty and Famines: An Essay on Entitlement and Deprivation*. New York: Clarendon Press, Oxford University Press.

Serra, Narcís, and Joseph E. Stiglitz. 2008. *The Washington Consensus Reconsidered: Towards a New Global Governance*. New York: Oxford University Press.

Shaw, E. 1973. *Financial Deepening and Economic Development*. New York: Oxford University Press.

Shleifer, A., and R. Vishny. 1993. "Corruption." *Quarterly Journal of Economics* 108 (August): 599–617.

Singer, H. 1950. "The Distribution of Gains between Investing and Borrowing Countries." *American Economic Review* 40 (May): 473–85.

Skidelsky, R., and F. Martin. 2011. "For a National Investment Bank." *New York Review of Books* 58 (7) (April 28): 26–29.

Soludo, C. C., and T. Mkandawire. 2003. *African Voices on Structural Adjustment*. Trenton, NJ: Africa World Press.

Stiglitz, J. E., and B. C. Greenwald. 2014. *Creating a Learning Society: A New Approach to Growth, Development, and Social Progress*. New York: Columbia University Press.

Stiglitz, Joseph. 1998. "The Role of the Financial System in Development." Paper presented at the 4th Annual Bank Conference on Development in Latin America and the Caribbean, June 29.

Strom, S. H. 1989. "'Light Manufacturing': The Feminization of American Office Work, 1900–1930." *Industrial and Labor Relations Review* 43 (1) (October): 53–71.

Sula, O., and T. D. Willett. 2009. "The Reversibility of Different Types of Capital Flows to Emerging Markets." *Emerging Markets Review* 10 (4) (December): 296–310.

Suret-Canale, Jean. 1971. *French Colonialism in Tropical Africa, 1900–1945*. London: C. Hurst.

Swann G.M.P., M. Prevezer, and D. Stout, eds. 1998. *The Dynamics of Industrial Clustering*. Oxford: Oxford University Press.

Syverson, Chad. 2011. "What Determines Productivity?" *Journal of Economic Literature* 49 (2): 326–65.

Tanzi, V. 1998. "Corruption around the World: Causes, Consequences, Scope, and Cures." *IMF Staff Papers* 45 (December): 559–94.

Taylor, L. 1981. "IS/LM in the Tropics: Diagrammatics of the New Structuralist Macro Critique." In *Economic Stabilization in Developing Countries*. Edited by W. R. Cline and S. Weintraub. Washington, DC: Brookings Institution, 465–506.

Taylor, L. 1988. *Varieties of Stabilization Experience*. Oxford: Clarendon Press.

———, ed. 1993. *The Rocky Road to Reform*. Cambridge, MA: MIT Press.

Thomas, M. A. 2015. *Govern Like Us: U.S. Expectations of Poor Countries*. New York: Columbia University Press.

Thorbecke, W., and N. Salike. 2013. "Foreign Direct Investment in East Asia." *RIET Policy Discussion Paper Series* no. 13-P-003 (March). Tokyo: Research Institute of Economy, Trade, and Industry.

Timmer, C. P. 1988. "The Agricultural Transformation." In *Handbook of Development Economics*. Edited by H. Chenery and T. N. Srinivasan. Vol. 1. Amsterdam: Elsevier Science Publishers, 276–331.

———. 2014. "Managing Structural Transformation: A Political Economy Approach." WIDER Lecture. Helsinki: UNU-WIDER.

U.S. Department of Justice. 2006. *Report to Congress on the Activities and Operations of the Public Integrity Section for 2006*. Washington, DC.

UNCTAD (United Nations Conference on Trade and Development). 1992. *World Investment Report: Transnational Corporations as Engines of Growth*. New York: United Nations.

———. 2013. *World Investment Report 2013: Global Value Chains: Investment and Trade for Development*. Geneva.

UNIDO (United Nations International Development Organization). 2009. *Industrial Development Report 2009—Breaking In and Moving Up: New Industrial Challenges for the Bottom Billion and the Middle-Income Countries*. Vienna.

———. 2013. *Industrial Development Report 2013—Sustaining Employment Growth: The Role of Manufacturing and Structural Change*. Vienna.

United Nations. 2007. *Good Governance Practices for the Protection of Human Rights*. New York: Office of the High Commissioner for Human Rights.

Vogel, Ezra F. 2011. *Deng Xiaoping and the Transformation of China*. Cambridge, MA: Harvard University Press.

Wade, R. 1990. *Governing the Market: Economic Theory and the Role of Government in East Asian Industrialization*. Princeton, NJ: Princeton University Press.

Wang, J. Y., and M. Blomström. 1992. "Foreign Investment and Technology Transfer: A Simple Model." *European Economic Review* 36:137–55.

Wang, Y. 2009. "Development Partnerships for Growth and Poverty Reduction: A Synthesis of the First Event Organized by the China-DAC Study Group." Beijing: International Poverty Reduction Center in China, October 28–29.

Watts, J. 2005. "The Tiger's Teeth." *Guardian*, May 25.

Webb, Sidney, and Beatrice Webb. 1978. *The Letters of Sidney and Beatrice Webb*. Edited by N. MacKenzie and J. MacKenzie. Cambridge: Cambridge University Press.

Wei, S. J. 1996. "Foreign Direct Investment in China: Sources and Consequences." In *Financial Deregulation and Integration in East Asia*. Edited by T. Ito and A. Krueger. Chicago: Chicago University Press.

Whalley, John, and Xiliang Zhao. 2010. "The Contribution of Human Capital to China's Economic Growth." NBER Working Paper no. 16592. New York: NBER.

White, Anna. 2011. "Top Ten Banker Jokes." *Telegraph* (London), December 8.

White House. 2013. *Foreign Direct Investment in the United States*. Washington, DC, 2013.

Wignaraja, Ganeshan. 2013. "Asian Infrastructure Development Needs and a Way Forward." Presentation at the Business Forum 8th Transport Ministerial Meeting. Tokyo, September 4, 2013. http://www.adbi.org/files/2013.09.04.cpp.wignaraja.asian.infrastructure.dev.way.forward.pdf.

Williamson, John. 1990. "What Washington Means by Policy Reform." In *Latin American Adjustment: How Much Has Happened?* Edited by J. Williamson. Washington, DC: Institute for International Economics.

———. 2002. "Did the Washington Consensus Fail?" Paper presented at the Center for Strategic & International Studies. Washington, DC, November 6. http://www.iie.com/publications/papers/williamson1102.htm.

Woolcock, Michael. 2012. "Dueling Development Visions: Shaping the World Bank for the Future." Blog post, April 13. http://blogs.worldbank.org/developmenttalk/what-exactly-is-development.

World Bank. 1982. *World Development Report Agriculture*.

———. 1986. *World Development Report*.

———. 1989. *World Development Report 1989: Financial Systems and Development*. New York: Oxford University Press.

———. 1995. *Bureaucrats in Business: The Economics and Politics of Government Ownership*. New York: Oxford University Press.

———. 2002. *Transition, the First Ten Years: Analysis and Lessons for Eastern Europe and Former Soviet Union*. Washington, DC.

———. 2005a. *Economic Growth in the 1990s: Learning from a Decade of Reform*. Washington, DC.

———. 2005b. *Review of World Bank Conditionality*. Washington, DC, September.

———. 2008. *World Development Report Agriculture*. Washington, DC.

———. 2012. *World Development Report 2013: Jobs*. Washington, DC.

———. 2013. *Doing Business 2013*. Washington, DC.

———. 2014. *Country Partnership Strategy for Georgia, FY 2014-FY 2017*. Report no. 85251-GE. Washington, DC.

World Economic Forum. 2011. *The Global Competitiveness Report 2011–2012*. Geneva.

———. 2012. *The Future of Manufacturing: Opportunities to Drive Economic Growth*. Davos, Switzerland.

———. 2013. *Enabling Trade: Valuing Growth Opportunities* (in collaboration with Bain & Company and the World Bank). Geneva. http://www3.weforum.org/docs/WEF_SCT_EnablingTrade_Report_201 3.pdf.

Worldwide Governance Indicators. http://info.worldbank.org/governance/wgi/#home

WTO (World Trade Organization). 2014. *World Trade Report 2013*. Geneva.

Zeng, D. Z., ed. 2010. *Building Engines for Growth and Competitiveness in China: Experience with Special Economic Zones and Industrial Clusters*. Washington, DC: World Bank.

———. 2012. "SEZs in Africa: Putting the Cart in Front of Horse?" *Let's Talk Development*, April 9.

Zhang, X. 2012. "Clusters as an Instrument for Industrial Policy: The Case of China." Paper presented at the International Economic Association (IEA)—World Bank Roundtable "New Thinking in Industrial Policy." World Bank, May.

Zhang, X., and D. Hu. 2011. "Overcoming Successive Bottlenecks: The Evolution of a Potato Cluster in China." IFPRI Discussion Paper 01112. Washington, DC: International Food Policy Research Institute.

Zhang, X., J. Yang, and T. Reardon. 2015. "Mechanization Outsourcing Clusters and Division of Labor in Chinese Agriculture." IFPRI Discussion Paper no. 01415 (February). Washington, DC: IFPRI.

Zoellick, R. B. 2010. "The End of the Third World? Modernizing Multilateralism for a Multipolar World." Speech at the World Bank–International Monetary Fund Spring Meetings. Washington, DC, April 14.

Index

Note: Italicized pages refer to figures and tables

ambitious pragmatism: agglomeration and,
183–84, 190, 233, 248, 257, 282–86,
294; agriculture and, 158, 160–70, 175,
178–79, 186, 195, 328n1, 328n2; China
and, 158–60, 169–76, 187, 190–93,
199–201, 329n7, 330n18; clusters and,
185; comparative advantage and, 166,
177, 184, 191, 194–95; competition
and, 173, 187, 191; cooperation and,
187; delayed gratification and, 192–98;
diversification and, 13, 71, 122, 127,
133, 177–79, 183–84, 210, 232, 248,
339n22; economic development and,
157, 160–69, 176, 178, 183, 189, 191;
education and, 178, 181–82, 193, 195,
329n6, 329n11; endowment structures
and, 160, 185, 193–97; Equatorial
Guinea and, 158–59; externalities and,
162, 180, 183–84; failure and, 158, 160,
164, 166, 168, 173; global value chains
(GVCs) and, 168–69, 187–89; governance and, 197; gross domestic product
(GDP) and, 159, 164, 172, 179, 182,
190, 193–95, *196–97*; health issues and,
159, 186, 188, 329n6; human capital
and, 178–81, 186, 197–98; industrialization and, 160, 162, 175–80, 184–92,
194–95; infrastructure and, 165, 168,
175–76, 181, 186–87, 197, 329n9;
innovation and, 161, 167, 177–81, 189,
192–93; institutions and, 158, 161, 163,
165–68, 176–77, 181, 187, 197–98,
328n1, 329n11; International Monetary Fund (IMF) and, 161, 330n18;
management and, 195; manufacturing
and, 162–63, 167–68, 178–96, 330n16,
330n17; natural resources and, 158,
175–76, 180, 198; Nkrumah and,
157–58, 160; oil and, 159, 190, 330n18,
330n19; poverty and, 158–64, 166–71,
178, 186, 314–16, 329n6; privatization
and, 161; productivity and, 162–69,
173, 178–88, 191, 198; prosperity and,
161, 168, 170, 172, 174, 176, 189, 197–
98, 330n16; protection and, 189–90,
195; randomness and, 161; reform and,

160–61, 165, 168; regulation and, 161,
165, 168, 178; rehabilitating, 314–16;
romanticizing rural poverty and, 166–
69; sectoral shifts and, 178–79; Sherlock Holmes syndrome and, 197–98;
stability issues and, 161, 174; structural
change and, 176–92; subsidies and, 164,
166, 195; success and, 159–60, 163–64,
171–80, 184, 188, 191–94, 198; sustainability and, 171, 177, 182, 185–87; taxes
and, 165–66, 186, 195; technology and,
161–69, 176–82, 187, 189, 192–93,
329n11, 330n20; transportation and,
162, 168, 187–88, 191; understanding
global dynamics and, 169–76; unemployment and, 158, 178, 185; United
States and, 173–75, 180, 190, 193–201;
World Bank and, 159, 161–62, 164,
169–70, 186, 328n1, 329n5
American Society of Civil Engineers, 322n2
Andean Trade Promotion Act, 270
Angwafo, Mwanka, 12
APEC economies, 174
Argentina, 39, 111–13, 254–55, 307
Aschauer, D., 22
Asian Development Bank, 327n7
Asian Miracle, 256
Attar, Farid, 310–11, 320
Austen, Ralph, 78
Austin, Gareth, 81
Australia, 180, *263*, 264
automobiles, 128, 196, 206, 269
Ayyagari, Meghana, 91–92, 250
Azerbaijan, 26, *27*

backward linkages, 6, 14, 215, 240, 295,
297, 306, 338n21
backwardness, 18, 130, 132, 181, 198,
316–20, 330n20
Bahrain, 127
Bangladesh, *27*, 132, 333n17; ambitious
pragmatism and, 169, *170*, 187; foreign
direct investment (FDI) and, *93–94*, 238,
240, 318; globalization and, 278, 289;
labor-intensive industries and, 231–32,
319; Rana Plaza and, 231; stability of, 95

Bank for International Settlements, 327n7
barbershops, 1–2
Barro, Robert, 29, 88
Baucus, Max, 329n7
Bauer, P. T., 79–80
beauty salons, 1–2
Becker, Gary S., 60
Begin, Menachem, 202–3
Belarus, 26, 121, 326n3
Belgium, 128, 280
Benin, *105*, 156
Bertola, Giuseppe, 31
Bessen, James, 268
Bhutan, *27*, 41
binding constraints: comparative advantage and, 9; coordination and, 3; human capital and, 34–35; implementation guidelines and, 25–26, 34–35, 77, *87*, 91–100, *104*, 110, 206–10, 217–32, 246, 267; infrastructure and, 25–26, 34–35, 77, *87*, 90–100, *104*, 110, 206–8, 210, 214, 220, 246, 267, 326n5; policy prescriptions and, 87, 90–100, *104*, 110; random search for true, 90–97; rational selection and, 217–32; removing, 9, 14, 217–32
Blagojevitch, Rod, 49
Boeing, 262–64, 336n7
Bole International Airport, 333n18
Bolivia, 29, 35, 41, 103–8, 118, 280, 292
Bond, Michael Harris, 38–39
Borges, Jorge Luis, 254–55, 307
Botswana, 58, 124, 156, *172*, 314
Bourguignon, François, 47, 93
Boycko, Maxim, 54
Brazil, 320, 329n9; ambitious pragmatism and, 169, *170*, *172*, 176, 187, 191; Doing Business ranking of, 26; globalization and, 287, 307; as large middle-income economy, 18, 130; procrastination stereotype of, 39; structural transformation in, 124; total factor productivity and, 40
Bretton Woods, 76, 100, 141–42, 144, 161
bribery, 20–21, 50–53, 58, 61, 63
bubbles, 267

Burkina Faso, *27*, 76, *105*, 156
Burundi, 29, 35, 41, *105*, 156

C&H Garments, 241
Calderon, Cesar, 24
Calderon, Gabriel, 112
Cambodia, *27*, 318
Cameron, James, 117, 120
Cameroon, 33, 36, 49–50, *105*, 124, 144, 156
Camp David agreements, 202–3, 252
Canada, 244–45, *263*
Canning, D., 22
capitalism, 81, 162, 231–32, 279
Capitol Punishment (Abramoff), 48
Caribbean Basin Initiative, 270
Caro, Robert, 48
Carter, Jimmy, 202–3, 252
Cecchetti, Stephen, 67
Central African Republic, *105*, 126–27, 129, 133–34, 156, 327n6
Chad, *27*, *105*, 144, 156
Chang, Ha-Joon, 37–38
China: agriculture and, 9–12; ambitious pragmatism and, 158–60, 169–76, 187, 190–93, 199–201, 329n7, 330n18; Deng Xiaoping and, 33–35, 159–60, 289–90; Doing Business rankings and, 26, *27*; education and, 32; financial development and, 46; foreign direct investment (FDI) and, 236–40; globalization and, 190, 257, 266–67, 284–91, 306–7, 335n2, 336n8, 337n17, 338n20; growing export market of, 174; growth models and, 120–24, 130; Hong Kong and, 34, *172*, 193, 238–39, 323n8; human capital and, 32–35, 41; implementation guidelines and, 206, 221, 232, 237–42, 247, 252–53, 333n16; Lao Tzu and, 207; management and, 10, 34; manufacturing and, 18, 326n8; natural resources and, 34–35, 289; oil and, 190, 267; Penang, 285–86; policy prescriptions and, 311, 317–20, 326n8; potatoes and, 9–12; poverty and, 169; Qiaotou, 284–85, 337n17; School of Economics

China (*continued*)
    and Management, 10; transitional economy of, 5; transportation and, 25
China Development Bank, 240
Chirac, Jacques, 49
Chuhan-Pole, Punam, 12
Clarks, 240
Clemens, Michael, 327n8
climate change, 187
clusters: ambitious pragmatism and, 185; backwardness and, 318; Bollywood and, 281; boosting production/trade and, 279–87; Chinese potatoes and, 11–12; electrical-electronic, 285–86; export-processing zones (EPZs) and, 246–49, 285–86, 288, 293, 305; fragmentation and, 271–72, 285–86, 291, 336n11; globalization and, 256, 271, 279–308, 337n15, 337n18; growth models and, 123; Hollywood and, 281, 283–84; implementation guidelines and, 211, 214, 219–20, 233, 240, 246–49, 334n24; industrial parks (CBIPs) and, 298–307, 339n22; policy prescriptions and, 317–18; randomness and, 279–87; rational selection and, 214, 219–20, 233, 240, 246–49; Silicon Valley and, 280–81, 283; special economic zones (SEZs) and, 214–15, 237, 241, 245–49, 247, 253, 256, 273, 287–307, 325n5, 334n24, 339n22; spillover and, 273, 280, 288, 292, 294, 306–8
Côte d'Ivoire, 13, 80, 121–22, 124, 144, 156
Collier, Paul, 139, 271
Colombia, 38, *170*
colonial economics, 77–82, 324n1
Commonwealth of Independent States (CIS), 121
Communism, 33–34, 175, 239, 253
comparative advantage: agriculture and, 10–14; ambitious pragmatism and, 166, 177, 184, 191, 194–95; coordination and, 133–37; financial development and, 45, 61, 64, 74; following, 133–37; globalization and, 255–58, 272, 274,

284, 287, 289–99, 305; growth models and, 113, 119, 121–40; human capital and, 30, 35–36; identifying sectors with, 215–17; implementation guidelines and, 203–4, 207–8, 212–17, 227–28, 236, 240–42, 249–50, 253; latent, 3–6, 9, 11, 14, 18–19, 28, 30, 96, 99, 129, 133, 135, 138, 194, 213–16, 227–28, 249, 255, 298, 305, 321n3, 321n4, 339n22; policy prescriptions and, *85*, *87*, 96–99, 103, 312, 316–19; rational selection and, 212, 215–17, 227–28, 236, 240–42, 249–50, 253; revealed (RCA), 216–17; special economic zones (SEZs) and, 287–99
competition: ambitious pragmatism and, 173, 187, 191; clusters and, 280–81 (*see also* clusters); comparative advantage and, 5 (*see also* comparative advantage); country vs. corporate, 173–74; entrepreneurs and, 130; globalization and, 280–84; growth models and, 131, 135, 326n5; implementation guidelines and, 206, 212, 218, 220, 233, 238; policy prescriptions and, 76, 82, *104*, 319, 325n5; regulation and, 321n4; spillover and, 273, 280, 288, 292, 294, 306–8
Conference of the Birds, The (Attar), 310–11, 320
Congo, 34, 55–59, *105*, 156
Constantinescu, C., 260
convergence, 88, 171, 175, 196, 278
Cooper, R. N., 198, 200
cooperation: ambitious pragmatism and, 187; globalization and, 4, 262, 269, 272–73; growth models and, 142
coordination: comparative advantage and, 133–37; constraints and, 3; externalities and, 3, 83, 113, 125–37, 180–83, 233, 242, 245, 250–51, 294; failure and, 83, *85*, 99, 109; game theory and, 335n30; globalization and, 294, 339n22; implementation guidelines and, 233, 242, 245, 250–51, 335n30; increased credit and, 119; infrastructure and, 313; innovation and, 180–83; missed opportunities and,

Engel's Law, 164
Enterprise Surveys, 30, 91, 326n8
entrepreneurs: Africa and, 1–2, 24; competition and, 130; cooperatives and, 285; corruption and, 51–52, 65; decline of warrior, 78–79; drive of U.S., 4; endowment studies and, 126; financial development and, 51, 66; government dependency and, 230; Investment Climate Assessments (ICAs) and, 91; managerial capabilities and, 96, 319; manufacturing and, 189; Negev Desert Israelis and, 9; risk-return ratio and, 2–3; self respect and, 2; South Africa and, 1–3; subsidies and, 130; supply chain issues and, 233, 244, 284; sustainability and, 3; technical capabilities and, 96, *96, 219*; transaction costs and, 3–4
Equatorial Guinea, *27, 105,* 156, 158–59
equity: financial development and, 70, 72, 74; foreign direct investment (FDI) and, 332n11; globalization and, 300, 303–4; growth models and, 132, *149;* implementation guidelines and, 240, 332n11; infrastructure and, 22; market optimality and, 70; portfolio debt flows and, 332n13; regulation and, 74; total factor productivity (TFP) and, 22
ethics, 2, 58, 157, 261
Ethiopia, 24, *27, 105, 196,* 320, 326n8; aid addiction and, 156; aviation services and, 333n18; footwear industry of, 123; foreign direct investment (FDI) and, 239–41, 318; GDP of, 26; governance issues in, 289; growth models and, 123, 156; land tenure and, 301; poverty of, *170,* 221, 320; worker incentives and, 41
Etounga-Manguelle, Daniel, 39
European Commission, 243
European Union, 12, 270, 331n8
Evolution of the Japanese (Gullick), 38
exchange rates, 173, 325n3; financial development and, 63–64; globalization and, 266–67, 274, 296; growth models and, 117–19, 140; implementation guidelines and, 222–25; policy prescriptions

and, *93–94,* 102, *104,* 106, 109; rational selection and, 222–25
export composition, 180
export-processing zones (EPZs), 246–49, 285–86, 288, 293, 305, 319
export specialization indices (ESI), 216–17
externalities: agglomeration and, 183–84; ambitious pragmatism and, 162, 180, 183–84; comparative advantage and, 133–37; coordination and, 3, 83, *86,* 113, 125–37, 180–83, 233, 242, 245, 250–51, 294; economic diversification and, 183–84; economic linkages and, 6; financial development and, 60–61, 64, 67; globalization and, 281, 285, 294, 296, 305, 337n16, 339n22; government compensation and, 5; growth models and, 113, 125–37; human capital and, 37; implementation guidelines and, 233, 242, 245, 249–51; innovation and, 180–83; limited subsidies and, 249–52; missed opportunities and, 130–33; policy prescriptions and, 83, *85,* 98–99, 109, 313, 317; state facilitation and, 13; sustainability and, 126–30; technology and, 180–83

factor costs: globalization and, 292; growth models and, 122, 129; implementation guidelines and, 214, 218–20; policy prescriptions and, 317; transaction costs and, 3, 6, 214, 218–19, 292, 321n4
failure: ambitious pragmatism and, 158, 160, 164, 166, 168, 173; bank, 71; coordination, 83, *85,* 99, 109; donor, 84, *86–87,* 302–3; globalization and, 254, 291–92, 294–95, 298, 302–3; government, 13, 83–84, *85–86,* 302–3, 313; implementation guidelines and, 205, 213, 224–25, 242, 248; market, 42, 82–84, *85,* 121, 130, 138, 224, 302–3, 312–13; mechanics of, 110, 113, 120, 122, 130, 135, 138, 141, 328n13; policy prescriptions and, 89, 98–99, 109, 312–14; protection and, 312–13; regressions and, 90; special economic zones (SEZs)

failure (*continued*)
and, 291–92, 294, 296–98, 302–3;
structuralism and, 312–13; subsidies
and, 312–13; Washington Consensus
and, 21, 312–14
farmers. *See* agriculture
Farole, Thomas, 289, 291–92
financial development: China and, 46;
comparative advantage and, 45, 61, 64,
74; corruption and, 46–64, 71; Doing
Business indicators and, 12, 26, *27*, 47,
91, 107, *124*, 159, 239, 246, 261, 314,
326n4; education and, 66; endowment
structures and, 64, 73–74; entrepreneurs
and, 51, 66; equity and, 70, 72, 74; externalities and, 60–61, 64, 67; foreign aid
and, *59*; gross domestic product (GDP)
and, 59–60; health issues and, 51;
human capital and, 66; incentives-compatible policy and, 60–64; industrialization and, 57, 65, 70; innovation and, 13,
36, 42, 68 (*see also* innovation); institutions and, 44–74; intellectual mimicry
and, 65–74; International Monetary
Fund (IMF) and, 46; management and,
56, 59, 66, 68; modernization and, 80,
82, *85*, *87*, 109, 121, 131, 161, 192, 205,
224–25, 269, 287; natural resources
and, 54, 63, 73; opportunity cost and,
22–23, 55–57; poverty and, 57–58, 62,
65–66, 71–72; productivity and, 47,
59, 66–67; prosperity and, 45, 57, 64,
66; protection and, 64, 83–84, *85*, *87*,
109; redefining structure for, 70–74;
reform and, 44, 61, 71–72; regulation
and, 46, 50–51, 60, 63, 65–67, 71, 74,
324n6; risk and, 46, 64, 66–68, 70–74;
special economic zones (SEZs) and, 215,
237, 241, 247, 253, 256, 273, 287–92,
298–307, 325n5, 334n24; stability
issues and, 46, 60, 69, 72; subsidies
and, 61, 63–64, 136; sustainability
and, 56, 72–74; taxes and, 54, 56, 60;
technology and, 54; transaction costs
and, 71; transitions and, 5, 9, 61, 106,
108–9, 131, 159–60, 163, 253, *277–78*;

underdeveloped financial institutions
and, 65–74; United States and, 49–52,
57, 71; unpleasant truths about, 44–74;
World Bank and, 47, 56, 71
firm size, 70, 73, 96, *96*, 127, *219*, 250
five-year development plans (FYDPs), 210
food security, 164, 186
foreign aid: addiction to, *59*, 113, 137–56;
control group for, 150; Country Policy
and Institutional Assessment (CPIA)
and, 148–49; decreasing returns and,
139; dependency on, 139–41; financial
development and, *59*; GINI index and,
152, 154; growth models and, 113, 137–
47; HIPC and, 148–49, 331n7; hysteresis and, 147–48; implementation guidelines and, 227; Meltzer Report and, 138,
327n7; meta-economics and, 141–46;
official development assistance (ODA)
and, 141–42, 146–48, 156; performance
and, 148–56; policy framework papers
(PFPs) and, 141; policy issues and, 141–
46; policy prescriptions and, 91; Sachs
on, 138–39; trust and, 143–46
foreign direct investment (FDI): addiction
to, 327n9; agglomeration economics
and, 233–34; attracting, 233–35; backwardness and, 318; Bangladesh and,
238; China and, 236–40; controlling
stakeholders and, 332n13; definition of,
332n11; endogenous growth theories
and, 235; equity and, 332n11; Ethiopia
and, 239–41; globalization and, 285,
288–89, 291, 304, 307, 338n20; growth
identification and facilitation framework (GIFF) and, 232–41; growth
models and, 123, 136; Hong Kong and,
238–39; implementation guidelines and,
214, 232–41, 247–48, 332nn11–16;
infrastructure and, 307–8; Korea and,
237–38; Mauritius and, 238–39; policy
prescriptions and, 100, 102, *104*, 313–
14, 317–19, 325n5, 325n6; poverty and,
307; rational selection and, 232–41;
special economic zones (SEZs) and,
338n20; United States and, 332n12

foreign value added (FVA), 275, *276*, 337n13

forward linkages, 6, 240, 295, 338n21

Foster-McGregor, Neil, 272–73, 275

fragmentation, 271–72, 285–86, 291, 336n11

France, 49, 79, 128, 145, 193, 195, *197*, 237, *263*, 264, 280, 325n3, 326n5, 333n19

free markets, 83, 108, 161, 313

freeports, 306

G7 countries, 175, 266

Gabon, 32, *105*, 156

Galbraith, John Kenneth, 160

Gambia, 80, *105*, 156

Gates, Bill, 167

Gates Foundation Africa Strategy, 167

Gbago, Laurent, 144

General Agreement on Tariffs and Trade (GATT), 259–60

Georgia, 106

Germany, 37–38, 58, 128, 193, 195, *197*, 237, 267, 322n2, 332n9, 333n19

Gerschenkron, Alexander, 18, 65, 134

Ghana, *27*, 32–33, 36, 39, 58, *105*, 121–24, 143, 156–60

GINI index, *152*, 154, 337n15

Glaeser, Edward, 61

globalization: agriculture and, 264, 266, 270, 273, 285, 289, 300, *309*, 335n3, 337n18, 337n19, 338n21; analytics of interdependence and, 198–201; backwardness and, 316–20; boosting production/trade and, 279–87; Borges and, 254–55, 307; China and, 190, 257, 266–67, 284–91, 306–7, 335n2, 336n8, 337n17, 338n20; clusters and, 256, 271, 279–308, 337n15, 337n18; comparative advantage and, 255–58, 272, 274, 284, 287, 289–99, 305; competition and, 280–84; cooperation and, 4, 262, 269, 272–73; coordination and, 294, 339n22; corruption and, 293, 295–96, 299, 305–7; credibility and, 270–79; diet and, 9; duty and, 247, 270, 290, 306, 334n25, 336n10; economic

development and, 279, 281, 287, 289, 292, 295, 304, 336n10; education and, 268, 291, 300, *309*; endowment structures and, 279, 293, 296, 300; equity and, 300, 303–4; export-processing zones (EPZs) and, 246–49, 288; externalities and, 281, 285, 294, 296, 305, 337n16, 339n22; factor costs and, 292; failure and, 254, 291–92, 294–95, 298, 302–3; foreign direct investment (FDI) and, 285, 288, 289, 291, 304, 307, 338n20; fragmentation and, 271–72, 285–86, 291, 336n11; General Agreement on Tariffs and Trade (GATT) and, 259–60; Generalized System of Preferences (GSP) and, 270, 334n25, 336n10; governance and, 46–47, 281, 287, 289, 291, 293, 296, 305, 308; gross domestic product (GDP) and, 257–60, 289, 338n20; growth models and, 129–30; health issues and, 261, 286, *309*; human capital and, 29–30, 281, 287, 291; industrialization and, 260, 266, 272, 289; industrial parks and, 273, 293, 298–308; infrastructure and, 266, 280–81, 284–94, 297–308, 337n18, 339n24; innovation and, 267–69, 272, 278–82, 287, 302, 308; institutions and, 254, 256, 273, 279, 283, 286–88, 291, 295–307, 336n6, 337n15, 338n20; lower costs from, 187; management and, 262, 268, 273, 280, 296–97, 300; manufacturing and, 259, 262, 264, 267–73, 277–78, 282–89, 299, 303, 306, *309*, 335n3; natural resources and, 266, 270, 289, 292; oil and, 267, 289, 336n8; poverty and, 257, 288, 300, 307; privatization and, 301, 304; productivity and, 269–73, 280, 287–88, 300; prosperity and, 289, 307–8; protection and, 257–61, 264–65, 293, 296–99, 305, 339n22; randomness and, 279–87, 292–93, 297; reform and, 278, 286, 290, 300–1, 305; regulation and, 261, 267, 281, 288, 290, 295–99, 302–4, 335n1, 335n5; special economic zones (SEZs) and, 214–15,

Growth Commission, 15–16, 212
growth identification and facilitation
framework (GIFF): continual technical/
industrial change and, 213–14; education and, 227–29; endowment structure
and, 214; firm constraints and, 217;
foreign direct investment (FDI) and,
232–41; implementation guidelines and,
232–45; manufacturing and, 214–15;
rational selection and, 213–17, 221,
225–45, 246, 248; self-discovery by private firms and, 242–45; unemployment
and, 225–29
growth models: agriculture and, 122, 127,
132, 139; China and, 120–24, 130;
clusters and, 123; comparative advantage
and, 113, 119, 121–40; competition
and, 131, 135, 326n5; convergence and,
88, 171, 175, 196, 278; cooperation
and, 142; coordination and, 125–37;
corruption and, 120, *132*; economic
development and, 113–17, 120, 124–25,
132–34, 136, 139, 148; education and,
127, 134, *152*, 327n8; elusive analytics
of, 87–90; equity and, 132, *149*; externalities and, 113, 125–37; factor costs
and, 122, 129; failed opportunities and,
130–31; flaws of standard, 113–20;
foreign aid and, 113, 137–56; foreign
direct investment (FDI) and, 123, 136;
GINI index and, *152*, 154, 337n15;
globalization and, 129–30, 258 (*see
also* globalization); global value chains
(GVCs) and, 119; governance and,
120, 127, 132; gross domestic product
(GDP) and, 114, 126–28, 131, 134,
138, 148–49, *151–52*, 327n6, 328n14;
health issues and, 127, *152–53*, 154,
327n8; heterogeneity and, *86*, 89–91,
94–96, 110, 325n7; human capital and,
127, 131–35, 139; industrialization
and, 117, 128, 134; infrastructure and,
124, 127–28, 132–39, 150, 154, 156,
326n5, 327n8; innovation and, 13, 36
(*see also* innovation); institutions and,
113–14, 125–26, 130–34, 138, 140–45,

148–49; International Monetary Fund
(IMF) and, 114, 126, 141–44, 328n13;
Keynesian, 198, 200, 223; Khan-Knight,
114–19; laziness and, 22, 37–43, 310;
linear approach and, 26, 45; Malthusian
conditions and, 171; management and,
143, 149; manufacturing and, 126–27,
130; meta-economics and, 141–46; natural resources and, 125–26, 129, 131; oil
and, 127–28, 144; populism and, 117–
18; poverty and, 132, 134, 137–41, 143,
152; privatization and, 121; productivity
and, 125–26, 149; promises/limitations
of, 97–100; prosperity and, 113, 117,
126–28; protection and, 121, 130–31;
reform and, 100–10, 112, 120–21, 130–
32, 144, 327n7, 328n13; regulation and,
119, 133, 135, 140, 326n5; revisionism
and, 120–25; Sherlock Holmes syndrome and, 197–98; stability issues and,
113–25, 140, 142, 145, 149–50, *151*,
155, 156; standard, 113–20, 123–26,
130–31, 135, 137, 140–41; structural
change and, 176–84; sustainability and,
126–30, 176–84; taxes and, 126, 137,
151; technology and, 113, 126–27,
129–35, 138; transaction costs and, 134,
137; transportation and, 133; understanding global dynamics and, 169–76;
United States and, 129; unrealistic standard growth and, 113–16; World Bank
and, 122, 141–45, 327n7, 328n13
Guess, 240
Guinea, *105*, 156, 158
Guinea-Bissau, *105*, 156
Gullick, Sidney, 38

H&M, 240
Hai, Helen, 241
handicraft, 217, 269
Harding, T., 235
Haussmann, Ricardo, 97, 188, 271, 278
health issues: ambitious pragmatism and,
159, 186, 188, 329n6; drugs and, 58, 75,
106, 141, 327n9; financial development
and, 51; food security and, 164, 186;

health issues (*continued*)
  globalization and, 261, 286, *309*; growth
    models and, 127, *152–53*, 154, 327n8;
    hospital mistakes and, 87; human capital
    and, 29–30, 34, 37; implementation
    guidelines and, 207, 212; nutrition and,
    153, 154, 186, 329n6; policy prescrip-
    tions and, 75, 79, 84, 87–88, 102, *104*,
    314; total factor productivity (TFP)
    and, 22; transportation and, 23
heavily indebted poor country (HIPC),
  148–49, 331n7
Heckman, James, 28
heterogeneity, *86*, 89–91, 94–96, 110,
  325n7
Hewlett Packard, 286
Hidalgo, C., 189, 191
Hitachi, 286
Hobson, John A., 80–81
Hofstede, Geert, 38–39
Hollywood, 1, 39, 281, 283–84
Holy Land, 7
Honduras, 289
Hong Kong-China, 34, *172*, 193, 238–39,
  323n8
Hopkins, A. G., 78
Houphouet-Boigny, Félix, 122
housing, 188, 266, 301
Hu, Dinghuan, 11
Huajian, 240, 241
human capital: ambitious pragmatism and,
  178–81, 186, 197–98; backwardness
  and, 18, 130, 132, 181, 198, 316–20,
  330n20; binding constraints and,
  34–35; China and, 32–35, 41; comparative advantage and, 30, 35–36; Deng
  Xiaoping and, 33–35, 159–60, 289–90;
  direct/indirect measurement of, 322n5;
  economic development and, 30, 35–39,
  43; education and, 28–39, 42–43 (*see
  also* education); endowment structures
  and, 31, 35–36; externalities and, 37;
  financial development and, 66; globalization and, 29–30, 281, 287, 291; governance and, 18, 29–30; gross domestic
  product (GDP) and, 31–33, 40; growth

models and, 127, 131–35, 139; health
  issues and, 29–30, 34, 37; implementation guidelines and, 208, 210, 225, 228,
  235, 249; industrialization and, 25, 32,
  40; infrastructure and, 28, 33–34, 37,
  41; innovation and, 36, 42; institutions
  and, 29–31, 43; lack of, 18; laziness and,
  22, 37–43, 310; management and, 34,
  38–39; manufacturing and, 30, 34–35,
  37, 41; natural resources and, 29–30,
  322n5; policy prescriptions and, *85–86*,
  103, *104*; poverty and, 36–37, 43; privatization and, 26; productivity and,
  23–24, 28–29, 37–43; prosperity and,
  30–31, 34; skilled labor and, 25, 28, 36,
  42, 154, 158, 185, 210–11, 245–46,
  248, 250, 272, 280, 282, 286, 292, 319,
  323n11; Solow residual and, 29; stock
  measurement of, 322n5; structural
  change and, 31, 35–36; talent and, 4, 29,
  36, 54, 112, 243, 255; taxes and, 35–36;
  technology and, 28, 30, 33–36, 41–42,
  325n4, 330n20; training and, 10, 13, 28,
  31, 35–36, 41, 228–31, 236, 250, 301,
  306, 326n8, 337n18; transportation
  and, 23–26, 33; United States and, 31,
  40–42; weak base for, 6, 18, 22, 28–37,
  43, 210, 225–26, 317, 318
human rights, 53, 59
Hume, David, 322n8
Huntington, Samuel, 39, 53
Hussein, Saddam, 14–15
Hynes, Williams, 324n2
hysteresis, 2, 147–48, 321n1

Iceland, 288
illegal behaviors, 21, 50, 60, 106, 250, 263
Imbs, J., 183–84
implementation guidelines: agriculture and,
  208–12, 216–17, 228, 232, 251, 331n2,
  333n18, 334n25, 334n29; binding
  constraints and, 25–26, 34–35, 77, *87*,
  91–100, *104*, 110, 206–10, 217–32,
  246, 267; Camp David agreements
  and, 202–3, 252; China and, 206,
  221, 232, 237–42, 247, 252, 333n16;

clusters and, 211, 214, 219–20, 233, 240, 246–49, 334n24; comparative advantage and, 203–4, 207–8, 212–17, 227–28, 236, 240–42, 249–50, 253; competition and, 206, 212, 218, 220, 233, 238; coordination and, 233, 242, 245, 250–51, 335n30; corruption and, 205, 218, 235, 249; economic development and, 203–4, 206, 211–13, 224, 236, 241, 250, 334n24; education and, 207–8, 212, 226–29, 239; endowment structures and, 206, 212–15, 225, 231, 247, 249; equity and, 240; exchange rates and, 222–25; externalities and, 233, 242, 245, 249–52; factor costs and, 214, 218–20; failure and, 205, 213, 224–25, 242, 248; finding right entry points and, 212–52; firm self-discovery and, 242–45; foreign aid and, 227; foreign direct investment (FDI) and, 214, 232–41, 247–48, 332nn11–16; global value chains (GVCs) and, 204, 252; governance and, 208, 215, 218, 235, 239–40, 246, 253; gross domestic product (GDP) and, 206, 209–10, 214, 220, 226, 253; growth identification and facilitation framework (GIFF) and, 232–45; health issues and, 207, 212; human capital and, 208, 210, 225, 228, 235, 249; human creativity and, 202–3; industrialization and, 205–6, 209, 211–12, 331n5; infrastructure and, 204, 207–8, 210, 218, 221–30, 235–41, 246–53, 333n18, 334n24; innovation and, 214–15, 218, 233, 242, 244–45, 250–52, 335n31; institutions and, 204, 207–8, 211–12, 223–25, 237, 242, 249–50, 331n6; International Monetary Fund (IMF) and, 223–24, 331n7; job creation and, 229–30; management and, 212, 227, 233, 235, 249, 332n11; manufacturing and, 209–17, 222, 227–28, 232, 235–50, 253, 332n12, 335n31; natural resources and, 235, 249–50; new firm incubation programs and, 232–41; oil and, 206; poverty and, 204–5, 208,

210, 223–24, 228, 232, 241, 253, 331n4, 331n7; productivity and, 203, 210–11, 219–20, 230–34, 239, 246, 248, 250; prosperity and, 203–7, 212–13, 231, 247, 253; protection and, 205, 234, 242; randomness and, 203–4, 207, 211, 223, 246, 251–52; rational selection and, 204–12 (*see also* rational selection); reform and, 207–12, 217–20, 226–27, 230, 235, 238, 246–47, 335n31; regulation and, 218, 222, 226, 228, 231, 246, 248, 334n24, 335n31; special economic zones (SEZs) and, 214, 237, 241, 247, 253, 334n24; stability issues and, 207–8, 212, 223, 229–30, 235, 331n7, 332n13; subsidies and, 205–6, 230, 242, 249–52; success and, 203–7, 213–14, 220–22, 225, 227–28, 231, 235–45, 248–53; supply chains and, 245; sustainability and, 205–6, 224, 227, 243, 331n7; taxes and, 206, 214, 223, 227, 247–52, 335n31; technology and, 210–16, 231–39, 242–45, 248, 250–52, 334n24; transaction costs and, 214, 217–19, 226; transportation and, 224; unemployment and, 205, 211, 220, 223, 225–32; United States and, 206, 221, 234, 237, 247; World Bank and, 236, 239, 332n11
incompetence, 57–60
incubation programs, 232–41
India, *27*, 51, 242; ambitious pragmatism and, 169, *170*, 176, 187, 191, 195–96, *197*; globalization and, 256, 295, 307; growth models and, 124, 130; human capital and, 36, 38; poor business environment of, 16, 25, 320, 323n8
Indonesia, 16, 18, 124, 130, 169, *170*, *172*, 195, *196*, 206, 320
industrialization: ambitious pragmatism and, 160, 162, 175–80, 184–95; delayed gratification and, 192–98; financial development and, 57, 65, 70; globalization and, 260, 266, 272, 289; global value chains and, 25, 119, 168–69, 187–88, 204, 252, 256, 264, 267, 270–79, 286, 317–18; growth models and, 117, 128,

industrialization (*continued*)

134; human capital and, 25, 32, 40; implementation guidelines and, 205–6, 209, 211–12, 331n5; paradox of, 160–66; policy prescriptions and, 81–82, 101, 319; poverty and, 18; prosperity and, 18; special economic zones (SEZs) and, 214–15, 237, 241, 245–49, 253, 256, 273, 287–307, 325n5, 334n24; structural change and, 176–92

industrial parks, 6, 19, 123; ambitious pragmatism and, 192; cluster-based (CBIPs), 298–307, 339n22; globalization and, 273, 293, 298–308, 337n12, 338n20; implementation guidelines and, 214–15, 219, 221, 226, 236–40, 247–48, 253; policy prescriptions and, 317–19

industrial policy: clusters and, 281; European Commission and, 243; import-substitution strategy and, 213; Obama on, 335n31; sector-targeted, 213; self-discovery and, 243; success of Chinese agriculture and, 11

Industrial Revolution, 3, 7, 9, 16, 30, 79, 162, 178, 268, 284

inequality, 66, 106, 154, 186–87, 268

information and communications technologies (ICTs), 230–31

infrastructure: Africa and, 24–26; agriculture and, 12–14, 24–25; aid institutions and, 322; ambitious pragmatism and, 165, 168, 175–76, 181, 186–87, 197, 329n9; ASCE report card for, 322n2; backwardness and, 18, 130, 132, 181, 198, 316–20, 330n20; binding constraints and, 25–26, 34–35, 77, *87*, 91–100, *104*, 110, 206–8, 210, 214, 220, 246, 267, 326n5; comparative advantage and, 3 (*see also* comparative advantage); as convenient culprit, 22–28; coordination and, 313; creative destruction and, 3, 126, 191, 252; deficit of, 18, 24, 37, 247–48; delayed gratification and, 192–98; economic development and, 3–4; enabling government and, 3; endowment structure and, 3, 18, 31, 35–36,

64, 73–74, 103, 113, 127–36, 160, 185, 193–97, 206, 212–15, 225, 231, 249, 279, 293, 296, 300, 319; equity and, 22; financial development and, 70–74; foreign direct investment (FDI) and, 307–8; gap of, 3, 24–25, 28, 317; globalization and, 266, 280–81, 284–94, 297–308, 337n18, 339n24; growth models and, 124, 127–28, 132–39, 150, 154, 156, 326n5, 327n8; hard, 4–5, 133–34, 249, 313; human capital and, 28, 33–34, 37, 41; implementation guidelines and, 204, 207–8, 210, 218, 221–30, 235–41, 246–53, 333n18, 334n24; industrial parks and, 6, 19, 123, 192, 214–15, 219, 221, 226, 236–40, 247–48, 253, 273, 293, 298–308, 317–19, 337n12, 338n20; irrigation and, 8, 10, 24, 165, 168, 321; islands of excellence and, 26, 28; localized, 12; optimality and, 70–74; policy prescriptions and, 81, 92–96, *104*, 107, 313, 317–18; productivity and, 12 (*see also* productivity); as real constraint, 3, 22–28, 317; reform and, *104*; skilled labor earnings and, 323n11; soft, 4–5, 133–34, 249, 313; solving issues of, 221–22; structural change for sustained growth and, 176–84; structuralism and, 6, 78, 82–84, *85*, *87*, 114, 117, 120, 130, 194, 258, 311–14; successful transitions and, 5; transaction costs and, 22, 24, 321n4; United States and, 322n2; weak institutional environment and, 4, 6, 65, 204, 208, 223

innovation, 68; ambitious pragmatism and, 161, 167, 177–81, 189, 192–93; coordination and, 180–83; delayed gratification and, 192–98; externalities and, 180–83; globalization and, 267–69, 272, 278–82, 287, 302, 308; growth diagnostics and, *87*; human capital and, 36, 42; implementation guidelines and, 214–15, 218, 233, 242, 244–45, 250–52, 335n31; Industrial Revolution, 3, 7, 9, 16, 30, 79, 162, 178, 268, 284; latecomers and, 194; policy prescriptions

and, 315–16; QWERTY keyboard and, 282–83, 292; research and development (R&D) and, 42, 233, 237, 252, 338n20; structuralism and, *85*; sustained growth and, 126, 130; transportation and, 13
Institute of Medicine, 87
institutions: aid, 114, 138, 322n1; ambitious pragmatism and, 158, 161, 163, 165–68, 176–77, 181, 187, 197–98, 328n1, 329n11; cluster-based industrial parks (CBIPs) and, 300–1; coordination and, 133–37; economic development and, 3; externalities and, 133–37; financial development and, 44–74; globalization and, 254, 256, 273, 279, 283, 286–88, 291, 295–307, 336n6, 337n15, 338n20; governance and, 61 (*see also* governance); growth diagnostics limitations and, 97–100; growth models and, 113–14, 125–26, 130–34, 138, 140–45, 148–49; human capital and, 29–31, 43; implementation guidelines and, 204, 207–8, 211–12, 223–25, 237, 242, 249–50, 331n6; infrastructure and, 322 (*see also* institutions); intellectual mimicry and, 65–74; International Financial Institution Advisory Commission and, 327n7; Pavlovian errors in assessing, 44; policy prescriptions and, 75–76, 79–92, 95–106, 109, 316, 319; prosperity and, 3–4, 6, 18–19; reform and, *104*; underdeveloped financial, 65–74; underdeveloped political, 45–64; unpleasant truths about, 44–74; weak, 4, 6, 65, 204, 208, 223
Intel, 286
Inter-American Development Bank, 327n7
interest rates, 68, 71, 98–99, 102, *104*, 106, 115, 119, 222–23, 229, 304, 308
International Financial Institution Advisory Commission, 327n7
International Labour Organization (ILO), 171
International Monetary Fund (IMF): ambitious pragmatism and, 161, 330n18; financial development and, 46; growth models and, 114, 126, 141–44, 328n13;

implementation guidelines and, 223–24, 331n7; performance criteria of, 328n13; policy prescriptions and, 103–6, 326n10
interventionism, 77
Investing across Borders, 325n6
Investment Climate Assessments (ICAs), 91
Ireland, 193, 247, 288, 290–91, 306
irrigation, 8, 10, 24, 165, 168, 321
Irwin, Douglas, 258–59
Italy, 31–32, 145, *263*, 264, 280, 284

Japan: ambitious pragmatism and, *172*, 173, 191, 193, 196, *197*; corruption and, 49; delayed gratification and, 193; financial development and, 49, 52; globalization and, *263*, 264, 267, 274, 286, 305; growth models and, 129, 145; human capital and, 34, 38; implementation guidelines and, 237, 242; Industrial Revolution and, 16; laziness and, 38
Javorcik, B. S., 235–36
Jemio, Luis Carlos, 106
Jiang, Ye, 72
Jiang Zemin, 290
job creation, 91, 96, 106–7, 185–87, 210, 213, 229–30, 290–92
Jordan, Michael, 298
Joseph, Richard, 60, 295
Juma, Calestous, 24

Kabou, Axelle, 39
Kagame, Paul, 159, 241
Katz, Lawrence, 42
Kazakhstan, 26, 326n3
Keefer, Philip, 54
Kempes, Mario, 112
Kenya, 24, 36, *105*, 124, 156
Keynesianism, 198, 200, 223
Khan, Mohsin S., 114–19
Kharroubi, Enisse, 67
King, Martin Luther, Jr., 2
Kiswahili, 35
Klapper, Leora, 66
Knack, Stephen, 54
Knight, Malcolm, 114–19

332n11; incompetence and, 57–60; managerial expertise and, 6, 233, 319; policy prescriptions and, 96, 107, 317, 319, 326n8; privatization and, 8; School of Economics and Management, 10; World Governance Indicators (WGIs) and, 12, 46–47, 62

Mandri-Perrott, Cledan, 304

mangoes, 12–14, 242, 321n6

Mankiw, Gregory, 29

manufacturing: ambitious pragmatism and, 162–63, 167–68, 178–96, 330n16, 330n17; boosting production/trade and, 279–87; China and, 18, 326n8; climate change and, 187; education and, 30–31; entrepreneurs and, 189; export pessimism and, 189–91; fragmentation and, 271–72, 285–86, 291, 336n11; future of, 188–89; globalization and, 259, 262, 264, 267–73, 277–78, 282–89, 299, 303, 306, 309, 335n3; globalization and, 187 (see also globalization); global value chains and, 25, 119, 168–69, 187–88, 204, 252, 256, 264, 267, 270–79, 286, 317–18; growth models and, 126–27, 130; human capital and, 30, 34–35, 37, 41; implementation guidelines and, 209–17, 222, 227–28, 232, 235–50, 253, 332n12, 335n31; inequality and, 186–87; policy prescriptions and, 82, 85, 87, 96, 107, 313, 317, 319, 324n2, 326n8; prosperity and, 9, 18; rational selection and, 209–17, 222, 227–28, 232, 235–50, 253; rule of law and, 187; special economic zones (SEZs) and, 214–15, 237, 241, 245–49, 253, 256, 273, 287–307, 325n5, 334n24; structural change and, 178–92; sustainability and, 186–87; tariffs and, 64, 108, 125, 174, 196; transportation and, 191–92; United States and, 335n31; value added and, 12, 127, 139, 173, 180–88, 233, 274–78, 286, 288, 305, 319, 330n13, 330n17, 332n12, 334n27, 337n13

Maradona, Diego, 112

market fundamentalism, 6, 83, 313

Marshall, Alfred, 65, 248, 279–85, 294, 308, 334n26

Marshmallow Test, 192–94

Marxism, 78, 80, 181

Mattoo, A., 260

Mauritania, 105, 156

Mauritius, 5, 36, 105, 121, 123, 156, 193, 238–39, 247, 267, 286, 289, 318–19, 332n10

Mauro, Paolo, 54

Mayer, Colin, 70

Mayer, Thierry, 261

Medicare, 87

Meltzer Report, 138, 327n7

Menotti, Cesar Luis, 111–13

Messer, Ellen, 9

Mexico, 39, 118, 169, 170, 187, 292

Milesi-Ferretti, Gian Maria, 267

Millennium Development Goals, 209

Mischel, Walter, 192

MIT Poverty Action Lab, 84, 314

MKUKUTA, 210

modernization: colonialism and, 80; delayed gratification and, 192–98; structuralism and, 80, 82, 85, 87, 109, 121, 131, 161, 192, 205, 224–25, 269, 287; sustainability and, 82

Mogae, Festus G., 58

Monga, Célestin, 6, 17, 95, 198–99, 213, 267, 329n8

monopoly rent, 64, 135, 252, 296

Morales, Evo, 106

Moses, 7

Mozambique, 26, 27, 105, 156, 329n9

Mukherjee, Arpita, 295

Murphy, K. M., 54

Mutharika, Bingu wa, 36–37

Myanmar, 27, 29, 35

Myrdal, Gunnar, 323n8

Naipaul, V. S., 2

NASA, 87

National Semiconductor, 286

Naturalizer, 240

natural resources: ambitious pragmatism and, 158, 175–76, 180, 198; Arabian

natural resources (*continued*)
Gulf and, 36, 126, 129; China and, 34–35, 289; financial development and, 54, 63, 73; Ghana and, 158; globalization and, 266, 270, 289, 292; growth models and, 125–26, 129, 131; human capital and, 29–30, 322n5; implementation guidelines and, 235, 249–50; investment and, 29, 35, 54, 129, 175–76, 235, 249, 266; Prebisch-Singer hypothesis and, 180, 258, 329n12; rent seeking and, 34; structural change and, 176–84

Negev Desert, Israel, 7–9, 11

Nehru, Jawaharlal, 256

Netherlands, 112, 193, 195, *196–97*, 206, 237, 282

new structural economics: corruption and, 64; foreign aid addiction and, 137 private firm entry and, 64; transformations in suboptimal conditions and, 18. *See also* structuralism

New Structural Economics (Lin), 6, 64

Nguesso, Denis Sassou, 55–59

Niger, 80, *105*, 143, 156

Nigeria, *93–94*, 95, *105*, 156, 169, *170*

Nkrumah, Kwame, 121, 157–58, 160

nontariff measures (NTMs), 261–62, 335n5, 336n6

Norway, 29, 41, 61

Nurkse, Ragnar, 162, 175

nutrition, *153*, 154, 186, 329n6

Obama, Barack, 32, 49, 58, 174, 234, 335n31

official development assistance (ODA), 141–42, 146–48, 156

offshoring, 240–41, 336n11

oil: ambitious pragmatism and, 159, 190, 330n18, 330n19; Bahrain and, 127; Chad-Cameroon pipeline and, 144; China and, 190, 267; Congo and, 56; Equatorial Guinea and, 159; exports and, 84, 190, 267, 330n18, 336n8; globalization and, 267, 289, 336n8; growth models and, 127–28, 144; implementation guidelines and, 206; Japan and, 267;

policy prescriptions and, 84, 321; price changes and, 127, 289, 330n18; Saudi Arabia and, 127

opportunity cost, 22–23, 55–57

Organization for Economic Cooperation and Development (OECD) countries, 8, 100–1, 109, 226, 339n24

Pack, Howard, 257, 265, 267

Page, Tim, 245

palm oil, 79, 122

Panama, *27*, 40

Paris Club, 331n7

paternalism, 46, 58, 144

path-dependent equilibrium, 282–83, 321n1

PAVCOPA, 13

Pavlovian behavior, 44

peanuts, 8, 80

peasants, 33–34, 36, 39, 81, 161

Peru, 280

Plato, 16

Poirson, Hélène, 54

police, 1, 20–21, 28, 58

policy framework papers (PFPs), 141

policy prescriptions: agriculture and, 80, *104*, 107; backwardness and, 316–20; binding constraints and, 87, 91–100, *104*, 110; Bretton Woods and, 76, 100, 141–42, 144, 161; China and, 311, 317–20, 326n8; clusters and, 317–18; colonial economics and, 77–82; comparative advantage and, *85*, *87*, 96–99, 103, 312, 316–19; competition and, 319, 325n5; corruption and, 92–96, 102, *104*, 107, 325n3; decision trees and, 97–98; delayed gratification and, 192–98; deregulation and, 83, *85*, 102, *104*, 119, 161, 222, 267, 326n5; economic development and, 75–78, 81–82, *85–87*, 88–89, 92–93, 102, 304, 311–18; economic development approaches and, 82–87; education and, 82, 84, 96, 98, 102, *104*, 314–15; elusive analytics of growth and, 88–91; endowment structures and, 103, 319; externalities and, 83, *85*, 98–99, 109, 313, 317;

Rajan, R. G., 69

Rana Plaza, 231

randomness, 18; ambitious pragmatism and, 161; cluster theory and, 279–87; control trials and, 17, 84, *86*, 156; corruption and, 1, 20; economic miracles and, 252; globalization and, 279–87, 292–93, 297; growth models and, 113–16; implementation guidelines and, 203–4, 207, 211, 223, 246, 251–52; labor and, 3; policy prescriptions and, 77, 84, *86*, 91–97, 311, 314; true binding constraints and, 91–97; white noise and, 15

rational selection: choosing what not do do and, 204–12; clusters and, 214, 219–20, 233, 240, 246–49; comparative advantage and, 212, 215–17, 227–28, 236, 240–42, 249–50, 253; constraint removal and, 217–32; cost of border formalities and, 222; endowment structures and, 212–15, 225, 231, 247; exchange rates and, 222–25; externalities and, 249–52; finding right entry points and, 212–52; firm self-discovery and, 242–45; foreign direct investment (FDI) and, 232–41; growth identification and facilitation framework (GIFF) and, 213–17, 221, 225–45, 246, 248; job creation and, 229–30; manufacturing and, 209–17, 222, 227–28, 232, 235–50, 253; new firm incubation programs and, 232–41; sectors with latent comparative advantage and, 215–17; simplifying trade procedures and, 222; solving infrastructure issues and, 221–22; special economic zones (SEZs) and, 214, 245–49; subsidies and, 249–52; transparency and, 222; unemployment and, 225–32

Reardon, Thomas, 284

recession, 71, 84, 118, 122, 175, 189–90, 223, 259, 303, 307, 321n2

reform: agriculture and, 14, 161, 165–66; ambitious pragmatism and, 160–61, 165, 168; available funding and, 207; blanket, 208; disruptive, 19; financial development and, 44, 61, 71–72;

globalization and, 278, 286, 290, 300–1, 305; gradual, 8; growth models and, 112, 120–21, 130–32, 144, 327n7, 328n13; implementation guidelines and, 207–12, 217–20, 226–27, 230, 235, 238, 246–47, 335n31; infrastructure and, *104*; institutions and, *104*; policy prescriptions and, 76, *87*, 89–91, 97, 100–10, 315, 325n5; politics and, 6; rural, 9; stabilization framework for, 102; structural, 16, 18, 76, 102, 161, 176–84; tax, 102, *104*; Washington Consensus and, 4, 21, 26, 71, 83–86, 91, 99–100, 103, 108–9, 114, 120–24, 130–31, 311–14, 325n3; without growth, 100–10

regulation: ambitious pragmatism and, 161, 165, 168, 178; competition and, 321n4; deregulation and, 83, *85*, 102, *104*, 119, 161, 222, 267, 326n5; equity and, 74; financial development and, 46, 50–51, 60, 63, 65–67, 71, 74, 324n6; globalization and, 261, 267, 281, 288, 290, 295–99, 302–4, 335n1, 335n5; growth models and, 119, 133, 135, 140, 326n5; implementation guidelines and, 218, 222, 226, 228, 231, 246, 248, 334n24, 335n31; policy prescriptions and, 83, *85*, 91–96, 102, *104*, 106, 325n5, 325n6; productivity and, 41; prosperity and, 3–4, 20; transaction costs and, 3

rent seeking: corruption and, 45, 54–55, 61–62, 64, 104, 242, 252, 292, 296, 301, 305–7; mitigating risks of, 64, 305–7; natural resources and, 34; special economic zones (SEZs) and, 305–7; state capture and, 45

repression, 58, 71, 74, *104*, 125–26

research and development (R&D), 42, 233, 237, 252, 338n20

revisionism, 120–25

Ricardo, David, 18, 219

risk: Chinese potato crops and, 9; entrepreneurs and, 3; excess-capacity situations and, 23; financial development and, 46, 64, 66–68, 70–74; personal tolerance of, 66; relativism and, 46; rent seeking and,

risk (*continued*)
  64, 305–7; state capture and, 64; traffic violations and, 21; universalism and, 46
risk-return ratio, 2–3
roads, 3, 338n21
Rodrik, Dani, 89, 107, 178–79, 278, 319
Rolls-Royce, 269
Romer, P. M., 54
Rose-Ackerman, Susan, 54
Rosenstein-Rodan, P., 82
rule of law, 46, 58, 132, 187, 234
Rumsfeld, Donald, 14–15
Russell, John, 38
Russia, 58, 121, 193, 326n3
Ruta, M., 260
Rwanda, *27*, 156, 159, 241, 318, 326n5
Ryder, Guy, 171

Sachs, Jeffrey D., 138–39
Sadat, Anwar, 202
Sahel, 12
Said, Edward, 47, 77
Sanchez-Robles, B., 22
Sao Tome, *105*, 156
Sarkozy, Nicolas, 39–40
Saudi Arabia, 127
School of Economics and Management, Lanzhou University, 10
Schopenhauer, Arthur, 47
Schumpeter, Joseph, 65, 126, 178, 181
Seagate, 286
seaports, 23, 303
sectoral shifts, 178–79
self-discovery, 242–45
self employment, 107, 334n29
Senegal, 39, 80, *105*, 124, 156, *196*, 206
Serven, Luis, 24
service sectors, 9, 107, 163–64, 169, 185
Sestito, Paolo, 31
Shaw, Edward, 65
Sherlock Holmes syndrome, 197–98
Shleifer, A., 50
shocks, 166, 299–300, 321n1, 330n19
Siemens, 286
Sierra Leone, *105*, 156
Silicon Valley, 280–81, 283

Singapore, 323n8; Deng Xiaoping and, 34; economic performance of, 26, *27*; globalization and, 267, 291; global value chains and, 317; growth models and, 126–29, 133, 327n6; investment climate of, *93–94*, 94–95; sustained growth in *172*;
Singer, Hans, 258
Sirima, Bissiri, 76
slavery, 7, 78–79, 81, 324n2
Slovenia, 121
small and medium-sized enterprises (SMEs), 72, 243
Smith, Adam, 22, 65, 109, 125, 280, 282–83
Smokey Mountain garbage dump, 232
social capital, 136, 327n8
socialism, 38, 106, 120, 208
Solow, Robert, 16, 29, 178, 181
Somalia, *105*, 156
Sony, 286
Sousa, José de, 261
South Africa, 1–3, 25–26, 81–82, 156
Soviet Union, 33–34, 108, 120, 131, 213, 326n3
Spain, 280, 292, 333n19
special economic zones (SEZs): clusters and, 287–307, 339n22; comparative advantage and, 287–99; corruption and, 296, 305–7; duty and, 247, 270, 290, 306, 334n25, 336n10; failure and, 291–98, 302–3; foreign direct investment (FDI) and, 338n20; globalization and, 253, 256, 273, 287–307; government intervention and, 296; guiding principles for, 298–300; implementation guidelines and, 214, 237, 241, 245–49, 253, 334n24; location of, 293–94; policy prescriptions and, 325n5; political capture and, 296; rational selection and, 214, 245–49; rent seeking and, 305–7; specialized, 293 (*see also* industrial parks); success and, 215, 237, 241, 247, 253, 256, 273, 287–92, 296–307, 325n5, 334n24
Spence, Michael, 15, 212

spillover, 174, 237–38, 248, 273, 280, 288, 292, 294, 306–8

Sri Lanka, 292

stability issues: agriculture and, 161; ambitious pragmatism and, 161, 174; financial development and, 46, 60, 69, 72; globalization and, 266, 304; growth models and, 113–19, 121–25, 140, 142, 145, 149–50, *151*, *155*, 156; implementation guidelines and, 207–8, 212, 223, 229–30, 235, 331n7, 332n13; policy prescriptions and, 76, 84, *85*, 93–96, 100–3, *104*, 106, 108, 313; prosperity and, 5, 15; reform framework for, 102

stagnation, 30, 106, 126, 162, 259, 265, 268

state capture, 45, 51, 61–62, 64, 120–21, 242, 249, 296

Stiglitz, Joseph E., 3, 66, 109, 181

structural adjustment programs (SAPs), 100, 102, *105*, 107

structural change: ambitious pragmatism and, 176–92; delayed gratification and, 192–98; externalities and, 183–84; industrialization and, 176–92; manufacturing and, 178–92

structuralism, 6, 78; ambitious pragmatism and, 194; development approaches to, 82–85, *86*; export composition and, 180; externalities and, 183–84; failure and, 312–13; growth models and, 114, 117, 120, 130; globalization and, 258; modernization and, 80, 82, *85*, *87*, 109, 121, 131, 161, 192, 205, 224–25, 269, 287; policy prescriptions and, 311–14; production structure and, 179–80; reform framework for, 102; sectoral shifts and, 178–79; sustained growth and, 176–84

subsidies: agriculture and, 8, 11; ambitious pragmatism and, 164, 166, 195; disguised, 313; entrepreneurs and, 130; export, 328n4; externalities and, 249–52; failure and, 312–13; financial development and, 61, 63–64, 136; globalization and, 295–96, 305; health care and, 37; implementation guidelines and, 205–6,

230, 242, 249–52; nonviable firms and, 125, 130–31; policy prescriptions and, 83–84, *85*, *87*, 99–100, 102, *104*, 109, 136; rational selection and, 249–52; repression and, 125; sustainability and, 5, 136, 296, 312–13; transitory, 5

success: ambitious pragmatism and, 159–60, 163–64, 171–80, 184, 188, 191–94, 198; benefits from crises and, 254–55; Borges and, 254, 307; Chinese potatoes and, 9–12; cooperation and, 4, 187; financial development and, 44–45, 47, 53, 63; globalization and, 254–56, 260–63, 266–67, 281–92, 296–307; implementation guidelines and, 203–7, 213–14, 220–22, 225, 227–28, 231, 235–45, 248–53; Malian mango and, 12–14, 242, 321n6; Menotti and, 111–13; Negev Israelis and, 7–9, 11; policy prescriptions and, 75, 81–82, 89, 100–1, 106, 110, 311, 316–19; secrets of, 111–13, 118, 123, 125, 128–31, 135–37, 146; special economic zones (SEZs) and, 215, 237, 241, 247, 253, 256, 273, 287–92, 296–307, 325n5, 334n24

Sudan, *105*, 156

sugar, 122, 166

Suharto, 206

Sukarno, 206

Sula, O., 333n14

Sun, Xifang, 72

supply chains: backward linkage and, 215; decentralization of, 187; entrepreneurs and, 233, 244, 284; globalization and, 262, 291, 297, 317; government, 10; implementation guidelines and, 216, 220, 233, 243–45; limited clustering and, 297; rail and, 243–44; reducing barriers in, 317

supply-side approach, 42, 69, 109, 114–15, 119

Suret-Canale, Jean, 324n2

sustainability: agriculture and, 23, 160–66; ambitious pragmatism and, 171, 177, 182, 185–87; consumption and, 186–87; coordination and, 126–30; Easterly

United States: African Growth and Opportunity Act (AGOA) and, 247, 270, 334n25; agriculture and, 8; ambitious pragmatism and, 173–75, 180, 190, 193–201; corruption and, 48–49, 52; drive of entrepreneurs in, 4; economic development and, 25; education and, 31; financial development and, 49–52, 57, 71; foreign direct investment (FDI) and, 332n12; globalization and, 257, 263, 266–70, 274, 280, 335n2, 336n8; growth models and, 129; human capital and, 31, 40–42; implementation guidelines and, 206, 221, 233–34, 237, 248; income gap in, 40, 321n2; Industrial Revolution and, 16; infrastructure report card for, 322n2; International Monetary Fund (IMF) and, 327n7; manufacturing and, 335n31; policy prescriptions and, 84, 87–88, 312, 314, 318

U.S. Agency for International Development (USAID), 13, 328n1

U.S. Federal Reserve, 266–67

U.S. Generalized System of Preferences (GSP), 270, 334n25, 336n10

utility maximization, 17–18

utility prices, 221, 302

Uzbekistan, 121, 326n3

value added: agriculture and, 12; ambitious pragmatism and, 173, 180–88, 330n13, 330n17; domestic (DVX), 275, *276*, 337n13; foreign, 275, *276*, 337n13; globalization and, 274–78, 286, 288, 305, 337n13; growth models and, 127, 139; international markets and, 127; manufacturing and, 12, 127, 139, 173, 180–88, 233, 274–78, 286, 288, 305, 319, 330n13, 330n17, 332n12, 334n27, 337n13

Vanuatu, 26

Vatican, 49

Venables, Anthony, 271

Vietnam, 5, 26, *27*, 121, 124, 157–58, 287, 289, 318, 320, 326n8

Vigano, Carlo Maria, 49

Vishny, R., 50

Vogel, Ezra, 33–34

Voltaire, 169

Wacziarg, R., 183–84

War of the Worlds, The (Wells), 159

Washington Consensus, 4, 71; Bolivia and, 103–8; expanded version of, 83–84; failure and, 21, 130–31, 312–14; Georgia and, 106; growth models and, 114, 120–24, 130–31; International Monetary Fund (IMF) and, 103; linear approach to, 26; market fundamentalism and, 83–84, 313; MIT Poverty Action Lab and, 84; policy prescriptions and, 83–84, *85–86*, 91, 99–100, 103, 108–9, 311–14, 325n3; poor implementation issues and, 21; privatization and, 26; reform and, 106; revisionism and, 121; tariffs and, 108; Williamson on, 83, 99–102

waste, 39, 59–60, 159, 232, 321n5, 335n31

Webb, Beatrice, 38

Wells, H. G., 159

West Africa, 78–79, 82, 166, 324n2

"Where Has All the Education Gone?" (Pritchett), 29–30

White, Anna, 65

Willett, T. D., 333n14

Williamson, John, 83, 99–101

Wolfowitz, Paul, 56

Woolcock, Michael, 84, 314

World Bank: agriculture and, 161–62; ambitious pragmatism and, 159, 161–62, 164, 169–70, 186, 328n1, 329n5; benchmarks of, 328n13; Census of Investment Promotion Agencies and, 235; Comprehensive Development Framework and, 143; Doing Business indicators and, 12, 26, *27*, 47, 91, 107, *124*, 159, 239, 246, 261, 314, 326n4; Enterprise Surveys and, 30, 91, 326n8; financial development and, 47, 56, 71; globalization and, 291, 336n6; growth models and, 122, 141–45, 327n7,